European Communication Research and Education Associatic

This series consists of books arising from the intellectual work of ECREA members. Books address themes relevant to the ECREA's interests; make a major contribution to the theory, research, practice and/or policy literature; are European in scope; and represent a diversity of perspectives. Book proposals are refereed.

Series Editors
Nico Carpentier
François Heinderyckx

Series Advisory Board
Denis McQuail
Robert Picard
Jan Servaes

The aims of the ECREA are

a) To provide a forum where researchers and others involved in communication and information research can meet and exchange information and documentation about their work. Its disciplinary focus will include media, (tele)communications and informatics research, including relevant approaches of human and social sciences;

b) To encourage the development of research and systematic study, especially on subjects and areas where such work is not well developed;

c) To stimulate academic and intellectual interest in media and communication research, and to promote communication and cooperation between members of the Association;

d) To co-ordinate the circulation of information on communications research in Europe, with a view to establishing a database of ongoing research;

e) To encourage, support and, where possible, publish the work of young researchers in Europe;

f) To take into account the desirability of different languages and cultures in Europe;

g) To develop links with relevant national and international communication organizations and with professional communication researchers working for commercial organizations and regulatory institutions, both public and private;

h) To promote the interests of communication research within and among the Member States of the Council of Europe and the European Union;

i) To collect and disseminate information concerning the professional position of communication researchers in the European region; and

j) To develop, improve and promote communication and media education.

Selling War

Selling War

The Role of the Mass Media in Hostile Conflicts from World War I to the 'War on Terror'

Edited by Josef Seethaler, Matthias Karmasin,
Gabriele Melischek and Romy Wöhlert

First published in the UK in 2013 by
Intellect, The Mill, Parnall Road, Fishponds, Bristol, BS16 3JG, UK

First published in the USA in 2013 by
Intellect, The University of Chicago Press, 1427 E. 60th Street,
Chicago, IL 60637, USA

A catalogue record for this book is available from the
British Library.

Cover designer: Edwin Fox
Copy-editor: MPS Technologies
Production manager: Tim Mitchell
Typesetting: Planman Technologies

ISBN 978-1-84150-610-4
ECREA Series ISSN: 1753-0342

Printed and bound by Hobbs, UK

Contents

Preface

Perspectives on the Changing Role of the Mass Media in Hostile Conflicts

Matthias Karmasin, Gabriele Melischek, Josef Seethaler and Romy Wöhlert

War and communication appear to be essential and universal features of the *conditio humana*. It may be cynical to claim that war is communication, but from an anthropological viewpoint, violence can be seen as being a specific form of communication. From a historical perspective, it is evident that communication has often led and still leads to war. The culture of war is indeed shaped by communication – from the written and nonwritten rituals of mutual respect and disrespect to the definition of legitimate violence and the cunning manipulation of this definition and to the attempts to restrain the damage that conflicting parties inflict on each other.

It is obvious that the mass media have dramatically changed the nature of communication in society in general. Since the emergence of the mass press in the late nineteenth century, almost all forms of social, political and economic life have been shaped and reshaped by the media, replacing other social institutions such as the family, school and the church as providers of information and moral orientation. This seems to be true for war as well. War has always been one of the favorite subjects of the mass media. Fear and hatred, the feeling of security as well as political mobilization have depended on and still depend on perceptions of reality. Developing technologies and evolving information environments have, however, provoked substantive changes in the role of the media in mediating wars, and thus in shaping these perceptions of reality.

In this book, we want to reconstruct these developments following the thesis that there is a duality between the changes in warfare and the (technical) possibilities of communicating these events. War has been an important factor in the evolution of new forms of social communication, and at the same time new means of communication have altered the relationship between war and the mass media. In the end, it is not only a technical but also a social and cultural process.

This book is the first to bring together international scholarship to explore the changing relationships between war, the media and the public both from multidisciplinary perspectives and over a lengthier time period, beginning with World War I and concluding with the so-called 'War on Terror'. In discussing a wide variety of theoretical concepts and methodological tools for analyzing the nature of these relationships and in presenting a broad range of research results, this book will make an important contribution to scholarly debates on the role of the mass media in modern warfare. These approaches address broad areas of research, from the role of traditional media to blogs, warlogs and eyewitness journalism, from war correspondence to embedded journalism, from propaganda to war PR and information warfare. Moreover, various aspects of the media economy and media ethics, as well as cultural studies approaches, are integrated into the discussion.

By combining rigor and accessibility, this book also aims at introducing students to this innovative area of research. As a textbook for students, each chapter provides a brief introductory summary, a list of key points brought up in the text, study questions that can be used for discussions or as topics for essays and as a guide to further readings on the subject (including web links, if available).

Introduction

The book starts with a thorough overview by Philip Seib of war, the media and the public sphere. His chapter explores how the perception of war in the public sphere is influenced by the media and, more precisely, how the news media define and perform their social function in relation to war. It points to the fact that it is not only the way in which journalists deliver news about war to the public that affects how people think about war. Information and its impact on the public are also influenced, to a varying extent, by the medium that conveys the message. The impact of newspaper articles differs from that of a live television report from the battlefield, which in turn differs from an amateur's YouTube video, not just in terms of production but also in terms of access and consumption. Obviously, changes in the media environment and its technologies affect the nature of news journalism, the role of professional communication and the way media messages are perceived by the public.

'Never Such Innocence Again': Propaganda and Total War

Changes can be reflected on most accurately when they are contrasted with historical developments. This seems to be true for William Howard Russell, who covered the Crimean War (1854–56) for *The Times* and was the first 'war correspondent' in the modern sense of the term. This applies to the pictures of fallen soldiers in the Battle of Gettysburg of 1863 during the American Civil War and also to the German-French War of 1870–71 and the beginning of modern propaganda. Of course, these changes could not have taken place without technical innovations such as the telegraph, photography and the possibilities of the mass press to *re-produce* the reports from the front line. However, as Reinhard Stauber shows, the publication and illustration of these wars, the 'reality' of the atrocities of war, changed the way respective societies framed the war and dealt with its consequences. The famous poem on World War I, 'Never Such Innocence Again' by Philip Larkin, might also apply to the mobilization of the public spheres during the World War I, which was globally covered by the media. The 'Great War' marked a significant change in the mediatization of war.

War was no longer a 'gentlemen's disagreement'. On the contrary, the respective public opinions viewed the enemy as the incarnation of evil, which precluded compromise and only considered unconditional surrender as a satisfactory outcome. War was not only waged on the battlefield; it also fought for acceptance and – in the words of Lyotard – for metahistory: the struggle to determine the dominant interpretation of war. In his remarks on the semantic sliding of the concept of war, Diego Lazzarich points out that the narration of war became one of the main cognitive categories of modern war itself.

The struggle for the framing of war, as well as the framing of the war experience itself, was not over when the World War I ended in 1918. Rather, it became a dominant topic, especially in Germany, Austria and Italy, where it affected the political climate and public discourse. Political compromise no longer seemed possible or even rational. John Dewey addresses this point in his essay 'The Eclipse of the Public', published in 1927, when he states that this war also devastated the public sphere.

In actual fact, the importance of propaganda and censorship was on the increase during the 'short 20th century' (Eric Hobsbawm). In 'total war', the public sector tried to involve the entire society, thus eliminating the distinction between public and private. In particular, Nazi Germany focused on propaganda after the experiences of the World War I, based on the assumption that the superior propaganda of the Allies played a significant role in the German defeat. One aspect of total war was total propaganda, the attempt to control all forms of public content, even jokes and posters, and to monitor everything, including private conversations. Basing themselves on different sources, that is, the official 'Reports from the Reich' as well as *Feldpost* ('field post') letters, Jürgen Wilke and Clemens Schwender try to understand how people used the media during World War II, how they processed media content and how they reacted to it.

But even democracies like the United Kingdom and the United States devoted major resources to their efforts to form public opinion, despite the fact that the premises of a pluralistic society with more or less independent media made complete success in this endeavor more difficult. The delicate balance between freedom of opinion and patriotic needs, between an open society and national security, has dominated the debate in the western world ever since. Nevertheless, in the 1950s, propaganda was still the dominant form of public communication. There was no substantial change on either side of the conflict. The media were seen as an important factor, but not as part of military strategy.

Visual Turn, War PR and the Changing Relationships between Politics, Media and the Public Sphere

After the first 'television war' in Vietnam, it seemed clear that the media played a decisive role not only in the perception of war on the home front but also in the success of war. Indeed, Vietnam did change something: the media culture and the culture of war converged. The Vietnam War and its influence on popular culture and, conversely, the influence of popular culture on the war have been intensively discussed. The war became part of the rock 'n' roll culture of the 1960s – not only in the United States. It was fought and remembered in pictures and metaphors of rock 'n' roll. In his book *Dispatches* Vietnam reporter Michael Herr illustrates this point: 'Out on the street I couldn't tell the Vietnam veterans from the rock 'n' roll veterans.' Media culture, popular culture and the culture of war were closer than ever.

This contributed to the myth that the United States was not beaten on the battlefields in Vietnam but rather on the home front. The media were seen as strong, influential and decisive, but also as hard to control or manipulate using traditional forms of propaganda. One has to take a closer look, however, at the relationship between the media, policy and public opinion. As Daniel C. Hallin points out, the contradiction between the rhetoric of total war used to mobilize public support and the reality of a limited war is important in understanding the changing patterns of public opinion during the Vietnam War as well as the recurrent patterns of public opinion during post-World War II conflicts in general. Not only for soldiers and their families, but also for the public at large, it is difficult to accept the notion of a limited war, the idea that one is risking his or her life for a cause to which the nation is not fully committed. The disillusioning reality of Vietnam led to the end of propaganda and the beginning of war PR.

There are several major aspects of this development. First of all, a total war between nuclear powers was no longer a reasonable alternative. Conventional wars were limited and there was an international consensus for preventing them from escalating into a third world war. The ensuing 'revolution in military affairs' placed the stress on PR and on the efforts not only to justify war but also to market war as 'just wars'. Magnus-Sebastian Kutz focuses on this debate emerging at the time about the theory of a 'just war'.

On the media level, Vietnam marked a visual turn. By putting a face on war, television and photojournalism have brought the unimaginable to life. Nick Út's famous Pulitzer Prize-winning photograph of a young girl running naked on a road after being severely burned on her back by a South Vietnamese napalm attack is an outstanding example of the newly exercised power of the media to define reality. Valérie Gorin discusses the iconography of those media-created images of war between the 1960s and the 1990s and links it to a 'rhetoric of compassion', while Romy Fröhlich emphasizes an often overlooked aspect of the ongoing changes in the mass-mediated pictures of war, namely, the gender-stereotypical war coverage and the role of women in times of war, which she found to be decisively related to the status and the role that women are accorded in society as a whole.

The end of propaganda and the beginning of war PR meant far-reaching consequences for the interplay of politics, the media and the public, which again, as Josef Seethaler and Gabriele Melischek argue, was subject to change because of the end of the Cold War and the new political uncertainties it brought about. Moreover, the so-called CNN (or Al Jazeera) factor associated with 24-hour live coverage of conflicts around the globe fortified the effects of this visual turn and may be seen as accounting for new developments such as 'embedded journalism' and 'Pentagon TV'. The motto is no longer propaganda but instead the media professionalization of the armed forces, no longer control of information but marketing, no longer lying but failing to tell the whole truth, no longer censorship but mental embedding and self-censorship. This raises new and somehow disturbing questions about the future of journalism in this area as well as about the nature of the public sphere and thus of democratic society. After Vietnam, the media in general, and the electronic media in particular, became part of military strategy. Robert M. Entman makes this oppressively clear: from now on, war has to be sold to the public – even at the cost of any kind of realism.

Globalization and the 'Postmodern' War of Images

Under the premises of globalization and digitalization, we are once again witnessing a change in the technical possibilities of communication and a change in the nature of warfare. On the one hand, wars are no longer fought by regular armies only but also by paramilitary groups, criminals and regular armed forces alike. The outcome of this development is characterized as 'postmodern', 'atypical' or, more recently, as 'asymmetrical war'. On the other hand, time has become 'real' and space is distorted by the simultaneous global media coverage of conflict and violence. In this sense, as Diego Lazzarich puts it in his historical overview at the beginning of the book, the Persian Gulf War can be said to be the first 'live war' in that it enabled massive emotional participation in the event. It was, however, participation in an event cleansed of death so as not to endanger public support for military action.

Thus, the double-faced role of the mainstream media becomes more obvious than ever: they reflect particular perceptions of reality and form them at the same time. In so far as war reporters are and will continue to be integrated into their respective culture and community (and are accordingly biased), media conflict appears in tandem with military conflict. The media are missiles. Stephan Russ-Mohl argues that, in a globalized world, media networks, because they constitute some of the 'big linkers', have become even more decisive in influencing the progress of a war by fighting a 'war of images' (although he concedes that it is conceivable, at least to a certain extent, that new forms of media criticism will spring up from the 'blogosphere').

More than ever, the aims and strategies of this new warfare depend on particular perceptions of reality. But, while the deliberative public discourse on war and conflict would require more factual information, these forms of 'mediated discourse' are not about facts but rather about images – or, to put it more accurately, according to Philip Hammond, about the 'right' or the 'humanitarian' image. Not only are governments paying closer attention to image and its presentation, journalists too are joining this narcissistic search for meaning. When a war or a so-called 'Operation Other Than War' (OOTW) starts and ends, the soldier and the terrorist are defined publicly and part of a more or less globalized discourse. It is up to the media to decide whether the 'War on Terror' was a success or a failure, whether Israel had waged war or just carried out a police action, whether the resolution of the war in Bosnia-Herzegovina was 'just' or whether the engagements in Afghanistan and Iraq were a victory or a defeat – and, even more complicated, for whom. Both the home front and public opinion worldwide depend on these media framing strategies that the parties in a conflict seek to adopt in order to make the most out of their marketing efforts. The chapters by Nel Ruigrok, Wouter van Atteveldt and Janet Takens as well as by Dennis Lichtenstein and Claudia Nitsch deal with the role of the media in conflict dynamics such as it can be seen in various international conflicts and from different methodological viewpoints.

While conflict parties spend a great amount of resources in shaping public opinion, direct intervention is not only impossible but also not necessary, since the mass media are economically motivated to meet audience expectations and the needs of the advertising industry. Moreover, journalists have incentives to produce or simply reproduce marketable content as cheaply as possible. If the audience accepts the sound bites from Pentagon TV, the PR spins of the conflicting parties, and fake news as breaking news and are satisfied with it, then there is no economic motivation to change. This presents a challenge for professional ethics and decent journalism, as Roman Hummel shows. And quite obviously, not all players can cope with this challenge – because of the different types of infrastructure, the deficits in the professional education of war correspondents and the mental embedding of journalists. Under such circumstances, investigative reporting is replaced by framing strategies that were previously experienced as successful.

Similar to state institutions, non-state actors have also come to terms with the media culture. Since wars can no longer be thought outside a media frame, we are led to assume that hostile engagements and terrorist acts are staged for media effects – at least to a certain extent. The events of 9/11 fueled the debate on the mediatization of terror. While some see the rise of a new form of terrorism, others just see the 'CNN effect' spreading to this form of asymmetrical and atypical war. In this context, Brigitte L. Nacos throws light on the mass-mediated debate on torture in post-9/11 America by assuming that there are links between mass media content, on the one hand, and attitudes about torture among policy-makers and the general public, on the other. She paints a disturbing picture of the limitations of public discourse – even in democracies. We have to remember, however, that 'mediatized' war is still about life and death. And there is only one way to cope with conflicts: by breaking the spiral of hostility.

* * *

Editing this book and working with so many committed people has been a pleasure and a privilege. This collection has evolved out of a conference on 'War, Media, and the Public Sphere', which took place at the Austrian Academy of Sciences on March 6–7, 2009 and was organized by the Commission for Comparative Media and Communication Studies and the Department of Media and Communications Science at the University of Klagenfurt. However, this book does not simply represent the proceedings from the 2009 event. Instead, all papers were heavily revised and updated according to the needs of a textbook for students. We would therefore like to express our deepest gratitude to all contributors to this volume for their thought-provoking and insightful chapters. (To some articles, items like further reading lists and web links were added by the editors.) We would also like to thank Nico Carpentier, the anonymous reviewers and all the people from the European Communication Research and Education Association (ECREA) for their valuable comments and suggestions. We are very happy that this volume is included in the ECREA Book Series. Many thanks to Melanie Marshall and Tim Mitchell from Intellect for their valuable help during the editing process. We are especially indebted to Anja Löbert and her colleagues from Textworks Translations, Manchester, who did an excellent job in proofreading the manuscript, and to Cíntia Maria Fonseca da Silva for assisting us in the final stages of preparing the book for publication. Last but not least, we owe special thanks to Henkel Central Eastern Europe for funding not only the conference but also the printing of the book.

Introduction

Delivering War to the Public: Shaping the Public Sphere

Philip Seib

Summary

The ways that news about war is delivered to the public profoundly affect how people think about war. That may appear counterintuitive; after all, the information itself, not its method of delivery, would seem to be what matters. But information and its impact are influenced to varying extents by the medium that carries the message. A newspaper analysis differs from a live television report from the battlefield, which in turn differs from an amateur's YouTube video, not just in the craft that has gone into the messages or even their specific content, but also in how they are received by their audiences.

This chapter examines war and the media – primarily the news media but also, to a limited degree, the role of non-news media. Relying primarily on examples drawn from conflicts in which the United States has been involved, the chapter is designed to stimulate thinking about how war's place within the public sphere is influenced by media and, more particularly, how the news media define and perform their societal role related to war. As years have passed, the definition of 'news media' has expanded, as has the definition of 'journalist', with the population of each growing significantly. These changes make more complex the evaluation of how news is received by the public. Another factor in the effects of news is the larger social context of information flow, which includes non-news elements such as entertainment – in this field the television, cinema and other products that address war-related topics. As with news, entertainment's effects vary: a *Rambo* may stimulate a thirst for (vicarious) combat, while a *Saving Private Ryan* may encourage appreciation of the horrific nature of war. Whatever the particular entertainment vehicles may be, those that depict war become part of the inventory of images and ideas that shape the public sphere. In this way, non-news messages as well as journalism help build the environment in which news is received. These are ingredients of the multifaceted process of constructing opinions about war.

Relationships among News Media, Civilian Policy-Makers and the Military[1]

How the public perceives war depends in part on the relationships that the news media have with the government. Several important questions must be addressed:

- During wartime, what happens to journalists' adversarial relationship with government?
- Should it be set aside altogether, or at least moderated?

- To what extent do the responsibilities of citizenship/patriotism supersede those of journalism?

To use as an example the run-up to the Iraq War and the conflict's early stages in 2003, a case can be made that a de facto collaboration existed between the Bush administration and most US news organizations. Following the attacks of September 11, 2001, many in the news media were eager to follow the government's lead, wherever that might take them, without doing the journalist's basic job, which is to ask questions.

It is really that simple. When the White House says Iraq possesses weapons of mass destruction, you ask, 'How do you know that?' When you get an answer, you do not simply accept it, but you follow up with more questions and you look for more sources, engaging in a dialectic exercise that can be hard work but is the essence of journalism.

This sounds like a lesson that can be quickly taught to someone just beginning the study of journalism, but some of the best news organizations in America, such as the *New York Times* and *The Washington Post* consistently failed to meet this basic standard.

Such a failure is not an esoteric matter. When sloppy journalism prevails, the public suffers because government influence expands to fill the vacuum left by the news media's nonperformance. In considering how the public sphere responds to war, effects of this imbalance should be evaluated carefully.

Sometimes news organizations reexamine their assumptions and assertions, and find them to be wanting. Such was the case with the *New York Times* in 2004. Although the newspaper deserves credit for its introspective undertaking, the systemic problems its senior editors found underscore the dangers of journalistic nonchalance.

In a 'From the Editors' critique, the *New York Times* said it had published 'an enormous amount of journalism that we are proud of' about the war, but admitted that

> we have found a number of instances of coverage that was not as rigorous as it should have been. In some cases, information that was controversial then, and seems questionable now, was insufficiently qualified or allowed to stand unchallenged. Looking back, we wish we had been more aggressive in re-examining the claims as new evidence emerged – or failed to emerge.

The analysis said,

> Editors at several levels who should have been challenging reporters and pressing for more skepticism were perhaps too intent on rushing scoops into the paper [...] Articles based on dire claims about Iraq tended to get prominent display, while follow-up articles that called the original ones into question were sometimes buried. In some cases, there was no follow-up at all. ('The *Times* and Iraq', 2004)

In effect, the *New York Times*, like many other American news organizations, had retreated from its proper place within the public sphere, ceding ground to the government.

That proper place is a spot from which the news media can monitor discourse and encourage a broad array of voices to participate in debate. One role of the press is to present those voices to a larger public as an intelligible chorus rather than an undecipherable cacophony. In this case, most of the voices came from the Bush administration or those who shared the administration's interests. That means there is little contest for the public's support; the intellectual terrain on which issues should be debated is left barren. People can choose to believe the administration's case or not, but they are far more likely to believe it if there is no comparably accessible counterpoint.

In this desolate public sphere, policy-makers intent on having their way are more likely to succumb to the temptation to present conjecture as fact and even concoct 'evidence' to support their claims. If they know they are unlikely to encounter consistent press pushback, expedience becomes more alluring.

To remain with the *New York Times* case, it is useful to examine some of the internal debate at the paper. Daniel Okrent, the *New York Times*'s public editor (an ombudsman of sorts), was more forceful in his analysis of the Iraq coverage than the writers of the 'From the Editors' piece had been. He wrote, 'To anyone who read the paper between September 2002 and June 2003, the impression that Saddam Hussein possessed, or was acquiring, a frightening arsenal of W.M.D. seemed unmistakable' (Okrent, 2004). Some of the *New York Times* coverage, noted Okrent, 'was credulous' and 'much of it was inappropriately italicized by lavish front-page display and heavy-breathing headlines', while stories that 'provided perspective or challenged information in the faulty stories were played as quietly as a lullaby'. Okrent went on to point out that 'war requires an extra standard of care, not a lesser one'. Some reporting, he wrote, relied far too heavily on anonymous sources, and 'other stories pushed Pentagon assertions so aggressively you could almost sense epaulets sprouting on the shoulders of editors' (Okrent, 2004).

Why does this happen? Only rarely is there evidence of premeditated collusion between a journalist and government officials. More often it is a function of laziness and other kinds of sloppy procedures as well as reluctance to defy what appears to be the popular mood of the moment. In post-9/11 America, being patriotic seemed to require marching in step with the Bush administration's parade toward war with Iraq. The longer that opposition to war was marginalized, the firmer the support for the Bush policy became and the harder it was for contrarian journalists to gain traction.

Once the invasion of Iraq began in March 2003, news media ties to the government became even closer as a result of the Pentagon's system of embedding journalists with combat units. This meant that about 700 members of the press corps would live, work and travel with military units for weeks, or even months. The audience for this venture, said the Pentagon, was both the American public and 'the public in allied countries whose opinion can affect the durability of our coalition, and publics in countries where we conduct operations, whose perceptions of us can affect the cost and duration of our involvement' (US Department of Defense, 2003: 1–2).

Guidelines for the 'embeds', as they came to be known, were relatively reasonable. Journalists could not report about specific numbers of troops or plans for upcoming operations.

5

They were expected to refrain from publishing names or photographs of individual casualties, at least until next of kin had been notified.

Although Pentagon spokespersons talked about 'a free press in a free society', they acknowledged pragmatic reasons for the embed program. Having reporters on the battlefield would reduce the chances that the enemy could rely on disinformation – about who was inflicting civilian casualties, for example – and would perhaps provide such vivid depictions of American military prowess that Iraqi forces would be demoralized and surrender (Salamon, 2003). Perhaps most important, favorable coverage would bolster support for the war within the United States.

During the initial days of the invasion, the embeds delivered close-up descriptions of the fighting. But a study conducted by the Project for Excellence in Journalism (2003) found that television stories from embedded reporters during the first week of the war featured 'all the virtues and vices of reporting only what you see'. The study found the following:

- 94 percent of the stories were primarily factual rather than interpretive.
- 60 percent of the reports were live and unedited.
- In 80 percent of the stories, viewers heard only from the reporters, not from soldiers or other sources.
- 47 percent of the stories described battles or their results.
- The reports avoided graphic material – not one of the stories in the study showed pictures of people who had been hit by weapons fire.

The report found that the war as presented by embedded television journalists was like 'reality itself – confusing, incomplete, sometimes numbing, sometimes intense, and not given to simple story lines' (Project for Excellence in Journalism, 2003: 12).

'Reporting only what you see' might not, on first hearing, seem like such a bad thing. It sounds like a basic definition of objectivity: factual, unembellished coverage. But good journalism includes an appreciation of nuance and an ability to place 'what you see' in a broader context. Jack Fuller, president of Tribune Publishing Co., said that the television coverage was 'utterly riveting' but that 'it also demonstrated that there is a difference between seeing and understanding' (Sharkey, 2003: 20).

That difference affects the perception of war within the public sphere. The coverage provided plenty of snapshots, often of Hollywood-style combat with American soldiers as action heroes wielding massive firepower. But seldom was there substantive reporting about civilian casualties or how Iraqis were responding to the invasion. Convenient episodes such as the toppling of Saddam Hussein's statue in Baghdad became iconic, while bloody chaos remained outside the camera's focus. This means the public was often seeing a contrived version of war, and so their feelings about the conflict, and particularly its political elements, were affected accordingly.

Embedded reporters frequently adopted the perspective of the troops they accompanied. *The Orange County Register*'s Gordon Dillow (who had been in the army during the Vietnam

War) said, 'Isolated from everyone else, you start to see your small corner of the world the same way they do'. This shared outlook can affect the substance and tone of coverage. Dillow wrote,

> I didn't hide anything. For example, when some of my marines fired up a civilian vehicle that was bearing down on them, killing three unarmed Iraqi men, I reported it – but I didn't lead my story with it, and I was careful to put it in the context of scared young men trying to protect themselves. Or when my marines laughed about how .50-caliber machine gun bullets had torn apart an Iraqi soldier's body, I wrote about it, but in the context of sweet-faced, all-American boys hardened by a war that wasn't of their making. And so on. The point wasn't that I wasn't reporting the truth; the point was that I was reporting the marine grunt truth – which had also become my truth. (Dillow, 2003: 33)

'My marines'. 'My truth'. Dillow's choice of words shows how sometimes the line between journalist and participant became blurred, both as a matter of self-image and in story content. This kind of coverage presumably reinforces the inclination to support the war, an opinion that is held by a sizable bloc of the public, particularly during the early stages of the conflict.

If the news media become an adjunct of the military, serving in more of a public relations role than a journalistic capacity, the flow of information to the public will almost certainly take on a militaristic coloration. When this is overtly reinforced by the government, the public has little chance to develop an informed alternative viewpoint.

The Dillow case provides a useful illustration of how the media affect the relationship between the state and civil society. Instead of occupying neutral terrain between the two, which arguably is the appropriate place for the news media, journalists periodically edge cozily close to the government. This creates an imbalance of influence that is intrinsically undemocratic, removing an important check on government power and thus changing the political dynamic of the public sphere.

Media Evolution and the Public Psyche

The relationship between war reporting and the public has a long history. Homer's rendition of the Trojan War has given his audience an appreciation of wartime heroism. Herodotus and Thucydides were early practitioners of the craft and made clear the relationship between combat and politics. Centuries later, Matthew Brady and his colleagues presented visual images of the battlefield to the public, and during the following century the arrival of electronic media brought warfare even more vividly into citizens' homes.

No longer could anyone be truly distant from combat. As World War II began, the first electronic installment of 'living-room war' arrived on radio waves, most notably in the work of Edward R. Murrow. Reporting from the rooftops of London during air raids, Murrow delivered the sounds of war as well as his own dark poetry about how Britons endured the blitz. Bringing news in this form so explicitly into the lives of the public affected how people looked at government and policy. Speaking at a tribute to Murrow in 1941, Archibald MacLeish said, 'you burned the city of London in our houses and we felt the flames that burned it. You laid the dead of London at our doors and we knew the dead were our dead' (Seib, 2006: 148). The power of this relatively new medium was reshaping public perceptions of the war of the moment and warfare generally.

About two decades later, television brought visual images of the Vietnam War into the living room. Michael Arlen, television critic of *The New Yorker*, wrote that on the TV screen 'we were watching, a bit numbly perhaps (we have watched it so often), real men get shot at, real men (our surrogates, in fact) get killed and wounded' (Arlen, 1982: 82–3). Viewers were close and yet removed, Arlen continued, watching the war 'as a child, kneeling in a corridor, his eye to the keyhole, looks at two grownups arguing in a locked room – the aperture of the keyhole small; the figures shadowy, mostly out of sight; the voices indistinct'. Television provides and controls that keyhole view of war: episodic flashes that lack context, blood that never splashes onto the living-room rug and vanishes altogether when the channel is changed (Arlen, 1982: 82–3; Seib, 2002: 31).

What did this television presence mean in terms of the relationship between state and civil society? Media coverage did not, in itself, generate revulsion toward the war. Although some policy-makers sought to blame news coverage for 'losing' Vietnam (a notion that survives in some quarters to this day), that grossly overstates the media's clout. The failure of the US war effort was a matter of policy, not press. The debate about this was long and often fascinating, and cannot be pursued in detail here. Instead, consider this appraisal by Clark Clifford, secretary of defense during the latter stages of Lyndon Johnson's presidency:

> Contrary to right-wing revisionism, reporters and the antiwar movement did not defeat America in Vietnam. Our policy failed because it was based on false premises and false promises. Had the results in Vietnam approached, even remotely, what Washington and Saigon had publicly predicted for many years, the American people would have continued to support their government. (Clifford, 1991: 474)

Clifford's statement is a valuable reminder that political institutions, not the news media, are the principal players in shaping the public's expectations about policy. The news media can point out unfulfilled promises and blatant untruths, and that is an invaluable part of the democratic structure. It is, however, a supporting role.

Supporting, but still important. Without the news media, war would intrude far less significantly into the public's consciousness. Thanks to new media technologies, war has now become a regular visitor in the living room, and to keep the audience better informed – or perhaps better entertained – combat is now sometimes presented in real time. Coverage of the 1991 Gulf War featured live reports, and by the time of the 2003 invasion of Iraq improved technology and more intense competition among news organizations fostered extensive real-time combat coverage.

A principal challenge facing news organizations reporting live from a combat zone or anywhere else is adhering to the adage, 'Get it first, but first get it right'. When the deadline is always 'Right now!' important elements of journalism might be jettisoned. Corroboration, detail, analysis, context – all these are crucial to good news coverage, but sometimes there is just not time for them if your primary goal is to 'get it first'.

As American units raced toward Baghdad during the early days of the 2003 Iraq invasion, American viewers could turn on their televisions during the early morning hours and watch live battles. Embedded reporters took advantage of satellite technology to feed often engrossing real-time reports to their audience. This was a new, more exciting version of living-room war.

The American public apparently enjoyed the adrenalin surge this coverage provided. These were heady times for the Bush administration, as well; the media coverage reinforced the administration's message that the war was achieving its objectives. Journalists seemed happy with their quasi-military role and news organizations rarely found time for critical voices.

But beneath the surface, volcanic forces were building that were about to change the nature of journalism forever.

New Media and the Public Sphere

During the first days of the Iraq war, a US soldier who identified himself as 'L. T. Smash' began writing a blog, with entries such as this: 'Saddam Hussein fired a couple of those Scuds that he doesn't have at me this afternoon. He missed.' During the first week of the war, 'Smash's' website was attracting 6,000 visitors a day. Other blogs were posted by military personnel, Baghdad residents, politicians and journalists who supplemented their regular coverage with more personal reporting. Howard Kurtz of *The Washington Post* characterized the battlefield blogs as 'idiosyncratic, passionate, and often profane, with the sort of intimacy and attitude that are all but impossible in newspapers and on television' (Kurtz, 2003).

Blogs alter the balance that has long existed between the news media and the public. Along with other Internet-based material, blogs amplify voices that previously went unheard or did not even speak because they assumed they would not be noticed. For information consumers, blogs offer a different view of events than traditional news media provide, and sometimes that difference is refreshing in its style and substance. Blogs exponentially increase the diversity of information sources. Just as the growth of cable news channels expanded the ideological spectrum of broadcast journalism, so do blogs offer niches dedicated to subject matter that is presented with various degrees of expertize. Some who peruse the blogosphere do not take most of the material seriously, but some find blogs that they trust as news sources comparable to those of traditional media.

Particularly in countries with government-controlled or otherwise limited news media, such as Egypt and Iran, blogs can open up public discourse in unprecedented ways. This is not to say that blogs in and of themselves are going to bring democracy to those countries, but the tripartite government–public–media relationship has the chance to be better balanced. That is an important, if not conclusive, step forward.

In democracies during wartime, blogs might undermine government attempts to shape the news media's approach to conflict coverage. Opposition voices will have a venue and although any individual blog's audience will probably be relatively small, bloggers' cumulative effect may have an impact (especially if their reports are picked up and amplified by larger media organizations). As a result, legitimizing a war and mobilizing public support may become more difficult for government. During the 2002–03 period when the Bush administration was planning the Iraq War, blogs' pervasiveness and sophistication had not yet reached their height. Going to war today might prove a more politically difficult task.

There are times when war is just and necessary. Even in that situation a democratic government should be expected to make a compelling case for war and should be prepared to address objections that arise in all forms of media. It can be argued that the growing media population, as exemplified by blogs and other online mechanisms, provides security to democracy by compelling government to make its case in a way that can enlist the support of various bloggers as well as the *New York Times* editorial board.

Enriching and making more diverse and complex the range of new media are video blogs such as YouTube. During the Iraq War, YouTube was used by the US military to display positive images of the American presence in Iraq, but other YouTube offerings showed American troops engaged in 'extremely violent, anti-social activities' (Christensen, 2008: 156). Swedish scholar Christian Christensen observed of the YouTube effect that, 'in an era of instantaneous global online distribution systems and cheap, simple media production, the dominance of traditional, centralized, and hierarchical modes of information dissemination, public diplomacy and propaganda can no longer be taken for granted' (2008: 157).

This YouTube example illustrates how government is being forced by the rise of new media to enter into overt, direct competition with nongovernmental information sources. During the days when conventional news organizations monopolized the supply of information to the public, the government could exert influence in more subtle ways, such as providing or withholding access and deluging the news media with briefings and other information that would be delivered to the public. For the government, the news media served as little more than a conveyor belt. In the newly expanded information universe, government can no longer rely exclusively on channeling its message through the news establishment and will need instead to engage the public more directly.

In terms of representations of war, this constitutes a significant change in how war is viewed by the public and how government interacts with its citizenry. 'Storytelling power' has become much more diffuse, and, as Christensen noted, YouTube videos showing abuse of civilians and other acts of wanton violence have great impact because 'they reveal a side of military activity that is meant to be hidden from the citizens who both fund the war and vote for the politicians who support it' (2008: 172). With these stories available to a large (and global) public, government may find its credibility suffering and opposition to its policies gaining strength. Images such as those that can be found on YouTube and those emanating from the Abu Ghraib torture scandal can break down public faith in government and accelerate the progression from skeptical tolerance of government pronouncements to outright distrust and opposition.

The media's evolution has built momentum during the first years of the new century, and by making war information more accessible and more diverse has shaped not only the present but also the future of the public sphere.

Looking Ahead

The media, broadly defined, will continue to play a significant role in the legitimization or stigmatization of conflict. One aspect of this is the visual imagery of war. Most mainstream media present sanitized depictions of war. The feeling of news executives seems to be that the public should not be discomfited by too much blood. American news organizations are particularly squeamish about graphic images. Sometimes Hollywood provides more accurate renderings of conflict.

This is not merely a matter of 'tastefulness'. If the public is presented with war-fighting as a nice, neat enterprise, why not do it more often? Why care about 'collateral damage' (a rather obscene term), if it appears to be limited to a few buildings knocked down? 'Shock and awe' is a clever turn of phrase, but it has dreadful meaning for those who are caught up in it.

In Iraq, Gaza, Afghanistan and elsewhere, conflict takes place that is far more gruesome than most publics are asked to consider. The news media have become so concerned about the presumed delicacy of their audience that one must turn to contemporary motion pictures to find more realistic depictions of warfare. That will benefit viewers' digestion if they watch a newscast at dinnertime, but it does not aid the public's understanding of the nature of war.

As well as needing to decide what limits there should be on the content of conflict coverage, information providers of all kinds must come to grips with the realities of media globalization. This takes shape in numerous ways. Satellite television has a vast worldwide audience, and the 'digital divide' is slowly but steadily narrowing as Internet service reaches more parts of the world. Cell phone service, however, is already pervasive and has become the vehicle of choice for many millions of those gathering and disseminating information. Whatever the tools, worldwide media growth is accelerating on many levels.

Part of this expansion involves an 'Al Jazeera effect' through which upgraded regional media deliver news in ways that are more credible than those of 'outsiders'. For instance, coverage of the recent conflict in Gaza by the Arab satellite news channels was received differently than reporting by western news organizations. 'Seeing ourselves through our own eyes' is important, and seeing 'our own' conflicts in this way alters the public sphere. To again use the Gaza conflict as an example, in addition to providing graphic images of civilian casualties within Gaza, many Arab news organizations were sharply critical of some

Arab governments' hands-off policy toward the Palestinians. Such coverage was a significant factor in inflaming the politics of the region and presents a lesson about the media as an engine of change, or at least a contributor to volatility.

This case underscores the importance of how news is presented, meaning – in this instance – by whom it is presented. A case can be made that localized news significantly alters the government–news media–public relationship whether in the Arab world, Latin America, sub-Saharan Africa or other places that have long endured a public sphere shaped (and even controlled) by colonial and other outside influences.

Add to print and broadcast media the Internet-based information sources, with their interactive capabilities, and the ability to cover war, in the journalistic sense, may be expanded. 'Citizen journalists' with cell phone cameras are one example of this. Suppose they had been in Rwanda in 1994 – would they have made a difference?

The 'small wars' (which seem anything but small to those caught up in them) may now emerge from relative invisibility and make their presence felt within the public sphere. Then, global publics – governments and citizenry – will need to decide how to respond. To paraphrase MacLeish's comment about Murrow, when the media lay the dead from distant places at our doors will that distance narrow and will the public take notice and demand a response?

Any projections about global activism should be made with great caution. Media-induced compassion fatigue can be debilitating, and the cries to 'do something' can fade quickly. But the world will not be able to pretend that it does not know. In 1938, Neville Chamberlain chose to abandon Czechoslovakia to Adolf Hitler rather than intervene in 'a quarrel in a faraway country between people of whom we know nothing'. In the era of new media and an enlarged public sphere, no people and no conflict are so far away that we can claim to know nothing about them.

But the absence of ignorance does not ensure the presence of wisdom. Part of our task as scholars is to foster the emergence of wisdom.

Key Points

- News media should monitor societal discourse and encourage a broad array of voices to participate in the debate about societal issues, and they should critically ask questions and use more than just government sources in their answers.
- Nonetheless, how the public perceives war depends nowadays on the particular relationship that the news media have with the government: In the Iraq War of 2003, most voices came from the Bush administration or those who shared the administration's interests, and the news media simply adopted the government positions, which allowed the government to expand its influence by filling the vacuum left behind by the news media.
- The resulting imbalance of influence is intrinsically undemocratic and removes an important check on government power, which in turn alters the political dynamics of the public sphere.

- During the Iraq War of 2003, the 'embedded journalism' being sold by the government as factual and unembellished coverage close to the actual events was, however, unable to place 'what you see' into a broader context of understanding and was correspondingly lacking in substantive reporting, for example, reporting from the civilian perspective (i.e., casualties) or from the Iraqi perspective.
- The new media stepped in to take over the controlling role that news media should play, and Internet blogs, for instance, offered a different view of events than the traditional news media provided, thus exponentially increasing the diversity of information sources.

Study Questions

1. How were civilian policy-makers, the news media and the military connected during the 2003 Iraq War, and what were the effects of this connection on objective war coverage of the official news media, taking into account, for instance, the aspect of 'embedded journalism'?
2. What new forms of news coverage on war emerged from the one-sided situation of news coverage during the 2003 Iraq War – for example, in the area of the new media such as blogs, YouTube and so on?
3. During 2002/03, when the Bush administration was planning the Iraq War, the pervasiveness and sophistication of blogs had not yet reached their height. In light of the rapid development of those media, discuss whether going to war today might prove a more politically difficult task, and what new forms of public engagement and interaction with citizenry would have to be developed by governments in order for them to gain public support for their policies.

Further Reading

Allan, Stuart and Barbie Zelizer (eds) (2004) *Reporting War. Journalism in Wartime*. London: Routledge.

Rid, Thomas (2007) *War and Media Operations. The US Military and the Press from Vietnam to Iraq*. London: Routledge.

Seib, Philip (2004) *Beyond the Front Lines. How the News Media Cover a World Shaped by War*. New York; Basingstoke: Palgrave Macmillan.

——— (2006) *Broadcasts from the Blitz. How Edward R. Murrow Helped Lead America into War*. Washington, DC: Potomac Books.

——— (ed) (2010) *War and Conflict Communication*. 2 vols. London; New York: Routledge.

Thussu, Daya K. and Des Freedman (eds) (2003) *War and the Media. Reporting Conflict 24/7*. London; Thousand Oaks, CA: Sage.

Tumber, Howard and Frank Webster (2006) *Journalists Under Fire. Information War and Journalistic Practices*. London: Sage.

Websites

Center for Public Integrity: www.publicintegrity.org
PEW Research Center, Project for Excellence in Journalism: Studies, commentaries and backgrounders on war and terrorism carried out by PEW: www.journalism.org/ra_by_media/*/*/67

References

Arlen, Michael J. (1982) *Living-Room War*. Harmondsworth; New York: Penguin Books.
Christensen, Christian (2008) 'Uploading Dissonance. YouTube and the US Occupation of Iraq', *Media, War & Conflict* 1(2): 155–75.
Clifford, Clark (1991) *Counsel to the President. A Memoir*. New York: Random House.
Dillow, Gordon (2003) 'Grunts and Pogues. The Embedded Life', *Columbia Journalism Review* 42(1): 32–33.
Kurtz, Howard (2003) 'Webloggers Signing On as War Correspondents', *The Washington Post*, March 23, 2003.
Okrent, Daniel (2004) 'The Public Editor. Weapons of Mass Destruction? Or Mass Distraction?', *New York Times*, May 30, 2004.
Project for Excellence in Journalism (2003) 'Embedded Reporters. What are Americans Getting?', http://www.journalism.org/node/211 (February 19, 2009).
Salamon, Julie (2003) 'New Tools Make War Images Instant but Coverage No Simpler', *New York Times*, April 6, 2003.
Seib, Philip (2002) *Going Live. Getting the News Right in a Real-Time, Online World*. Lanham, MD: Rowman & Littlefields.
———— (2004) *Beyond the Front Lines. How the News Media Cover a World Shaped by War*. New York; Basingstoke: Palgrave Macmillan.
———— (2006) *Broadcasts from the Blitz. How Edward R. Murrow Helped Lead America into War*. Washington, DC: Potomac Books.
Sharkey, Jacqueline E. (2003) 'The Television War', *American Journalism Review* 25(4): 18–27.
'The *Times* and Iraq' (2004), *New York Times*, May 26, 2004.
US Department of Defense (2003) 'Public Affairs Guidance on Embedding Media during Possible Future Operations/Deployments in the U.S. Central Command's Area of Responsibility', www. defense.gov/news/Feb2003/d20030228pag.pdf (March 12, 2010).

Note

1   Some of the material related to the Iraq War is drawn from Seib (2004).

PART I

'Never Such Innocence Again': Propaganda and Total War

War and the Public Sphere

European Examples from the Seven Years' War to the World War I

Reinhard Stauber

Summary

I n recent times, historical research – and, most notably, the concept of *Erfahrungsgeschichte* ('the history of experience') – is acknowledging the role of the mass media in shaping the knowledge and the images of reality that are present in society. That is particularly true in times of war when the media enjoy privileged access to information. Based on the examples of four European wars between 1750 and 1918 (The Seven Years' War, the Crimean War, the Franco-Prussian War of 1870–71 and the World War I), this chapter outlines the techniques and forms in which the media reported on war in the past few centuries. It attempts to illustrate the fact that conjuring up images of the enemy and arming the citizenry against real and presumed opponents has always been an important tool in creating in-groups while excluding 'the others'. In the course of the nineteenth century, the notion of the 'nation' developed into an absolute value that could not be questioned and thus became the highest and the sole reference point for the loyalty of political associations and their leaders. It thus emerged that war and nation-building or nation-state-building were very closely associated with one another. The experience of war counts as one of the central nation-building factors in modern times, and the incorporation of the nation into the events of war would be unthinkable without the nineteenth-century mass media and their accounting of the events in words and images.

Introduction

War, as Karmasin (2007) has recently explained, is a deadly and ever-present extreme state of human existence. Not least for this reason, they are also media and communication events that have had an enormous impact since the beginning of the historical tradition (Karmasin, 2007: 11; see also Daniel, 2006a; Köppen, 2005; Knieper and Müller, 2005; Preusser, 2005; Löffelholz, 2004; Hartwig, 1999; Imhof and Schulz, 1995).

The media and communication sciences can contribute to research on the close interconnections between a media culture and war, but the historical sciences also have a part to play. Over the past ten years, the concept of *Erfahrungsgeschichte* ('the history of experience') has been extended beyond the evidence of actors, eyewitnesses and those directly affected ('the experience of war') to include the process of medial transmission to a wider audience (Buschmann and Carl, 2001). The mass media have a key function in shaping the knowledge that is present in society: they create images of reality that stamp experience and become particularly effective in certain contexts, especially when such media enjoy privileged access to information, as is (or seems to be) the case in times of war.

'In modern times societies are increasingly integrated, in terms of communication, via the mass media' (Buschmann, 2001: 102). The European wars of the 1850s and 1860s gave the role of the mass press a sudden boost and placed newspapers at the center of public communication. By 1850 at the latest, politics recognized that the press was indispensable as an instrument of political mobilization (Buschmann, 2001: 113). Thus war became a fixed component of the contemporary world of the imagination – not only as a military event but also with respect to its political, social and historical contexts. Wars and crises were not only communicative events of the first rank but also screens on to which the clash of opinions between political world images and various social views were projected.

In this chapter, I shall present four European examples between 1750 and 1918 in order to outline the techniques and forms in which the media reported on war.

The Eighteenth Century – The Seven Years' War

Even in the eighteenth century, current political news was disseminated most quickly and widely by the daily or weekly press. The development of this medium in the context of the seventeenth-century 'communication revolution' can, it seems, be attributed in part to the high proportion of war-related reportage in early newspapers and to the interest of urban elites in particular in this sort of information (for an overview, see Wilke, 2005). Events of the Thirty Years' War, such as the storming of the city of Magdeburg, which was reduced to ashes in 1631, or the conclusion of peace in 1648, were early large-scale media events with a European dimension (Schultheiss-Heinz, 2004; Wrede, 2004; Blitz, 2001).

This trend continued in the eighteenth century and was promoted by the evolving enlightened and critical public sphere. The Seven Years' War, which was fought in a number of theaters of war in Europe and overseas between 1756 and 1763, was a major event. One of the leading German-language newspapers of the period, the *Unpartheyischer Correspondent*, published in Hamburg, increased its average print-run from 1,500 to more than 10,000 between 1730 and 1780.

I shall discuss some of the main features of war reporting in the eighteenth-century press by taking as an example the Austrian monarchy's oldest newspaper, the *Wiennerisches Diarium* (from 1780 on renamed the *Wiener Zeitung*), founded in 1703 and privileged by the imperial court. The court supplied information exclusively to the *Wiener Diarium*, and the paper was justifiably considered the official mouthpiece of Viennese politics (Gestrich, 2006).

Usually published twice a week, the newspaper ran to eight pages in length. In times of war, however, extensive reports and supplements meant that it regularly doubled or tripled in size, news about Austria, France (its most important ally), and its main enemy, Prussia, forming the main focus of interest. 'Detailed news about the other belligerent powers was frequently conveyed by [regular] correspondents in the respective capitals, rather than coming from the "front"' (Gestrich, 2006: 26f). Thus, the news did not originate with war reporters in the real sense of the word. A time lag of ten to fourteen days between the occurrence of an event and it being reported on in the press was the rule.

About one-third of the reports were devoted to things that would hardly arouse interest today, such as the deployment and redeployment of troops, that is, the semipublic side of preparations for war, which could be observed on the spot with relatively little risk. There were fewer reports about armed conflicts and battles (about 15 percent), and only 3 percent of the reports concerned war crimes in the broadest sense, especially plundering and forced requisitions. It is hardly surprising that the *Wiennerisches Diarium* concentrated on such acts committed by Prussian troops, which points to the propaganda function of the manner in which news is selected.

The *Wiener Diarium*'s main sources for its war reports were the field journals and war diaries kept by the Austrian army. Written at the headquarters of operational units (and incidentally, not always by high-ranking soldiers), they were sent to the Viennese court, which passed parts of them on to the press. The journals were 'composed in a very neutral tone, and reported a great deal about troop movements, officers' achievements, and promotions. Battles, as a rule, were described in a distanced manner, as if from the perspective of a general watching from the top of a hill' (Gestrich, 2006: 33). In certain cases, for example in 1760, when Prussia firebombed Dresden, a royal residence defended by the Austrians, the consequences of acts of war became visible to the civilian population. The perspective of the ordinary soldier, by contrast, was completely missing.

The Crimean War 1853–56 – The First Media War?

By the nineteenth century, newspapers were the standard medium of war reporting, and they continued to play this role. The Crimean War was the first European war that readers could find information about by reading newspaper reports filed regularly by correspondents writing from the midst of events – that is, reports from the front in the real sense, using the first-person perspective of a participant, in words or images. All the major London newspapers had at least one reporter with the troops at the front and in Constantinople – and thus the independent journalistic genre of war reporting was born (Daniel, 2006b; Knightley, 2004; Lambert and Badsey, 1994; Münkler, 1992; Royle, 1987).

The flood of different images turned the Crimean War into a spectacle of visual representation (Keller, 2007; Smith, 1978):

- In addition to the traditional battle pictures such as those commissioned, for example, by the weekly *Illustrated London News* (with sales of 200,000 in 1855), there were a large number of relatively inexpensive lithographs, retouched in color, and often available only after a few weeks. They included, for example, William Simpson's iconic representation of Florence Nightingale as the 'Lady with the Lamp'.

- In a huge panorama in Leicester Square, Londoners could experience the Battle of Alma, fought on September 20, 1854, at the end of the same year; Madame Tussaud put Florence Nightingale on display; and the battles of the siege of Sevastopol were recreated in sound and light shows.
- Photography, so far, still played a minor part in this flood of images of a distant war (Holzer, 2003a). Photographers had been present on the spot since the spring of 1855, but their products were of little interest to current reporting as there was no technical means of reproducing photographs in newspapers. Roger Fenton photographed the life of troops behind the lines, in vegetable gardens and with military bands, and he left more than 300 portraits of officers. Furthermore, James Robertson and Felice Beato documented the destroyed fortifications of Sevastopol after it was captured in September 1855 (Paul, 2004: 61–5; Keller, 2003).

In Britain, an open and highly controversial public debate accompanied the decision, taken by Aberdeen's government at the end of 1853, to join France in granting the Ottoman Empire armed support against Russia. Other topics that attracted wide public attention were whether Britain's preparations for war were adequate; the strategy followed by the commander-in-chief Lord Raglan, after the landing of the Black Sea expeditionary forces (approx. 30,000 strong) in 1854; the logistical problems at the theaters of war; or the sanitary conditions and especially the atrocious medical care for British soldiers. The popularity of the war against the empire of the Russian tsar, who was presented as a sort of archenemy, was stoked by all the British newspapers and served to conceal the transition to an offensive war in the summer of 1854, a step marked by the decision to besiege the fortress of Sevastopol in the Crimea. But from the turn of the year 1854–55 the leading articles in all the print media became clearly more critical of the war ('national suicide', according to *The Times* of January 25, 1855, Daniel, 2006b: 55), and Prince Albert, consort of Queen Victoria, increasingly became a target for xenophobic journalists.

The Times occupied a special position – it had something like a public–private partnership with the government in Westminster. Strongly capitalized and peerlessly well informed about events in the capital and worldwide, it was the newspaper of choice in the City of London, where it sold up to 60,000 copies, and the most widely read newspaper worldwide for international news. In addition, during the 1850s it was something like the government's mouthpiece vis-à-vis an unstable House of Commons, riven by special interests. As early as 1852, Henry Reeve, a *Times* leader writer and Privy Council official, had written to Foreign Secretary Granville: 'This nation is a good deal enervated by a long peace, by easy habits of intercourse, by peace societies and false economy. To surmount the dangerous consequences of such a state, the Government will require the support of public opinion' (Daniel, 2006b: 41f).

Unlike Queen Victoria, who advised against paying too much attention to journalists, the British prime ministers of the Crimean War period, Aberdeen and Palmerston, were clearly aware 'that the times are gone when politics was able to dispense with the press' (Daniel, 2006b: 57).

The Times' proximity to the arcane area of politics, the information passed to it and, not least, the financial strength of its owner, John Walter III, meant that its editors were confident that as a moral authority and Europe's conscience, they had a claim to influence politics. Indeed, they felt a moral imperative to do so: 'A newspaper such as *The Times* is in the position rather to confer than receive favours, and rather to act as the umpire than the tool or the instrument of party' (Daniel, 2006b: 55).

The Crimean War was at the beginning of William Howard Russell's (1820–1907) career as special correspondent for *The Times*. Previously the paper's parliamentary reporter, from February 1854 on he accompanied the British Expeditionary Corps for more than two years. Later he worked for the paper in India, during the American Civil War, at Königgrätz in 1866 and Sedan in 1870, and in 1879 he was in South Africa for the *Daily Telegraph*.

Working for *The Times* opened every door for Russell. In March 1861 he was received in Washington by President Lincoln, who said, 'The *London Times* is one of the most significant powers in the world – I cannot think of anyone who has more power, except perhaps the Mississippi. I look forward to getting to know you as its ambassador' (Russell, 2000: 208).

And in July 1870 Bismarck personally told the *Times* correspondent, who had paid him a courtesy visit in Berlin before his journey to Lorraine, 'You will travel. I cannot give you an order; that is a matter for the War Minister. A decree has been issued that in principle press correspondents are not permitted to accompany our army. But you are an exception and will shortly receive your credentials' (Russell, 2000: 287; see also Daniel, 2004; Atkins, 1911).

Russell and Edwin Lawrence Godkin, who reported from the front for the *Daily News*, unsparingly conveyed the negative conditions they found, including those on their 'own' side. 'To this extent, the reputation of war reporting as a journalistic genre that informs and speaks the truth, a reputation which goes back to the Crimean War, has a core of reality' (Daniel, 2006b: 61).

Yet for future generations of war reporters who, consciously or not, allowed themselves to be used in the service of their own 'patriotic' cause, this core of reality could become an expedient lie to get them through life.

The vividness and drama that characterized the reports by Russell and Godkin can be attributed to the relatively great freedom of movement that journalists enjoyed in the military theaters and depended on their individual ability in finding the right people to talk to. As a rule, reports were sent to London by post, which meant that the information had a transmission time of two to three weeks. The Crimea was not integrated into the continental telegraph system until April 1855, and even then correspondents only exceptionally telegraphed their reports because of the high costs involved (see Kaufmann, 1996).

British war reporters in the Crimean War obtained much of their information from regimental officers. These were already known to British newspapers as the authors of letters to the editor, and they were not sparing in their criticisms of the commander-in-chief Lord Raglan and his general staff. Thus a new sort of pressure was exerted on the leading generals, and politics could interfere in strategic questions with ever shorter reaction times. Raglan, 66 years old at the time and a protégé of Wellington's, had last seen active service at Waterloo in 1815. He considered himself responsible only to his supreme commander, Queen Victoria, and was neither able nor willing to deal with these new conditions:

> Instead of sending reports from the theatre of war written with an eye to capturing the attention of the reading public, he continued to file his extremely dependable but boring dispatches. Instead of receiving reporters from the front working for the big London papers in his headquarter in the Crimea, he snubbed them by ignoring them. (Daniel, 2006b: 49)

Until February 1856, when the war was practically over, correspondents' reports were not formally censored. Raglan complained about Russell's reports because they revealed details of troop positions to the enemy side, which could have security implications. However, there appeared to be no reaction from the editorial board in London, and the government could not afford to take any measures that, however remotely, might have looked like a restriction on freedom of the press.

Finally, it should be mentioned that the Crimean War precipitated the first charitable appeal launched by the media in military history (see Wilke, 2008). In 1854 John Delane, editor of *The Times*, established a relief fund in his newspaper to provide money for better medical treatment for British soldiers. This drew public attention to an aspect of the war that was not specifically strategic or political, and inspired Florence Nightingale to set off for Scutari, where the biggest British military hospital was located, with 38 nurses on October 21, 1854. Officially, she was acting on the instructions of the British War Ministry.

She was not the only private individual acting to demonstrate that civilian commitment and competence could achieve more than the clogged-up military bureaucracy. Alexis Soyer demonstrated the efficiency of his catering service in providing meals for the troops in the Crimea and, in the spring, the company Peto, Brassey & Betts constructed a section of railway line between the harbor of Balaklava, where the British supply ships landed, and the troop positions outside Sevastopol. But Austen Henry Layard's suggestion that the government should instruct a private army to conduct the war (made in the House of Commons in July 1854) was certainly unrealistic.

Germany 1870–71 – The Media Production of National Unity

> The war of 1870–71 is one of the first in history to be followed and influenced by public opinion from the start.
>
> (Becker, 2001: 47)

The telegraph now played the central role in the transmission of news during wartime, especially since the railways made it possible to deploy troops more rapidly, thus making quicker communications necessary. But the telegraph was also important in communications between the 'front' and the 'home front'. The so-called *Königliche Depesche* (royal dispatch) developed into a popular ritual. In this dispatch the supreme commander, King Wilhelm of Prussia, reported important events from his headquarters to his consort Augusta in Berlin, who was formally Prussia's regent in his absence.

From the city palace in Berlin, these texts were passed on to newspaper editors, who printed them as posters that were then displayed so that large numbers of people could read them. Naturally, they were also printed in the newspapers. More detailed information generally only followed a few days later, in the form of army reports and reports from their own correspondents who, as a rule, could not use the telegraph and had to rely on the army postal services (see Koch, 1978).

Among the war reporters were experienced men such as Russell, who again reported for *The Times*, and Friedrich Wilhelm Hackländer, who worked for the *Augsburger Allgemeine Zeitung*. Others hired themselves out to newspapers out of a love of adventure or a sense of political mission, even though up to that point they had only experienced war in books. One example was the writer Gustav Freytag, a writer who was already well known. He reported for his own weekly, *Die Grenzboten*, from the headquarters of Crown Prince Friedrich of Prussia.

He was an exception. Compared with their British colleagues, German reporters were at a disadvantage. 'As civilians who did not wear a uniform, had no military rank, and moved around the theatre of war largely independently' (Becker, 2006: 70), they often encountered mistrust. Their copy was often reprinted by other newspapers that ignored the laws of copyright, and the authors frequently recycled their own reports in war books or memoirs that they put together. Examples in this case are Freytag and the well-known novelist Theodor Fontane (Daniel, 2005).

The war correspondents themselves, such as Hans Wachenhusen, were fully aware of the dilemma they faced between writing lively descriptions and their lack of an overview of the whole strategic picture. They were also conscious of the fact that while their eyewitness accounts might have enormous atmospheric density, the information value of these accounts as far as understanding the larger context was concerned was limited.

No effective press censorship was exercised in the 1870–71 war, but this was unnecessary on the German side because a dual 'internal censorship' ensured that the reportage had the desired patriotic thrust. First of all, all newspapers in principle supported the war against France and the policy of national unification; there was nothing like the attempt by *The Times* in 1854–55 to put pressure on its own government. And second, all correspondents knew that about eight days after publication, their reports would be read by military staffs and soldiers in many quarters. They therefore avoided any overt or critical descriptions. Furthermore, in 1870 they mostly had their own side's victories to report, which meant that 'on the whole, they could write the truth without having to hurt anyone too much' (Becker, 2006: 71).

Pictorial reportage continued to be largely the domain of the 'battle painters', known at the time as *Specialartisten* ('special artists'). Their drawings were sent to newspaper editors by the army postal service, and were then, as a rule, transformed into woodcuts. Two weeks after the depicted events the drawings were ready to be published. One section of the print media, led by the *Gartenlaube*, an illustrated family paper that had been published since 1853, placed special emphasis on this constant stream of visual material and thus significantly enhanced its circulation. During the war it achieved print-runs of 300,000, which meant that as many as three million people might actually have seen each copy (Wildmeister, 1998). There were also short-lived publications that profited from the news boom during wartime and specialized in graphics. They had martial names such as *Deutsche Kriegszeitung* or *Der Deutsche Volkskrieg*.

The *Specialartisten* also had opportunities to make use of their war drawings again following their return 'from the field' in the form of representative paintings, which a suitably primed bourgeois civil society gladly bought. Photography, which was not yet technically advanced enough to capture rapidly moving scenes, still played a secondary part in current reportage. Nonetheless, in the form of postcards and portraits, it played an important role in the communication between those in the field and those back home (Becker, 2001: 380–482; Bock, 1982; see also Paret and Fliessbach, 1990: 177–210).

The density of information in word and image, the regularity with which it was delivered, its rapid utilization by the mass media, and the broad appeal it had among the population would, it seems, allow us to speak of an independent media reality of war during the campaign of 1870. This dictated particular themes and patterns of perception and interpretation, not only among the audience at home but also in the theater of war itself. As Becker (2006) has pointed out, 'By [also] obtaining an overview with the aid of these publications, soldiers at the same time acquired patterns of interpretation with whose assistance they came to terms, to whatever degree, with their own experience' (Becker, 2006: 73).

Thus a sort of 'interpretative community' was created, linking the army and home, and this community was central to the political dimension of the war from a Prussian-German point of view. The main and crucial theme of the media reality of 1870 was the nation, and in this case more specifically the creation of the German nation by means of a war under Prussian leadership. The war anticipated the creation of the nation, which had not yet been founded formally, as a community of experience and as a space of common experience. This played a crucial role in binding the army, politics and society together into one indissoluble unit. The war set the stage for the southern German states to move over to the side of politics centered on Berlin and for the founding of the German Kaiserreich at the beginning of 1871. It was no accident that the new polity chose the day of the capitulation of Sedan (September 2, 1870) as its national day. A central interpretative plank of the successful foundation of the *kleindeutsches Reich* (the implementation of the 'small German' solution) was to link the 1870 War of Unification closely with Napoleon's military defeat in the 'wars of liberation' of 1813–15. This conjured up Germany's triumph – at last – over the 'archenemy' France, and made it possible to foreground Prussia's role in the supposed national rebirth of Germany (Buschmann, 2003: 25–53; Becker, 2001: 292–376).

War reporting placed itself in the service of this idea, fulfilling the function of allowing the home front to participate in the experience of soldiers as intensely as possible, while, conversely, keeping soldiers in close contact with those at home.

Even in the run-up to the war, the Prussian king's honor and the alleged insult delivered to him by French diplomacy were conflated with the entire nation's honor. In a letter dated August 1870, the great lawyer Rudolf von Jhering, in Vienna at the time, described how he read five newspapers everyday at home, while still finding time to go to town and read even more papers or study the latest bulletins on display. There was no time for academic work, he wrote. He thought of the war constantly and dreamed about it at night. He noted uneasily that he was degenerating and beginning to wish evil on the French. Finally, claiming that he was 'taking part' in this war himself ('I hope it is the last for me'), he came close to equating his experience of the war as a newspaper reader with that of a soldier (Becker, 2001: 49f).

At the same time, the army postal service kept up communications between the home country and the front. In addition to 100 million letters and postcards and more than two million parcels, it also carried newspapers to the troops (estimates put the figure at more than three million copies). Unlike the lengthier wars that came about later, the seven-month-long campaign of 1870–71 did not represent a substantial break in soldiers' lives. They continued in their familiar social roles and repeatedly found themselves addressed as sons, husbands or fathers in letters and cards. Special collections were organized to ameliorate their suffering and, especially around Christmas of 1870, efforts were made to emphasize the solidarity between soldiers and their families.

The images that reached home also played an important part in this. These images depicted neither the horrors of war nor soldiers drowning their boredom in alcohol. Rather, they showed bourgeois men in uniform who had interrupted their professional activities for a certain time in order to serve the nation while attempting to retain the small-town comforts of their familiar environment. This sent a signal to the families that the men in uniform who were shown playing cards, washing their clothes, reading the newspaper or writing letters were the same men they knew, who were addressing the large common mission that the war represented, without changing as a result (Paul, 2004: 37–45, on 'comfortable war'; Becker, 2003).

Creating this fiction of a unified nation and making it possible for those at home to experience the closeness between the army and the people by rapidly bridging the gap between the theater of war and home was the new and probably most important function of media communication in the Franco-Prussian War of 1870–71: 'Soldiers and civilians were similar to each other, took an interest in each other, and identified with each other' (Becker, 2006: 81).

The World War I – Journalists as the Mouthpiece of the Military

In the view of the military high commands in both Paris and Berlin, the war that started in 1914 and was to become the 'catastrophe of Europe' no longer had room for neutral, critical observers reporting from the front. Rather, war correspondents were expected to be part of a patriotic mission. They were expected to take sides and, acting as mediators between home and the front, to contribute to their own side's war effort, thus functioning as a sort of additional weapon in the generals' hands. During the mobilization period, Helmuth von Moltke, chief of the German general staff in 1914, described the press as an 'indispensable means for the conduct of war' (Lindner-Wirsching, 2006: 132f; see also Mruck, 2004; Quandt and Schichtel, 1993). Having reporters closely tied to the political and military leadership promised advantages in the battle for national and international public opinion.

In Berlin, a separate press service was set up through one division of the general staff (Lieutenant Colonel Walter Nicolai). It held daily press conferences and organized the accreditation of journalists for the areas around the front. At the same time, censorship regulations were issued. In October 1915, the War Press Office was set up under the direct control of the Army High Command. 'Its task was to influence the mood [...] at the front, in Germany, and in Germany's allied states through military reportage and propaganda' (Lindner-Wirsching, 2006: 116; see also Wilke, 2007; 1997: 79–125).

The generals in Berlin thus succeeded in keeping reportage and the transmission of news almost completely under their control and giving official army reports the status of a monopoly on information sources.

The French military leadership did not allow reporters at the front to accompany their own troops until the middle of 1917 (Britain allowed them in the spring of 1915). For extended periods during the war, the French press gleaned most of its information from foreign newspapers or from British and American correspondents (Farrar, 1998).

Berlin proved to be more generous in this regard, and its first journalists set off at the end of August (eight for the West, five for the East). They were 'pooled' in 'war correspondent quarters' and supervised by a general staff officer. The prerequisites included 'recognized patriotic views' and experience as an officer. They were not granted military status and they or their newspapers or agencies had to pay all their costs.

Trips to command posts or to the front could be undertaken only in military vehicles, in groups and accompanied by press officers, and journalists could really only speak to high-ranking staff officers and local commanders. The planning from above carefully ensured that there was no contact with fighting troops. Common briefings in the press quarters concerning several of the sometimes remote theaters of war resulted in a high degree of uniformity in the reporting. The 'common utilization of all available information' (Lindner-Wirsching, 2006: 121), a characteristic feature of the pool system, left no room for exclusive scoops of any sort. German war reports ('Kb') were also censored on the spot by press officers in the main headquarters. Subsequently, reports could be printed in German papers without additional checks (Rajsfus, 1999; Creutz, 1996; Koszyk, 1968: 68–83).

To start with, the ideas of war held by the reading public at home, as well as by reporters, were strongly shaped by their experience of the relatively short campaign against France in 1870–71. The technical mass warfare experienced by soldiers at the front in 1914–18, which provided relatively little action and soon ground to a halt in the trenches at the front, had little in common with this. 'The front journalists' haul of material, which was meager anyway, was reduced even further by self-censorship, external censorship, and lack of experience, so that many war reporters took recourse to embellishment and invention in order to fill pages' (Lindner-Wirsching, 2006: 123). When such reports arrived back at the front with the newspapers, the soldiers considered them to be much too positive.

The technical problems of reproducing photographs on newspaper printing presses had been solved by the 1890s and during the South African War of 1899–1902, and portable cameras such as Kodak Brownies were first used alongside heavy plate cameras on tripods.

But concerns about military secrecy meant that all the belligerent states initially imposed a ban on filming and photography, which meant that pictorial reportage was at first still in the hands of the painters and illustrators. Even if war photographers were allowed (in October 1914, there were 39 in Germany; as a comparison, the *Leipziger Illustrirte Zeitung* alone had 50 war painters in the field), war painting with its greater opportunities for shaping and dramatic concentration continued to be an indispensable part of pictorial reportage, while battle scenes regularly had to be 'recreated', that is, faked for the cameras. Photographs of the aftermath of fighting and occupation predominated. They also documented the damage inflicted on cities by artillery (Paul, 2004: 103–52; Holzer, 2003b; Eisermann, 2000; Zühlke, 2000; Hüppauf, 1998; Krumeich, 1994).

The French, who had regularly sent delegations of artists to the front since the end of 1914 ('missions artistiques aux armées'), deliberately opted for painting over photography to document the war as well as the impact of battles.

From the start of the World War I, there was, in addition to photography, regular film reportage in the form of newsreels, and eight camera teams alone were deployed on the German side, for example. Fighting on the most remote front was completely neglected, and filmed material was also subject to strict censorship. The supreme commands tried to keep the whole production process under their control. On the German side this resulted in the founding of the *Bild- und Filmamt* (BUFA, Image and Film Office), which had seven film crews at the beginning of 1917. On the French side, the *Section Cinématographique de l'Armée* (SCA), a division of the press office in the war ministry, was set up as early as April 1915, and in addition, there was a state-run picture agency for photographic documents. During the battle of the Somme in the summer of 1916, the *cinéoperateurs* were permitted near the front but were otherwise mostly engaged in filming fakes, since this 'staged war' could be handled better from a technical standpoint and conformed more closely with the public's expectations (Oppelt, 2002: 99–163).

A German–French comparison shows that war correspondents in the World War I had a similar understanding of their roles and worked in very similar conditions:

- They had to prove themselves committed 'patriots' before they could be accredited as journalists.
- They had to allow themselves to be 'embedded' in the pool system organized by the military.
- They had to submit to censorship.
- And they had to accept that in general they would stay on the fringes of the action.

The standardization of the information they were given and the expansion of the theaters of war meant that it was impossible for individuals to be responsible for the content of information reports.

It seems that the rules governing the way in which the general public gains its image of war from the mass media have hardly changed since 1914–18, almost 100 years ago. The power of images has, of course, grown immeasurably stronger. The technical innovations in twentieth-century media, from the moving images of newsreels and the TV war of the cameras to war blogs posted on the Internet, increasingly determine how war is seen, how its purpose is interpreted and how it is remembered.

War and Nation

Some final remarks: conjuring up images of the enemy and arming a people against real and assumed opponents has always been a central tool in creating in-groups and excluding 'the others'. During the nineteenth century, the 'nation' developed into an absolute value that could not be questioned. It became the highest and the unique reference point for the loyalty of political associations and their leaders. And through the same process it emerged that war and nation-building or nation-state-building were very closely associated with one another. The case of the 1870–71 war in particular shows how a war against the supposed 'archenemy' France provided a screen on to which all ideological streams could project their notions of political and symbolic participation in the nation – from the conservatives and the liberal-democratic side to the women's movement and the attempts for Jewish emancipation (Buschmann, 2003: 41).

'The modern nation was born of war' (Buschmann and Langewiesche, 2003: 9). This is true of the way in which specific nation states were formed. Almost all were created out of wars in the nineteenth or twentieth century (the separation of Norway from Sweden in 1905 is one of the few exceptions). It is also true of the social interpretation of these creation stories. The national historical constructs of the nineteenth and twentieth centuries, which sometimes delved far back into the past, assigned war a central role as the creator of the nation and anchored it deeply in the historical-mythological arsenal of their own genesis and self-image.

A flood of ephemeral writing, lectures, history textbooks, historical painting, monuments and parades, but above all the impact of the mass press, conferred on war – and this includes the specific pathos of 'death for the fatherland' – its rank as 'the reference point for collective memory, a field on which political loyalty can be demonstrated, or the symbolic place where the future is formed' (Buschmann and Langewiesche, 2003: 9). The experience of war counts as one of the central nation-building factors in modern times, and the incorporation of the nation into the events of war would be unthinkable without the nineteenth-century mass media and their representation, in words and images, of the events of war.

Key Points

- The development of the daily and weekly press in the context of the seventeenth-century 'communication revolution' can be attributed in part to the high proportion of war-related reportage in the early newspapers and the interest of the urban elites in this sort of information in particular.
- The European wars of the 1850s and 1860s (e.g., the Crimean War) gave the role of the mass press a sudden boost, placed newspapers at the center of public communication, and made politics recognize that the press was indispensable as an instrument of political mobilization.
- Creating the fiction of a unified nation and making it possible for those at home to experience the closeness between the army and the people by rapidly bridging the gap between the theater of war and home was the most innovative and perhaps the most important function of media communication during the Franco-Prussian War of 1870–71.
- The example of 1870–71 in particular shows how a war against the supposed 'archenemy' France provided a screen on to which all ideological streams could project their notions of political and symbolic participation in the nation – from the conservatives and the liberal-democratic side to the women's movement and the attempts for Jewish emancipation.

Study Questions

1. What parallels can be found between the rules for German and French war correspondents in the early twentieth century (during the World War I) and present-day guidelines for embedded journalists (e.g., during the 2003 Iraq War), and what limits of objectivity for war correspondents can be identified in those rules?
2. What impact do the changing technical tools for visually representing war scenes during the three centuries outlined in this chapter have on the images of war that were created and hence on the public's perception of war?

3. Compared with the historical examples given in this chapter and beyond, how important are the mass media of today in involving the respective nation in the events of war, thereby promoting nation-building and the shaping of a national identity?

Further Reading

Cooke, John B. (2007) *Reporting the War. Freedom of the Press from the American Revolution to the War on Terrorism*. New York: Palgrave Macmillan.

Knightley, Phillip (2004) *The First Casualty. The War Correspondent as Hero and Myth-Maker from the Crimea to Iraq*. Baltimore, MD: Johns Hopkins University Press.

Markovits, Stefanie (2009) *The Crimean War in the British Imagination*. Cambridge, UK; New York: Cambridge University Press.

McLaughlin, Greg (2002) *The War Correspondent*. London; Sterling, VA: Pluto Press.

Young, Peter R. and Peter Jesser (1997) *The Media and the Military. From the Crimea to Desert Strike*. Basingstoke: Macmillan.

References

Atkins, John B. (1911) *The Life of Sir William Howard Russell, the First Special Correspondent*. London: J. Murray.

Becker, Frank (2001) *Bilder von Krieg und Nation. Die Einigungskriege in der bürgerlichen Öffentlichkeit Deutschlands 1864–1913*. München: Oldenbourg.

——— (2003) 'Die "Heldengalerie" der einfachen Soldaten. Die Lichtbilder in den deutschen Einigungskriegen', pp. 39–56 in Anton Holzer (ed.) *Mit der Kamera bewaffnet: Krieg und Fotografie*. Marburg: Jonas.

——— (2006) 'Deutschland im Krieg von 1870–71 oder die mediale Inszenierung der nationalen Einheit', pp. 68–86 in Ute Daniel (ed.) *Augenzeugen. Kriegsberichterstattung vom 18. zum 21. Jahrhundert*. Göttingen: Vandenhoeck & Ruprecht.

Blitz, Hans-Martin (2001) 'Frühe Konstruktionen eines deutschen Vaterlandes. Tradition und Bedeutung antifranzösischer Feindbilder im Siebenjährigen Krieg', pp. 139–52 in Thomas Höpel (ed.) *Deutschlandbilder – Frankreichbilder. 1700–1850. Rezeption und Abgrenzung zweier Kulturen*. Leipzig: Leipziger Universitätsverlag.

Bock, Sybille (1982) 'Bildliche Darstellungen zum Krieg von 1870–71', Dissertation, Freiburg, Albert-Ludwigs-Universität Freiburg.

Buschmann, Nikolaus (2001) '"Moderne Versimpelung" des Krieges. Kriegsberichterstattung und öffentliche Kriegsdeutung an der Schwelle zum Zeitalter der Massenkommunikation (1850–1870)', pp. 97–123 in Nikolaus Buschmann and Horst Carl (eds) *Die Erfahrung des Krieges. Erfahrungsgeschichtliche Perspektiven von der Französischen Revolution bis zum Zweiten Weltkrieg*. Paderborn: Schöningh.

——— (2003) *Einkreisung und Waffenbruderschaft: Die öffentliche Deutung von Krieg und Nation in Deutschland 1850–1871*. Göttingen: Vandenhoeck & Ruprecht.

Buschmann, Nikolaus and Dieter Langewiesche (eds) (2003) *Der Krieg in den Gründungsmythen europäischer Nationen und der USA*. Frankfurt; New York: Campus.

Buschmann, Nikolaus and Horst Carl (eds) (2001) *Die Erfahrung des Krieges. Erfahrungsgeschichtliche Perspektiven von der Französischen Revolution bis zum Zweiten Weltkrieg*. Paderborn: Schöningh.

Creutz, Martin (1996) *Die Pressepolitik der kaiserlichen Regierung während des Ersten Weltkriegs. Die Exekutive, die Journalisten und der Teufelskreis der Berichterstattung*. Frankfurt; New York: P. Lang.

Daniel, Ute (2004) 'Der Gallipoli-Effekt, oder: Zum Wandel des Kriegsberichterstatters vom Augenzeugen zum Aufklärer', pp. 181–94 in Daniela Münkel and Jutta Schwarzkopf (eds) *Geschichte als Experiment. Studien zu Politik, Kultur und Alltag im 19. und 20. Jahrhundert*. Frankfurt; New York: Campus.

―――― (2005) 'Bücher vom Kriegsschauplatz. Kriegsberichterstattung als Genre des 19. und frühen 20. Jahrhunderts', pp. 93–121 in Wolfgang Hardtwig (ed.) *Geschichte für Leser. Populäre Geschichtsschreibung in Deutschland im 20. Jahrhundert*. Stuttgart: Steiner.

―――― (ed.) (2006a) *Augenzeugen. Kriegsberichterstattung vom 18. zum 21. Jahrhundert*. Göttingen: Vandenhoeck & Ruprecht.

―――― (2006b) 'Der Krimkrieg 1853–1856 und die Entstehungskontexte medialer Kriegsberichterstattung', pp. 40–67 in Ute Daniel (ed.) *Augenzeugen. Kriegsberichterstattung vom 18. zum 21. Jahrhundert*. Göttingen: Vandenhoeck & Ruprecht.

Eisermann, Thilo (2000) *Pressephotographie und Informationskontrolle im Ersten Weltkrieg. Deutschland und Frankreich im Vergleich*. Hamburg: Kämpfer.

Farrar, Martin J. (1998) *News from the Front. War Correspondents on the Western Front, 1914–18*. Thrupp, Stroud, Gloucestershire: Sutton.

Gestrich, Andreas (2006) 'Kriegsberichterstattung als Propaganda. Das Beispiel des "Wienerischen Diarium" im Siebenjährigen Krieg', pp. 23–39 in Ute Daniel (ed.) *Augenzeugen. Kriegsberichterstattung vom 18. zum 21. Jahrhundert*. Göttingen: Vandenhoeck & Ruprecht.

Hartwig, Stefan (1999) *Konflikt und Kommunikation. Berichterstattung, Medienarbeit und Propaganda in internationalen Konflikten vom Krimkrieg bis zum Kosovo*. Münster: Lit.

Holzer, Anton (2003a) 'Den Krieg sehen. Zur Bildgeschichtsschreibung des Ersten Weltkriegs', pp. 57–70 in Anton Holzer (ed.) *Mit der Kamera bewaffnet: Krieg und Fotografie*. Marburg: Jonas.

―――― (ed.) (2003b) *Mit der Kamera bewaffnet. Krieg und Fotografie*. Marburg: Jonas.

Hüppauf, Bernd (1998) 'Fotografie im Ersten Weltkrieg', pp. 108–23 in Rolf Spilker, Bernd Ulrich and Manfred Brockel (eds) *Der Tod als Maschinist. Der industrialisierte Krieg, 1914–1918*. Bramsche: Rasch.

Imhof, Kurt and Peter Schulz (eds) (1995) *Medien und Krieg, Krieg in den Medien*. Zürich: Seismo.

Karmasin, Matthias (2007) 'Krieg – Medien – Kultur. Konturen eines Forschungsprogramms', pp. 11–34 in Matthias Karmasin (ed.) *Krieg – Medien – Kultur. Neue Forschungsansätze*. München: Fink.

Kaufmann, Stefan (1996) *Kommunikationstechnik und Kriegführung 1815–1945. Stufen telemedialer Rüstung*. München: Fink.

Keller, Ulrich (2003) 'Authentizität und Schaustellung. Der Krimkrieg als erster Medienkrieg', pp. 21–38 in Anton Holzer (ed.) *Mit der Kamera bewaffnet: Krieg und Fotografie.* Marburg: Jonas.

—— (2007) *The Ultimate Spectacle. A Visual History of the Crimean War.* Amsterdam: Gordon and Breach.

Knieper, Thomas and Marion G. Müller (2005) *War Visions. Bildkommunikation und Krieg.* Köln: Halem.

Knightley, Phillip (2004) *The First Casualty. The War Correspondent as Hero and Myth-Maker from the Crimea to Iraq.* Baltimore; MD: Johns Hopkins University Press.

Koch, Ursula E. (1978) *Berliner Presse und europäisches Geschehen 1871. Eine Untersuchung über die Rezeption der grossen Ereignisse im ersten Halbjahr 1871 in den politischen Tageszeitungen der deutschen Reichshauptstadt.* Berlin: Colloquium Verlag.

Köppen, Manuel (op. 2005) *Das Entsetzen des Beobachters. Krieg und Medien im 19. und 20. Jahrhundert.* Heidelberg: Universitätsverlag Winter.

Koszyk, Kurt (1968) *Deutsche Pressepolitik im Ersten Weltkrieg.* Düsseldorf: Droste.

Krumeich, Gerd (1994) 'Kriegsfotografie zwischen Erleben und Propaganda. Verdun und die Somme in deutschen und französischen Fotografien des Ersten Weltkrieges', pp. 117–32 in Sabine R. Arnold, Ute Daniel and Wolfram Siemann (eds) *Propaganda. Meinungskampf, Verführung und politische Sinnstiftung (1789–1989).* Frankfurt: Fischer.

Lambert, Andrew D. and Stephen Badsey (1994) *The Crimean War.* Stroud: Alan Sutton.

Lindner-Wirsching, Almut (2006) 'Patrioten im Pool. Deutsche und französische Kriegsberichterstatter im Ersten Weltkrieg', pp. 113–40 in Ute Daniel (ed.) *Augenzeugen. Kriegsberichterstattung vom 18. zum 21. Jahrhundert.* Göttingen: Vandenhoeck & Ruprecht.

Löffelholz, Martin (ed.) (2004) *Krieg als Medienereignis II. Krisenkommunikation im 21. Jahrhundert.* Opladen: Westdeutscher Verlag.

Mruck, Tanja (2004) *Propaganda und Öffentlichkeit im Ersten Weltkrieg.* Aachen: Shaker.

Münkler, Herfried (1992) 'Schlachtbeschreibung: Der Krieg in Wahrnehmung und Erinnerung. Über "Kriegsberichterstattung"', pp. 176–207 in Herfried Münkler (ed.) *Gewalt und Ordnung. Das Bild des Krieges im politischen Denken.* Frankfurt: Fischer.

Oppelt, Ulrike (2002) *Film und Propaganda im Ersten Weltkrieg. Propaganda als Medienrealität im Aktualitäten- und Dokumentarfilm.* Stuttgart: Steiner.

Paret, Peter and Holger Fliessbach (1990) *Kunst als Geschichte. Kultur und Politik von Menzel bis Fontane.* München: Beck.

Paul, Gerhard (2004) *Bilder des Krieges, Krieg der Bilder. Die Visualisierung des modernen Krieges.* Paderborn: Schöningh; München: Fink.

Preusser, Heinz-Peter (ed.) (2005) *Krieg in den Medien.* Amsterdam: Rodopi.

Quandt, Siegfried and Horst Dieter Schichtel (1993) *Der Erste Weltkrieg als Kommunikationsereignis.* Giessen: Justus-Liebig-Universität.

Rajsfus, Maurice (1999) *La Censure Militaire et Policière (1914–1918).* Paris: Cherche midi.

Royle, Trevor (1987) *War Report. The War Correspondent's View of Battle from the Crimea to the Falklands.* Edinburgh: Mainstream.

Russell, William H. (2000) *Meine sieben Kriege. Die ersten Reportagen von den Schlachtfeldern des neunzehnten Jahrhunderts.* Frankfurt: Eichborn.

Schultheiss-Heinz, Sonja (2004) *Politik in der europäischen Publizistik. Eine historische Inhaltsanalyse von Zeitungen des 17. Jahrhunderts.* Stuttgart: F. Steiner.

Smith, Karen W. (1978) *Constantin Guys. Crimean War Drawings, 1854–1856.* Cleveland: Cleveland Museum of Art.

Wildmeister, Birgit (1998) *Die Bilderwelt der 'Gartenlaube'. Ein Beitrag zur Kulturgeschichte des bürgerlichen Lebens in der zweiten Hälfte des 19. Jahrhunderts.* Würzburg: Bayer. Blätter für Volkskunde.

Wilke, Jürgen (ed.) (1997) *Pressepolitik und Propaganda. Historische Studien vom Vormärz bis zum Kalten Krieg.* Köln: Böhlau.

—— (2008) *Massenmedien und Spendenkampagnen. Vom 17. Jahrhundert bis in die Gegenwart.* Köln: Böhlau.

Wilke, Jürgen (2005) 'Krieg als Medienereignis. Zur Geschichte seiner Vermittlung in der Neuzeit', pp. 83–104 in Heinz-Peter Preußer (ed.) *Krieg in den Medien.* Amsterdam: Rodopi.

—— (2007) *Presseanweisungen im zwanzigsten Jahrhundert. Erster Weltkrieg, Drittes Reich, DDR.* Köln: Böhlau.

Wrede, Martin (2004) *Das Reich und seine Feinde. Politische Feindbilder in der reichspatriotischen Publizistik zwischen Westfälischem Frieden und Siebenjährigem Krieg.* Mainz: P. von Zabern.

Zühlke, Raoul (ed.) (2000) *Bildpropaganda im Ersten Weltkrieg.* Hamburg: Kämpfer.

Discourses of War

Diego Lazzarich

Summary

The irruption, in modernity, of the masses on to the political scene brought about a deep change in the way war is thought and fought. From an operation carried out with the use of a restricted number of troops, modern war has increasingly become an event that requires the total involvement, whether direct or indirect, of the people in a state. This historical-political change strongly contributed to transforming war from a purely military activity to a cultural event. Notwithstanding the varying nature of the media used over the course of history, modern war has always been preceded and accompanied by a discourse: a set of narratives and images capable of imposing, on the public sphere, a historically specific concept of war in order to attain popular support. Through the analysis of the three different yet inescapably connected discourses of war, it can be observed how the concept of war has continually undergone a process of semantic sliding during the twentieth century.

The first half of the century was characterized by the circulation of a discourse that conveyed a positive idea of war, exalting its mortiferous nature and heroic dimension. War thus became socially accepted, and though taking on different nuances in each individual country, Europe was pervaded by the idea that war could regenerate a continent considered by many as old and tired. After the two world wars, the tragic historical consequences associated with this discourse and the development of weapons of mass destruction contributed to the development of a very different concept of war. The event that had triggered so much enthusiasm until the mid-twentieth century became a dangerous and potentially catastrophic event that produced constant international tension and consequently shifted war on to a strictly virtual plain. Only with the end of the Cold War was there a return to that type of war that is actually materially fought; this time, however, the discourse that developed around the concept of war appears to have reversed the terms that had been dominant in the first half of the century. The penetrating role of the media imposes the dominant idea, in the public sphere, that war is a cold, aseptic event: it appears as an operation that aims exclusively at restoring a violated normality through absolute technological precision.

Communicating Modern Wars

The relation between war and communication extends throughout the twentieth century, branching out during the course of western history with increasing intensity and becoming more relevant over time, to the point of becoming, today, an inescapable and problematic issue that challenges and questions the very political categories of modernity. Although the impact of this relationship explodes on the scene during World War I, its origin can be traced back to the early modern period. Indeed, already with the French Revolution, it is possible to observe what historian Mosse (1990) called the 'myth of the war experience'. This means that, for the first time in modernity, the experience of war was transformed into a myth: in Barthes's definition, a 'system of communication', a 'message', a 'way of signifying' and giving 'form' (Barthes, 1957: 191).

The main aim of the French Revolution, namely, the subversion of the political order through a transfer of power from one individual (the monarchy) or a few (the aristocracy) to the many (democracy) was linked to a process of narration capable of transmitting an image of war that involved more and more people (Furet, 1978: 90). Some revolutionaries began describing in a positive manner their participation in the Revolution, and did not do so in personal diaries but rather in gazettes, hence influencing the public sphere. This public dimension must be considered to be the economic-political-communicational space that Habermas sees as coinciding with the rise of the middle class in Europe (Habermas, 1962). Thanks to this short circuit between war and the public sphere, the concerns of the revolution not only reached and drew in a great number of people but it also launched a completely new phenomenon at the time: the voluntary enlistment of thousands of young and cultured Europeans (Mosse, 1990).

With the 'myth of the war experience' described by Mosse, the public sphere seems to have become linked with war from the very inception of the modern political project, thus giving life to a relationship destined to grow with time, finally showing its most powerful effects in the war experiences of the twentieth century.

In order to understand the deep causes underlying this phenomenon, it is first necessary to analyze the very nature of that event that today we define as 'war'. Ernst Jünger's reconstruction of the concept is fundamental in this respect. This German writer, taking a cue from the extraordinary novelty represented by World War I, wrote an essay entitled *Die totale Mobilmachung* ('The Total Mobilisation', 1930), in which he observed that the wars previous to World War I were led exclusively by the monarchs, with the use of a restricted number of soldiers led by a trusted commander, with no need for the approval of political representatives, for the involvement of Parliament, nor, for that matter, for the approval of the people. These wars required only a partial mobilization and a limited use of state resources, thanks to both the way in which war was conducted and, to a certain degree, the calculability of armaments and costs (Jünger, 1930).

But with the disappearance of a 'warrior caste', with the defense of the nation in the hands of 'everyone who, generally speaking, is apt for war' and with the great increase in war expenses, the mechanism needed more and more to 'involve the abstract forms of the mind, of money, of the "people", in short, the powers of a rising national democracy', through the 'act of mobilisation' (Jünger, 1930: 16). The war previously led by the sovereign and by few other men under the sovereign's control disappears altogether with the emergence of total war, a conflict in which any distinction between the military and civilian aspect is erased (Ludendorff, 1935).

In such a historical-political context, war, which until 1914 had been thought of exclusively as 'an armed action', takes on a new architecture comparable to 'a gigantic process of work' through which, in a much more articulate way, 'alongside the armies facing each other in the battlefields, new types of armies are formed: the army of transporters, of suppliers, the industry of armaments: in general, the army of work' (Jünger, 1930: 17).

The shift from partial to total war involves everyone within the state, directly or indirectly, in the war process. In order to channel all national social resources, 'total mobilization' is necessary, an act 'through which it is possible, using one single command over a control panel, to merge together the forces – such a diffused and ramified network of energies – of modern life, into the greater current of the energy of war' (Jünger, 1930: 18).

From that moment on, total mobilization appears to be the sole key to military success, the actual means by which war is won. Whether or not a country's people are asked to fight or to support the war financially or even just politically, total mobilization means, essentially, that the people legitimize what is determined by their rulers.

In this fundamental process, which is at the basis of modern war, communication is cast in a completely new light, since it appears as one of the most suitable means of motivating the population and getting it involved in a political design; indeed, it proves to be the vital means by which total mobilization can be realized. Thus, communication becomes an agent that, when injected into society, has the power to awaken the population, motivating it and orienting its energies toward a given end. In particular, communication is made more effective through a narration that creates a design, a plan in which people can feel included, in which they acquire a shared feeling, where they become the main actors in the story. This requires a portrayal of the way in which everyone can contribute to the war process, showing the public how this can happen, defining the individual steps necessary, and creating a sense of cohesion among all of the individual contributions.

Clearly then, the narration of war becomes one of the main cognitive categories of modern war itself because, to paraphrase Barthes, there is not, there has never been, anywhere, a popular war without a narrative.[1] More than just a story, however, we should speak of the narrative of war as an actual discourse, following Foucault's use of the term (Foucault, 1969): whereas 'Saussure and Barthes were interested in relatively small, isolated units of representation (language/sign systems), Foucault was interested in larger systems of representation' (Procter, 2004: 60). Thus, following Stuart Hall (1986) and the paradigms of cultural studies, by the term 'discourse' we can indicate 'a whole cluster of narratives, statements and/or images on a particular subject that acquire authority and become dominant at a particular historical moment' (Procter, 2004: 60). If we use the term 'discourse', and not simply 'narration', we immediately provide the sense of a more expressly political dimension of representation, of that process of knowledge production that 'imposes' how a given phenomenon is acknowledged and interpreted. The use of the term 'discourse' reveals one of the most deeply adhered and hidden political factors of this relationship between war and the public sphere.

What follows is a genealogy of the discourses of war that have been produced around three of the key conflicts of the twentieth century: World War I, the Cold War and the 1991 Persian Gulf War.

Regeneration and Heroism

By the beginning of the twentieth century, Europe had experienced solid international stability for several decades, which had also led to significant economic, political and social growth. This essentially progressive trend came to a halt with the propagation, in the public sphere, of a discourse aimed at placing war back at the center of the political debate.

In Italy, this discourse began to flourish thanks to publications such as *Leonardo* (1903–07), *Il Regno* (1903–06), *Lacerba* (1913–15) and *La Voce* (1908–16). These journals were a means of circulating the opinions of a group of intellectuals who, by attacking the 'debauched who love easy living', sought to challenge and eventually destroy economic and political peace and stability by affirming that the bourgeois lifestyle distorted and weakened mankind. As Marinetti eloquently wrote, 'Humanity is a mass of erotic and bloody instincts, overwhelming and rapacious, painfully caged by fear, society, convenience' (Marinetti, 1987: 496).

War appeared to many to be the fastest and most radical means of destroying a society considered to be tired and tiresome, given the conviction that 'only when every faith will have been destroyed, a new culture will be born; only when chaos will be perfect, then the new order will be formed, and, with it, a new balance' (Papini, 1919: 98).

The new discourse that was spreading within the public sphere at the beginning of the twentieth century was about to assign a new meaning to the term 'war', in relation to modernity. War came to be understood both as a political tool, used to modify European state morphology, and as a spiritual device, creating the 'dominant ideology of a vigorous renovation' that could 'purify Italian life' (Febbraro, 1998: 18). Order and peace, which had been the dominant values for intellectuals in the two previous centuries, thus began to lose their primacy and be replaced by their exact opposites.

An important contribution to this change came from the Futurist movement, which, already in its manifesto, published on February 20, 1909 in *Le Figaro*, stated, 'We will glorify war – the world's only hygiene – militarism, patriotism, the destructive gesture of freedom-bringers, beautiful ideas worth dying for' (*Le Figaro*, February 20, 1909).

Futurism offered the possibility of elaborating an actual esthetics capable of glorifying, using different languages, the positive value of war as well as its irreducible vital and saving essence: 'The world's only hygiene!' (Marinetti, 1909: 9). Alongside these declamatory and idealizing nuances, there was also the 'muscular and emotional espousal of war as exuberant gymnastics, recreational and competitive space-time, sports match [...] vital impulse [...] proof of existence: war for the sake of war' (Isnenghi, 1970: 23).

War was transformed into a hymn to life, 'power of youth, heroism, impulse, resistance [...] violence of bloody instincts' (Marinetti, 1987: 496). Thus the way was paved for war to be transformed from being a feared and fearful event to becoming a welcomed, sought-after and desired event: 'We shall go to war dancing and singing' (Marinetti, 1915: 19).

Through such concerted intellectual effort, the positive meaning attributed to war became a dominant value in the public sphere as well, thus transforming the supporters of peace into a dangerous and negative force field. Hence the seeds of warmongering rhetoric were sewn: a culture of war that would quickly and vigorously spread all over Europe and come to represent the matrix for the subsequent myth of war as a regenerating experience.

This new discourse of war appeared first in Italy, but the same rhetoric pervaded the debate in other countries as well. Spain, Portugal and France were among those countries where the press contributed to this positive reading of war within the public sphere. In England, too, the idea of war 'seduced' certain intellectuals and artists, as the first issue of the journal *Blast*, published in 1914, proves. Members of the Vorticist movement, in its inspiration and intent closely allied with Futurism, declared the 'enthusiastic adhesion to conflict', seeing war as the 'very focus of its aesthetic programme', exalting the capacity of war to 'purify the idea of nation from the waste of the bourgeoisie, from the romantic and rural stereotypes and to let the artist, finally, realize his full individuality, free from the burden of social constrictions' (Marzola, 2005: 30).

In Germany the discourse of war became an actual *Kriegsideologie* ('war ideology', Mann, 1986: 96). Many politicians, scientists, artists, writers and journalists placed war at the center of ideological discourse (Mommsen, 2000: 41–58), based on the conviction that war was the only means by which a new political, economic, social and philosophical order could be created, dismantling a world considered by that time to be degenerate and in which, as George Simmel wrote, money was the measure of all things (Simmel, 1900).

War appears to combine many of the values with which Germany identified (Mann, 1918; Losurdo, 2001), so much so that World War I became a battle between two antithetic visions of the world: the mercantile and modern vision of the Entente Powers on the one side and Germany's spiritualistic, antidemocratic, antiegalitarian and antimaterialistic vision on the other. It became, in short, an authentic war of faiths, a *Glaubenskrieg* ('religious war', Sombart, 1915: 195).

The most effective and cogent description of the meaning that war had acquired during that period in Germany comes from Max Scheler: 'War re-establishes in our consciousness the true, realistic relationship between life and death.' It puts an end to the blindness, or rather to the voluntary blindness, with which we face death, ending the 'repression and concealment' that was carried on through 'the deceptive veil of a vital praxis that had become a dull habit' (Scheler, 1915: 82; also in Losurdo, 2001: 20–1).

This *Kriegsideologie* enabled a fundamental cultural shift, one that would also later deeply influence the discourse produced during World War II: the direct association of war with death, both terms taking on a positive value. Because death itself offers one the opportunity to discover the true value of life, war must no longer be feared; it is an opportunity to be in touch with death. In this case, the notion that war is the principal means of restoring a truer relationship with life takes shape; it becomes the means by which an existential equilibrium can be attained.

In fact, this discursive elaboration would later send millions of people into the battlefields as volunteers in search of such a regenerating experience. This same discourse, indeed, was also able to resist the ruins of World War I and to pervade the rhetoric of war used by both totalitarian and democratic regimes. By then, war was seen as an entirely normal event in modern social life. This grand discourse of war, which was capable of making an event that was so mortiferous and destructive an essential part of social normality, ended with the end of World War II and was replaced by a new form of discourse that was bound to modify profoundly, once again, the idea of war.

The Scenario of War

An important change in the perception of war took place during the period commonly referred to as the Cold War. With the onset of the nuclear age, the world was suddenly forced to confront a new situation, one that was determined by the impossibility of using all the military equipment then in existence, since that would have meant very likely the complete destruction of humankind. This new dimension of war would deeply modify the concept of war itself, which was to become no longer a regenerating event to be faced in a heroic manner but simply a matter of technology, one with thoroughly nihilistic potential.

This view was propagated in the public sphere through a broad debate encompassing diverse intellectuals and opinions. One of the most important contributors to the debate was Bertrand Russell, with his pacifist campaign. The British philosopher underlined how the enormous and excessive power of nuclear weapons made the classic categories of conflict irrelevant, such as that between winners and losers, since, in the event of a nuclear war, both the former and the latter would simply be united in one deadly fate (Russell, 1961). Norberto Bobbio took a similar viewpoint in this respect, claiming that a thermonuclear war could not be compared with any conventional war because in a war of this type everyone would lose. This principle could lead to one choice only: the impossibility of war (Bobbio, 1977: 39–42).

The concept of war thus began to be linked to an apocalyptic sphere that found its grammar in fear. In this vision's trail, a type of discourse began to spread that affirmed in numerous ways how such a war could lead only to destruction.

The western public was plunged into an atmosphere of fear that deeply influenced the life choices of millions of people. Indeed, the political choices of citizens were influenced by not only this environment but also everyday decisions. Fear was so widespread that millions of families in the United States got used to the idea that fathers were planning to have an atomic shelter installed, that mothers were stocking up on accessories and food supplies for the basement, and that their children were undergoing atomic bomb drills at school. As historian Laura McEnaney writes, the atomic bomb marked a completely new era that deeply modified American society, transforming citizens into soldiers faced with the development and implementation of actual defense plans, and with their front yards transformed into front lines. This atmosphere, it must be stressed, was not caused by individual paranoia but, instead, promoted by the 1950 founded US Federal Civil Defense Administration, which, among others, encouraged citizens to imagine and prepare for the present and future in case of a nuclear attack (McEnaney, 2000).

One of the most obvious manifestations of this fear linked to the outbreak of a nuclear conflict was the phenomenon of nuclear shelters that started in 1961, with an intense debate involving various intellectuals, politicians and scientists, among whom were Herman Kahn, J. Robert Oppenheimer and Henry Kissinger. Discussions on atomic shelters began proliferating and gave life to the dilemma defined by *Business Week* as 'to dig, or not to dig'. The debate was reported and amplified by the media, and it pervaded US society. A sense of this profound transformation in American culture can be detected in the proliferation of articles in journals and magazines as varied as *The Yale Review, Architectural Record, Good Housekeeping, Catholic National, Successful Farming* and *Time* (Rose, 2001: 1).

The entire US public sphere found itself immersed in a discourse of war that was so amplified by the media that it reached an unprecedented level of penetration. Through the diffusion of a microphysical phenomenon, a dominant discourse spread across the entire western world, assuming the form of an incontrovertible truth and becoming the dominant political discourse for decades.

The shifting of war on to the terrain of apocalyptic magnification and fear caused a profound change in the way war itself was interpreted. Whereas the previous experience of war had linked it to a realm of mainly material destruction, the Cold War was mainly characterized by psychological factors (Aron, 1962: 212).

Being at war came to mean less the conflict itself and more the visualization of what might happen should combat occur. This atmosphere of fear was generated and intensified by a great imaginary discourse leading to a continual production of new scenarios.

A particularly relevant contribution to the development of this perception of war in the public sphere came from various authors, one of the most noteworthy being Herman Kahn. In his famous book *Thinking About the Unthinkable*, the author articulated (positive) hypotheses on possible post-thermonuclear war scenarios. For example, the nuclear fallout was described by Kahn simply as one of many incidents of life; the resulting birth defects were depicted with the corollary explanation that these would not bring about the extinction of humankind because the majority of the survivors would not be affected, since they would not be touched by many of the other consequences of war (Kahn, 1962). The creation of possible scenarios also led to the compilation of statistics on the number of potential victims in a nuclear attack and on the amount of time that might be required for a nation to recover. Kahn claimed that the United States would need a recovery period of five years in the event of ten million victims, while if the number of victims ended up being 80 million, 50 years might be necessary for such a recovery (Lapp, 1962: 113).

Although it was also framed on a theoretical level, the debate stimulated by Kahn had precisely the opposite aim of that triggered by Russell and Bobbio. Indeed, these latter intellectuals anticipated a catastrophe in their efforts to delegitimize any political attempt to simply think about the hypothesis of nuclear war; the vision proposed by Kahn, by contrast, had the effect of showing the calculability and rationality of such a potential war, in that it took the same route taken by various Soviet authors (Chaliand, 1990: 1349–89).

Within this framework, both the detractors and the supporters helped shift war on to a completely virtual level of reality. The enormous power of nuclear weapons strengthened not so much the use of force itself as it did the threat of it (Montanari, 2004: 215). This is why McLuhan defined the Cold War as an electronic battle of information and images (Savarese, 1992: 103–13).

The Cold War itself became one great scenario. The novelty factor of the period was so heightened that conflict scholars such as General Lucien Poirier and General Pierre Joxe defined the Cold War as a 'semiotic war', also using the expression 'strategic gesticulating to define it'. Joxe explained that war was being transformed into a strategy aimed at indicating the field of possibilities opened up by conflict, a virtual arena in which to demonstrate one's determination and intentions to the Other, that is, 'making known that, in the event of […] one is able to […] and one has the firm intention to […]' (Joxe, 1983: 24).

The Cold War was, strictly speaking, a war of signs, so much so that we can speak of an actual semiotics of war. Thus, a virtualization of war was initiated, a phenomenon that would modify the dimensions and the meaning of war itself to the point that war, as interpreted using the classic categories, became only one among many other 'ways of practicing violence' (Poirier and Chaliand, 1997: 38). At that point, strategy no longer meant solely the management of logistics and armaments, because material strength became one among other possible options of strategic action, which also included '"semiotic weapons" such as threat, dissuasion, manipulation, feeling' (Montanari, 2004: 218). In this sense, Felix Guattari aptly speaks of the purely simulatory character of the period (Guattari, 1997).

The Cold War thus became a huge discursive production that by constantly posing war as the object of discourse ended up repeatedly and incessantly producing scenarios of a conflict without ever really actualizing these scenarios. The enclosure within a virtual realm of reality stood, in the end, as the very substance of war. In the Cold War, virtualization was, strictly speaking, an actualization of war, but of a war that, in fact, was not a war. A profound modification of the category of war was underway as well as an emptying-out of the very same term with respect to the classic and modern concepts of war. War lost its typically militaristic character and acquired the characteristic features of a communicative event, one that was no longer an accessory element but rather one fully strategic and intrinsic to war itself.

Without an actual battlefield or the direct experience of the troops, the western public sphere began to associate war with a purely mediatic dimension in which war became the idea of war, or what 'common sense'[2] recognized as truth. If it was a war, it was fought on the terrain of the public sphere, marking yet another change in the concept and the perception of war in the West.

The Gulf War

With the Persian Gulf War, an entirely new phase in the way the discourse of war was produced and communicated began. On January 17, 1991, a coalition of twenty states, headed by the United States of America, began bombing Iraq as a reaction to the August 1990 invasion of Kuwait. At 2:38 a.m., Operation Desert Storm began and, at the very same moment and thanks to CNN, the live coverage of the bombing of Baghdad was delivered to every household in the world.

If McLuhan defined Vietnam as the 'first television war' (McLuhan, 1968: 134), the Persian Gulf War can be said to be the first 'live war' since, for the first time in history, technology allowed one to show a conflict in real time. This process was made possible thanks to what Paul Virilio calls 'absolute velocity' (Virilio, 1995): the obliteration of space brought about by a technology capable of producing a tele-presence, a long-distance presence. Millions of spectators found themselves suddenly thrown into the battlefield, watching the bombings in the very same moment as they were taking place.

As Habermas has observed, the unprecedented media coverage of the Persian Gulf War was responsible for the equally exceptional involvement of the public sphere, with its massive emotional participation in the event (Habermas, 1991: 4).

The mediatic dimension of the event, along with the live rendition of it, played a key role in how the public perceived what was taking place. Everybody, in fact, had the feeling they were being given access to a continuous flux of images, the very continuity of which had the power to legitimize the truthfulness of such images (much the same way that an uncut, continuous video shoot guarantees the 'reality' of what we are watching).

Indeed, this produced an effect of complete transparency between the war and its viewers. The same feeling was further enhanced by the way in which the army conveyed what was happening to the public. The press conferences were in fact used to provide detailed descriptions of the attacks and the weapons involved. In what very nearly resembled a high-tech exhibition, the press was presented with the military equipment used in combat: the F-117 Stealth, the first plane in the world that was invisible to radar; remote-controlled bombs, also called 'intelligent bombs', capable of striking with ultimate precision; or the satellite system for constantly and minutely mapping the territory.

For the first time, the army appeared to open up to civil society with unprecedented transparency. Even the pilots' viewpoints from their planes were shared with the public, showing clips of air raids in which, in a deafening silence, the missiles hit their targets, the images strikingly resembling those of certain war games.

Alongside this new method of communicating war, another new element emerged on the part of army officials: the use of a language that constantly underlined and affirmed the cold neutrality of military operations, the almost aseptic character of the conflict that pointed to the thaumaturgical, healing power of military operations. Such healing power was in fact evoked through the use of such expressions as 'surgical operations' to define the accuracy of the bombing operations (Lakoff, 1991).

Particularly striking was the will to deliver a message in which war was read not so much as a hostile action against an enemy but as a beneficial operation aimed at healing and liberating people from some evil force that had taken over part of the organism being targeted. A new concept of war was thus born that would also be used in subsequent wars, which were also legitimized as operations with the beneficial aim of exporting democracy.

Juxtaposing the reconstruction of combat and the military semantics adopted, we notice that the Gulf War was presented as a 'clean war' dominated more by technology than by man: a 'post-heroic' war, as the political analyst Edward Luttwak (1996) defined it. A war, in short, the infallible computerized logic of which generated provisional models able to anticipate scenarios in which any potential mistake was avoidable, including the most unpleasant mistake of all: death. It was hardly a coincidence that the victims of war operations were referred to using the term 'collateral damage', thus drying up any remaining drop of blood in the communication of a war that had already crowned its immortal hero on the altar of the mass media: technology.

The Gulf War with its technological system was presented as the paradigm of the war of the future in which 'optronic software, microchips, computers and so on become [...] the new protagonists of the battle field' (Husson, 1991: 99).

Such a communication strategy had a striking impact on the formation of the public sphere. All over the world, the media were sucked into this stratum of communication, into reporting information that was simply delivered to them by the army, and thus re-enforcing a liminal dimension in which war was posited somewhere halfway between reality and science fiction. An interesting example of this phenomenon is a newspaper article in which the following is stated: 'It was the first, real Star Wars battle, Saddam Hussein its Darth Wader, its black knight of death' (Caretto, 1991: 11).

The media thus contributed to validating the representations of war offered by the military, opposing virtually no resistance. Furthermore, from the front line, the embedded journalists merely confirmed the information given during the press conferences.

All of these factors substantiated a discourse aimed at conveying an image of war that was new, but also positioned inside an old theoretical framework. As political theorist Michael Walzer has stated, the 'air raid campaign' was presented 'in a language that combined technical jargon and just war theory'. It was even underlined that the pilots were 'respectful of the moral aspects' so as to limit the number of civilian victims. Everything in the representation of war contributed to legitimizing it as a just war, an operation conducted following the precepts of the doctrine: *ius ad bellum* (the right to wage war) and *ius in bello* (observance of the rules of conduct in war) (Walzer, 2004: 85–6). The operations were overall presented as characterized by moderation and with the recognized, legitimate aim of restoring the international order that had been violated with the invasion of Kuwait – the same motivation that led authors like Bobbio (1991: 22–3) and Habermas (1991: 8) to publicly support the idea of the legitimacy of war.

Many different pieces combined perfectly to produce a discourse of war that found a surprisingly successful response in the public sphere. The discourse elaborated was such that even an acute historian like Eric Hobsbawm, in a 1999 interview, spoke of the development of military technology and of how this modified war operations, stating that 'from the Gulf War on, we know […] that high technology produces a much more precise and selective ability to destroy', thus avoiding 'devastating and bloody conflicts'. The British historian describes the Gulf War as a conflict characterized by a technological imprint in which the intelligent bombs are capable of choosing specific targets and avoiding others. The technological factor was interpreted by Hobsbawm not as a formal input but as a basic and substantial one, destined to transform the nature of conflict itself. As the author argues, high technology indeed 'restores the distinction – disappeared in the twentieth century, when the wars were progressively more directed against civilians – between combatants and non-combatants' (Hobsbawm, 2001: 12).

Hobsbawm's observations lead us to the heart of the issue. He sees in the Gulf War a high-tech conflict in which the Jüngerian paradigm of total war is modified and invalidated. This recalls the orderly – not absolute – *guerre en forme* described by Carl Schmitt (Schmitt, 1950), when wars were fought only between armies and civilians were stricken only occasionally or accidentally, and never for strategic purposes.

The Gulf War was presented to the western public as a new war: cleansed of the gross imprecision of early twentieth-century weapons that had left behind so many casualties, cleansed of the devouring will to power that had fed previous modern wars, taken out of the insidious swamps of a field battle. Thus, a discourse capable of imposing a new idea of war took shape, one in which technological precision brought back the possibility of a distinction between the military and civilian, in which air raids were capable of avoiding any useless bloodshed. Here, a calculating rationality confined war operations inside a space where any mortiferous feature was removed and obliterated. The Gulf War was presented as unerringly the war of its own era – not only because it appeared to be the perfect offspring of the high-tech world but also (and foremost) because it seemed like the only possible, the only acceptable, war.

The Semantic Sliding of the Concept of War

If we compare the three discourses of war just analyzed, we can observe how, in the course of the twentieth century, the concept of war has undergone a semantic sliding. Using the language of linguistics, we may say that war is like a signifier that has undergone a re-signification process, which has brought about a deep change in its meaning. War must be thought of then as a sign that, like all signs, refers to something else. 'When we are faced with something that appears as a sign, we can assume its meaning, but the meaning is determined only if it is positioned inside a contextual structure that makes it a signifier' (Natoli, 2005: 116).

Indeed, the aim of the discourse of war itself appears to be that of creating the context in which the sign (war) is determined. While in the early twentieth century war was signified as a regenerating experience, in 1991 it was transformed into a neutral event aiming at restoring normality. 'If we take the two ends of our discourse and draw a line across them, we immediately see the transformation that war undergoes.' (Lazzarich, 2008: 46)

War (which is also, as we have seen, a sign, from the Greek word *sêma*) slides from one semantic field, made of concepts such as death, danger, suffering, blood and heroism, to another in which the dominant concepts are technique, rationality, coldness, security, precision and asepticity. This shift in meaning takes place through a process in which the event of war finds itself superimposed on a virtual and basically mediatic dimension of reality.

What we must investigate is whether the concepts of war conveyed by the discourses that have been analyzed here have actually accompanied the phenomenology and the individual experiential dimension of war. In short, has war actually been what these discourses have narrated, or has there been a detachment between the events of war and the narration thereof?

We know today that the discourse that aims at presenting war as heroic and regenerating is refuted by the reality of combat. Already during World War I, indeed, battles were characterized more by technique than by heroism. As Jünger wrote in one of his first novels, war had become an 'arithmetic calculus', a 'bloody fight of production and apparatus', in which what counted was not the heroic gesture but rather the quantity of munitions shot in the field so that the enemy was unable to dig a new trench. In such a war, even death 'passed above fields like the clouds of a storm' without giving the soldiers of either army the opportunity to 'see the enemy in the face' (Jünger, 1979: 12).

As Adorno observed, in a conflict in which cold and hard steel had become the main means by which armies fought each other, 'the body's incongruity with the mechanical warfare made real experience impossible' (Adorno, 2005: 54), de-substantiating both the role and the classic image of the soldier traced by a certain epics of war.

The discourse of war as a regenerating event found its limit in the reality of war itself. What was left of such discourse, however, heavily influenced European history up until World War II, especially with respect to the association of war and death. The totalizing experience of World War I influenced European culture to such an extent that it made war and death into two events so inevitable and habitual that an attitude of immunized acceptance emerged, in particular toward those fascist movements that promoted violence and military symbolic as a daily practice (Mosse, 1990: 210).

The very relevance and the consequences of this broader discourse on war marked the inception of a psychological and cultural process whereby war became divorced from its own consequences. The dramatic effects of World War II and its pervasive unacceptability within the public eventually made it impossible to re-propose a discourse that promoted war, such as the one that had circulated so widely in the first half of the twentieth century.

With the burden of horror left by two world wars, intellectuals were very likely to oppose the idea of a nuclear war. It is, indeed, difficult to say to what extent the nuclear threat, which was central to the discourse of the Cold War, was real. Some scholars like Hobsbawm voiced doubts about the real threat during that period, stating that such a discourse had been produced and promoted mainly by the United States for reasons of domestic politics and international stability (Hobsbawm, 1994: 268). Nonetheless, the aim of such discourse was a different one: namely, that of transforming a vaguely mediatic front into a real war front and of propagating a new idea of war in the public sphere. The influence of this discourse was so significant and durable that on January 4, 1991, in the midst of the Gulf crisis and a few days from the expiration of the ultimatum, Baudrillard wrote an article in *Libération* in which he stated that a 'real' war could not take place because it would be too obscene for the western public, who were by then used to thinking of war only in virtual terms.

Although his prediction was evidently proven wrong, paradoxically Baudrillard was not entirely wrong in his analysis. The discourse around the 1991 war assumed precisely this level of (virtual) reality as the basis of its development.

War reporters have testified that, by a careful policy of censorship, control and falsification of representations, the army was able to organize a communication strategy aimed at creating a narration of the events that was realistic but hardly real. The perceived supposed transparency of the war description was only one step in a well-implemented strategy. For instance, it was later revealed that, from the JIB (Joint Information Bureau) in Dharham, Saudi Arabia, where the briefings took place (and where the headquarters of the Allied Forces was also located), officials selected restricted pools of journalists, all of them Anglo-Saxon, who, after having passed censorship, were to report to their colleagues about their embedded missions with the army. Journalists who opposed such restrictions were arrested (Fontana, 2004: 124). After the end of the war, moreover, the public found out that the official sources had silenced or deliberately manipulated most of the information, such as, for example, the facts regarding the number of civilian victims or the insufficient accuracy of 70 percent of the so-called intelligent bombs (Fracassi, 2007: 127).

Alongside this type of censorship and manipulation, there is evidence in the Gulf War of a more sophisticated level of communication, aimed at the authentic creation of events and incidents. A well-known public relations firm, Hill & Knowlton, was hired to carry out an unprecedented media campaign addressed to the US public. In order to reach its goals, the agency not only created events but also manufactured news items, such as the famous incident reported by President Bush in which Iraqi soldiers were said to have killed babies found in incubators in the Kuwait City hospital. Furthermore, the firm made sure that any image was censored in which war was associated with its death-bearing effects.

This all took place amidst the guilty silence of the world's media. According to studies carried out by Edward Herman, during Operation Desert Storm, the news reports and references in one of the most important newspapers in the United States, the *New York*

Times, in 79 percent of the cases was derived solely from the US government or affiliated organizations (the Pentagon, the CIA, etc.); in 20 percent of the cases it came from other official sources; and in only 1 percent of the cases was it derived from independent sources or experts (Herman, 1999). This was so true that Howell Raines, editor of the *New York Times*, openly admitted at the end of the war having acted unprofessionally and superficially (Kohn, 2003: 242).

The study of the discrepancies that accompanied the discourse of the Gulf War leads us to ask what actually happened and what the real relationship is today between war and the public sphere.

In his 1984 work entitled *War and Cinema. The Logistics of Perception*, Paul Virilio affirms that already back then we were witnessing 'a growing derealisation of military engagement. For in industrialized warfare, where the representation of events outstripped the representation of facts, the image [is] starting to gain sway over the objects, time over space' (Virilio, 1989: 1). Rudyard Kipling said that the first victim of war is truth, but during the Gulf War we were faced with something different, in which not only truth was the victim but also war itself, its very representation.

The level of manipulation was such that Baudrillard provocatively stated that the Gulf War had never taken place for the western consumer-spectator because non-bombs (surgical actions) had hit non-human beings (collateral damage) in the name of a contradictory nonideal (not harming others), which in turn covered unsaid things (control of oil resources and the security of Israel) (Virilio, 1995: 63).

If this analysis provides evidence of the semantic sliding of the concept of war, it also suggests that war is a cultural event, and as such it undergoes a signifying process through discourses that produce meaning. The question then is why such discourses become dominant in the public sphere not simply to inform but also to convey a false meaning of war,[3] and why, in short, war has repeatedly undergone a process of semantic sliding?

A simple answer is that while on the one hand war is still the only means to obtain certain results that are unattainable through international law, on the other, a western nation's inclination to go to war and accept its use has changed dramatically since World War II (and in the United States, even more strongly after Vietnam). If a state wants to wage war, it must first convince its people to support it, because war is a political act, but the sovereignty of a state lies with its people. Such a simple explanation, however, forces us to ask another question: In a democratic regime, should politics not represent the citizens? If so, how is this simple premise compatible with the recurring use of discursive practices aimed at silencing if not mystifying certain aspects of war?

Conclusion

The analysis of the discourses carried out so far makes us recognize that in the relationship between war and the public sphere another conflict is hidden, one that is possibly deeper and more structurally embedded in the state itself. As Gramsci suggests, the internal dynamics of the state are more complex than those traced by liberal thought (Gramsci, 1971). Behind the decisions of politics, there often lies not a common interest but rather a hegemonic social bloc: namely, the social groups that hold power. This explains why war is not conveyed through an informative discourse but rather through one that tries to produce the most acceptable representation of war according to common sense. If current common sense has assimilated the idea that war is a negative event because of its deadliness, it then becomes necessary to enter the 'practical, everyday consciousness of popular thought of the masses' (Hall, 1986: 23) and to transform that common sense by associating war with other concepts that are considered socially positive.

Since common sense 'is disjointed and episodic' (Gramsci, 1971: 362), the discourses of war must accommodate the fragmentary and diverse nature of the contexts and periods in which they are produced. They, too, must be disjointed and episodic in order to be absorbed by the popular thought of the masses. No matter how differentiated and contradictory they may be, all of these discourses will, in the end, operate to affirm the necessity of war. The most varied cultural means will be used in this process, and the public sphere will function as the initial, preliminary battlefield for any war. In modernity, winning the cultural battle in the public sphere has always been the prerequisite of starting a war.

Key Points

- Modern wars are accompanied by discourses that, through the media, impose specific concepts of war.
- The association of war with a positive, regenerating, heroic and mortiferous dimension is the main feature of the type of discourse that dominated the first half of the twentieth century.
- The Cold War was characterized by the idea that war is a catastrophic event that must be avoided, thus resulting in a virtualization and mediatization of conflict.
- With the Persian Gulf War, a new discourse of war was produced, one that was able to associate war with a technological, aseptic and neutral terrain.
- The semantic sliding of the concept of war is a linguistic-cultural process that war underwent throughout the course of the twentieth century.

Study Questions

1. What is a 'semantic sliding' of the concept of war?
2. Why are modern wars accompanied by particular discourses?
3. What is the difference between the discourse of war produced in the first half of the twentieth century and that of the Persian Gulf War of 1991?

Further Reading

Baudrillard, Jean (ed.) (1995) *The Gulf War Did Not Take Place*. Bloomington: Indiana University Press.

Chomsky, Noam and Edward S. Herman (2002) *Manufacturing Consent. The Political Economy of the Mass Media*. New York: Pantheon Books.

Fussell, Paul (1975) *The Great War and Modern Memory*. New York: Oxford University Press.

Gramsci, Antonio (1971) *Selections from the Prison Notebooks of Antonio Gramsci*. Edited by Quintin Hoare and Geoffrey Nowell-Smith. New York: International Publishers.

Kahn, Herman (1962) *Thinking About the Unthinkable*. New York: Horizon Press.

Lazzarich, Diego (2009) *Guerra e pensiero politico. Percorsi novecenteschi*. Napoli: Istituto Italiano per gli Studi Filosofici (donwnloadable on *Google Books*).

Leed, Eric J. (1979) *No Man's Land. Combat & Identity in World War I*. Cambridge; New York: Cambridge University Press.

Losurdo, Domenico (2001) *Heidegger and the Ideology of War. Community, Death, and the West*. Amherst, NY: Humanity Books.

Mosse, George L. (1990) *Fallen Soldiers. Reshaping the Memory of the World Wars*. New York: Oxford University Press.

Winter, Jay (1995) *Sites of Memory, Sites of Mourning. The Great War in European Cultural History*. Cambridge: Cambridge University Press.

References

Adorno, Theodor W. (2005) *Minima Moralia. Reflections on a Damaged Life*. London; New York: Verso.

Aron, Raymond (1962) *Paix et guerre entre les nations*. Paris: Calmann-Lévy.

Barthes, Roland (1957) *Mythologies*. Paris: Editions du Seuil.

—— (1994) *The Semiotic Challenge*. Berkeley: University of California Press.

Bobbio, Norberto (1977) *Il problema della guerra e le vie della pace*. Bologna: Il Mulino.

—— (1991) *Una guerra giusta? Sul conflitto del Golfo*. Venezia: Marsilio.

Caretto, Ennio (1991) 'La guerra del Golfo. Una battaglia da guerre stellari', *La Repubblica*, January 19, 1991: 11.

Chaliand, Gérard (1990) *Anthologie mondiale de la stratégie. Des origines au nucléaire*. Paris: Laffont.

Febbraro, Paolo (ed.) (1998) *I poeti italiani della 'Voce'*. Milano: Marcos y Marcos.

Fontana, Toni (2004) *Hotel Palestine, Baghdad. Nelle mani degli iracheni*. Milano: Il saggiatore.

Foucault, Michel (1969) *L'archéologie du savoir*. Paris: Gallimard.

Fracassi, Claudio (2007) *Sotto la notizia niente. Saggio sull'informazione planetaria*. Roma: Editori riuniti.

Furet, François (1978) *Penser la Révolution Française*. Paris: Gallimard.

Gramsci, Antonio (1971) *Selections from the Prison Notebooks of Antonio Gramsci*. Edited by Quintin Hoare and Geoffrey Nowell-Smith. New York: International Publishers.

Guattari, Félix (1997) *Piano sul pianeta. Capitale mondiale integrato e globalizzazione*. Verona: Ombre corte.

Habermas, Jürgen (1962) *Strukturwandel der Öffentlichkeit. Untersuchungen zu einer Kategorie der bürgerlichen Gesellschaft*. Frankfurt: Suhrkamp.

——— (1991) 'Der Golf-Krieg als Katalysator einer neuen deutschen Normalität', pp. 10–44 in Jürgen Habermas, *Vergangenheit als Zukunft*. Zürich: Pendo.

Hall, Stuart (1986) 'Gramsci's Relevance for the Study of Race and Ethnicity', *Journal of Communication Inquiry* 10(2): 5–27.

Herman, Edward S. (1999) *The Myth of the Liberal Media*. New York: P. Lang.

Hobsbawm, Eric J. (1994) *Age of Extremes. The Short Twentieth Century, 1914–1991*. London: Michael Joseph.

——— (2001) *Intervista sul nuovo secolo*. Roma: Laterza.

Husson, Jean P. (1991) *Programmi di guerra. Scenari e tecnologia nel conflitto del Golfo*. Firenze: Vallecchi.

Isnenghi, Mario (1970) *Il mito della Grande Guerra. Da Marinetti a Malaparte*. Bari: Laterza.

Joxe, Alain (1983) 'Stratégie de la dissuasion nucléaire', *Actes Semiotiques Bulletin* 25: 24.

Jünger, Ernst (1930) *Die totale Mobilmachung*. Berlin: Junker und Dünnhaupt.

——— (1979) *Sturm*. Stuttgart: Klett-Cotta.

Kahn, Herman (1962) *Thinking About the Unthinkable*. New York: Horizon Press.

Kohn, Bob (2003) *Journalistic Fraud. How the New York Times Distorts the News and Why It Can No Longer Be Trusted*. Nashville, TN: WND Books.

Lakoff, George (1991) 'Metaphor and War. The Metaphor System Used to Justify War in the Gulf', *Viet Nam Generation Journal Online* 3(3).

Lapp, Ralph E. (1962) *Kill and Overkill. The Strategy of Annihilation*. New York: Basic Books.

Lazzarich, Diego (2008) *Guerra e/è comunicazione*, in *Guerra e comunicazione*. Napoli: Guida: 5–67.

Losurdo, Domenico (2001) *Heidegger and the Ideology of War. Community, Death, and the West*. Amherst, NY: Humanity Books.

Ludendorff, Erich (1935) *Der totale Krieg*. München: Ludendorffs.

Luttwak, Edward (1996) 'A Post-Heroic Military Policy', *Foreign Affairs* 75(4): 33–44.

Mann, Thomas (1918) *Betrachtungen eines Unpolitischen*. Berlin: Fuscher.

——— (1986) 'Kultur und Sozialismus' in *Essays II*. Frankfurt am Main: S. Fischer Verlag: 93–103.

Marinetti, Filippo T. (1909) 'Manifiesto del Futurismo', *Le Figaro*, February 20.

——— (1915) *Guerra sola igiene del mondo*. Milano: Edizioni Futuriste di poesia.

——— (1987) *Taccuini (1915–21)*, Edited by Alberto Bertoni. Bologna: Il Mulino.

Marzola, Alessandra (2005) *Guerra e identità. Percorsi della letteratura inglese nel Novecento*. Roma: Carocci.

McEnaney, Laura (2000) *Civil Defense Begins at Home. Militarization Meets Everyday Life in the Fifties*. Princeton, NJ; Oxford: Princeton University Press.

McLuhan, Marshall (1968) *War and Peace in Global Village*. New York: Bantam.

Mommsen, Wolfgang J. (2000) 'Intellettuali, Scrittori, Artisti E La Prima Guerra Mondiale, 1890–1915', pp. 41–58 in Vincenzo Calì, Gustavo Corni and Giuseppe Ferrandi (eds) *Gli intellettuali e la Grande Guerra*. Bologna: Il Mulino.

Montanari, Federico (2004) *Linguaggi della guerra*. Roma: Meltemi.

Mosse, George L. (1990) *Fallen Soldiers. Reshaping the Memory of the World Wars*. New York: Oxford University Press.

Natoli, Salvatore (2005) *La verità in gioco. Scritti su Foucault*. Milano: Feltrinelli.

Papini, Giovanni (1919) *L'esperienza futurista*. Firenze: Vallecchi.

Poirer, Lucien and Gerard Chaliand (1997) *Le chantier stratégique. Entretiens avec Gérard Chaliand*. Paris: Hachette.

Procter, James (2004) *Stuart Hall*. London; New York: Routledge.

Rose, Kenneth D. (2001) *One Nation Underground. The Fallout Shelter in American Culture*. New York; London: New York University Press.

Russell, Bertrand (1961) *Has Man a Future?*. London: George Allen & Unwin.

Savarese, Rossella (1992) *Guerre intelligenti. Stampa, radio, TV, informatica. La comunicazione politica dalla Crimea al Golfo Persico*. Milano: F. Angeli.

Scheler, Max (1915) *Der Genius des Krieges und der deutsche Krieg*. Leipzig: Verlag der Weißen Bücher.

Schmitt, Carl (1950) *Der Nomos der Erde im Völkerrecht des Jus Publicum Europaeum*. Köln; Berlin: Greven.

Simmel, Georg (1900) *Philosophies des Geldes*. Leipzig: Duncker & Humbolt.

Sombart, Werner (1915) *Händler und Helden. Patriotische Gesinnungen*. München; Leipzig: Duncker & Humblot.

Virilio, Paul (1989) *War and Cinema. The Logistics of Perception*. London: Verso.

—————— (1995) *Absolute Velocity*. Interview held at the European IT Forum, September 5, Paris, www.mediamente.rai.it/mediamentetv/learning/ed_multimediale/english/bibliote/intervis/v/virilio.htm (January 2, 2012).

Walzer, Michael (2004) *Arguing About War*. New Haven, CT; London: Yale University Press.

Notes

1   In his *Introduction to the Structural Analysis of Narratives,* Barthes states: 'there are not, there have never been, any people anywhere without narrative' (Barthes, 1994: 95).

2   For a further elaboration of Gramsci's interpretation of 'common sense', see the section entitled 'The Semantic Sliding of the Concept of War' in this chapter.

3   On the problematic rule of the western liberal media during war, see Chomsky and Herman (2002).

Between Indifference and News Hunger

Media Effects and the Public Sphere in Nazi Germany during Wartime

Jürgen Wilke

Summary

From 1930 the National Socialist Party began forming an information service. Initially it was organized within the SS *Sicherheitsdienst* (Security Service, SD), but in 1939 it was transferred to the *Reichssicherheitshauptamt* (Reich Security Head Office, RSHA). Otto Ohlendorf entered the SD in 1936 and was appointed as head of Department III. This department was responsible for the domestic information service. The *Reports from the Reich* documented in the German Federal Archive can be seen as instructive sources for the opinion formation of the German population in the Third Reich. Published from October 1939, in particular in a column on 'The effects of general propaganda and of the control of the press and broadcasting' that was added to the 'Cultural sectors' section, they provide insight into the use, the evaluation and the effects of the mass media during World War II.

Introduction

War constitutes a state of emergency for a society. Before the actual engagement in war begins, civil rights are suspended or undermined. Military goals take precedence and direct behavior and actions. People are compelled to live under more complicated circumstances, and they are forced to bear special burdens and to accept restrictions. Material and personal sacrifices are demanded of them. The extent to which all this is the case, however, depends on other factors, for instance, the characteristics of 'the enemy', whether the war is waged in the home country or far away, and how much the individual is directly affected by it. In addition, the reasons for and the aims and legitimation of the war are significant. In general, the type of political system is also important. In democratic systems, conditions are different even in times of war than in authoritarian states and totalitarian dictatorships. In addition, the state of emergency may be short-lived, but it may also last for a considerable time if a war extends over years (or decades).

Wars have consequences for the public sphere and for public (and private) communication. This assumption will be examined with the help of a historical case. The case dates back nearly three-quarters of a century, but it has not lost any of its immense momentousness: the World War II. No other war in history has claimed such a large number of victims and left behind such a degree of destruction. The war was decisively caused by Germany, where the National Socialist Party had been in power since 1933. Even in that dictatorship, however, there was a public sphere and forms of articulating public opinion (Wirl, 1990). In this case, I think it is especially interesting to examine how the people used the media in World War II under such political circumstances, how they processed the media content and how they reacted to it. What effects did the media have on the public?

Opinion Research in the Third Reich: Organization and Sources

To answer these questions, we need to examine the primary sources. In democratic societies, the media themselves – the press, radio, television and so on – may be examined. Today, in addition, (independent) representative surveys are possible. For the Third Reich, however, these sources are lacking. From Hitler's seizure of power (the so-called *Machtergreifung*) in 1933, the Nazis strove to control the media and to make it an instrument of their propaganda (Abel, 1968; Wilke, 2007). As a result, the media can hardly be used to find out what people at that time really thought. In the 1930s, representative surveys were still in an early stage of development even in the United States, and they did not even exist in Germany. Nevertheless, even dictators want to know the opinions of their subjects. Thus, it is not surprising that even in the Third Reich there were efforts to obtain knowledge about this.

Since 1930, the National Socialist Party (NSDAP) had started to build up its own information service (Boberach, 1965: XIff; 1984a: 11ff; Herbst, 1982: 105ff, 182ff), intended to gather information about political enemies. The SS *Sicherheitsdienst* (Security Service, SD) emerged from this, which was headed by Reinhard Heydrich. After Hitler came to power, the work of the SD could be expanded to the state level. For this purpose, task sharing with the Gestapo, the state secret police of Nazi Germany, became necessary. Similarly to other sectors of the state administration, the main office of the SD expanded during the 1930s and the number of staff members increased. On September 27, 1939, it was merged with other departments, thus creating the *Reichssicherheitshauptamt* (Reich Security Head Office, RSHA).

Within this organization, Department III was responsible for the domestic information service. Its head was Otto Ohlendorf, who had been a member of the NSDAP since 1925 (Herbst, 1982: 182ff; Wildt, 2003). He entered the SD in 1936 and was mainly interested in trade and economic questions (which later took him to the Reich Economics Ministry, where he was temporarily deputy secretary of state). In 1941–42, Ohlendorf was head of one of the notorious SS task forces that, according to his own confession, killed 90,000 people in the Soviet Union. Subsequently, he was tried and sentenced to death in the so-called *Einsatzgruppen* Trial (Task Force Trial) in 1948 before being executed in 1951.

It was Ohlendorf who is said to have developed the SD into an 'opinion research institute of the dictatorship' (Boberach, 1984a: 11).[1] He considered 'an [...] objective information service as an important instrument without which no government of a large political system may get by in our age of highly complicated circumstances of life' (as cited in Boberach, 1965: 533).

Moreover, he considered such an information service necessary 'in a state which in its basic conception is based on the leadership system and does not provide for a corrective by parliamentary or journalistic institutions' (Boberach, 1965: 535).

The SD systematically gathered information and prepared reports aimed at informing the political leaders about the mood in the country. Ohlendorf saw a growing discrepancy between the promises of the NSDAP, on the one hand, and the actual reality, on the other. He wrote,

> I had in mind the creation of an organ which, instead of public criticism, would nonetheless make it possible for the governance to become acquainted with the opinions existing in the public and to follow them. In this sense, an outlet for unresolved tensions and a source of information about the urgent necessities of the lives of the people was what was ultimately sought (as cited in Boberach, 1965: 536).

Thus, this undertaking was definitely intended to stabilize the regime's power. The gathering of information was organized all over Germany with the help of 51 main branches and 519 branches of the RSHA. They depended on a large number of informants making observations and recording statements of opinion. As Ohlendorf stated later, the number of informants was approximately 30,000. A memo of the SD main section in Stuttgart (No. 168) of October 12, 1940 explained their task as follows:

> It has to be ensured that all sections of the population are constantly supervised regarding their moods and attitudes. In conversations, every informant has to seize every opportunity, in his family, among his friends and acquaintances and above all at his workplace, inconspicuously to learn about the actual impact on the public mood of all important domestic and foreign events and measures. Furthermore, the conversations of all Germans citizens in trains (commuter trains) and trams, in shops, at the hairdresser's, at newsstands, in government offices (food and coupon offices, employment offices, city halls etc.), at weekly markets, in bars, in companies and lunchrooms, constitute informative evidence in plenty, which in many cases is still observed insufficiently (as cited in Boberach, 1984a: 17).

According to Ohlendorf, 'in principle, professionally recognized persons with a good reputation, practising in the various areas of life (e.g., government officials, judges, doctors, teachers, scientists, economists, journalists, etc.), are chosen' as informants (as cited in Boberach, 1965: 537). They mostly fulfilled their tasks on a voluntary basis. The central evaluation and summarizing was done at Department III of the RSHA by a small circle of responsible officials (Boberach, 1965: 537).

While at first annual reports were sufficient, the outbreak of the war brought about reporting at shorter intervals. 'Periodic short-term information' for the Reich and party leaders 'about the political situation within the Reich and the mood of the population'

(Boberach, 1984a: 20) started with the first *Bericht zur innenpolitischen Lage* (Report on the domestic political situation) of October 9, 1939. From December 8, 1939 on, the reports were called *Meldungen aus dem Reich* (Reports from the Reich) and were subdivided into five parts (or temporarily six parts):

- General atmosphere and situation
- Enemies (omitted in summer 1940)
- Folklore and public health (from March 1940)
- Cultural sectors
- Law and administration
- Economy

From May 1940 on, the *Reports from the Reich* were numbered consecutively. The reports that had been published until then were numbered retroactively as 1 to 88. Furthermore, a column called 'Effects of general propaganda and of the control of the press and broadcasting' was added to the 'Cultural sectors' section (this column is especially important for this chapter). Until May 1940, three reports per week were published; afterwards, it was two, sometimes supplemented by larger reports on special, mostly current, questions in the annex. Each report referred to the period of time that had elapsed since the previous report.

The SD reports consisted of 12 to 45 pages. They were marked as top secret ('for the personal information of the addressee only'). It is not possible to reconstruct fully the list of people who received them. Their primary addressees were first of all Heydrich and the *Reichsführer-SS* (SS chief commander) Heinrich Himmler, but they were also sent to the Minister of Propaganda Joseph Goebbels and to other ministers or NSDAP *Reichsleiter* (National Leaders), such as Hermann Göring and Robert Ley, the head of the German Labour Front. The supreme command of the *Wehrmacht* (German Defence Forces) also received them. Obviously, Adolf Hitler was only informed indirectly by his deputy Rudolf Hess or by Himmler. The head of the Party Chancellery, Martin Bormann, apparently did not receive them. Bormann harshly criticized the SD reports as a 'mouthpiece of defeatism' because of the grave atmosphere they documented. In 1944, together with Robert Ley, he forbade all functionaries of the NSDAP and German Work Front from cooperating with the SD. Goebbels also saw 'a certain danger' in the SD reports, as he entrusted to his diary on April 17, 1943: '... as most readers of these reports do not have sufficient skill in political differentiation to distinguish a triviality from a substantial case' (as cited in Hano, 1963: 13).

This ban led in practice to the termination of the regular reports. After that, only SD reports on singular questions were published. The last documents of this kind originate from the end of March 1945. Nonetheless, as late as May 1945, facing the military defeat of Germany, Ohlendorf wrote a paper in Flensburg in which he offered his expertize and services to the caretaker government of the Reich under Admiral Dönitz and indirectly also to the victorious British: 'I have advocated the opinion that, especially at the present time, the government of the Reich needs such an instrument for its information, and that it is also necessary for a loyal and objective cooperation with the occupying power' (as cited in Boberach, 1965: 533). Ohlendorf emphasized again how important it was that – to serve the truth – the work of such an information service not be 'doctrinally biased' (Boberach, 1965: 537) but 'objective' and 'factually independent'. In retrospect, he admitted, 'However, this condition has not been achieved in any form' (as cited in Boberach, 1965: 535).

The aims, production and characteristics of the *Reports from the Reich* necessarily lead one to question their value as sources. Can they be regarded as authentic documents reflecting actual opinion formation in Germany during the war years? This question has solicited a good deal of controversy. It was at least Ohlendorf's intention to deliver an unvarnished picture of the atmosphere in Germany. Anything different would not have been useful for the political (and military) leaders in any event. In retrospect, Ohlendorf understood the reason for the minimal acceptance and internal criticism of the SD reports, especially in the evidence they provided of a negative pessimistic mood during the ongoing war:

Especially the Reich party leaders, the Reich Ministry of Propaganda, and some other authorities more strongly affected by public criticism have tried to hinder the work of the SD. These prejudices to a large extent resulted in the actual public opinion represented by the SD not reaching the decisive authorities, with the result that it could not be taken into consideration. This does not only apply to the individual departments and heads of department who were often inconvenienced by the claimed criticism, but unfortunately also to the central government of the Reich and the Führer himself, who took notice of the compiled facts, thoughts and ideas or were informed about them to an absolutely insufficient extent (as cited in Boberach, 1965: 538).

Nevertheless, the *Reports from the Reich* did not remain without effect: 'Numerous propaganda efforts can be considered to have resulted only from the SD reports, and even Hitler's speeches often resulted from SD reports or took up their topics' (Herbst, 1982: 187). For example, it can be demonstrated that the leading authorities of the broadcasting service reacted rapidly to criticism of their programs that was published in the late summer of 1940 by introducing new entertainment elements and long traditional broadcasts. A few weeks later the SD reports announced,

The current *music program* of the German broadcasting service increasingly finds approval. [...] It is above all gratefully welcomed that there are from time to time *dance music numbers* during the concerts. (No. 142, November 18, 1940; Boberach, 1984b, Vol. 6: 1776)

The possibility cannot be excluded – indeed it is rather probable – that in summarizing the SD reports, certain pieces of information were specifically selected, while some were withheld, misinterpreted or even distorted, simply due to wishful thinking or to please superiors. Ludolf Herbst argues that a correct picture of the mood within the population could hardly be drawn using spy-like methods in secrecy (Herbst, 1982: 187f). However, Otto Ohlendorf interpreted the negative reactions of the Nazi state and party machinery as an indication of the 'objectivity' of the SD reports. Given the necessary critical distance, it is now possible to assign 'a surprisingly high information value' (Steinert, 1970: 45) to the SD reports and to see them as instructive sources for the opinion formation of the German population in the Third Reich, above all in view of the absence of alternative sources (see Stöber, 1998).

The SD reports are documented in the German Federal Archive. A first selection was edited by Heinz Boberach in 1965. In 1984, he published a complete edition in seventeen volumes. One year later, Volume 18 offered an essential index. Further holdings from the Main State Archive in Koblenz were published later (Brommer, 1988). In any case, the *Reports from the Reich* were not the only means of 'opinion research' in the Third Reich. Herbst spoke of an absolutely 'rampant network of such information systems' (Herbst, 1982: 107). This included, among other things, reports by NSDAP local groups, some of which have been edited, those for Bavaria, for example (Broszat et al., 1977).

Paradoxes of Media Use and Factors of Media Effects

The secret reports of the SD are a source of information about how people in the Third Reich thought about a large number of topics. They prove that – unlike in August 1914 – there was no war enthusiasm at all to be perceived in Germany when World War II broke out in 1939 (Steinert, 1970: 91ff). In fact, feelings of depression, resignation, apathy and confusion, as well as the desire for freedom, were rampant. Soon doubts emerged about whether the war could be won. The military successes, however, caused spirits to rise but only temporarily. Above all, the supply situation was important. This cannot be further analyzed here, as we are primarily interested in information on the use, the evaluation and the effects of the mass media during World War II such as it is provided by the SD reports. In this context, one finds a curious paradox between indifference and avoidance, on the one hand, and news hunger and the search for information, on the other.

Indifference and Avoidance

As the SD reports prove, the confidence in victory that was prevalent in Germany in the summer months of 1941 dwindled from then on. People were prepared for the fact that the war in the East was not to be won before the onset of winter, although the media claimed precisely this. As a result, the attention being paid to the media by the general public rapidly decreased:

> In the reports from the districts it is unanimously said that *attention to the press coverage of the fighting in the East has subsided*. The population is prepared, reluctantly and somewhat

morosely, for the campaign against Bolshevism not coming to an end this year. (No. 219, September 11, 1941; Boberach 1984b, Vol. 8: 2746)

The spreading indifference hardened into an attitude of avoidance and even into a 'complete isolation from the political events' (No. 238, November 17, 1941; Boberach, 1984b, Vol. 8: 2997).

The reports from the districts reveal that large parts of the population increasingly react a little wearily and indifferently to all reports about the *development of the fighting in the East*. You could again meet other Germans not shrinking from admitting that they had not listened to the news the whole week and justifying this with statements such as, 'You don't miss anything at all'. There is often criticism that numerous partial results were presented rather strongly as successes without resulting in a coherent picture of the situation in the East and without developments becoming apparent which would lead to bigger decisions before the onset of winter. [...] The 'going on' about the partial successes by the broadcasting service, which we mentioned above, is repeatedly criticized. (No. 220, September 15, 1941; Boberach, 1984b, Vol. 8: 2762)

The tediousness of the mass media, which was the result of propaganda both with regard to content and to style, was also criticized:

As an example of a certain fatigue arising in the population with regard to the press and broadcasting coverage, it is repeatedly pointed out that the same news, with a nearly identically worded commentary, is presented in different broadcasts and in the press. (No. 112, August 5, 1940; Boberach, 1984b, Vol. 5: 1442)

The merging of the different regional broadcasting programs into one program for the *Reich* was met with rejection. The population reacted by switching off the programs, which prevented the desired results of broadcasting from occurring. In this situation it was assumed that foreign broadcasting was increasingly being listened to, although it was prohibited. The radios installed by the National Socialist government in public places for the collective reception of broadcasts also became less popular:

There are numerous reports that the news broadcasts in restaurants are meeting with an increasing apathy and indifference on the part of the guests present. Complaints about the indiscipline of the audience when news reports are broadcast in restaurants occur more and more often. (No. 129, October 3, 1940; Boberach, 1984b, Vol. 5: 1637f)

During the first weeks of the war, people in Germany were not particularly aware that the mass media struck a note of propaganda that was all-pervasive. Soon, however, this was increasingly perceived as annoying and uncomfortable, above all as the supply situation worsened in everyday life. People's skepticism mounted vis-à-vis the press:

In the reports, a series of voices supports the view that at the moment, the press does not have '*a great appeal*' with its outer appearance and its design regarding contents. Day after day, the newspapers are only briefly skipped over by many German citizens as they are *rather monotonous in their outer appearance* and they repeat some unvarying issues … with a few words changed and without any essentially new arguments. This frequently results in a certain satiation, as the information about these repeatedly treated questions was perceived as already sufficient.

[…]

It is often said that the layout of the German press with its *big headlines* published *every day* seems very blunt. […] Germans have become used to the newspapers *always* being published with big headlines, even when it turns out when reading them that the topics or messages that are treated below do not have the news value or the weight within the general scope of the war that the headlines themselves promise. The majority of newspaper readers have their own point of view and judgements regarding the appeal of the big headlines. (No. 371, October 23, 1943; Boberach, 1984b, Vol. 13: 5022)

In August 1940 the aversion to polemic glosses on England was reported: '*Only factual reports would still attract interest*' (No. 113, August 8, 1940; Boberach, 1984b, Vol. 5: 1452). Exaggerations turned out to be counterproductive when the phase of the war was relatively quiet and nothing decisive was happening:

According to the majority of reports from the individual areas of the Reich, the attitude of the population toward the news in the press and the broadcasting service is currently characterized by a very strong reservation. Many Germans are overcome with mistrust given the fact that all the news has 'in some way propagandistic overtones'. The 'listlessness' of German citizens is considerably determined by the fact that the individual news reports are about successes that have no importance as far as deciding the war is concerned. (No. 317, September 14, 1942; Boberach, 1984b, Vol. 11: 4199)

One month before that, the SD report had lapidary described the paradoxical information situation:

Newspapers and broadcasting hardly gain a hearing for their reports. The OKW [High Command of German Armed Forces] *report and more factual reports* of a military or political nature are urgently awaited. (*SD-Berichte zu Inlandsfragen* [SDB], August 12, 1943; Boberach, 1984b, Vol. 14: 5595)

News Hunger and the Search for Information

Alongside the attitude of indifference and avoidance, there was in Germany also a hunger for news and an active search for information during World War II. Apart from the public appearances of Adolf Hitler, war events had the biggest influence on media consumption. The beginning of the war had resulted in a run on the mass media, which, in turn, increased popular excitement:

> The whole mood is thus activated so that the [depiction of] events touching the German confrontation with the enemies in any form, be it in movies, the press, the broadcasting service, lectures, literature and the like are most popular. Thus, for example, there is spontaneous applause all over the Reich during the newsreels in the cinemas; thus, the regular evening unmasking of the English atrocity campaigns and lies on the radio is most warmly welcomed; [...] thus, in the press sector, the present [high] circulation of the newspapers can be explained by the strong desire for current news transmission although there is less time available. (No. 5, October 18, 1939; Boberach, 1984b, Vol. 2: 366)

The reports of the *Propaganda-Kompanien* (propaganda companies, PK) were especially popular. They had been established starting in 1938 and were first introduced during the invasion of Czechoslovakia (von Wedel, 1962). In a sense, these were 'embedded journalists', in that the PK correspondents were firmly integrated into the armed forces and were also trained to use weapons themselves. Their reports attracted 'brisk interest', since they enabled contact between the front and home and helped to prevent 'a drifting apart of front and home as was the case during the World War [I]' (No. 72, April 3, 1940; Boberach, 1984b, Vol. 2: 950). The PK reports were regarded as sensational, even spectacular, because the PK correspondents were actually involved in the fighting, which could be heard and seen. The population was said to show 'perfect admiration' (No. 87, May 14, 1940; Boberach, 1985, Vol. 4: 1130) for the work of the PK men. Even the announcements of German losses appeared to be confidence-building:

> The immediate announcement of the German losses had a favorable effect on the trust in the German coverage and was regarded as a sign, generally welcomed, that the government considered the German people to be inwardly strong and sufficiently steadfast to openly inform it even about heavy losses. (No. 76, April 12, 1940; Boberach, 1984b, Vol. 4: 983f)

For similar reasons, the reports about English air strikes on Berlin in the summer of 1940, which led to heavy losses on the German side and were answered with counterattacks, were very attentively noted. This ended a phase of distinct lack of interest in the media, with the result 'that the interest of the population in the coverage of press and broadcasting again is extraordinarily strong now' (No. 123, September 12, 1940; Boberach, 1984b, Vol. 5: 1564).

A true 'run' on the media, especially newsreels, was triggered by the attack on the Soviet Union in the summer of 1941. According to the SD reports, even in the spring, the news reports were already being 'observed with a really ravenous hunger' (No. 179, April 17, 1941; Boberach, 1984b, Vol. 6: 2206). This was shown by Hitler's frequent appearances in public. It was said in this situation that 'it is everywhere gratefully recognized that the *press and the broadcasting service take account of the news hunger in the population and fulfil the wishes of readers*' (No. 179, April 17, 1941; Boberach, 1984b, Vol. 6: 2204). At the same time, rumors about the worsening relationship with Russia spread as the press and the broadcasting service almost ceased reporting on the Soviet Union: 'In connection with this, the population dwells on the question why are the press and the broadcasting service no longer providing information about Russia? And what might be the reasons, even more than before?' (No. 175, March 31, 1941; Boberach, 1984b, Vol. 6: 2167).

In May 1941, the population for the first time speculated on a possible war against the Soviet Union. As before, the SD reports frequently mention the spreading of rumors, which had an important function in the Third Reich because of the suppression of free communication (see Dröge, 1970). That the newspapers no longer reported on the Soviet Union was seen as confirmation of the rumors that, among other things, reported an alleged 'revolution' between the supporters of Stalin and those of Molotov (No. 183, May 5, 1941; Boberach, 1984b, Vol. 7: 2260).

When Germany attacked the Soviet Union on June 22, 1941, the German media started a campaign against the former ally that had a significant effect on the population:

According to unanimous statements from several parts of the Reich, the impact of the reports from the front was a very extraordinary one. The depression existing at the beginning abruptly subsided after the first reports from the front. They have contributed considerably to the population's 'regaining its composure' by consistently making the extremely positive developments in the fighting discernible. (No. 197, June 26, 1941; Boberach, 1984b, Vol. 7: 2444)

As Nazi propaganda claimed, Germany had only acted in anticipation of an attack by the Soviet Union. German citizens now fuelled their great news hunger with 'curious expectations', poured into the cinemas assured of success, and devoured the PK reports (No. 199, July 3, 1941; Boberach, 1984b, Vol. 7: 2473; No. 200, July 7, 1941; Boberach, 1984b, Vol. 7: 2489).

In summer 1943, the (last) major German offensive at the Eastern front and the Allied landing on Sicily again awoke the interest of the whole German population:

In all reports it is emphasized that the news broadcasts and especially the Armed Forces' reports have not been listened to with such regularity in a long time and also that the newspapers were again being read attentively. This was done with a *serene interest and quiet objectiveness* which naturally, regarding the developments in Sicily, was not free from a certain concern about the further development of the fighting. (SDB, July 15, 1943; Boberach, 1984b, Vol. 14: 5472)

People were not satisfied with the coverage, however. They distrusted the news and asked for the publication of the 'whole truth':

The interest in news about the events of the war has even increased since the battle in the East and the landing of the enemy on Sicily. Every day the Armed Forces report is eagerly awaited, as is the distribution of the newspapers, which are taken out of the vendors' hands and are often sold out shortly after their appearance. [...] Because of the general deep concern about the course of the war and the desire for open information about the 'truth', even if it is hard, every word is 'examined most thoroughly'. (SDB, July 22, 1943; Boberach, 1984b, Vol. 14: 5510f)

In view of the uncertainty, the population tended to pay careful attention to the positioning as well as to the mentioning of names and details in the newspapers. It was common practice 'to read between the lines' (Boberach, 1984b, Vol. 15: 6065):

Great attention was paid to the form of those messages, which were conveyed without comment and frequently in not particularly prominent positions in the newspapers and which mentioned different details [...] almost marginally. From such passing mentions especially, the conclusion was drawn in reference to earlier experiences that these were important news items, and the most different combinations were made up between them. (No. 305, August 3, 1942; Boberach, 1984b, Vol. 11: 4034)

The decline of the credibility of Nazi propaganda necessarily made the media in Germany more and more ineffective during World War II. People rooted through the newspapers more and more critically. The inner agreement of the population with the media content that existed at the beginning of the war, and their voluntary acceptance of it, had dissolved completely:

The efforts especially of the press to present the military situation of Germany as favorable, despite the setbacks in the East and in Sicily and despite the intensifying air strikes of the enemy, are consistently checked for their arguments with suspicious attention. Many commentaries and individual news reports were described as being not convincing. (SDB, September 2, 1943; Boberach, 1984b, Vol. 14: 5700)

The feeling of unbearable uncertainty finally led to popular demands:

'*We do have a right to know what is going on*', or: 'What does propaganda gain if it does not come out with the truth? We will have to learn about the facts anyway, just as was the case regarding Stalingrad.' (SDB, August 2, 1943; Boberach, 1984b, Vol. 14: 5564)

Effects of Different Media Compared

During World War II, the German public had three media at its disposal: the press (especially the newspapers), radio broadcasting and newsreels. According to the rules of media research, there are significant differences between these media in terms of their function and effects. Because of its significant topicality, broadcasting in Germany was appreciated as the best medium for initially obtaining information. The press was seen as enabling a more 'in-depth' understanding of the news. In the case of newsreels, the information value provided took second place behind the emotional experience and the feeling of 'being a part of it'. These differences were emphasized over and over again in the SD reports and will be demonstrated here by a few examples out of many possible ones:

> The press manages to ensure that interest in it is not hampered, although it inevitably has to limp behind broadcasting as far as the [delivery of] the news is concerned. But [newspapers and so on] are eagerly taken up, especially for further reading. (No. 90, May 23, 1940; Boberach, 1984b, Vol. 4: 1165)
>
> The majority of Germans *again 'calmly studied'* the speech [by Hitler] to 'uncover the subtleties of the speech'. The day after the speech, the *demand for newspapers was extremely high.* (No. 323, October 5, 1942; Boberach, 1984b, Vol. 11: 4280)
>
> The variety, diversity and detail of the newsreels in the period mentioned and the very positive effect on the population again showed that the pictorial reports of the newsreels were often a more convincing and pervasive means of mood control than coverage by the press and broadcasting. (No. 197, June 26, 1941; Boberach, 1984b, Vol. 7: 2445)

Obviously the German population believed that film coverage was less likely to distort news for propaganda purposes. From this point of view, the newsreels appeared to be closer to reality:

> In different departments of the Reich it was universally ascertained that running a newsreel often immediately dispelled a detectable reservation or even a certain mistrust of the press and broadcasting reports [...], which were often described as being too 'propagandistic'. The pictorial reports of the newsreels [...] were followed with 'great astonishment'. According to various individual observations, the newsreels had a much more convincing effect than the press and broadcasting coverage of the same topics. (No. 379, April 29, 1943; Boberach, 1984b, Vol. 13: 5192f)

However, the newsreels also began to lose credibility. Serious rumors were induced by the fact that from December 2, 1942 on, Stalingrad was a topic that was no longer covered by the newsreels: 'In connection with the fact that for some time now there have been no more pictures from Stalingrad, it was repeated that our troops are locked up in Stalingrad' (No. 348, January 7, 1943; Boberach, 1984b, Vol. 12: 4634).

Alternative Information Sources

The secret reports of the SD concerning the prevailing mood and atmosphere in the Reich offer many indications of how the population used alternative information sources during World War II. The less the mass media offered the desired information or the less credible they became, the more frequently this occurred, since it was believed that they were merely instruments of official propaganda. According to the SD reports from the beginning of 1943, other sources appeared to be more credible: 'People make efforts not to confine themselves to the press and broadcasting service as sources of information, but instead try to gain a more accurate picture by gathering information from people on furlough and from letters from the front' (No. 353, January 25, 1943; Boberach, 1984b, Vol. 12: 4717).

In the months following Stalingrad, it was observed 'that the *population*' formed '*its picture of the situation independently of public control instruments with the help of "facts" they can access*' (SDB, October 21, 1943; Boberach, 1984b, Vol. 15: 5904). Stories of people on furlough and letters from those on active service, which were delivered by the army postal service, took over the information role of the media, and friends and acquaintances no longer talked about what they had learned from the press and broadcasting but rather about the contents of the army postal service letters. In terms of their effect, the latter by far surpassed the former:

> It could be said that the belief of many Germans in the steadfastness of the Eastern front is more strongly influenced by one single unfavorable letter from a soldier or the story of a single soldier on furlough than 'can be made up for by the press within one week'. (SDB, January 27, 1944; Boberach, 1984b, Vol. 16: 6287)

Foreign radio stations were another source of information, although listening to them was prohibited. Despite the threat of penalties, many people nevertheless switched on these programs. After the German successes at the beginning of the war, this was done out of the conviction that the reception of 'enemy media' could do no harm and that these media could no longer be taken seriously (No. 103, July 8, 1940; Boberach, 1984b, Vol. 5: 1356). When Hitler's deputy made his surprising flight to England, an SD report said, 'the desire for information on the Hess case obviously considerably loosened broadcasting discipline' (No. 126, September 23, 1940; Boberach, 1984b, Vol. 5: 1596). When the defeat at Stalingrad became clearer at the end of January 1943, while the media still stoked the hope of victory, Germans no longer hid the fact that they were listening to foreign radio stations. They were ready to pass on the things they had heard, 'to gossip about one or the other smear campaign', as it was put in one SD report (No. 355, February 1, 1943; Boberach, 1984b, Vol. 12: 4736). Obviously, people were no longer afraid to admit in public that they did something illegal. The administrative control of the public sphere was subject to inexorable erosion:

Because of the poor quality of the information about important events, there is a *growing feeling of alienation regarding propaganda*. Occasionally people virtually deduce an inner right from the scarce news reporting to override – as it is called – 'paternalism' and inform themselves using other sources. An extensive formation of rumors which hardly allows the public means of control to have an effect any more, among other things. (SDB, August 5, 1943; Boberach, 1984b, Vol. 14: 5573)

Key Points

- The SS *Sicherheitsdienst* (SD) started to systematically gather information and to prepare reports to obtain knowledge about the mood in the country. In view of the absence of alternative sources, and given the necessary critical distance, these *Reports from the Reich* can be seen as instructive sources for the opinion formation of the German population during the Third Reich.
- Examining the secret reports of the SD, various paradoxes in terms of media use and factors of media effects can be observed: on the one hand, attitudes of indifference and avoidance, on the other hand, a hunger for news and the search for information.

Study Questions

1. In the secret reports of the SD the differences between the three media at their disposal – the press (especially newspapers), radio broadcasting and newsreels – are emphasized. How would you characterize the differences in terms of their function and effects?
2. There are always tensions between the private and the public sphere, even when they are closely connected in various ways. Discuss the different characteristics of the relationships between both spheres within a democratic and an authoritarian/totalitarian system.

Further Reading

Bankier, David (1992) *The Germans and the Final Solution. Public Opinion under Nazism.* Oxford: Blackwell.

Kershaw, Ian (2002) *Popular Opinion and Political Dissent in the Third Reich. Bavaria 1933–1945.* New ed. Oxford: Oxford University Press.

Websites

The *Reports from the Reich* are available at 20th Century German History Online – National Socialism, Holocaust, Resistance and Exile 1933–1945: db.saur.de/DGO (Information: www.degruyter.com/view/supplement/9783110233261_Brochure_en.pdf).

The Third Reich – a short overview (by the US Holocaust Memorial Museum): www. ushmm.org/wlc/en/article.php?ModuleId=10007331.

References

Abel, Karl-Dietrich (1968) *Presselenkung im NS-Staat. Eine Studie zur Geschichte der Publizistik in der nationalsozialistischen Zeit.* Berlin: Colloquium.

Boberach, Heinz (1965) 'Einleitung', pp. IX–XXXI in Heinz Boberach (ed.) *Meldungen aus dem Reich. Auswahl aus den geheimen Lageberichten des Sicherheitsdienstes der SS 1939–1944.* Neuwied; Berlin: Luchterhand.

—— (1984a) 'Einführung', pp. 11–44 in Heinz Boberach (ed.) *Meldungen aus dem Reich 1938– 1945. Die geheimen Lageberichte des Sicherheitsdienstes der SS. Vol. 1.* Herrsching: Pawlak.

—— (ed.) (1984b) *Meldungen aus dem Reich 1938–1945. Die geheimen Lageberichte des Sicherheitsdienstes der SS.* Herrsching: Pawlak.

—— (ed.) (1985) *Meldungen aus dem Reich 1938–1945. Die geheimen Lageberichte des Sicherheitsdienstes der SS. Index.* Herrsching: Pawlak.

Brommer, Peter (ed.) (1988) *Die Partei hört mit. Lageberichte und andere Meldungen des Sicherheitsdienstes der SS aus dem Großraum Koblenz. Vol 1.* Koblenz: Landesarchivverwaltung.

Broszat, Martin, Elke Fröhlich and Falk Wiesemann (eds) (1977) *Bayern in der NS-Zeit. Soziale Lage und politisches Verhalten der Bevölkerung im Spiegel vertraulicher Berichte. Vol. 1.* Munich; Vienna: Oldenbourg.

Dröge, Franz (1970) *Der zerredete Widerstand. Zur Soziologie und Publizistik des Gerüchts im 2. Weltkrieg.* Düsseldorf: Bertelsmann-Universitätsverlag.

Hano, Horst (1963) 'Die Taktik der Pressepropaganda des Hitlerregimes 1943–1945. Eine Untersuchung aufgrund unveröffentlichter Dokumente des Sicherheitsdienstes und des Reichsministeriums für Volksaufklärung und Propaganda', Dissertation, Berlin, Free University Berlin.

Herbst, Ludolf (1982) *Der Totale Krieg und die Ordnung der Wirtschaft. Die Kriegswirtschaft im Spannungsfeld von Politik, Ideologie und Propaganda 1939–1945.* Stuttgart: Deutsche Verlags-Anstalt.

Steinert, Marlis G. (1970) *Hitlers Krieg und die Deutschen. Stummung und Haltung der deutschen Bevölkerung im Zweiten Weltkrieg.* Düsseldorf; Wien: Econ.

Stöber, Rudolf (1998) *Die erfolgverführte Nation. Deutschlands öffentliche Stimmungen 1866 bis 1945.* Stuttgart: Steiner.

von Wedel, Hasso (1962) *Die Propagandatruppen der deutschen Wehrmacht. Die Wehrmacht im Kampf.* Neckargemünd: Vowinckel.

Wildt, Michael (ed.) (2003) *Nachrichtendienst, politische Elite, Mordeinheit. Der Sicherheitsdienst des Reichsführers SS.* Hamburg: Hamburger Edition.

Wilke, Jürgen (2007) *Presseanweisungen im zwanzigsten Jahrhundert. Erster Weltkrieg, Drittes Reich, DDR.* Köln: Böhlau.

Wirl, Manfred (1990) 'Die öffentliche Meinung unter dem NS-Regime. Eine Untersuchung zum sozialpsychologischen Konzept öffentlicher Meinung auf der Grundlage der geheimen Lageberichte des SD über die Stimmung und Haltung der Bevölkerung im Zweiten Weltkrieg', Dissertation, Mainz, Johannes Gutenberg-University.

Note

1 The German sources in the following are translated by the author. Italics are taken from the original.

Perception of Newspapers and Magazines in Field Post Correspondence during World War II

Clemens Schwender

Summary

Feldpost (field post) letters are increasingly being recognized as documents of everyday communication. They give an insight into the emotions and motivations of the ordinary soldier and their families and partners. Written communication was the only opportunity for contact with those at home and vice versa. In the days of World War II, the *Feldpost* letter was about the only means of individual communication available to soldiers and their relatives and friends back home. Estimates based on existing invoices between the German *Wehrmacht* and the *Reichspost* indicate that during World War II about 30 to 40 billion items marked *Feldpost* were transported. Almost 100,000 of these letters are kept in the *Berlin Feldpost Archiv*. The chapter presents examples of how newspapers and magazines as well as their content are mentioned in *Feldpost* letters. The citations will be categorized and analyzed in order to understand their function during war, while considering that both media and letters were subject to censorship.

Introduction

Witnesses to the events of the World War II fall into two fundamentally different categories. There are those directly affected – the soldiers and civilians who personally experienced and endured the pitched battles, sustained fighting and bombardments. And then there are the professional reporters, who compile their reports for purposes of publication in newspapers, magazines, over the air or in the weekly cinema newsreel.

Both types of witness produce reports; the professionals produce them for a mass media public. Reports by press copywriters and photographers are subject to censorship, only such information being permitted to reach readers, listeners and film audiences as conforms to the system. The nonprofessionals are likewise subject to censorship, both official and internal, of their messages to families, friends and acquaintances.

Each category of witness makes use of the other. Reporters interview soldiers or others affected by the war. Soldiers and their families use the media. As the soldiers exchange information with their families and friends, the role of the media can be partly reconstructed through analysis of this source.

Field Post as a Source

To develop insight into the perspective of individuals is part of the repertoire of any historical scholarship seeking relatively precise results from its search for reality. A similar concern explains why research into the private correspondence of historically important personages has always been popular. What is singular is that, in the World War II context, one of the most valuable of all sources for the inside view of a system – namely, letters from and to the front line, for which German has the succinct collective term of *Feldpost* (field post) – was not appreciated at its true value by historians until very late in the day. Soldiers write to their families; families write to serving soldiers.

Everyday conversations generally vanish unrecorded, but this period's everyday was recorded, on paper: family chitchat and gossip, work, shopping, private and even intimate matters and of course the hardships and misery of war. During those years, it should be remembered, the field post letter was almost the only means of personal communication that linked serving troops with their family and social network at home.

The field post organization delivered letters, postcards, parcels and telegrams, also newspapers, magazines and even books. Sometimes other soldiers going on home leave or returning would carry an item or two with them, which would incidentally circumvent the censorship. Writing '*Feldpost*' on the envelope or wrapper would generally ensure free carriage. From time to time, however, the hazards of war might impose constraints on the field post service, locally or more generally (Gericke, 1971: 22–56).

Today field post correspondence enables us to learn about events and feelings that without it would have remained hidden. A full 60 years on, the letters have lost their original private *raison d'être*. Revisited now, they acquire a new significance – that of bearing witness to their era. Moreover, they are a unique source for all that was quotidian in the exceptional circumstances of war. The letters written by thousands of soldiers and their family members and friends afford an insight into conditions similar to those experienced by many other people at the time. Historians' study of them brings that normality to light once more.

Historical figures can be perceived, through their correspondence, as fragments of history. Through their letters, we come to know those who have shaped history while living their own individual histories. In their letters, history is presented: history unembellished and unfeigned, unjudged and uncommented. History on the epic scale and history in microcosm unfold side by side here, sometimes separated by no more than a comma.

Using extrapolations from extant *Wehrmacht* and *Reichspost* (national post) accounts records (Ueberschär, 1989: 301), it can now be reliably estimated that on the German side alone between thirty and forty thousand million items marked '*Feldpost*' were handled by the field post service during the World War II.

For decisions as to what to include in a letter and what to omit, censorship was a factor. It was overt: everyone knew post was censored. It was visibly recorded: provided a letter contained no serious infringements, it would be resealed and stamped with a notice that the message had been opened by the field post censor. Various passages in the letters might be blacked out or removed with scissors. They were to contain no names, no information on arms or on the state of provisioning as well as no military objectives or assessments. It was not until later that ideological issues became relevant (Ziemann, 1996: 164). But every soldier knew how small the risk was that a given letter, among the millions of others, would be opened by the field post censors.

The Watzlawick question – 'How real is reality?' – needs to be asked in relation to media-dependent communication. And it supports the contention that reality is not the basis for communication but its product. What the reality was can no longer be ascertained in detail and can therefore be treated as irrelevant. It is more important to know what those involved experienced from their own perspective and what thus is the basis of their perception. The point of interest is the subjective truth as individuals perceived it.

From our present-day perspective, we can take it that when individuals wrote in system-conformist terms this reflected their real stance because no one could compel them to make disclosures of that nature in a private communication. Where anyone comes out against the system, what they say can likewise be taken seriously, for this is criticism expressed in awareness of the risk of being caught. The only texts that do not permit interpretation are those that make no mention of system-relevant matters. In point of fact, the letters contain many system-conformist passages and many that express criticism, and all of these can be interpreted.

Nonetheless, the main determinant of what went into the letters, as well as of what was omitted, was the communicative relationship between writer and addressee. What one writes to one's mother will not be what one confides to friends and fellow soldiers. Where in the one case the writer's concern will be to send signals designed to cause minimum alarm, the other will allow him to describe this or that dangerous situation in which his enterprise has carried the day.

It is in the communication of suffering that soldiers impose frontiers beyond which is silence. This may be seen in the relatively rare instances where it is possible to compare and contrast diary entries with letters written at much the same time. For home the soldier's message is of forward-looking confidence; to his diary he confides the hardships and the danger. The problem of truth and reality thus does not begin with the retrospect of memory but goes back rather to the selection of content and of narrative style for different addressees.

Method

The *Feldpost-Archiv Berlin* (Berlin Field Post Archive) Joint Project is a collaborative undertaking by the Berlin Museum of Communications, which is responsible for the archiving, and a group of consultants made up of historians and media and communications experts, which promotes the use of the archived material for scholarly, educational and general cultural purposes. For the first time ever, individual eyewitness accounts dating from the World War II period are being systematically collected and made available to the world of scholarship.

At present the analysis can only be conducted as a qualitative study. Though based on over 10,000 letters, the study cannot be regarded as representative. Neither individual letter-writers nor individual letters had equal chances of inclusion in the sample. Wartime circumstances saw to it that many letters never reached their intended recipients. A more grievous loss, from today's perspective, is that many letters went to waste disposal more than 60 years after the war ended. Differing cultures of memory and stewardship have a bearing on whether the letters are even now still preserved by the families.

The important thing is accordingly not what was actually written by soldiers and their families, collected on some statistically meaningful basis; rather, the study's aim will have to be that of acquiring a sufficiently broad and diversified spectrum of material to permit insight into how individuals expressed themselves on the subject of the system and of their own experiences. The individuals featured have not been selected or specially emphasized, but they are all cases that entered the sample randomly.

A point needing emphasis here because of its methodological implications is that the letters were not written so that they might end up in a subsequent study: they fulfilled a purely private function. Moreover, they were written spontaneously, with no prescriptions regarding content or frequency. The research is thus methodologically speaking a noninvasive and nonreactive study of natural communication.

The Four Worlds

The long periods of separation lived through by soldiers serving in distant theaters – periods that might last several years – had implications extending beyond communication problems. There was a progressive erosion of the shared frameworks of reference that could otherwise have sustained dialog between correspondence partners. The upshot was that correspondents lived in four distinct worlds. First there was the world of the soldiers, limited to the front line and the *Etappe*, a holding area behind the front to which they might be stood down to rest or regroup; then there was their homeland, where their families and partners lived; then the world of combined future and past, to which allusion was frequent because the present was missing; and the fourth world was that of the media, where one could find some sense of shared synchronous experience.

The World of the Front

The world of the front was the world of the soldier. It was the world that was surely the most difficult to communicate to those not in it. The reasons for that are many and diverse. Communications sent by the soldiers were most likely to be influenced by censorship. Initially the rules did not apply to ideological matters, their purpose being to ensure that sensitive military information remained withheld from the enemy even if field post were to fall into his hands. It was thus a violation of orders to report anything concerning military objectives, military engagements, the nature or condition of weapons and other resources, or the names of comrades or higher ranks. Not even the current location could be divulged to those at home. The need of those at home to know how their loved ones were faring surfaced in letter after letter. Letters being unable to supply more than the scantiest of context detail, the media became an important information resource for the families and friends of serving troops: 'I do read the newspapers thoroughly, of course, particularly when there is news about the Wehrmacht' (3-2002-0349[1], October 29, 1940).

Newspapers and magazines were no less ubiquitous at and behind the front than were field post letters. They traveled through the same channels, for one thing. Those holding subscriptions could have their local and national papers sent out to them. This brought them an echo of everyday life in the homeland and a sense of being off duty. And an army surgeon attached to a field hospital writes of himself and a colleague: 'The evenings we spend sitting in our room – as we are doing now – and writing home – though he not quite as often as I, then he'll spend the time reading the newspapers – the *Rostocker Anzeiger* and *Lübecker Generalanzeiger*' (3-2002-7265, October 23, 1942).

There were also frontline newssheets, produced specifically for the troops. One example was *Mitteilungen für die Truppe* (Active Service News), publication of which had begun in April 1940. It was a more or less official communication from the *Oberkommando der Wehrmacht* (Army High Command), which aimed to bring *Wehrmacht* frontline troops the unvarnished facts about the military situation, in contrast to the propaganda produced for the families at home (Buchbender and Sterz, 1983: 25–6). A soldier on the Western front writes from France, for instance, 'I have a copy of yesterday's army newspaper here, I'll send it to you. It will give you an idea of how we get our news here, apart from the wireless service' (3-2002-0947, June 6, 1940).

What does a soldier know about the battle he has just taken part in, and what does he know about the war? His subjective view gives him no overview over the regional situation, much less the general situation. Rumors and uninformed gossip might be widespread, but the print media provided explicit information that could be cited. They also provided an overview covering the various fronts. Many soldiers learned in this way of the destruction of the 6th Army at Stalingrad and were able to discuss this event among themselves and also, by letter, with their families: 'In the mess of course there is a lot of talk about that bad business outside Stalingrad. Not that we know any more about it than what the newspapers said and what we heard on the wireless' (3-2002-7247, March 5, 1942).

Newspapers and other media are thus seen to be an important source of information even for those directly involved: 'Special communiqués the day before yesterday and again late yesterday: 12 mill. ton mark has been reached, newspaper reports and maps are every soldier's main interest' (3-2002-0947, June 18, 1941).

Soldiers could introduce their own experiences. A range of attitudes can be discerned: one stance is a simple mention. Here the writer draws attention to a particular article or picture. This means he also has to send the newspaper too, complete or in sections, or else has to be sure his addressee has access to the relevant issue of the paper. This makes direct reference possible, and then a debate. The exchange of information may also be accompanied by esthetic or emotional judgments, on the basis of which correspondents can engage in comparing notes:

> The newspaper supplement of 22.7. has a photo captioned 'Unsere Soldaten wissen sich zu helfen' (Our soldiers can handle it), can you please cut it out and put it with my other photos. It's part of the Mot. Section of our bttr. You won't have guessed that, but that's what it is. (3-2002-0947, August 6, 1941)

A second type of stance involves the writer applying his personal expertize to the content of the article. This may be expressed in any of a number of ways. First of all, it can happen that what the writer already knows at first hand is confirmed by newspaper articles – and thus in fact by official sources. Press reporters covering the events in question are introduced as witnesses to the writer's own experiences:

> Up at the front here you get to see nearly everything. On 30.8., 96 tanks were destroyed in the Division's sector. Russian attempts to break out are being successfully repulsed. They had that in the newspaper too. (3-2002-0947, September 18, 1941)
>
> I'm sending off a newspaper by the same post. Everything in it happened here. You'll recognise some of the names. Make sure you keep it for me. (3-2002-0947, August 6, 1941)
>
> I'm enclosing a frontline news-sheet with today's letter – the article about 'Todgespickte Erde' (Death-Dotted Earth) is interesting. The descriptions in it are of our sector and exactly fit what happened during our advance. I actually saw the tank-traps and bunkers it mentions myself, and I drove through the villages mentioned too. I can only confirm everything they have put in the article. (3-2002-0827, August 29, 1942)
>
> What the newspapers are printing about the 'Soviet paradise' is not exaggerated at all. (3-2002-0935, May 7, 1942)

In a somewhat diluted variant of this stance, reports as published are broadly endorsed, but the letter-writers add their own perspective. Rather than merely repeat the official reports, they emphasize their personal experience of events and in particular their own interpretations. When he adopts the role of expert, the chronicler reveals how he sees himself:

> But anyway I'll just pop a newspaper article in the post for you to see for yourself what all we have achieved here. What they don't mention is the huge effort it cost. But it's quite interesting to read if you're not in the Forces yourself. (3-2002-7127, September 3, 1941)
>
> All I really need to add is that you can take all the newspaper reporting about Russia as being absolutely true, even if they do make a great propaganda thing of it. It really is ghastly – not just is, it always has been. From what the local people have been

saying I've learnt quite a lot, but it doesn't add up to a rounded picture. (3-2002-0827, May 20, 1942)

Official reports are difficult to refute from the subjective point of view. Letter-writers can thus challenge only particular aspects of them, not the whole:

> At night we hear the British and French droning away above us, never see them by day, now and again we get a thump of heavy guns from very far away, we all keep our gas-masks on – that's our war. It's only the radio and the papers tell us there is action in the border zone. All we know about at first hand is how tough it was on those forced marches. (3-2002-0947, November 25, 1939)

Only rarely, in the letters studied, is actual doubt cast on the reports – and then only minimally. It would be unwarranted to infer an underlying skepticism from this: 'Whether the figure for the dead given in the newspaper cutting is actually correct, I don't know.' (3-2002-7130, September 22, 1942)

Some of the letter texts neatly illustrate their writer's insight into how media reality is constructed. This emerges in particular when newspaper reports clash with personal experience or when the writer observes a report in the making. Here a field surgeon is the clear-sighted observer:

> We had a visit today from a war reporter, peacetime senior editor of *Das schwarze Korps* (The Black Corps) newspaper, and a co-founder. He wants to do a piece about our field hospital, probably illustrated. But he says it is very tricky running articles on the subject of field hospitals, because policy is not to keep reminding the homeland unnecessarily about our serious – and that really is the word now, serious – losses, numbers of wounded etc. I think that is downright stupid – by now every last family in Germany has had at least someone wounded that was close to them, and anyway they know perfectly well after three years of war that a lot of the sacrifices we've had to make have been in blood. For goodness' sake, everyone at home has the greatest possible interest in how well our wounded are being cared for and treated at the front. So if you can show them a field hospital where everything is in tiptop order, then it's surely bound to be a good thing if you can show people that and say: 'Look, there's the exemplary standard of care our wounded are getting even in a field hospital out there, up near the front.' (3-2002-7265, October 23, 1942)

Elsewhere the same surgeon writes, 'It also explains why he [a medical colleague] agrees to treat any and every Russian who takes ill, and in that way gets a very good idea of what conditions are really like – and that's a very different matter from what you get to read in the newspapers' (3-2002-7265, November 9, 1942).

Those with their own experiences, or who read reports dealing with their immediate locality, might express themselves in rather critical terms about media content. In this quotation, the writer implies that media reports do not confine themselves to neutral and objective presentation of facts but serve an ideological purpose: 'The news reports about Cologne are horrifying. Even the newspapers are admitting there is enormous devastation' (3-2002-0827, June 27, 1942).

This example also illustrates the point that people learn to read between the lines and to distinguish between propaganda and first-hand reality.

The World of the Homeland

A first and obvious point is that letters from home were less influenced by the censorship. They were likewise subjected to random checks, it is true, but militarily there was really nothing to hide. Allied bombing raids were obvious locally, and whenever possible air raid warnings would be broadcast (Boberach, 1984: 6526).

The world back home was a familiar world to the soldier on the front line. In most cases, he was not at the front from choice but had been wrenched away from his family and social circle. He wanted to remain part of the world back home. He kept on asking questions, encouraging communication. Physically remote though he was, the letter medium enabled the man to remain part of the discourse. Letters could carry a wealth of detail relating to family and possessions. Sometimes the letter had to replace first-hand experience.

Letters are individual media. Letters from and to the front were the communicative links serving the organization of family and relationships. Everyday gossip and hearsay formed part of the exchange. These functions were more effectively fulfilled by field post letters sent from home than by those in the opposite direction. The people and places were known both to the writer and to the recipient.

Written communication made it possible for the man serving far from home to share personal information. Although he could not contribute to it, being currently without experience of his own in the private context, he was not excluded. Participation in gossip and hearsay is a mark of belonging. While the man still continues to be told the little details that make up everyday life, he will know he still forms part of the social group.

Newspapers and magazines played an important part in communicating the content of life in the homeland. They made it possible to keep continuously up to date with the topics currently under public discussion at home. As one letter reports, 'So I at least have the newspaper coming regularly and know what is going on back in Germany. And the delivery is like clockwork. I've not missed an issue so far. My 8 July paper came yesterday evening. That's four days delivery time' (3-2002-0947, July 14, 1940).

It was through the local papers that losses became public knowledge, as they carried the death announcements inserted by the families of soldiers killed in action. This resulted in the consequences of war growing ever plainer as it continued, the total casualties mounting while individuals would find more and more names of personal acquaintances appearing on the lists:

> Yes, the Eschwege paper, I wonder will it list the killed in action. And why not? It's our local newspaper, after all. There are four dead now from Wanfried alone, including two I was at school with. An NCO and a 2nd Lieutenant. Yes, it's a sad business. Who's going to get it next? (3-2002-0349, July 17, 1940)

In this way, the death announcement columns became the measure for the military situation and for the position at home resulting from Allied raids. However, the newspapers were prohibited from publishing more than fifteen death notices daily, so that private estimates could not provide an accurate gauge of current losses for any given region: 'Back to the famous 15 death announcements per day in the paper now they're not allowed to put more in, always Belgorod and Orel sometimes Lake Ladoga! Metzger-Röder's son is dead too – he was 19' (3-2002-7130, September 1, 1943).

Death notices for personal acquaintances thus directly prompted discussion of this kind of news:

> Just think, I saw in the Detmold paper today that Karl Henneberg, the 20-year-old lad from Lage, has been killed. An NCO with the flak battery I think, they were up on the Channel coast. You know, he's godfather to Gertraud Kampmann! I got to know his Mum that time at the Möllings'. You knew him well too, didn't you? Sooner or later you get the real horrors with all this going on. And now these prospects of the war spreading much further! (3-2002-0861, May 9, 1941)

Newspaper reports had the great advantage that one could cut them out and enclose them with a letter. They then served as confirmation of the handwritten news and as a basis for continued discussion. Soldiers on active duty and family members at home made use of them. Just as it was difficult to mediate the world of the front to the homeland, it was not easy either to adequately convey experiences lived through during the nights of bombing raids to loved ones on active service. But the hunger for information was equally great: 'I always want detailed news about the air raids on Berlin. Maybe send newspapers if they report on them' (3-2002-0827, March 16, 1945).

The Past and the Future

Relationships that are being sustained by exchange of letters have a past and a hoped-for future. They are set up for an indefinite period, and in spite of the separation have not come to an end, but they are being subjected to a severe testing. Communication is what determines the course and nature of partnerships and so helps to bridge the gap. The problem is that love not being nurtured in shared experiences can only survive where mutual trust is very strong. Memories of good times in the past and hopes of better times to come are used as arguments for keeping up friendships in spite of present separation. In the absence of a shared present, the consolation had to be reference to the past. Memories were wheeled on to lessen the pain of the separate present.

In this entire domain within the thematic material of the field post correspondence, the media including newspapers and magazines are irrelevant. Past and future in this context refer to personal memories and experiences not covered by the media.

Propaganda and the Media

In these circumstances, media events were the only opportunity apart from leave, and of course the letters, to share current experiences and to gain independent experience of the separated worlds of front and homeland. Feature films produced at Babelsberg ran in German cinemas and also helped distract and entertain German troops stationed in many areas elsewhere. Newspapers, magazines and books, such as – for example – those of Bertelsmann Publishing's *Feldpost* series (Lokatis, 1999), could be sent anywhere and were avidly consumed by the soldiers. It was thus possible for them to join in the public discourse. The radio was the only live medium that could be heard simultaneously on all sectors of the fronts and throughout the homeland. The sense of simultaneous reception united those who had been physically separated.

Among all the broadcast material, speeches by members of the Third Reich's ruling clique are of particular interest. These broadcasts provided material permitting analysis and interpretation of the current military and political situation – material that would be picked up and used by letter-writers. Such speeches were almost invariably reproduced in newspapers after the broadcast. People without access to a radio were thus able to participate to some extent in these live media events: 'Then I bought a newspaper which gave me the gist of the Führer's address. I hope you were able to hear it on the radio' (3-2002-0861, October 4, 1941).

As it was so easy to enclose newspaper cuttings with a letter, it was naturally a matter of course for the radio medium to be instrumental in this way in prompting debate: 'I'm enclosing quite an interesting article from the Easter weekend edition of the *DAZ*. Let me know some time what you think of it' (3-2002-0861, April 15, 1941).

Alongside the effect that media events have in bringing about synchronous experience, a further aspect with a bearing on relationships is that of esthetic judgment. While every individual has an ability to assess and judge that is more or less his or her own, discussion of such judgment is extremely important and takes up a considerable proportion of everyday communication. Esthetic judgments are spontaneous assessments of perceptions. They help an individual establish whether a partner views the world in a similar way. Similarity between assessments eliminates lengthy bargaining over how to reconcile interests. The more closely the partners approach unanimity in esthetic judgment, the fewer the disputes that may be expected, and the simpler the cooperation. Reciprocal confirmation of the shared attitude is an important element of communication within a partnership. As only shared perceptions can serve the process of bringing assessments closer to one another, media events are of special importance.

In the context of esthetic discussion, the field post letter medium had a system-stabilizing effect: debate over a changing attitude was extremely difficult. In direct oral dialog, which permits testing of specific arguments, attitudes will be presented, and in the event of their not being received as hoped can also be voluntarily amended. The written context, by contrast, tends to commit. The written word carries more weight. There were further limitations, too: the routes traveled from sender to recipient were long and uncertain; letters did not always arrive in the order of sending; arguments – and indeed disputes – were hindered by the constraints of the medium. This meant it was always simpler to persist with a stance once it had been adopted than to modify it in the course of dialog. As one could not assume that the other person's stance had changed, one naturally sought to further underline one's own known stance. And the whole thing thus became a self-referential system.

Propaganda and Media Effect

The material contained in the speeches of Hitler, Goebbels, Göring and other members of the ruling elite is known and has been sufficiently researched. However, there has as yet been very little study of the effects and subjective appropriation of propaganda. The SS Security Service reports are known, certainly (see Boberach, 1984), but their reliability is limited by their known ideological perspective. While taking due account of the problem of internal and external censorship, one can analyze field post letters with a view to establishing how the writers personally assess the political and military situation. Whenever comments relevant to this topic are volunteered by the writer for the recipient's benefit, they can be understood as personal disclosures and political statements.

Those involved at the time might even draw inferences from the very fact that given newspapers were for war-related reasons appearing less frequently or ceasing to appear at all: 'The front from the Western approach (in the Genoese Alps) will become more and more important. The war won't last much longer anyway. Newspapers have stopped coming and all we have now is the pathetic little weekly bulletin' (3-2002-7130, April 9, 1944).

As the quotations thus far have demonstrated, reactions are exceedingly complex, and every possible stance emerges. It can be observed that newspaper cuttings are used as evidence of personal involvement, personal stances and personal experience. This may be indicated in the context of endorsement of the newspaper material, but also – though more rarely – through expression of a negative view. Irony too, as a way of expressing rejection or private disaffection, might be used by the writers of this period:

And then there's a piece in the paper today telling us just what needs to be done if we are to cope with the food situation. Well then, as the Herr Reichsminister is so sure of that, we can all look to the future with confidence. All the same, if I were you I would lay up a few groceries for a rainy day. Someone might conceivably have got the sums wrong. (3-2002-7130, November 26, 1944)

I see from the paper it's our duty to sacrifice anything that we won't actually need before the end of the war. If they'd just give us notice – but it would have to be binding – of what date this war is going to end, then yes, we could talk business. (3-2002-7130, January 14, 1945)

Results

The selection presented here of extracts from field post letters can be interpreted as corroborative evidence for the uses and gratifications approach, which of course foregrounds the subjective appropriation of media content. Irrespective of whether individual stances are assenting or rejective, the writers can adduce newspaper reports and weave them into their lines of argument. It is particularly interesting that a period widely perceived as having been propaganda-dominated should have permitted such individualistic reception of the media. In a context that scarcely allowed variance of opinion, the material published was subjectively filtered, interpreted and appropriated. It cannot be said that there was any clear or straightforward propaganda effect. The interpretations of reality adumbrated in the printed publications do indeed offer agenda-setting hypotheses about the objects of their attention, but they in no way claim to be delivering the authentic interpretations. On that issue the readers form their own subjective judgments.

The publications also made it possible for the 'frontiers of silence' discussed at the beginning of this chapter to be crossed. Once something had been placed in the public arena, this frontier had been breached, and that could be understood as the license to incorporate the publicly aired material into one's own account of events. Interpretation and evaluation remained the responsibility of the writer, who would exercise it with greater or lesser openness and directness according to personality and situation, while also remaining mindful of the identity of the recipient.

If one accepts the idea of the four worlds to which the communications in field post letters relate, it can be observed that in three of them newspapers may be cited. The fourth, reference to the past or the future, has no such citations. For that to be possible, shared experiences of high emotional value would have to be involved. In the case of cinema, this is still quite conceivable, but in relation to printed material much less so.

Appendix: Other Uses for Newspapers

Illustrated magazines have pictures with the articles. The soldiers use them to embellish their quarters. Pictures of popular film stars thus have their place in military accommodation.

Newspaper serves numerous purposes besides reading. There are examples of it being used as a wallpaper replacement, as packaging material, as wadding to stop up cracks and holes or to bulk out an oversized beret. When there are no cigarette papers, it can even be used for machorka. A rolled-up newspaper is useful as a fly-swat. For one further use, finally, a quotation from the archived letters: 'Can you remember to put newspapers in the first parcel, there is no bumf here' (3-2002-1260, March 26, 1944).

We can see that the uses of newspaper are as wide-ranging and multifarious as the needs they meet. Just as the news content is absorbed, so also uses are found for the physical properties of the paper.

Key Points

- Field post letters that are systematically collected and archived by the Berlin Museum of Communications are increasingly being appreciated by historians as they permit insight into everyday communication during the World War II.
- Correspondents of field post letters lived in four distinct worlds: the world of the soldiers, their homeland where their families and partners lived, the world of combined future and past, and the world of the media.
- Field post letters enable us to reconstruct the role of newspapers, magazines and other media for the soldiers as well as their families and social networks at home.

Study Questions

1. There are two types of fundamentally different witnesses to the events of the World War II who produced reports: the soldiers and civilians who experienced the battles personally and the professional journalists who wrote for the media. Can you explain the difference between these reports?
2. How would you describe the role of the media in supporting the view that field post letters can be interpreted as corroborative evidence for the 'uses and gratification' approach?

Further Reading

Kilian, Katrin (s.a.) 'The Medium "War Letter" as an Object of Interdisciplinary Research. Archives, State of Research and Processing of the Source from the Second World War', www. feldpost-archiv.de/english/e8-kilian-diss.html (December 1, 2010).

Schwender, Clemens (s.a.) 'Letters between Home and the Front – Expressions of Love in World War II Feldpost Letters', www.feldpost-archiv.de/english/e8-loveletters.html (December 1, 2011).

Websites

Berlin Field Post Archive: www.feldpost-archiv.de/english/index.html.

References

Boberach, Heinz (ed.) (1984) *Meldungen aus dem Reich 1938–1945. Die geheimen Lageberichte des Sicherheitsdienstes der SS.* Herrsching: Pawlak.

Buchbender, Ortwin and Reinhold Sterz (eds) (1983) *Das andere Gesicht des Krieges. Deutsche Feldpostbriefe 1939–1945.* München: Beck.

Gericke, Bodo (ed.) (1971) *Die Deutsche Feldpost im Zweiten Weltkrieg, Band 1.* Berlin: Archiv für Deutsche Postgeschichte.

Lokatis, Siegfried (1999) 'Feldpost von Bertelsmann. Die Editionspraxis des Gütersloher Verlags im Dritten Reich', *Neue Zürcher Zeitung,* March 8.

Ueberschär, Gerd R. (1989) 'Die Deutsche Reichspost im Zweiten Weltkrieg', pp. 289–320 in Wolfgang Lotz (ed.) *Deutsche Postgeschichte. Essays und Bilder.* Berlin: Nicolai.

Ziemann, Benjamin (1996) 'Feldpostbriefe und ihre Zensur in den zwei Weltkriegen', pp. 163–71 in Klaus Beyrer, Hans-Christian Täubrich and Norbert Abels (eds) *Der Brief. Eine Kulturgeschichte der schriftlichen Kommunikation.* Heidelberg: Edition Braus.

Note

1 Figures following quotations are classmarks identifying the source in the Berlin Museum of Communications Field Post Archive.

PART II

Visual Turn, War PR and the Changing Relationships between Politics, Media and the Public Sphere

Between Reporting and Propaganda

Power, Culture and War Reporting

Daniel C. Hallin

Summary

This chapter focuses on two themes. First, it attempts to define where propaganda fits into the larger picture of war and the public sphere, not overemphasizing the role of propaganda, but considering media coverage and the popular consciousness of war as rooted in culture and produced in a decentralized and substantially autonomous way. The second part of the chapter tries to explore to what extent American media coverage of war has or has not changed since Vietnam. On the one hand, focusing on the Iraq and Afghanistan wars, the pattern is strikingly, and distressingly, similar – distressingly because one would have thought that journalists and American society as a whole had learned from the Vietnam experience, but unfortunately that is only true to a limited extent. The pattern shown by the Vietnam war involved media coverage that was largely deferential to official representations and to the standard celebratory or at least sanitized framing of war coverage in the early period, followed by a shift, over a number of years, toward a more skeptical and pluralistic coverage that began with tactical arguments among political elites and moved on to relatively negative, if not particularly questioning, coverage. The Iraq War showed essentially the same pattern, and the timing was quite similar. This fact is distressing above all because in neither case can it be said that there was a full and open public debate about the decision to go to war in the first place. In the case of Afghanistan, the pattern is again similar, though more protracted, since the Afghanistan War was for several years eclipsed as a subject of public discussion by the war in Iraq. There were, in fact, important changes in how the American media covered war and foreign policy in the post-Vietnam period. The successful Gulf War went some way toward reversing them, however, and the September 11 attacks then substantially overrode them for some time, restoring something like the early Cold War media and public deference to official policy. Nevertheless, there are substantial differences between how the Vietnam War was covered and how the wars in Iraq and Afghanistan are covered, differences resulting from changes in culture (and specifically in media culture), the media industries and technology.

Propaganda and Culture

The title of the conference session for which this chapter was originally prepared was 'Between Reporting and Propaganda'. The concept of propaganda, of course, is one of the fundamental points of reference for understanding war and the public sphere. War, as a distinct form of social and political activity, has had deep impact on the public sphere, and one of the most distinctive aspects of that impact has to do with the way in which war planners attempt systematically to manage public opinion in wartime. Just as war has had deep impact on the development of science and technology, and the relation of the state to the latter, or many other aspects of the relations of state and society, so it has had deep impact on the public sphere; it has served as a crucible for the development of techniques for state management of public opinion. And propaganda, in the sense of conscious, instrumental use of communication to shape public opinion, is obviously an important force shaping media coverage of war. General Norman Schwarzkopf's live press conferences during the first Gulf War, for example, with the carefully selected smart-bomb videos that illustrated them, obviously had deep impact on the media coverage of that war, and on its representation more generally. In the aftermath of the September 11 terrorist attacks, US Defense Secretary Donald Rumsfeld developed ambitious plans to expand the information operations of the Defense Department (Schulman, 2006), and there is no question that the Iraq War could never have taken place without the Bush administration's campaign to disseminate information – false in this case, though not all propaganda is false – about Iraqi weapons of mass destruction and ties to al-Qaeda. More recently, we could point to the campaign, carried on by various actors, not necessarily centered in the US government, to promote the story of a crazy Iranian regime dead-set on acquiring nuclear weapons in order to lay the groundwork for military action against Iran (Umansky, 2008).

But this is only one piece of the story about war and the public sphere, and in my view not the most central one. A focus on propaganda is appealing, in part because analyses of media and war are often motivated to a large extent by a desire to expose manipulation and to press for a more open process of debate. In addition to that, the role of propaganda conflicts with dominant ethical norms about democratic communication and is therefore an effective focus for critical discourse. From an analytical point of view, however, to focus too narrowly on a top-down view of the way communication and opinion on war is formed, a view in which state officials are the only significant actors, leads us, in my view, to miss the depth to which war is rooted in culture, and political culture itself has become militarized, or shifts in this direction in time of war.

Here I would like to recap some of the arguments Todd Gitlin and I made in a study of television coverage of the Gulf War (Hallin and Gitlin, 1994). This study was part of a Social Science Research Council project on media and foreign policy (Bennett and Paletz, 1994). It was conducted largely by political scientists and communication scholars, and focused primarily on government management or influence on news coverage in the period of debate preceding the war. It included one article on the role of Hill & Knowlton, a public relations firm hired by the government of Kuwait to influence opinion, certainly one of the most important examples of the role of propaganda (Manheim, 1994). The research was excellent, but Gitlin and I thought it was missing the point in an important way, or at least was missing an important dimension. In the early discussion of the project, we realized that everyone else was planning to study the debate period that preceded the war, and no one was actually looking at the role of the media during the war itself. The emphasis was also primarily on elites, with the mass public present only as a dependent variable in survey-based analyses of opinion formation. We thought it would have been good to have an anthropologist or two doing ethnography out in American towns and neighborhoods where people were putting up yellow ribbons, giving blood and sometimes, especially at the beginning, participating in protests. We tried to fill the hole in a different way, by looking at television coverage of the war itself as a form of popular culture.

It is easy enough to see why scholars would focus on the debate period because democratic theory would say that that is when the media should make a difference. If there is a time when a strong democratic public sphere is really needed, it is in the period when a political decision to go to war is being debated, and if we are going to evaluate the degree to which the media act independently to facilitate democratic debate, this period is crucial. And yet, if we want to understand the formation of public opinion on the war, if we want to understand what war means in the popular consciousness and how a particular war and its representation shapes political culture, it is not clear that we are really getting at this by studying the representation of political debate in the prewar period. The American public was divided just about exactly 50–50 on the eve of the Gulf War. Within about a week, opinion had shifted to about 80 percent support for the war. This means that official management of opinion in the period of debate was of limited effectiveness: it did not create a consensus in support of a policy of war with Iraq. And we are left with the problem of explaining the huge shift in opinion that occurred after the actual start of the war.

Another way of explaining the significance of the approach we took has to do with the kinds of explanations that were typically offered for the character of war coverage. In the years following the war, when we were doing our research, journalists were often self-critical about the sanitized, glamorized, celebratory character of the reporting. A phrase I often heard in interviews and conferences devoted to the subject was, 'they played us like a flute', they meaning the military. Journalists were referring here to military management, which took the form both of restrictions on journalists – their movements were closely circumscribed during the Gulf War, and they were largely kept away from the actual fighting, for example – and on the kind of information management I referred to earlier, above all through the military's own press conferences. These things did matter, of course. But this explanation seemed to me an evasion of the journalists' own responsibility for the character of the reporting and a very simplistic understanding of how it was produced. Certainly military briefers or 'handlers' in the war theater had no role, for example, in the choices made by hundreds of news producers around the United States who were cooking up fancy graphics or in the activities of local journalists covering the flag-waving back in the United States. (Our study focused to a large extent on local television stations in the United States – the most important source of news for Americans – whose coverage was to a significant degree rooted in the 'home front', not in the theater of war.) In truth, it did not explain the reporting of journalists in the field, either, who participated quite actively in their own ways in producing the generally upbeat spectacle that was Gulf War coverage.

In Hallin and Gitlin (1994), we argued that once the war actually started neither public opinion nor media representation can be understood if we think of war simply as an 'extension of politics by other means' in Clausewitz's phrase; war becomes a form of popular culture, and is seen more as an arena of individual and national self-expression than a political policy. That is essential to understanding why opinion shifted so rapidly and dramatically once the war started: people did not change their opinion about the Gulf War as a political policy; they changed their whole frame of reference for thinking about what war meant and what it meant to have an opinion toward the war.

Once the war began, the media and the public were both caught up in a wave of enthusiasm for an extremely appealing drama, a collective enterprise with great cultural resonance. They were caught up in the story of ordinary American soldiers, common people suddenly at the center of history in a way they seldom are. Journalists reporting from the field told the story essentially from the soldiers' point of view and certainly celebrated them. They were caught up in the visual drama of technology, which provided exceptional material for television, far beyond the dull images that dominate most political reporting. The story of technology, like that of the soldiers, also seemed to project a sense of power and accomplishment. They were also caught up in the appeal of a celebration of community, an unusual, very participatory ritual of national unity that seemed to transcend everyday political life. This was manifested in coverage of community activities like putting up yellow ribbons and also in extensive coverage of the families of the soldiers, who, we argue, served as a kind of synecdoche in news coverage of the Gulf War, standing in for the public as a whole. We were also struck by the frequency of religious references in Gulf War coverage ('surface-to-air prayer'), and argue that popular consciousness during the war can be seen as a phenomenon of civil religion, in Durkheim's sense, treated by the media and public as a kind of sacred realm of community solidarity, in contrast to the normal conflict and corruption of political life.

The government did act in important ways to promote and facilitate these forms of representation, and obviously was conscious of their significance in many ways. It facilitated the celebration of technology by releasing the smart-bomb videos, for example, and actively promoted connections between hometown media and particular soldiers, which allowed local news media to 'humanize' and personalize their coverage. In other ways the military acted stupidly, in ways that reflected poor understanding of media and war. The exclusion of journalists from access to combat units, for example, was based on a false assumption, derived from mythology about Vietnam reporting, that journalists would report negatively if given access to the front. In fact, those restrictions served mainly to deprive them of much of the focus on the professionalism and bravery of the troops that has long been a staple of Anglo-American war reporting.

After the Gulf War, the military shifted away from this restrictive policy, introducing the more media-friendly policy of 'embedding' reporters with frontline units, which worked well for them in the Iraq War (Paul and Kim, 2004). The representation of war we identify here did not, however, result primarily from a top-down process of management by the state. The media themselves were highly active in producing it. This took place in many ways and at many levels – as individual journalists, for example, worked to produce what they saw as compelling stories, or from a very different direction, as the promotions departments of local television stations became involved in organizing rallies to support the troops, as they do also with other kinds of rituals of community solidarity like responses to natural disasters or rallies for local sports teams that become champions.

It is also important here to address the role of the public itself, and again, I would argue that a top-down model that sees public opinion as a passive response either to media representations or to manipulation by state propaganda is inadequate to understand what is going on. The public response to the war, including the rallying around the troops, was to a large extent a spontaneous movement of public opinion. The media had a role in producing it, of course, but they did not create it out of nothing. Media coverage has to be understood as to some extent a product of media response to public sentiments. Our interviews with journalists made it very clear that public opinion was a concern for them, and its influence was felt both positively and negatively.

There was great fear in the media during the Gulf War of being seen as insufficiently patriotic and insufficiently supportive of American troops; journalists felt considerable conflict over what their proper role was, whether they should be following standard professional norms of neutrality and the 'watchdog' role, or whether they should be reporting the war as part of what I have called the 'sphere of consensus' and playing a ritual role as celebrants of consensus. During the Gulf War the latter largely won out. That it did so was not merely a product of this negative influence of public opinion, the fear of being accused of lack of patriotism, but also as a result of a positive influence: many local journalists told us that they felt particularly gratified during the Gulf War at the appreciative response they got from members of the public for their coverage of the home front and their participation and facilitation of community solidarity activities; this emerged above all in their relations with families of the military personnel, who, again, were central characters in the coverage.

One final point has to be made about the public sphere during the Gulf War. The Gulf War has often been referred to as the war that, in Baudrillard's famous phrase, 'did not take place'. This point is usually connected with the strong role of image production and media management during the Gulf War, and what is usually meant is that the Gulf War was experienced more as a media spectacle than a real event. Baudrillard's (1995) point was actually more complex and not narrowly tied to media representations of the war. One of Baudrillard's arguments, for example, was the following: 'Unlike earlier wars, in which there were political aims either of conquest or domination, what is at stake in this one is war itself: its status, its meaning, its future' (Baudrillard, 1995: 32).

This is correct, I think, in that a primary concern for American policy-makers was to banish the 'Vietnam syndrome' and to establish that it was once again possible to use war as a political instrument, which required reestablishing a positive cultural meaning to war which they believe, not entirely accurately, to have been undermined by Vietnam.

They were successful in doing this in part because the war played so well in the media, and it was true that highly dramatic, aestheticized and pervasive representation of the Gulf War stood in contrast to the reality of a one-sided conflict. This has often led commentators to speak about the public reacting to contemporary war as a mere spectacle.

The point I would like to make here, however, is that even in the case of the Gulf War – which presents an extreme case due to the fact that it ended so quickly and therefore the phase of ground combat, in which the hard reality of war began inevitably to creep more fully into the reporting, remained very limited – this view is too simplistic. For the United States, at least, I do not believe we can understand the dynamics of public consciousness without taking into account the fact that people felt real fear about the level of casualties American forces would suffer. I should explain here that I live in a city with large military bases from which many Marines and sailors were deployed to the Gulf, so this is something I remember very clearly. This fear turned out to be largely unfounded, as Iraqi resistance was minimal. But it was very real, and the public reaction to the war – the strong intrusion of religion into the political public sphere, for example – cannot be understood without taking it into account. In some sense, the greatest power the state has to shape the public sphere in wartime is not the power over images and information but the power actually to place troops in a combat situation where their lives are at stake, and thus to set in motion a whole set of cultural responses by the troops themselves, the public, the media and other actors.

The central point I want to make here is that public consciousness on the Gulf War was not produced simply by a top-down process of state manipulation of information. It resulted from a complex, distributed process in which journalists and other media personnel and the mass public itself participated quite actively, a process that involved the mobilization of meanings deeply rooted in American culture. The public sphere is not manipulated from the outside in time of war. It is actually militarized in the sense that a long history of representations of war and of responses to it at different levels of society have produced structures of feeling, in Williams' (1977) sense that are largely self-reproducing.

I have focused here primarily on the Gulf War, which is of course a special case for various reasons, including most importantly the fact that it was a short, successful, mainly technological war with low casualties on the American side. Other meanings of war clearly come into play under other historical circumstances, as we shall see in the second section of this chapter. I have also focused on the United States, and of course the cultural meanings of war I am talking about here are not universal; they are to some extent distinctive to the United States or to some extent, perhaps, shared by the United States, Canada and Great Britain, which have somewhat similar histories as victors in World War II and (in the US and British case) also as imperial powers. I do think that some elements of this pattern would be applicable to other cases as well. One example might be the Russian intervention in Georgia in 2009, which also seemed to produce strong nationalist sentiments in the mass public and a public celebration of national prowess.

Changes Since Vietnam

In the second half of this chapter, I would like to address a question I am often asked, namely, to what extent American media coverage of war has or has not changed since Vietnam. Focusing on the Iraq and Afghanistan wars, I would have to say the pattern is strikingly, and distressingly, similar – distressingly because one would have thought that journalists and the society as a whole had learned from the Vietnam experience, but that is true only to a limited extent. The pattern of the Vietnam War involved media coverage that was largely deferential to official representations and to standard celebratory or at least sanitized frames of war coverage in the early period, followed by a shift, over a period of years, toward more skeptical and pluralistic coverage that began with tactical arguments among political elites and moved toward relatively negative, if not deeply questioning, coverage. This was essentially the pattern with the Iraq War, and the timing was quite similar; this fact is distressing above all in the sense that in neither case can it be said that there was a full, open public debate about the decision to go to war in the initial period.

The similarities even run down to the role of the same independent journalist, Seymour Hirsch, in breaking the story of war crimes that mainstream media resisted covering for an extended period (Umansky, 2006). In the case of Afghanistan, the pattern is again similar, though more protracted, since the Afghanistan War was for several years eclipsed as a subject of public discussion by Iraq. There were, in fact, important changes in the way the American media covered war and foreign policy in the post-Vietnam period. The successful Gulf War went some way toward reversing them, however, and the September 11 attacks then substantially overrode them for some time, restoring something like the early Cold War media and public deference to official policy.

Nevertheless, there are substantial and interesting differences between Vietnam coverage and Iraq and Afghanistan coverage, and I want to summarize some of them here. It should be kept in mind, first of all, that the Iraq and Afghanistan wars are on a much smaller scale than the war in Vietnam. There were 545,000 American troops deployed in Vietnam at the peak of the war, about three times the number in Iraq, and 58,000 Americans were killed in Vietnam, as opposed to about 5,000 in Iraq. Could the US government get the public to support a war on the same scale today, as they did in the 1960s?

I doubt it. The Iraq and Afghanistan wars are possible only because they are fought by a professional army and not by draftees, and because they are fought with much lower levels of American casualties than the Vietnam War. The public tolerance for American casualties is lower today than it once was, and this is related to some of the changes in culture, and specifically in media culture, that I will outline here.

- Coverage of dissent

In the early period of the Vietnam War, dissent and protest was almost entirely silenced in the mediated public sphere, either ignored or treated as treason. This is really not the case in the post-Vietnam period. Reporting on antiwar protest is marginalized in important ways (Reese, 2004), but it is also taken for granted as a normal part of the public sphere, and plays a significant role in contemporary war coverage, particularly in the prewar debate, as well as in the later collapse of consensus phase (e.g., Althaus, 2003).

- Soldiers, casualties and a populist media culture

One of the most striking differences between Vietnam coverage and coverage of contemporary wars is that Vietnam coverage, in the national media, did not include, to any significant degree, the kind of 'home front' coverage that dominates much of contemporary war reporting, including the focus on the families and the home communities of soldiers deployed to the war zone. This is related, I believe, to a general shift in media culture toward a more populist style, with greater attention to the ordinary person, and a strong attempt to connect stories with the concerns and points of view of ordinary citizens. This is in part a reflection of the shift toward a more competitive, market-driven media industry (Hallin, 2000).

It is also connected with what might be called the feminization of news and of culture: in the 1960s, war was seen as an affair of men, and the kind of extensive reporting on the women and children left at home – or men and children, in some cases as women are deployed – was not seen as an appropriate part of war reporting. Today, in the wake of the women's movement and a general shift from an earlier gendered conception of the boundary between public and private to a new and fuzzier concept that places greater weight on what were once considered private concerns, this part has high priority for the media.

What are the consequences of this shift? Baum (2003) in a book devoted to war and foreign policy coverage in 'soft news' venues, which have increasingly proliferated over the past generation, argues that it makes it increasingly difficult for policy-makers to get public support for interventionist foreign policy decisions, and that low tolerance for casualties may be related to the role of soft news.[1] My own view is that the humanization of news, that is part of the increasingly dominant soft news style, can cut different ways politically in war coverage. The upbeat focus on the way war strengthened the bonds of families with servicemen deployed to the Gulf War, which Gitlin and I identified as such a powerful theme in Gulf coverage, fits with this style, as do hero stories about individual soldiers. A focus on individual soldiers and their families can be a powerful force shifting war coverage into the sphere of consensus.

One way to think about the shift in public opinion at the beginning of the Gulf War, from a 50–50 division the day before the war to 80 percent support a week later, is to say that the object of public opinion changed: supporting the war ceased to mean supporting a political policy and meant instead supporting the troops. 'Up close and personal'[2] coverage of the war surely facilitates this – under the right circumstances. It is true, however, that it can also shift valence under different circumstances, and this is what happened later in the Iraq and Afghanistan wars, as the media devoted increasing attention to the human costs of the war. CBS, for example, closed news broadcasts on many occasions with an occasional profile on 'Fallen Heroes'. It does seem reasonable to assume that this is one of the reasons it is no longer possible to fight wars with casualties on the scale of Vietnam.

- Globalization of media and the public sphere

During the Vietnam War, the Vietnamese themselves, particularly ordinary citizens, rarely had a voice in American news coverage. They were seen but almost never heard. This does not appear to be the case in Iraq or Afghanistan coverage, where Iraqi and Afghan civilians are interviewed fairly often, and can often be heard complaining that the American invasion has made their lives worse or commenting on particular incidents that have caused civilian casualties. Civilian casualties are a fairly regular subject of news coverage, and this is reflected in the strong preoccupation of US and NATO commanders with the issue of civilian casualties caused by their forces. This is related, I believe, to the globalization of media – to the increasingly multilateral character of a media system, that is no longer dominated strictly by western media organizations, and to a cultural environment in which it is taken for granted that world public opinion does matter. The presence of CNN in Baghdad during the Gulf War – a presence that did on a few occasions produce reporting that departed from the sanitized coverage that dominated most Gulf War reporting – was one early manifestation of this change.

Another interesting manifestation of this is the fact that the Abu Ghraib story did not take off in the American media until the images circulated extensively in the Arab world. President Bush was forced to respond to them out of concern about their effect on Arab public opinion, and Bush's response then pushed them to the top of the news agenda in the United States (Umansky, 2006).

- Technology

Technology, finally, also has an important effect. In the wake of the Gulf War, most of the focus was on the ways in which technology enabled 'the birth of a new kind of military apparatus which incorporates the power to control the production and circulation of images as well as the power to direct the actions of bodies and machines' (Patton, 1995: 5). Today, however, we would have to balance that assessment with an emphasis also on the disruptive power of technology. The images of Abu Ghraib, for example, were taken by soldiers with digital cameras and eventually leaked to the media. This and many other kinds of decentralized, uncontrolled productions of images clearly play an important role today; this is one of the reasons it is impossible for policy-makers – and hence the media – to ignore civilian casualties.

One great irony about the Vietnam War is the fact that there was fairly extensive coverage of civilian casualties caused by American bombing in North Vietnam because of the presence of global media there, while there was extremely limited coverage of much more extensive bombing in South Vietnam deliberately targeted at the civilian population. No one could cover what happened in jungles and fields of rural Vietnam. Today, however, peasants would document such bombing with their cell phones and video cameras and post it on YouTube.

In discussing changes since Vietnam, I have obviously underscored a number of ways in which media coverage of war is more open than it was in the 1960s. It should be kept in mind, of course, that we are talking about a change from a public sphere that was extremely restricted, and it continues to be the case that there remains a strong tendency in time of war, in the United States at least, for the public sphere to lose independence relative to the state – not narrowly, as I have argued, through state intervention but through a deeper and more decentralized process in which the media and public are drawn into participation in the state-directed national enterprise of war.

Key Points

- Popular culture
- War communication
- Media coverage

Study Questions

1. How do journalists and the public as a whole actively participate in creating war images?
2. What lessons did the media learn from the Vietnam War?
3. To what extent is the public consciousness of war dependent on 'cultural memory'?

Further Reading

Bennett, Lance W. and David L. Paletz (eds) (1994) *Taken by Storm. The Media, Public Opinion, and U.S. Foreign Policy in the Gulf War*. Chicago: University of Chicago Press.

Chomsky, Noam (1994) *Media Control. The Spectacular Achievements of Propaganda*. Westfield, NJ: Open Media.

Hammond, William M. (1998) *Reporting Vietnam. Media and Military at War*. Lawrence, KS: University Press of Kansas.

MacDonald, Fred J. (1985) *Television and the Red Menace. The Video Road to Vietnam*. New York: Praeger.

Mandelbaum, Michael (1982) 'Vietnam. The Television War', *Daedalus* 111(4): 157–69.

Robinson, Piers (2002) *The CNN Effect. The Myth of News, Foreign Policy, and Intervention*. London; New York: Routledge.

Taylor, Philip M. (1997) *War and the Media. Propaganda and Persuasion in the Gulf War*. Manchester: Manchester University Press.

Thrall, Trevor A. (1994) *War in the Media Age*. Cresskill, NJ: Hampton Press.

References

Althaus, Scott L. (2003) 'When News Norms Collide, Follow the Lead: New Evidence for Press Independence', *Political Communication* 20(4): 381–414.

Baudrillard, Jean (ed.) (1995) *The Gulf War Did Not Take Place*. Bloomington: Indiana University Press.

Baum, Matthew (2003) *Soft News Goes to War. Public Opinion and American Foreign Policy in the New Media Age*. Princeton, NJ; Oxford: Princeton University Press.

Bennett, Lance W. and David L. Paletz (eds) (1994) *Taken by Storm. The Media, Public Opinion, and U.S. Foreign Policy in the Gulf War*. Chicago: University of Chicago Press.

Hallin, Daniel C. (2000) 'Commercialism and Professionalism in the American News Media', pp. 218–35 in James Curran and Michael Gurevitch (eds) *Mass Media and Society*. London: Arnold.

Hallin, Daniel C. and Todd Gitlin (1994) 'The Gulf War as Popular Culture and Television Drama', pp. 149–63 in Lance W. Bennett and David L. Paletz (eds) *Taken by Storm. The Media, Public Opinion, and U.S. Foreign Policy in the Gulf War*. Chicago: University of Chicago Press.

Manheim, Jarol B. (1994) 'Strategic Public Diplomacy: Managing Kuwait's Image during the Gulf Conflict', pp. 131–48 in Lance W. Bennett and David L. Paletz (eds) *Taken by Storm. The Media, Public Opinion, and U.S. Foreign Policy in the Gulf War*. Chicago: University of Chicago Press.

Patton, Paul (1995) 'Introduction', pp. 1–22 in Jean Baudrillard (ed.) *The Gulf War Did Not Take Place*. Bloomington: Indiana University Press.

Paul, Christopher and James J. Kim (2004) *Reporters on the Battlefield. The Embedded Press System in Historical Context*. Santa Monica, CA: RAND.

Reese, Stephen (2004) 'Militarized Journalism. Framing Dissent in the Gulf Wars', pp. 247–63 in Stuart Allan and Barbie Zelizer (eds) *Reporting War. Journalism in Wartime*. London: Routledge.

Schulman, Daniel (2006) 'Mind Games. How the Information War Distorts Reality and Pollutes the News', *Columbia Journalism Review* (May/June): 39–49.

Umansky, Erik (2006) 'Failures of Imagination', *Columbia Journalism Review* (September/October): 17–31.

——— (2008) 'Lost Over Iran. How the Press Let the White House Craft the Narrative about Nukes', *Columbia Journalism Review* 46(6): 26–30.

Williams, Raymond (1977) *Marxism and Literature*. Oxford: Oxford University Press.

Notes

1 Baum's argument is complex and depends in part on the idea that soft news expands the audience for news about foreign policy to less educated sectors of the public who in the United States are more likely to have 'isolationist' attitudes toward foreign policy. The examples he

focuses on include US policy in Bosnia and expansion of NATO. The dynamics may be very different in a period of active US involvement in a major war however. In that case, for one thing, all of the public is attentive to war news, but the framing of the story is probably also very different than in the kinds of examples Baum considers.

2 The phrase came from ABC Sports in the 1970s; part of the change in news conventions involved the migration of conventions from entertainment to news.

Just Wars and Persuasive Communication

Analyzing Public Relations in Military Conflicts

Magnus-Sebastian Kutz

Summary

Foreign and security policy, the media system and war itself have changed since the end of the Cold War. These changes and a related learning process have triggered a development at the organizational level, especially when one takes into account the fact that the media system has become faster and more networked. Precise information, clear and coordinated messages, and especially fast reactions have become vital in getting a message across to the public. 'Speed kills' – this phrase coined by Clintons' campaign team in 1992 to emphasize the importance of a rapid rebuttal of bad news – has become a core idea of PR management when intense media pressure is involved. The aim of the present chapter is to develop a model suitable for the analysis of the government public relations (PR) and propaganda used to justify and legitimize wars to the general public. It focuses on the contents of government PR as well as on the organizational measures taken to increase the influence on media reporting by the US administration as well as by the military. Both aspects are integrated into an analysis of the context and framework of PR: security policy, media systems and political culture. The PR of the US administrations during the wars in Kosovo, Afghanistan and Iraq are used to exemplify the model.

Introduction

Especially during the years of the George W. Bush presidency, there have been controversies about the justification of the Iraq War, often combined with allegations against the Bush administration, accusing them of having used 'propaganda' – meaning 'lies' and 'manipulation' – to gain public support for the intervention in Iraq.

Today it has become obvious that the White House and the Pentagon relied on faulty information, such as the idea that Iraq tried to acquire uranium in Africa and that Iraq had large stockpiles of chemical and biological weapons. Even former Secretary of Defense Colin Powell claimed that his speech to the United Nations (UN) was 'a blot' that 'will always be part of my record'.[1] Especially the Senate Select Committee on Intelligence (SSCI) and investigative journalists such as Seymour Hersh have published detailed research and information on the flaws of the intelligence process.[2]

The two previous wars led by the United States in Kosovo and Afghanistan did not involve any comparable controversy during their buildup and the first months of action. There were several reasons for the different public reaction. First, the rationales provided by the US administrations seemed more consistent with the goals of military action. Second, during the civil wars in former Yugoslavia, there had been massive atrocities against civilians, not only but certainly most clearly by the Serbian side, and the international community expected these atrocities to continue in Kosovo if military intervention did not take place.[3] Furthermore, the war in Afghanistan was triggered by the attacks on New York and Washington, DC, on September 11, 2001, and because the terrorists had a safe haven and support in Afghanistan, the decision to use military force found broad public support. In a Gallup Poll conducted directly after the beginning of the war in Afghanistan (November 8–11, 2001), a majority of 89 percent said that sending military forces to Afghanistan was not a mistake.[4]

Let us be clear: during the first months, the war in Iraq was also supported by the public. Yet this support declined after it became obvious that the goals could not be reached and that the justification behind the war was wrong. While in April 2003, 70 percent of those questioned said in a Gallup Poll that the war was worth fighting, this support declined to 51 percent one year later and to 33 percent in April 2007.[5] This demonstrates that every administration was able to gain initial popular support for military action. This chapter does not analyze media reporting per se or its influence on the public. Instead, it aims to examine what measures in terms of strategic communication were taken in order to justify and legitimize these wars and to exert as much influence as possible on the media.

The analysis proceeds in five steps: first, the terms 'public relations', 'persuasion' and 'propaganda' are defined and distinguished. On this basis, a model for public relations (PR) and propaganda analysis is developed, based on the philosophical notion of 'just war' and the framing concept. The relevant framework and context of communication is explained: it consists of key developments in the media system and basic aspects of US political culture. This framework forms the foundation for the empirical aspect of this chapter, which is – due to the limited space available – of a more illustrative and often anecdotal character. It focuses on two aspects: the organizational measures taken within the administration and the military to professionalize communication with the international media in a 24-hour media environment and, second, the actual justification of these wars. Especially this second aspect does not aim to expose 'lies' or 'failures' but rather to explain the basic messages and the framing used to legitimize military action.

PR, Persuasion and Propaganda

The terms 'propaganda' and 'public relations' have a long history and were closely associated with persuasion in the twentieth century. The term 'propaganda' emerged in the seventeenth century, when Pope Gregory XV founded the Saggregatia Congregatio de propaganda fide, which had the task of promoting the Roman Catholic faith. After the French Revolution, the usage of the term changed and the term served to describe ideologically and politically persuasive communication (Schieder and Dipper, 1984: 69–112). The first activities described as PR developed during the Industrial Age when large corporations tried to influence press reporting (St John, 1998: 38–40).

The rise of both concepts is closely connected with the World War I. US President Woodrow Wilson established the Committee on Public Information (CPI), which was responsible for establishing support for the war at home. PR professionals who shaped the industry in the 1920s and 1930s worked at the CPI: Ivi L. Lee, Carl R. Byoir and Edward L. Bernays. In an interview conducted in 1991 (the year of his 100th birthday), Bernays described the influence of the idea of propaganda during that time: 'When I came back to the United States I decided that if you could use propaganda for war you could certainly use it for peace. And propaganda got to be a bad word because of the Germans using it. So what I did was try to find some other words so we found the word "Counsel on Public Relations"'.

Harold D. Lasswell (1927: 27) defined propaganda as the 'management of collective attitudes by the manipulation of significant symbols', while Edward L. Bernays (1928/2005: 25) had a similar idea – even though he did not use the term 'manipulation'. He understood propaganda as a 'consistent enduring effort to create or shape events to influence the relations of the public to an enterprise, idea or group'. Following these ideas, Jowett and O'Donnell have described it as 'the deliberate, systematic attempt to shape perceptions, manipulate cognitions, and direct behaviour to achieve a response that furthers the desired intent of the propagandist' (Jowett and O'Donnell, 1999: 6).

A clear distinction between PR and propaganda became popular after World War II, as a reaction to propaganda in Nazi Germany.[6] PR is often associated with a normative idea of communication.[7] Even though these normative approaches are important for establishing an ethical standard, using them to define PR is complicated. There are various examples of PR firms not adhering to these standards, for example, working for nondemocratic states, promoting war or hiding the origins of the PR from the press that publishes the news (Kunczik, 2002: 36–7). For those reasons, the definition of Grunig and Hunt is probably the most suitable one: 'Public Relations is the management of communication between an organisation and its publics' (Grunig and Hunt, 1984: 7). This broad concept does not imply any normative idea of PR and allows one to focus on the core function of persuasive communication.

Despite these distinctions in terminology and definitions, both concepts have a lot in common. They both include the persuasive communication of organizations with the public in order to achieve a goal by promoting a certain interpretation. Shaping perceptions, manipulation and the neglect of truth can be inherent in both. But there are also differences: on the one hand, persuasive communication in dictatorships can be supported by censorship, sanctions and direct government control of the media – an idea that cannot be described by the term PR, which originates in the concept of a free press in the United States. On the other hand, there is a PR that provides information required for informed public discourse and the establishment of transparency. This kind of PR cannot be described as propaganda. So both concepts overlap in cases where persuasive communication in democracies fails to comply with ethical standards. In the following text, the term PR is used to include these aspects of propaganda as well.

As far as political communication in military conflicts is concerned, these ideas confront us with the following specific questions:

1. How are governments trying to persuade the public that the cause of a war is just and that military action is inevitable?
2. How do they try to shape the public interpretation of conflicts?
3. How do they try to gain the most possible influence on media reporting?
4. And what are the dominating constraints that shape PR in wartime?

A Model for PR Analysis in Wartime

The understanding of war has changed several times from the twentieth to the early twenty-first century: industrialized warfare began during the World War I, the World War II left Europe in ruins, the Cold War brought fear of nuclear war and destruction, and in its aftermath European armies were redesigned for a battle of *matériel* between countries and alliances. Since 1990, the understanding of war has changed again. Wars have become increasingly fought 'out of area'. Especially since NATO changed its strategic concept from one of 'flexible response' to one of 'flexible intervention',[8] troops have more frequently been called upon to intervene in local conflicts such as the Balkan wars and to fight asymmetric wars against insurgents such as in Afghanistan and Iraq.[9]

During the past century, warfare changed and became 'post-heroic warfare' (Luttwak, 1995). Western societies have experienced the destruction of two world wars in Europe, US soldiers died in large numbers on these battlefields and the United States suffered more than 58,000 casualties in the Vietnam War (National Archives, 2007). These experiences were combined with a significantly declining birthrate, so '[t]he loss of a youngster in combat, however tragic, was therefore fundamentally less unacceptable than for today's families, with their one, two, or at most three children. Each child is expected to survive into adulthood and embodies a great part of the family's emotional economy' (Luttwak, 1995: 115). Thus the pressure to legitimize wars has increased, and the number of soldiers killed in action has declined.

The wars of the twentieth century have triggered a development at the normative as well as the theoretical level: the 'Triumph of Just War Theory', as Michael Walzer has called an essay he wrote in 2002. The concept of 'just war' has a history that reaches back to antiquity and has its roots in the writings of Augustine, who outlined the ideas that were later on adopted by Thomas Aquinas in the Middle Ages and then matured until the end of the seventeenth century.[10] The concept again became influential in the aftermath of the World War II, initiated by the debate in Great Britain about the bombing campaign against German cities and the huge amount of civilian casualties in the German population (Rengger, 2002: 355).

The most significant influence, however, came from the debate about the Vietnam War in the United States. The political debate about the war was not only fuelled by its costs in money and lives of American soldiers but also by how the war was fought by the US military and the lack of consideration for Vietnamese civilians, which peaked – at least in the public's perception – with the My Lai Massacre. The experience of Vietnam ushered in a debate on morality, especially on the political left. But for the military the question also arose: did the moral failure or the way the war was fought lead to defeat in Vietnam? This debate funneled into the academic debate about the theory of 'just war' in political science and philosophy, which began following the end of the war and reshaped the way wars are fought. Nowadays laser-guided bombs are used, bombs that are expected to hit military targets precisely, and the military tries not to harm civilians, while the 'just war' theory is used to justify wars (Walzer, 2002: 928–32).

The concept of 'just war' has two aspects: *jus ad bellum* – the right to go to war – and *jus in bellum*, which defines how combatants are supposed to act. The latter is based on two core principles. The proportionality of means suggests that the relation between the military objective and the harm done especially to civilians and the civilian infrastructure should be balanced, while noncombatant immunity refers to the obligation to make a distinction between soldiers and irregular fighters, on the one hand, and civilians who are not participating in the conflict, on the other, in an attempt to prevent harm to the latter.

The first aspect – *jus ad bellum* – is based on seven core principles, which set the standards for a just decision to go to war (Rengger, 2002: 358):

1. Just cause: Is the reason for going to war just?
2. Legitimate authority: Do those who make the decision to go to war have the authority to make that decision?[11]
3. Right intention: Is the intent only to be found in the just cause or are there other (illegitimate) interests for going to war (e.g., to acquire territory)?
4. Proportionality of means and ends: Is it disproportionate to use force to achieve a goal? Does the amount of force (that is) needed to achieve a goal stand in no just relation to the goal?
5. Last resort: Can the problem only be solved by force or are there other peaceful ways to achieve the goal?
6. Reasonable hope of success: Can success be expected?
7. Aim for peace: Are there plans to return to a peaceful relationship between the conflicting parties as soon as possible?

Especially *jus in bellum* is – as the lessons from the two world wars and Vietnam have shown – already an integral part of military strategy. This does not mean that military strategy in recent wars necessarily complied with the ideas of *jus in bellum*. But the emphasis on 'surgical strikes' and the intensive use of technology to produce precision weapons show that a lot of effort is being made to comply with these requirements. The basic problem that often arises in practice, however, is that a distinction between combatants and noncombatants is only possible when the lives of soldiers are put at risk – a risk no commander likes to subject his soldiers to. Nevertheless, wars, it is thought, should be fought in a just way (Walzer, 2002: 936–38).

But many of the principles underlying *jus ad bellum* also play a vital role, a fact that is reflected, for example, in the discussions concerning the necessity of an authorization by the UN Security Council for the wars in Iraq in 2003 and in Kosovo. Hence the idea of 'just war' is so well integrated into the debate about war in western societies that it can be assumed that the idea and its underlying principles are key features in the debate about war. Thus one would expect that these principles may be found in the public justification of wars by governments and the military.

Because these principles of 'just war' are basic theoretical ideas and presumably rudimentary patterns of justification, it is also necessary to understand how they are connected to the actual conflict as well as to public understanding. The 'framing' approach offers a clue to this. Framing means 'selecting and highlighting some facets of events or issues, and making connections among them so as to promote a particular interpretation, evaluation and/or solution' (Entman, 2004: 5). Frames thus have four key functions:

1. Defining effects or conditions as problematic
2. Identifying causes
3. Conveying a moral judgment
4. Endorsing remedies or improvements

While Entman applies the term 'frame' to texts, frames are essentially based on schemas – interpretive processes of the human mind. Schemas are 'clusters and nodes of connected ideas and feelings stored in memory' (Entman, 2004: 7). They are connected in knowledge networks that link information (Kintsch, 1998: 412). A vital factor in the success of a frame is its cultural congruence. The more a frame is clearly congruent with a schema that dominates the political culture, the more readily it will be accepted. If it is incongruent, it will be blocked. Thus, in order to dominate the interpretation of events, it is important to establish frames that have as much cultural congruency as possible. The White House and the administration in general are the most powerful actors in establishing frames (Entman, 2004: 9–17). As a result, the administration's exclusive knowledge of security issues is a definite advantage, especially with respect to foreign and security policy.

The relationship between PR and the press can be explained by the intereffication model, which is outlined in Figure 1 (Bentele et al., 1997: 225–50). This model suggests a two-way relationship between PR and journalism. Actors on the micro-level, as well as departments and offices on the meso-level and journalistic and PR systems on the macro-level, adapt to each other and make adjustments in order to ease communication and make

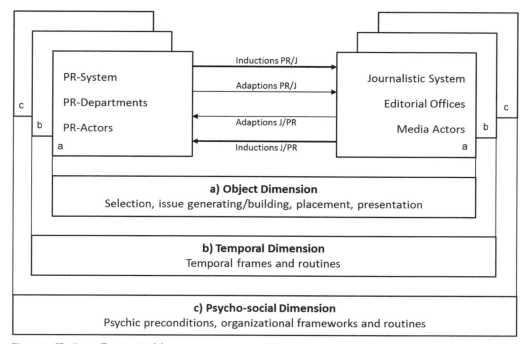

Figure 1: The Intereffication Model.
Source: Bentele and Nothaft (2007: 36).

it successful. At the same time, there are also inductions, which are defined as 'intended and directed communication offers or stimuli', for example, when a newspaper is supplied with information, press releases, exclusive interviews and so on, or when a PR actor is granted special media access.

As Figure 1 also shows, these adaptations or inductions take place in three dimensions: the 'object dimension' (a), which focuses on the contents of PR publications or media reporting, for example, press releases are more likely to be published when they are written to meet specific media needs; the 'temporal dimension' (b), PR offices usually adapt to the editorial deadlines of newspapers or the rapid reactions of the news channels; and the 'psycho-social dimension' (c), the organizational frameworks or routines in PR departments are altered to accommodate the needs of the media (Bentele and Nothaft, 2007: 36).

Based on this, the suggested model for the analysis of war-PR employs and adapts key ideas of the intereffication model (see Figure 2). Since this chapter focuses on government and military PR and the justification of wars, two columns can be distinguished: the 'organization of PR' and the 'justification of wars'.

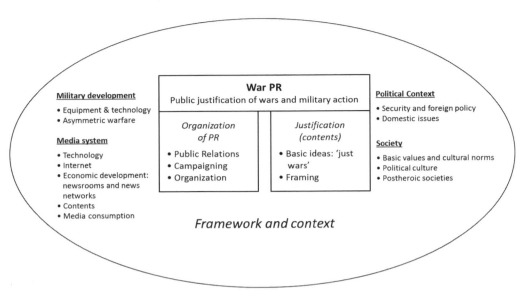

Figure 2: An Approach to Analyzing PR in Military Conflicts.

The column 'organization of PR' incorporates the inductions and adaptations in the psycho-social dimension as well as in the temporal dimension. In PR organizations, adaptations are made on an individual and on an organizational level regarding temporal routines and organizational frameworks in order to exert as much influence as possible on the media system. The development of the media system at the economic (e.g., cost-cutting in newsrooms) and technological level (e.g., satellite transmissions, the Internet, social networks) makes constant adaptation necessary. For instance, the development of news networks changed the temporal routines, which were previously closely tied to the cycle of newspapers and the evening news.

The justification of wars (the second column of the model in Figure 2) represents the content of PR and is comparable to the 'object dimension'. Here the analysis is primarily based on public statements and the speeches of administration officials. These texts provide the basic rationale – the 'just war' – as well as the framing of the situation. They are bound to a context of foreign and security policy, political culture, the content and structure of media reporting as well as domestic policy and military developments. It can be expected that administration representatives mainly focus on the *jus ad bellum* in order to justify their decision to go to war, while military representatives focus on the *jus in bellum* to prove that they are complying with the relevant norms.

Last but not least, the analysis has to include the organizational aspects of PR as well as the content of PR. Hence both are influenced by the framework and context that consists of military developments, the political context, the media system and the society. These factors need to be described in order for one to understand their impact on war-PR.

Framework and Context: Media Systems and Political Culture

There are several aspects that have an impact on PR in military conflicts (see again Figure 2). The development of 'security and foreign policy' is important for war-PR, since it constitutes the political decisions that require justification. The key developments following the end of the Cold War were the changes in NATO strategy previously mentioned as well as the 2002 shift to the concept of preemptive defense in US national security strategy (the so-called Bush-Doctrine).[12]

At the same time, a rapid 'development of military technology', usually described as a 'revolution in military affairs' (RMA), took place. The associated weapon technologies made it possible at least to approach the ideal of *jus in bellum* by conducting precise attacks on targets, while providing camera footage that could later be published to prove the warring party's military might, as well as its concern for civilians. Also, the emergence of 'asymmetric warfare' against non-state actors is an important political and military factor that has to be taken into account when justifying wars.

Furthermore, 'domestic issues' have an impact on PR campaigns in conflicts. This can be shown by the political situation in the United States before the war in Kosovo. US President Clinton had just gone through the impeachment trial, and so allegations arose that his engagement in Kosovo was also motivated by the desire to divert attention from his domestic problems. But the most important factors for PR in military conflicts are 'political culture' and – obviously – the 'media system'.

As shown in the previous section, cultural congruency is a key criterion for successful framing. On the one hand, this means that the framing of a conflict should be in line with the political schemas of the audience, for example, their knowledge of Iraq's aggression against Kuwait and the use of chemical weapons against Iran and the Kurdish population by the Iraqi government under Saddam Hussein. This does not mean – to take the example of the Balkan wars – that the audience has to be fully informed and possess sophisticated knowledge of these conflicts, for example, comprehensive information concerning the atrocities of both sides during the Balkan wars. On the other hand, in order to establish a successful frame, it is necessary to link it to core values and the political culture.

The most important aspect of the 'political culture' of the United States has been described by Robert N. Bellah as 'Civil Religion in America'[13] (Bellah, 1967). Even though faith plays an important role in US society, religious faith has been secularized as it became associated early on with the political system by the founding fathers and was transformed into a faith in values and political institutions. 'Though much was selectively derived from Christianity, this religion is clearly not itself Christianity' (Bellah, 1967: 7). It has rituals such as the Pledge of Allegiance, prophets like the founding fathers, martyrs like the former presidents Lincoln and Kennedy, places of worship (e.g., the Jefferson Memorial or Arlington Cemetery) and holy scriptures (e.g., the Declaration of Independence). Although many of its symbols are derived from the Christian faith (especially the Old Testament) and no president fails to mention God, it is not common to refer to Christ. Also some key beliefs of this civil religion are defining as far as US self-perception is concerned: the idea of the 'shining city upon a hill' and the 'new Jerusalem' equates Europe with Egypt and America with the Promised Land to which God has led the people to establish an order that should be an example to the world (Vorländer, 2008: 200–04). As Bellah summarized,

> Behind the civil religion at every point lie biblical archetypes: Exodus, Chosen People, Promised Land, New Jerusalem, Sacrificial Death and Rebirth. But it is also genuinely American and genuinely new. It has its own prophets and its own martyrs, its own sacred events and sacred places, its own solemn rituals and symbols. (Bellah, 1967: 18)

Several of these motifs can be found in the political deliberation that occurs in the United States, and often even opposing views refer to these ideas. A message framed by these ideas can easily activate a network of schemas regarding values. It could suggest a solution that is in line with those values that are so deeply ingrained in American political traditions, or it could show that a particular event contradicts these same values.

The other mayor constraint on PR is the 'media system'. A key factor in the success of a message is not only the framing but also its transmission to the media system. As a result, the PR has to adjust to the 'economic and technological development' of the media system.

In recent decades, some key changes have taken place on the level of 'technological development'. Not only the success of the Internet, which made international news and government information easily accessible and established new ways of participating,[14] but also the new transmission technologies for television are important in this regard. The technological capacity to transmit news reports via satellite changed the speed with which news from a conflict could reach the TV screens in the United States. Also, portable satellite dishes as well as satellite phones made it possible to report live from the battlefield during the 2003 Iraq War. Finally, TV satellites and satellite dishes heightened the availability of the international media, especially in the Middle East, thus triggering the founding of news channels such as Al Jazeera.

This leads to the 'economic development' of the media system. Most influential here was the rise of news networks, first in the United States and later all over the world. Twenty-four-hour news reporting especially changed the speed with which news could be distributed. It is no longer enough simply to react to the news within the time frame of newspaper production or that of the network evening news. In order to establish a successful frame or to counter bad news in cases of crisis communication, it is necessary to react as quickly as possible.[15] This is especially important in the case of international crises, when reporting is ongoing across several different time zones.[16]

The rise of new players and the 'Internet' has also had an economic impact on traditional news outlets such as newspapers, magazines and the evening news. Competition has increased, traditional electronic and print media have lost customers, and newspapers in particular are struggling now that classified ads have moved to the Internet. These losses have led to deep cuts in newsrooms, leaving less time for journalists to validate information, search and check news, and work on investigative reporting, while at the same time the pace of news has accelerated.[17]

Organizing PR: Strategic Information Management[18]

Before the Kosovo conflict, it was predicted that the attacks on the Serbian military would not last long and that there would be rapid success, but the military operation faced numerous obstacles. Weather conditions were bad and the Serbian military did not use its radar-guided air defense system as expected. Without being able to track the radar of the air defense units, it was impossible to destroy them, and so NATO planes had to work from high altitudes in order to protect themselves. This reduced the efficiency of the air force, whilst NATO had already ruled out the use of ground troops.[19] Since no ground forces were in Kosovo and no journalists could get there in their company, no images were available from the battleground outside of gun camera footage. At the same time, the Federal Republic of Yugoslavia published footage especially of civilian casualties and the destruction of infrastructure caused by the attacks. In doing so, their most important tool was the Eurovision News Exchange, a network of European public broadcasting companies for footage exchange, which accounts for a significant portion of the footage used by public TV broadcasters.

Thus, the dominant pictures at the beginning of the war were gun camera footage from NATO and pictures of civilian casualties in Yugoslavia, thus undermining NATO's credibility. This changed when refugees started to flee from Kosovo and their suffering as well as the refugee camps became a dominant feature of the coverage, which helped shape public perception and supported NATO's storyline.

NATO headquarters were responsible for the PR during the war. Within the first few weeks of the conflict, it became obvious that NATO's Office of Information and Press (OIP) was not equipped to handle such intense media interest. It only had three members, including the Spokesman Jamie Shea, and therefore lacked the capacity to handle the situation, while often being cut off from the required military information. As a result, the failures of NATO became a serious problem for NATO's attempts to justify the war. The attack on a refugee trek in Kosovo and the bombing of a bridge while a train was crossing it triggered intensive reporting and public criticism, especially since NATO at first denied and later on had to admit mistakes, and because communication between the OIP and the Supreme Headquarters Allied Powers Europe (SHAPE) did not work.

Since the media reporting was shaped by the rapidity of the news networks and took place across several time zones, it was not only the classic media cycle in the United States that had to be handled. If an incident occurred in Europe at 7 or 8 a.m. local time, it would already lead the morning news in the United States. Once this was realized by Washington, DC, and London, three steps were taken. Telephone conferences were used to exchange information and synchronize messages between the spokespeople of the participating countries (usually from the United States, the United Kingdom, Germany, France and Italy). NATO press conferences and the administration were coordinated to fill up as much airtime as possible, as news networks switched to these events. And – most important – a PR operation called the Media Operation Centre (MOC) was set up at NATO headquarters by the British spokesman Alastair Campbell and the White House Press Secretary Joe Lockhart in order to back up NATO's PR while spokesman Jamie Shea remained in place (Schreiber et al., 1999: 80).

About 30 members were working in several 'cells' (Jertz, 2001: 83):

- A 'Planning and Coordination Cell' responsible for strategic aspects
- A 'Media Monitoring Cell', evaluating media reports
- A 'SHAPE Liaison Cell' responsible for internal communication, making sure that all the required information was available to the PR staff
- And a 'Writers and Research Cell', responsible for research and ghostwriting

The PR officials considered two aspects to be vital for the stabilization of public support: first, the availability of images underlining their storyline, that is, that the attacks were needed in order to stop atrocities, and second, that the new structures provided by the MOC had made communication between NATO and the media function at last.

Two years later, after the terrorist attacks on New York and Washington, DC, of September 11, 2001, the Afghanistan War began on October 7, 2001. The problems were basically the same: the United States had almost no 'boots on the ground', only Special Forces were operating in Afghanistan, and it was difficult to allow journalists to accompany them. In addition, the war took place in a different time zone, so media reports could originate at any time from Asia and the Middle East, Europe and the United States; handling the international media was also required, Al Jazeera in particular. As the first Arabic news network at the time, Al Jazeera was the only TV station able to report from Kabul, Afghanistan and the region.

The two steps taken by the White House and the Pentagon were simple: on the one hand, Coalition Information Centers (CIC) were established in Washington, DC, London and Pakistan.[20] They were able to work with local journalists, monitor local media and react within the time zones. On the other hand, initial steps were taken to 'embed' journalists within the military, and a small number of journalists were allowed to join the Special Forces operating in Afghanistan, once the US media insisted on this.

During the preparation of the war against Iraq, several steps were taken within the US administration. The key political decisions were made within the White House, the Department of Defense and the Department of State. As illustrated in Figure 3 in the left-hand column, the war and the communication campaign were planned on '(1) a strategic level' within the White House Iraq Group, consisting of spokespersons, the White House Communication Director, the chiefs of staff and members of the National Security Council (NSC). Also, two

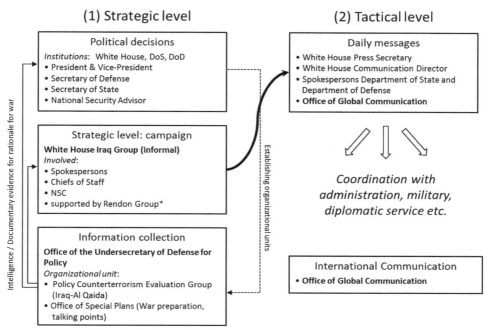

* The support of the Rendon Group is asserted by media reports, but was denied by the Rendon Group

Figure 3: Information Management before and during the 2003 Iraq War.

*The support of the Rendon Group is asserted by media reports but was denied by the Rendon Group.

units within the Department of Defense were established in order to collect information from the intelligence services, which supported the rationale for the war. Those two units – the Policy Counterterrorism Evaluation Group and the Office of Special Plans – were located at the office of the Undersecretary of Defense for Policy.

This process had been subject to criticism, since on the one hand faulty information backing the decision to go to war was provided by these offices, and on the other hand, the vetting process of the intelligence agencies was bypassed, and first-hand information was made available to the White House without further assessment, a process Seymour Hersh described as 'stovepiping' (Hersh, 2003a, 2003b).[21]

PR on '(2) a tactical (daily) level' (see Figure 3, right-hand column) was conducted by PR officials within the administration, but the efforts to coordinate messages were not as intense as during the Kosovo War. As it became obvious from the experiences in Afghanistan since 9/11, the world press had become increasingly important to the US administration, so a new office was established at the White House. While previously the White House had focused on the US media, the Office of Global Communication[22] was set up to establish a better relationship by focusing on the international media and granting noticeably improved access to White House officials and the president.

The decision that received most attention in the run-up to and during the actual conduct of the Iraq War was the embedding of journalists within the troops. Especially in the US military, the relationship with the media had been distorted, as a result of the experiences in Vietnam when media reports about atrocities against civilians had changed the public's perception of fighting a just war. Thus, there had been resistance against granting reporters access to the battlefield, and the US invasions of Grenada and Panama in the 1980s had taken place solely on camera.

During the Persian Gulf War in 1991, journalists' access was organized in a pool system, allowing only very restricted access to the war arena. Reports had to be approved before publication. In addition, transmitting them to newsrooms was a complicated and tedious process so that information was often outdated before it could even be published. Only the Marine Corps – which had always needed to cooperate with the media because of the competition with other parts of the military – granted improved access anywhere comparable to the embedding that occurred in the 2003 Iraq War. This was a successful move because the coverage of the accompanying reporters was favorable and did not violate security concerns. These experiences enabled a learning process within the military and the Department of Defense that became part of a development within the Department to open up the military to the media, which was now regarded as part of information operations (Rid, 2007).

Media representatives were allowed to accompany ground forces to the battlefield and to report without censorship or having their reports reviewed. They had to agree to 'ground rules', a catalog of restrictions regarding strategic information (goals, locations etc.) and the protection of soldiers or prisoners of war, which thereby limited their reporting. If they failed to comply, they could lose their accreditation and be removed from the unit (Department of Defense, 2003). The embedding of journalists has drawn criticism, especially as their closeness to the troops often seemed to influence their reporting. Reports often focused on cursory information and live transmissions from the battlefield without sufficient background information because giving out strategic information such as locations, destinations, targets or equipment could have endangered military operations. This was the main type of friction that occurred between war reporting and the needs of the military. Embedding was a success during the Iraq War, even though it was perceived beforehand as a risk. Live images from the battlefield dominated the news during the war, which left less room for independent reports such as those from Al Jazeera, for example.

'Our Cause Is Just' – The Iraq War

In the following section, the war against Iraq is used to exemplify the adjustment of the 'just war' theory and the 'framing' concept to the justification of the war by the US administration. In a first step, persuasive communication before the war started is analyzed in order to determine whether the seven core principles of the *jus ad bellum* can be identified in speeches of President George W. Bush between September 2002 and March 2003. An analysis of the framing of the war follows, going back to the events of September 11, 2001 and the framing of the so-called War on Terror. The aim here is to show how the terrorist attacks and the war against Iraq were integrated into a network of common knowledge and linked to the political culture in the United States – particularly the previously cited 'civil religion' – in order to establish the notion of the 'enemy'. The third step will be to show whether and how the ideas of *jus in bellum* were integrated in speeches and public statements of the president and the Secretary of Defense Donald Rumsfeld.

The empirical data are drawn from two sources. It is based in part on an earlier analysis (Kutz, 2006) that explained the rhetorical justification of the war but did not make use of the 'just war' theory. Information is drawn from a preliminary qualitative analysis that was part of a comparative research project targeting the justification of the wars in Kosovo, Afghanistan and Iraq in Germany and the United States.

In this section, examples are used to underpin the main line of argumentation. The documents used originate from the period between September 2002, when the intention to go to war was made public, and the fall of Baghdad in April 2003. In addition, four speeches of George W. Bush are used. Three of these were given in September 2001 in response to 9/11, and the fourth is the State of the Union speech given on January 29, 2002, which for the first time shifted the focus from the 'war against terror' to Iraq, by depicting it as a part of an 'axis of evil'.

I shall not discuss whether the justification provided by the Bush administration stuck to the facts or whether there was any manipulation. The persuasive communication of the administration on several occasions focused on facts that supported their rationale, while information contradicting it was left out (Kutz, 2006: 93–121). The focus was placed on weapons of mass destruction (WMD) because 'we settled on the one issue that everyone could agree on', as Paul Wolfowitz stated in an interview with *Vanity Fair* (Wolfowitz, 2003). Many of the key decision makers were obviously convinced of a link between Saddam Hussein and al-Qaeda, as Richard Clarke reported with regard to Wolfowitz (Clarke, 2004: 231–43). The flaws in the intelligence process based on ideological convictions are an important factor, too (Kutz, 2006, 2010).

The core task of the rationale for the 2003 Iraq War was to explain why the decision to go to war was just. There were three core arguments depicting the war as having a just cause[23] and a fourth mixed one:

1. Iraq has WMD and is prepared to use them.[24]
2. The Iraqi regime is cooperating with terrorists, including al-Qaeda, and was possibly involved in the terrorist attacks against New York and Washington, DC.[25]
3. The Iraqi regime is brutally oppressing the Iraqi people.
4. The fourth argument is a combination of the first two, namely, the possibility that Iraq handed WMD over to al-Qaeda or to other terrorist organizations.

This line of argument was established in the State of the Union Speech of George W. Bush on January 29, 2002:

Iraq continues to flaunt its hostility toward America and to support terror. The Iraqi regime has plotted to develop anthrax, and nerve gas, and nuclear weapons for over a decade. This is a regime that has already used poison gas to murder thousands of its own citizens – leaving the bodies of mothers huddled over their dead children. This is a regime that agreed to international inspections – then kicked out the inspectors. This is a regime that has something to hide from the civilized world.[26]

The argument was that a heavily armed, hostile country that oppressed its people was threatening the United States with WMD, which could potentially be used by terrorists. In several speeches, most notably in the State of the Union Address of January 28, 2003 before the war started, but also in his first radio address of March 22, 2003 after the war had started, George W. Bush used the phrase 'just cause' in connection with the decision to go to war, stating that 'our cause is just, the security of the nations we serve and the peace of the world'.[27]

Two important aspects of the rationale are the proportionality of means and ends as well as the usage of war as a last resort. Since there had not been any direct threat from Iraq against the United States, the war would be a preemptive strike to prevent the Iraqi regime from acquiring the capacity to attack. At the same time, Iraq was depicted as willing to use WMD against the United States. The alleged link between al-Qaeda and Iraq was key to this argument. It suggested that an attack on the United States could happen at any time without warning, while Iraq did not have to fear retaliation. The Iraq could 'provide some weapons and training to them, let them come and do his dirty work, and we wouldn't be able to see his fingerprints on his action'.[28]

The argument was that the Iraqi regime wanted to attack the United States and that this could happen at any time. At the same time, the threat was described as increasing, with Bush arguing that 'the danger to America from the Iraqi regime is grave and growing. The regime is guilty of beginning two wars. It has a horrible history of striking without warning'.[29] If the United States did not react fast, the consequences could be disastrous. The president described this threat in a speech on October 7, 2002 in which he stated that 'facing clear evidence of peril, we cannot wait for the final proof – the smoking gun – that could come in the form of a mushroom cloud'[30] – before Congress authorized the use of force.

Another key argument was that of proper authority. Because the United Nations Security Council (UNSC) is the legitimate authority in international law for authorizing the use of force, the United States tried to win its approval but failed. Especially Colin Powell's appearance in front of the Security Council drew a lot of attention. His speech had the character of a final speech of the prosecution in a jury trial. It could, therefore, have been staged to give the impression that the UN was unwilling and unable to act in the face of evidence and in order to weaken the Council's authority in the eyes of the US public.

Accordingly, the rationale focused on Resolution 1441, which passed the UNSC by unanimous vote and which demanded that Iraq disarm. In a radio address on February 8, 2003, the day after Colin Powell's presentation, George W. Bush portrayed the UNSC as unwilling to act:

Having made its demands, the Security Council must not back down when those demands are defied and mocked by a dictator. The United States would welcome and support a new resolution making clear that the Security Council stands behind its previous demands. Yet, resolutions mean little without resolve. And the United States, along with a growing coalition of nations, will take whatever action is necessary to defend ourselves and disarm the Iraqi regime.[31]

How much the 'just war' theory influenced the rationale for the Iraq War can be seen in an excerpt of the State of the Union Address delivered by George W. Bush on January 28, 2003, which also shows the last of the speeches to mention the principles of *jus ad bellum* – the aim for peace and the reasonable hope for success, depicted by the mention of military might:

We seek peace. We strive for peace. And sometimes peace must be defended. A future lived at the mercy of terrible threats is no peace at all. If war is forced upon us, we will fight in a just cause and by just means – sparing, in every way we can, the innocent. And if war is forced upon us, we will fight with the full force and might of the United States military – and we will prevail.[32]

The actual framing of the war in Iraq was also a key aspect of the rationale. It was in turn linked to the framing of 9/11. The day after the attacks, Bush already told the public they 'should not expect one battle, but a lengthy campaign, unlike any other we have ever seen'.[33] During his address to the nation on the evening of September 11, 2001, he contrasted the terrorists with the United States's own perception of itself as a 'new Israel', a perception deeply rooted in the country's civil religion: 'America was targeted for attack, because we're the brightest beacon for freedom and opportunity in the world. And no one will keep that light from shining.' At the same time, he depicted the situation as a struggle between good and evil: 'Today our nation saw evil, the very worst of human nature.'[34] By contrast, the terrorists were referred to as 'enemies of freedom', this last category being a core value in the United States. Similarly, in a speech to a joint session of Congress on September 20, 2001, Bush stated,

Americans are asking, why do they hate us? They hate what we see right here in this chamber – a democratically elected government. Their leaders are self-appointed. They hate our freedoms – our freedom of religion, our freedom of speech, our freedom to vote and assemble and disagree with each other. [...] These terrorists kill not merely to end lives, but to disrupt and end a way of life. With every atrocity, they hope that America grows fearful, retreating from the world and forsaking our friends. They stand against us, because we stand in their way.[35]

By contrasting the attacks with the United States's own perception of itself, a concept of the enemy was created that was clearly at odds with the core values of American democracy and civil religion.[36] Iraq was placed in the context of the War on Terror, administration officials alleged a link between Iraq and al-Qaeda, and – as mentioned above – it was predicted that Iraq might provide terrorists with WMD. These allegations associated the knowledge concerning 9/11 with the war against Iraq, while Saddam Hussein was placed at the center of the argument as the key enemy, which in turn made a distinction between the Iraqi people and the regime of Saddam Hussein possible.

Right before and after the beginning of the war in Iraq, the American president as well as the Secretary of Defense characterized the conduct of war as 'just' by focusing on two aspects. The efforts of the United States to provide humanitarian aid as well as the concern for civilians were emphasized. This second aspect was addressed in two steps. The first was to assure that the United States was taking every precaution not to harm civilians. The second step emphasized that the Iraqi regime placed military equipment deliberately in civilian areas and used Iraqis as 'human shields'. In several speeches, the citizens of Iraq were called upon to stay in their homes and to avoid military facilities, and the care being given to prisoners of war was underlined. In his address to the nation after the attacks began, George W. Bush declared on March 19, 2003,

> The people you liberate will witness the honorable and decent spirit of the American military. In this conflict, America faces an enemy who has no regard for conventions of war or rules of morality. Saddam Hussein has placed Iraqi troops and equipment in civilian areas, attempting to use innocent men, women and children as shields for his own military – a final atrocity against his people. I want Americans and all the world to know that coalition forces will make every effort to spare innocent civilians from harm.[37]

Conclusions and Outlook

The purpose of this chapter was to give an overview of the PR practice and the type of persuasive communication used by the US governments to justify wars. In accomplishing this, the attempt was made to sketch a model suitable for such an analysis. In order to understand this particular type of communication, it is necessary to examine strategic PR at the organizational level as well as to examine in a broader context the content of political communication such as it is presented in speeches and press conferences.

Foreign and security policy, the media system and war itself have changed since the end of the Cold War. These changes and an associated learning process have triggered developments at the organizational level, especially when one takes into account that the media system has become faster and increasingly networked. Precise information, clear and coordinated messages and especially fast reactions have become key to getting a message across to the public. 'Speed kills' – the phrase coined by the Clinton campaign team in 1992 to emphasize the importance of a rapid rebuttal of bad news – has become a core idea of PR organization in the face of intense media pressure. The establishment of the MOC during the Kosovo War illustrated the importance of these organizational measures. Without a large team that can handle all the tasks such as research, internal communication, media monitoring or strategic planning, it becomes impossible to handle a crisis that the world press focuses on.

Especially the experiences after 9/11 changed the views held within the US administration: while before the focus lay on the United States, the international media were now regarded as more or less equally important, and the cross-linkage between the international media, international support and the US media became obvious. As a reaction, first the CICs were established, later on the Office of Global Communication (OGC) in the White House.

The military, however, went through a learning process dating back to Vietnam. It was realized that in modern information management it is no longer possible to seal the armed forces off from the press. These learning processes were combined with the new Secretary of Defense and his staff pressing for the opening, which led to the idea of 'embedding'. But journalists who report live from the battlefield cause problems for the military. If strategic information is published, the goals of the operation as well as the lives of the soldiers become endangered. This conflict cannot be solved, and it inevitably leads to another conflict: reports have to be stripped of key information if they are to be published in order to protect the interests of the military, in which case the reporting may become superficial. Therefore, it is a key task for journalists as well as editors to handle the restrictions transparently and to focus instead on in-depth information rather than on fast and exclusive news or pictures.

The justification of the Iraq War as explained above leads to another question: is a war just, simply because it is possible to justify it to the public?

While the Clinton administration did not lose support even in the face of many obstacles during the Kosovo War, the majority of the US population still does not think it was a mistake to send troops to Afghanistan. As a Gallup report in 2009 showed, even though support has declined over the past eight years, still a majority of over 60 percent of those interviewed declare that the war was not a mistake (Gallup Poll, July 10–12, 2009). In contrast, the approval rating of the war in Iraq has dropped, with more than 60 percent of US population opposing it. Two reasons may be cited here: on the one hand, the loss of more than 4,000 soldiers' lives contradicts the post-heroic portrayal of war. On the other hand, the rationale that depicted the decision to go to war as in line with *jus in bellum* has proved itself wrong. No WMD were found, no connection between al-Qaeda and the Iraqi government was uncovered, and the Iraqi people were freed only to suffer subsequently from a civil war.

Nevertheless, the rationale worked to gather initial public support. It included all key aspects of 'just war' theory and framed the war so as to make it readily understandable to the US public. This also provides a key example useful in the analysis of the justification of wars as well as in the study of political communication. Everything worked perfectly until George W. Bush declared the mission to be 'accomplished', but the war itself did not end. In the months following, all key assumptions of the administration proved themselves to be wrong, and PR alone cannot heal disastrous political failure.

Key Points

- The justification of wars is highly influenced by their framework and context, and here especially by media development, political culture and basic values of society.
- Nonstop 24/7 news cycles, international media reporting throughout various time zones as well as the availability of live pictures via satellite from the battlefield make it necessary to provide adequate PR structures in the time zones where the wars are fought, in order to enact immediate influence on the interpretations of events.
- The justification of wars is based on two aspects: basic normative ideas provided by 'just war' theory and a framing congruent to political culture.

Study Questions

1. How would you distinguish between 'public relations' and 'propaganda', and how would you apply these terms to the justification of a current or historic military conflict?
2. Is it possible to apply 'just war' theory in order to make a decision whether to go to war or not? Is such a normative theory suitable for making such a decision, or is it only suitable for gaining public support?
3. How would you explain the 'framing' concept, using an example you are familiar with? Explain how cultural congruency has been achieved. Could another frame have been applied that would have contradicted the suggested solution or interpretation?

Further Reading

Bellah, Robert N. (1967) 'Civil Religion in America', *Daedalus* 96: 1–21.

Bentele, Günter and Howard Nothaft (2008) 'The Intereffication Model. Theoretical Discussions and Empirical Research', pp. 32–48 in Ansgar Zerfass, Betteke van Ruler and Krishnamurthy Sriramesh (eds) *Public Relations Research. European and International Perspectives and Innovations*, published as a Festschrift for Prof. Dr. Günter Bentele, University of Leipzig, on the occasion of his 60th birthday in March 2008. Wiesbaden: VS.

Cunningham, Stanley B. (2002) *The Idea of Propaganda. A Reconstruction.* Westport, CT: Praeger.

Entman, Robert M. (2004) *Projections of Power. Framing News, Public Opinion, and U.S. Foreign Policy.* Chicago, IL: University of Chicago Press.

Grunig, James E. and Todd Hunt (1984) *Managing Public Relations.* New York: Holt, Rinehart and Winston.

Kutz, Magnus-Sebastian (2006) *Public Relations oder Propaganda? Die Öffentlichkeitsarbeit der US-Administration zum Krieg gegen den Irak 2003.* Münster: Lit.

Münkler, Herfried (2004) *The New Wars.* Oxford: Polity.

Rid, Thomas (2007) *War and Media Operations. The US Military and the Press from Vietnam to Iraq.* London: Routledge.

Silberstein, Sandra (2002) *War of Words. Language, Politics and 9/11*. London; New York: Routledge.

Tumber, Howard and Frank Webster (2006) *Journalists Under Fire. Information War and Journalistic Practices*. London: Sage.

Walzer, Michael (2002) 'The Triumph of Just War Theory (and the Dangers of Success)', *Social Research* 69: 925–44.

Websites

Homepage of the Bush administration (preserved by National Archives): georgewbush-whitehouse.archives.gov.

Homepage of the William J. Clinton Presidential Library and Museum: www.clintonlibrary.gov/archivesearch.html.

Pew Research Center's Project for Excellence in Journalism's annual report on the state of the news Media: stateofthemedia.org.

US Department of Defense: www.defense.gov.

Website with resources on 'just war' theory: www.justwartheory.com.

References

Bahador, Babak (2007) *The CNN Effect in Action. How the News Media Pushed the West Toward War in Kosovo*. New York: Palgrave Macmillan.

Bellah, Robert N. (1967) 'Civil Religion in America', *Daedalus* 96: 1–21.

Bentele, Günter and Howard Nothaft (2007) 'The Intereffication Model. Theoretical Discussions and Empirical Research', pp. 32–48 in Ansgar Zerfass, Betteke van Ruler and Krishnamurthy Sriramesh (eds) *Public Relations Research. European and International Perspectives and Innovations*, published as a Festschrift for Prof. Dr. Günter Bentele, University of Leipzig, on the occasion of his 60th birthday in March 2008. Wiesbaden: VS.

Bentele, Günter, Tobias Liebert and Stefan Seeling (1997) 'Von der Determination zur Intereffikation. Ein integriertes Modell zum Verhältnis von Public Relations und Journalismus', pp. 225–50 in Günter Bentele and Michael Haller (eds) *Aktuelle Entstehung von Öffentlichkeit. Akteure-Strukturen-Veränderungen*. Konstanz: UVK Medien.

Bernays, Edward L. (2005, originally 1928) *Propaganda*, with an introduction by Mark Crispin Miller. New York: lg Publishing.

Brown, Chris, Terry Nardin and Nicholas J. Rengger (2002) *International Relations in Political Thought. Texts from the Ancient Greeks to the First World War*. Cambridge: Cambridge University Press.

Bussemer, Thymian (2005) *Propaganda. Konzepte und Theorien*. Wiesbaden: VS.

Clarke, Richard A. (2004) *Against All Enemies. Inside America's War on Terror*. New York: Free Press.

Cunningham, Stanley B. (2002) *The Idea of Propaganda. A Reconstruction*. Westport, CT: Praeger.

Department of Defense (2003) *Public Affairs Guidance on Embedding Media during Possible Future Operations/Deployments in the U.S. Central Command Area of Responsibility*, http://www.defenselink.mil/news/Feb2003/d20030228pag.pdf (December 19, 2011).

Dietzsch, Stefanie and Ursula Kocher (2003) '... To Fight Freedom's Fight. George W. Bushs Kriegsrethorik', pp. 117–29 in Manfred Beetz, Joachim Dyck, Wolfgang Neuber and Gert Ueding (eds) *Krieg und Rhetorik*. Tübingen: Niemeyer.

Entman, Robert M. (2004) *Projections of Power. Framing News, Public Opinion, and U.S. Foreign policy*. Chicago, IL: University of Chicago Press.

Grunig, James E. and Todd Hunt (1984) *Managing Public Relations*. New York: Holt, Rinehart and Winston.

Hans-Bredow-Institut (2004) *Internationales Handbuch Medien*. Baden-Baden: Nomos.

Hersh, Seymour (2003a) 'Selective Intelligence', *The New Yorker* May 12, 2003.

—— (2003b) 'The Stovepipe', *The New Yorker* October 28, 2003.

Jertz, Walter (2001) *Krieg der Worte – Macht der Bilder. Manipulation oder Wahrheit im Kosovo-Konflikt*. Bonn: Bernard & Graefe.

Jowett, Garth and Victoria O'Donnell (1999) *Propaganda and Persuasion*. Thousand Oaks, CA: Sage.

Kintsch, Walter (1998) *Comprehension. A Paradigm for Cognition*. Cambridge: Cambridge University Press.

Kunczik, Michael (2002) *Public Relations. Konzepte und Theorien*. Köln: Böhlau.

Kutz, Magnus-Sebastian (2006) *Public Relations oder Propaganda? Die Öffentlichkeitsarbeit der US-Administration zum Krieg gegen den Irak 2003*. Münster: Lit.

—— (2010) 'Die US-amerikanische Öffentlichkeitsarbeit zur Rechtfertigung des Irak-Kriegs im Kontext neokonservativer Ideologie', pp. 41–64 in Una Dirks (ed.) *Der Irak-Konflikt in den Medien. Eine sprach-, politik- und kommunikationswissenschaftliche Analyse*. Konstanz: UVK.

Lambeth, Benjamin S. (2001) *NATO's Air War for Kosovo. A Strategic and Operational Assessment*. Santa Monica, CA: RAND.

Lasswell, Harold D. (1927) 'The Theory of Political Propaganda', *American Political Science Review* 21: 627–31.

Loquai, Heinz (2003) *Weichenstellungen für einen Krieg. Internationales Krisenmanagement und die OSZE im Kosovo-Konflikt*. Baden-Baden: Nomos.

Luttwak, Edward (1995) 'Toward Post-Heroic Warfare', *Foreign Affairs* 74(3): 109–22.

Meyer, Philip (2004) *The Vanishing Newspaper. Saving Journalism in the Information Age*. Columbia: University of Missouri Press.

Münkler, Herfried (2004) *The New Wars*. Oxford: Polity.

National Archives (2007) *Statistical Information About Casualties of the Vietnam War*, www.archives.gov/research/military/vietnam-war/casualty-statistics.html (December 19, 2011).

National Commission on Terrorist Attacks upon the United States (2004) *The 9/11 Commission Report. Final Report of the National Commission on Terrorist Attacks upon the United States*, www.9-11commission.gov/report/911Report.pdf (December 19, 2011).

Regan, Richard J. (1996) *Just War. Principles and Cases*. Washington, DC: Catholic University of America Press.

Rengger, Nicholas J. (2002) 'On the Just War Tradition in the Twenty-First Century', *International Affairs* 78: 353–63.

Rid, Thomas (2007) *War and Media Operations. The US Military and the Press from Vietnam to Iraq.* London: Routledge.

Ronneberger, Franz and Manfred Rühl (1992) *Theorie der Public Relations. Ein Entwurf.* Opladen: Westdeutscher.

Schieder, Wolfgang and Christof Dipper (1984) 'Propaganda', pp. 61–112 in Otto Brunner, Werner Conze and Reinhart Koselleck (eds) *Geschichtliche Grundbegriffe. Band 4: Historisches Lexikon zur politisch-sozialen Sprache in Deutschland.* Stuttgart: Klett-Cotta.

Schreiber, Sylvia, Alexander Szandar and Thomas Tuma (1999) 'Dr. Jekyll und Mister Hyde', *Der Spiegel* May 17, 1999.

Senate Select Committee on Intelligence (SSCI) (2004) *Report on the U.S. Intelligence Community's Prewar Intelligence Assessments on Iraq,* intelligence.senate.gov/iraqreport2.pdf (November 25, 2011).

—— (2006a) *Report of the Select Committee on Intelligence on Postwar Findings about Iraq's WMD Programs and Links to Terrorism and How They Compare with Pre-War Assessments Together with Additional Views.* 109th Congress, 2nd Session, Senate Report 109–331. September 8, 2006, intelligence.senate.gov/phaseiiaccuracy.pdf (December 19, 2011).

—— (2006b) *Report of the Select Committee on Intelligence on the Use by the Intelligence Community of Information Provided by the Iraqi National Congress Together with Additional Views.* 109th Congress, 2nd Session, Senate Report 109–330, September 8, 2006, intelligence. senate.gov/phaseiiinc.pdf (December 19, 2011).

Silberstein, Sandra (2002) *War of Words. Language, Politics and 9/11.* London; New York: Routledge.

St John, Burton, III (1998) 'Public Relations as Community-Building Then and Now', *Public Relations Quarterly* 43(1): 34–40.

Thomass, Barbara (2007) *Mediensysteme im internationalen Vergleich.* Konstanz: UTB.

Vorländer, Hans (2008) 'Politische Kultur', pp. 196–236 in Peter Lösche (ed.) *Länderbericht USA.* Bonn: Bundeszentrale für politische Bildung.

Walzer, Michael (2002) 'The Triumph of Just War Theory (and the Dangers of Success)', *Social Research* 69: 925–44.

Wolfowitz, Paul (2003) 'Deputy Secretary Wolfowitz Interview with Sam Tannenhaus', *Vanity Fair* May 9, 2003.

Notes

1   *Colin Powell on Iraq, Race, and Hurricane Relief,* ABC News, September 8, 2005, http:// abcnews.go.com/print?id=1105979 (April 25, 2012).

2   Especially the reports of the Senate Select Committee on Intelligence (SSCI) on the intelligence process during the buildup to the Iraq War are important (SSCI, 2004, 2006a, 2006b). Hersh's coverage of the intelligence work in the office of the Undersecretary of Defense for Policy is also important.

3   For an overview of international crisis management during the Kosovo conflict, see Loquai (2003).

4   See www.pollingreport.com/afghan.htm (April 25, 2012).

5   See www.pollingreport.com/iraq2.htm (April 25, 2012).

6   For a history of the term 'propaganda', see Cunningham (2002) and Bussemer (2005).

7   For a normative approach to public relations, see Ronneberger and Rühl (1992); the self-portrayal of professional associations (e.g., the Public Relations Society of America) is also often shaped by these ideas.

8   The concept of 'flexible response' was based on the idea that NATO forces would react flexibly to an attack by the Warsaw Pact, meaning they could use nuclear weapons to stop an overwhelming conventional invasion by the Soviet military in Europe. The term 'flexible intervention' was coined in imitation of the concept of 'flexible response' when out-of-area military operations became part of NATO strategy in 1999.

9   For an overview and explanation of these 'new wars', see Münkler (2004).

10 An overview and excerpts may be found in Brown et al. (2002).

11 For a detailed discussion of 'just war' decisions and cases, especially regarding legitimate authority and just cause, see Regan (1996).

12 For an overview, see Kutz (2006: 67–74).

13 As Bellah states, the term 'civil religion' originates from Rousseau's *Social Contract* (Bellah, 1967: 5).

14 The development of participatory communication technologies, usually summarized as 'Web 2.0', has become an important factor in recent years. It is not relevant to the case studies that focus on the years 1999–2003 but must be taken into account for current and future developments.

15 See also Bahador (2007) for an analysis of the influence of the CNN effect on the Kosovo War.

16 The *International Media Handbook* of the Hans-Bredow-Institute (2004) is a key publication in media research. Thomass' (2007) introduction to the comparison of media systems also helps to outline core aspects.

17 Meyer (2004) shows the impact on newspapers. The annual survey 'State of the News Media', conducted by the Pew Research Center, provides an in-depth analysis of current developments; see www.stateofthemedia.org.

18 The following section is based in part on interviews conducted with former high-ranking members of the Clinton and Bush administrations.

19 For an assessment of NATO's military strategy in Kosovo, see Lambeth (2001).

20 For an overview of articles related to the CICs, see Source Watch's 'Coalition Information Center', www.sourcewatch.org/index.php?title=Coalition_Information_Center (April 25, 2012).

21 The sources have been investigated by the SSCI (2006a, 2006b). For an overview, see Kutz (2006: 81–8; 2009).

22 The OGC started work in September 2002 and was established by a presidential directive in January 2003 (Kutz, 2006: 77–81).

23 This includes the right intention, a line of argument that mainly can be claimed against a war. When, during demonstrations against the war, slogans such as 'No war for oil' were displayed,

they were based on the allegation that the US administration did not reveal their true intentions for going to war. For an overview of the basic reasons for the decision to go to war, see Kutz (2006: 61–75). For an insider's view of the US administration, see Clarke (2004: 265).

24 Transcripts of FBI interviews with Saddam Hussein published in 2009 by the National Security Archive suggest that the Iraqi regime also claimed to have WMD for deterrence purposes against Iran: see www.gwu.edu/~nsarchiv/NSAEBB/NSAEBB279/index.htm (April 25, 2012).

25 The connection was made either indirectly, by talking about Iraq in the context of the 'war on terror', or it was based on an alleged meeting between Mohammed Atta and the head of Iraqi intelligence in Prague. This allegation was withdrawn from the talking points when information surfaced suggesting that Atta was in the United States at the time of the meeting and that the source might have been wrong (SSCI, 2006a: 94–100). The report of the 9/11 Commission published in 2004 denies the link between Iraq and al-Qaeda (National Commission on Terrorist Attacks upon the United States, 2004).

26 *President Delivers State of the Union Address*, January 29, 2002, http://georgewbush-whitehouse.archives.gov/news/releases/2002/01/20020129-11.html (April 25, 2012).

27 *President Discusses Beginning of Operation Iraqi Freedom*, March 22, 2003, http://georgewbush-whitehouse.archives.gov/news/releases/2003/03/20030322.html (April 25, 2012).

28 *Iraq Must Disarm Says President in South Dakota Speech*, November 3, 2002, http://georgewbush-whitehouse.archives.gov/news/releases/2002/11/20021103-3.html (April 25, 2012).

29 *President: Iraqi Regime Danger to America is 'Grave and Growing'*, October 5, 2002, http://georgewbush-whitehouse.archives.gov/news/releases/2002/10/20021005.html (April 25, 2012).

30 *President Bush Outlines Iraqi Threat*, October 7, 2002, http://georgewbush-whitehouse.archives.gov/news/releases/2002/10/20021007-8.html (April 25, 2012).

31 *President's Radio Address*, February 8, 2003, http://georgewbush-whitehouse.archives.gov/news/releases/2003/02/20030208.html (April 25, 2012).

32 *President Delivers 'State of the Union'*, January 28, 2003, http://georgewbush-whitehouse.archives.gov/news/releases/2003/01/20030128-19.html (April 25, 2012).

33 *Remarks by the President in Photo Opportunity with the National Security Team*, September 12, 2001, http://georgewbush-whitehouse.archives.gov/news/releases/2001/09/20010912-4.html (April 25, 2012).

34 *Statement by the President in His Address to the Nation*, September 11, 2001, http://georgewbush-whitehouse.archives.gov/news/releases/2001/09/20010911-16.html (April 25, 2012).

35 *Address to a Joint Session of Congress and the American People*, September 20, 2001, http://georgewbush-whitehouse.archives.gov/news/releases/2001/09/20010920-8.html (April 25, 2012).

36 Regarding the framing of 9/11, see Dietzsch and Kocher (2003) and Silberstein (2002).

37 *President Bush Addresses the Nation*, March 19, 2003, http://georgewbush-whitehouse.archives.gov/news/releases/2003/03/20030319-17.html (April 25, 2012).

An Iconography of Pity and a Rhetoric of Compassion

War and Humanitarian Crises in the Prism of American and French Newsmagazines (1967-95)

Valérie Gorin

Summary

This chapter explores the rhetoric of compassion in media framings of humanitarian crises in a historical and cultural perspective across space and time. It shows the first results of an exploratory analysis of media narratives and images of war between the 1960s and the 1990s. Benefiting from the cover of the mass media, modern humanitarianism has played a controversial role in raising public opinion and influencing politics and has contributed to the appearance of the 'victim' concept and its representation in the media throughout the twentieth century, along with images of pain and death. 'Victimization', or the tendency to induce a hierarchy among victims, offers an immediate reading of such humanitarian crises according to a simplified and Manichean scheme. But since media representations insist on producing figures of innocent suffering such as women and children, their narratives and images often fall back on older collective references and memories. Using 'framing mechanisms' as methodological tools, these results provide representations that favor Christian iconography and historical parallels such as World War II. These representations act as means of qualifying the crises and result ultimately in the moral condemnation of them. While there are clear distinctions in how conflicts are treated when they emerge in western as opposed to Third World countries, on how the ethnic victims' background is presented, and on how the paradigm of distance and proximity is dealt with, these media framings are all aimed at relieving suffering, are based on universally shared values, but are at the same time at risk of resorting to reductive schemes.

The Media and Humanitarian Crises: A Growing Sense of Victimization?

At the beginning of 2009, the conflict between Israel and Hamas in the Gaza Strip[1] emblematized a recurrent dilemma in how wars are covered on an international level. While the Israel Defence Forces (IDF) for strategic reasons[2] had limited media access to Gaza, it had also tried to prevent the international public from seeing too much blood and death.

Nevertheless, the few journalists who managed to get into the Gaza Strip[3] started to send videos and pictures of wounded men and women and, in doing so, highlighted the discussion about civilians being taken as targets both by the Israeli army and Hamas militants. This framing was strengthened even further by the story of Ezzeldeen Abu Al-Aish, a Palestinian doctor who worked in Israel. He lost three daughters and a niece when they were killed by an Israeli shell. While he was providing live reports on Channel 10 every night by phone from the Gaza Strip, his tragedy took place right in front of international viewers on January 16, 2009. It was widely broadcast by international news organizations, thus revealing increased media interest in the collective or individual suffering of others. After the rush of foreign journalists into Gaza immediately following the opening of the border, it even seemed that the war reporting on Gaza was unusually condensed and focused mainly on the human costs of the conflict. The resulting stories were focused on individual, family-scale tragedy, such as this article from *Time*:

> You can measure the destruction in Gaza by the number of bombs dropped or buildings flattened or the price to rebuild it all, but the real cost lies within people like Abed Rabu, whose pain and sense of loss are apparent from the moment you meet him. [...] Israel has begun investigating some of the more egregious allegations about civilian deaths, which are multiplying as Gaza picks itself up from the rubble. (Tim McGirk and Jebel Al-Kashif, 'Voices from the Rubble', *Time*, January 29, 2009)[4]

What is shown by these war 'anecdotes' elicits sociological consideration: far more than a man's suffering, it is the father figure that is being focused on and the loss of his children. While this is hardly unique to this war, as we read in recent studies on the use of children in international news coverage (Moeller, 2002; Wells, 2007), this type of framing reveals a growing concern for children as 'innocent victims':

> A story that uses children is seemingly transparent in its meaning. Dead children [...] have become too familiar icons at the turn of the millennium. Today's disasters, which are hard to follow even with a scorecard, are made more comprehensible and accessible by the media's referencing of children – even if that focus on children is a false or distorted consciousness, a simulacrum of the event. (Moeller, 2002: 37)

The 'media's referencing of children' is not new and is part of the history of modern humanitarianism. Western sensibilities toward the innocent victims of war were already characteristic of the aftermath of World War I.[5] Benefiting from the cover of the mass media, modern humanitarianism has played a controversial role in arousing public awareness and influencing politics (Minear et al., 1996; Robinson, 2001). It has thus contributed to the appearance of the 'victim' concept and its representation in the media during the twentieth century, together with the associated images of pain and death.

'Victimology' or 'victimization' then offers an immediate reading of the various types of people involved in humanitarian crises by dividing them into a simplistic scheme of 'villains', 'victims' and 'heroes' (this refers to humanitarian actors in the field). This has raised the concern of Rony Brauman, a former head of Médecins Sans Frontières (MSF),[6] who produced a series of documents (Brauman, 1993; Brauman and Backmann, 1996) in which he discusses the concept of 'the purity of the victim status':

> [The media insist on] the symbolic level of the 'victim status' [...], this one being considered as a victim only when he or she is seen as an effigy of unfair suffering, of hurt innocence. Victim of a cruel nature, of an absurd war – others' wars are always absurd –, of merciless armed gangs, of a bloody dictator, but pure victim, non-participant.[7] (Brauman and Backmann, 1996: 24)

Trapped in what may be considered an insensitive iconography, the media representations of humanitarian crises insist on compassion 'clichés' that have in fact been perpetuated over time. Therefore, an effort should be made to gain better historical understanding of these types of framing.

This chapter explores the rhetoric of compassion from a humanitarian perspective across space and time. If recent works have shown the salience of a sensationalist, emotional and compassionate discourse in the media reporting of recent conflicts (Moeller, 1999), they still lack a deeper understanding of the historical and cultural perspective (Mesnard, 2002). Indeed, if media representations insist on figures of innocent suffering, such as women and children, their narratives and images often fall back on older collective references and memories. The media discourses have then helped to sustain the persistence of stereotypes and 'clichés' in social representations of the 'self' and 'the other'.

The aim of this chapter is to propose the first results of an exploratory analysis of media narratives and images of war between the 1960s and the 1990s. Four humanitarian crises resulting from armed conflicts were chosen with the intention of drawing on a historical and geographical perspective: the Biafra Civil War and famine (1967–70);[8] the Lebanon War (1975–90), which is limited here, however, to the specific period that involved international military intervention (1982–84);[9] the Bosnian War as part of the general conflict in the Balkans (1992–95);[10] and the Somali Civil War and famine.[11]

Based on an analysis of 'framing mechanisms' (Ghanem, 1996) taken from a sample composed of major illustrated reports between 1967 and 1993, the analysis will focus on a particular medium that consists of four international and national newsmagazines: *Time*, *Newsweek*, *Le Nouvel Observateur* and *L'Express*. This empirical comparative study will help us to understand the media representations of civil wars over time (from the late 1960s to 1970s to the 1990s) and space (western and African spheres), especially when it comes to conflicts in the Third World.[12] This study focuses on the concept of framing and its semio-pragmatic applications surrounding the visibility of the 'pain of others' (Sontag, 2002) in order to underline how collective memory is deeply rooted in the media shaping of international conflicts.

Framing Pity in Media Narratives and Pictures

The frames used by journalists cannot be distinguished from social representations, both of them influencing each other symbolically in the way they shape and understand events, especially when they involve distant cultures and worlds: 'Framing is concerned with the way interests, communicators, sources, and culture combine to yield coherent ways of understanding the world, which are developed using all of the available verbal and visual symbolic resources' (Reese, 2003: 11). The symbolic aspect in these media representations of international events, particularly with respect to armed conflicts that generate humanitarian emergencies, can hardly be underestimated.

Humanitarian action is a modern concept that is closely allied with charity, that is, those forms of helpful acts that have appeared in older societies since the rise of Christendom. Christian iconography thus includes countless images illustrating gestures of pity and devotion, from saints to madonnas, scenes of *pietà* persistent throughout the twentieth century. In addition, biblical metaphors of the Apocalypse have since made their way into contemporary media language, thereby participating on a broad linguistic scale in the depiction of horror.

Nowadays, talking about humanitarian action involves in fact summoning up a particular iconic imagery, a sort of factual referent that in words and images summarizes a given situation at a specific time:

Action is not separable from representation, to the point where the latter is decisive for the first. Rescuing a victim (or, more modestly, donating so that lives can be saved), or resorting to media to denounce what civilians are subjected to, ask from me to call at the threshold of action, before its beginning. Then, during its development, a set of representations – also of myself – that support my decision, guide my practice and provide myself and others with the necessary presence for its recognition. (Mesnard, 2002: 8)[13]

These factual referents that are specific to collective memories have not only been based on Christian iconography but also on older media events and sensationalist reports that have involved history since then. Sometimes characterized by a politics of the spectacle and denounced as a 'charity business' by some nongovernmental organizations (NGOs) such as MSF, these media representations of humanitarian crises are linked to the history of the live report and the competition between newsmagazines and television. After the first broadcast wars such as that in Vietnam in the 1960s, the living-room war effect emphasized the visible aspect of reality, whether it be still or moving images aimed at summarizing events.

Photojournalism had to respond to the competition from television, first by insisting on content, with newsmagazine reporters having a little more time in the field than other reporters to carry out a more detailed analysis of the situation; second, by using visual and title effects to enhance the scoop, such as the famous slogan of *Paris Match*: 'The weight of words, the impact of pictures.' By working in difficult and stressful situations in the context of armed conflicts, journalists are tempted to use older schemes of perception in order to try and summarize the ins and outs of a crisis:

> News must be immediate, dramatic and novel. Stories are simplified and personalized, with viewers or readers encouraged to identify with characters or to make judgements about them. There is titillation, in the sexual sense, or in the wider sense of arousing excited curiosity, through emphasis on the horrific – blood, injury and violence. Readers' responses are affected by language, tone, style and delivery. (Berrington and Jemphrey, 2003: 227–28)

One way to measure this emphasis on the horrific aspects of humanitarian crises is to analyze the 'framing mechanisms' that have been identified by Salma Ghanem (1996). Pictures, titles, quotes and subheadings reveal a particular *mise-en-scène* that helps to identify the salient aspects of media representations of an event. Hence, framing mechanisms were systematically analyzed in this empirical comparative study of approximately 500 illustrated reports, all published in the two major newsmagazines in the United States (*Time* and *Newsweek*) and two in France (*Le Nouvel Observateur* and *L'Express*).

In an initial step, a classic thematic content analysis done using data analysis software (Atlas.ti) was used to identify the general framings used in newsmagazines, especially those involving the humanitarian side of these conflicts. Then, in a second step, a semio-pragmatic analysis was conducted on those 'framing mechanisms' that reenforce the humanitarian aspects, by examining both pictures and the semantics of titles and quotations: 'through their systematic choices of word and image, the media not only expose audiences to the spectacles of distant suffering but also, in so doing, simultaneously expose them to specific dispositions to feel, think, and act toward each instance of suffering' (Chouliaraki, 2008: 372).

In their reports of suffering, the media – sometimes unconsciously – rely on the proximity-distance paradigm between spectators and victims, thus playing a role in the way the public perceives events:

> The spectator is, compared to the media, in the position [...] of someone to whom a proposition of commitment is being made. [The statements and images from the media combine] a description of the suffering and an expression of a particular way to be concerned about it, they propose to the spectator a precise mode of emotional, linguistic and conative commitment. (Boltanski, 1993: 215)[14]

Though we will not insist here on the effect of the media on the public and the implications that media content have for potential action, it is important to underline how these framings involve a graduation, or hierarchy, in the emergency level that is proclaimed and in the characterization of the specific crises. This process is divided by Boltanski into three topics, or schemes of functioning: the topic of denunciation, the topic of sentiment and the esthetic topic (Boltanski, 1993: 91–189).

If esthetics are particularly significant in evoking images of pity, the two other topics function as means of labeling persecutors, provoking moral condemnation, encouraging military intervention (the topic of denunciation) and depicting victims and emotions (the topic of sentiment), as has been stated by Chouliaraki:

> Two dimensions of the spectator–sufferer relationship are relevant to the analysis of the 'eloquence' of pity, its production in meaning. These are the dimensions of proximity-distance and watching-acting. How close or how far away does the news story place the spectator vis-à-vis the sufferer? How is the spectator 'invited' by the news story to react vis-à-vis the sufferer's misfortune – look at it, feel for it, act on it? (Chouliaraki, 2008: 374)

Consequently, the following questions derived from these concepts are related to the identification of these specific humanitarian framings:

1. Is there any significance given to the suffering of innocents?
2. Are there any specific visual framings?
3. What about the rhetoric used?
4. Are there any differences between US and French newsmagazines?

The 'Topic of Denunciation': Crises Qualifications and Moral Condemnation

Labeling a conflict with the term 'massacre' or 'genocide' is scarcely insignificant and often recalls a past event that is still present in people's memory. As we have pointed out before, historical parallels play an important role in the way journalists characterize conflicts, parallels that are in fact an essential part of the history of humanitarian action. In his study of the representation of victims in collective memory, the French historian Philippe Mesnard (2002) has identified two memorable and disruptive periods in the history of conflicts during the twentieth century.

The first one is related to World War II and the genocide of European Jews. Absolute symbols of 'total war' and the failure of western democracies to confront barbarism, the large-scale bombings of cities and civilians, the endless sieges and battles, and the massive human losses have been a turning point in the war reporting. Above all, pictures of Nazi concentration and extermination camps and the scale of the Jewish genocide represented a unique moment in history (Zelizer, 1998). As a result of the horror and incredulity this event provoked, any comparison with a previous conflict was made impossible, marking this genocide as the ultimate reference point of atrocity.

The second turning point identified by Mesnard occurred in the late 1960s, somewhere between the Biafra Civil War and the Vietnam War. Both of these conflicts took place at a time when newsmagazines were competing with television, thus marking this period as the 'golden era' of photojournalism. Characteristic of these distant wars was that reports of civilians' slaughter formed a memorable point at a time of an impressive social and political activism in western societies.[15] It was emblematic of the appearance of war casualties involving innocents, with iconic images of the starving African child and the Napalm girl in Vietnam.[16]

References to World War II and the Jewish genocide are frequent in the reports analyzed in this study, both implicitly and explicitly. As the Biafra crisis exploded in media coverage during the summer of 1968, that is, at the height of the famine, the parallels drawn between the situation of Ibos rebels and the Jews were frequent. They were considered 'the Jews of Africa' (*Le Nouvel Observateur*, February 14, 1968: 14) and have been called the victims of 'the largest pogrom in contemporary African history' ('Martyrdom and Birth of a Nation', *Le Nouvel Observateur*, August 26, 1968: 18–9). At the same time, a discussion of the definition of genocide arose in political circles in France, mainly due to the activism of young French doctors such as Bernard Kouchner (who will later found MSF). Many pictures, however, by focusing on close-ups of starving children gathered along the walls of huts, played on the limits of the parallels, as this caption in *Time* indicates: 'In this land, the choice seems to be between starvation and slaughter' ('A Bitter African Harvest', July 12, 1968: 20). The question of genocide will regularly appear later on, especially in the case of Bosnia and the issue of ethnic cleansing.

When it comes to urban and guerrilla fighting, such as in Beirut during the Lebanese War, the parallels were obvious between the situation in Beirut and the famous city sieges and the brutality of World War II. Indeed, at the beginning of the Israeli surprise offensive on Beirut in the summer of 1982, the city was seen as 'the new Stalingrad' ('Beirut: The Palestinian Agony', *L'Express*, June 25, 1982: 62–3). At the time of the slaughter in Sabra and Chatila in September 1982, parallels with the atrocities of 1939–45 were re-enforced, and the Palestinian refugee camps were compared with 'ghettos', the 'indiscriminate massacre of women, old people and children' with a 'pogrom' ('For the Honor of Israel …', *Le Nouvel Observateur*, September 25, 1982: 38), and persecutors even tried to erase evidence of the events: 'And when it was over, they attempted, in a manner reminiscent of World War II, to destroy the evidence by bulldozing the bodies into makeshift common graves' ('The New Lebanon Crisis', *Time*, September 27, 1982: 8–12).

It seems that this explosion of violence is not understandable in the late twentieth century, which has also seen the rise of human rights and the end of long-lasting conflicts in western societies. For European readers, this violence cannot be explained and brings humanity back to its primitive origins, such as it appears again in the massacres and ethnic cleansing during the Bosnian War: 'Many of Sarajevo's 300,000 remaining residents are wondering why outside powers are permitting such primitive violence to unfold on the very doorstep of a postmodern Europe that has supposedly outgrown it' ('The Siege of Sarajevo', *Newsweek*, July 6, 1992: 22–3).

Witnesses, particularly aid workers who are sometimes witnesses of daily killings in the field, are not sparing with the parallels, sometimes unbelievable, they draw to the past, when barbarism was common in the practice of war, long before any law of war had been established. Thus, a Red Cross worker talks of 'going back to the Middle Ages' when speaking of the rescue of civilians, while Rony Brauman questions western passivity in the face of 'butchery [...] at the doors of Europe' (*Le Nouvel Observateur*, June 4, 1992: 64–6).

Such war crimes, whether they be the slaughter of civilians or ethnic cleansing, demand punishment at a higher level, and hence reenact the memories of World War II and the prosecution for crimes against humanity, which *L'Express* calls 'the impossible new Nuremberg' (*L'Express*, February 4, 1993: 18–9) of war crimes in Bosnia. This was already the case after the massacre of Sabra and Chatila, all newsmagazines having covered the investigation and its conclusion in 1983. 'The Verdict is guilty' (*Time*, February 2, 1983: 6–14) indicates a clear universal condemnation as pictures of disemboweled bodies remind readers of the intolerable, blind violence against innocents.

Later on, parallels with the pictures of Nazi camps are clearly obvious in the case of the so-called 'death camps' in Bosnia in August 1992: 'Life and death in the camps' (*Newsweek*, August 17, 1992: 13–4), 'The spectre of the camps ...' (*Le Nouvel Observateur*, August 6, 1992: 40–1), 'Must it go on?' (*Time*, August 17, 1992: cover). These metaphors are clearly amplified by iconic images of emaciated bodies behind wire fences, reminding one of Bergen-Belsen and Auschwitz.

Such graphic and semantic violence demands intervention, which is the second step in media discourses. The question of western intervention in such conflicts is fundamental. It did not happen in the case of Biafra; at the time, action was mainly limited to medical and food supplies being provided by humanitarian associations such as the Red Cross. Indeed, western intervention in the form of military-humanitarian operations has occurred more frequently in the 1990s, although they were mainly discussed in political and diplomatic spheres (Price and Thompson, 2002). An increasingly central actor on the international scene, the United Nations (UN), had already sent a coalition of foreign powers to Lebanon in 1978.[17]

For Bosnia, it was asked, 'Why Europe is paralysed?' (*Le Nouvel Observateur*, June 4, 1992: editorial), or 'Should the West go to Sarajevo?', while the Serbian outrages were compared with Nazi atrocities: 'We don't even have the strength to look at those pictures of "ethnic cleansing", that in the past the whole world – or almost – would have fought' (*L'Express*, December 18, 1992: editorial).[18]

Partly influenced by the involvement of Bernard Kouchner, then Secretary of Humanitarian Action in the French government, western nations helped to provide emergency aid through 'humanitarian corridors'.[19] Although a UN coalition had intervened beginning in March 1992, difficult stories of the martyrdom of civilians shot in cross fire and pictures of dead bodies in the streets of Sarajevo during the summer of 1992 made the UNPROFOR (United Nations Protection Force) look ineffective in a place where 'there's no peace to keep' ('Bosnia: The US Does Little for the War's Victims', *Newsweek*, August 23, 1993: 16).

By contrast, while the UNOSOM (United Nations Operation in Somalia) coalition was disregarded because of its useless actions in Somalia at the same time, the continual violence against civilians and the rising famine called for a humanitarian operation that led to the media-glorified US intervention in December 1992.[20] Instead of relief aid workers, figures of soldiers replaced the humanitarian delegates in the field, and big cover pages celebrated the new modern hero: 'As Operation Restore Hope begins, Somalis want the US to stay long enough to fix not just their diet but also their society' ('Great Expectations', *Time* special report, December 21, 1992: 32–5).

Such stories of US soldiers acting as new aid providers were often accompanied by pictures framing a crowd of young, smiling Somalis, shaking hands with foreigners in fatigues. A silent crowd, one could say, as they waited for food. They were almost never offered a chance to express themselves in the lines of the foreign press, although this was not true of the victims in Sarajevo. This reenforces a perceptible colonialist stereotype in the western media, as Chang et al. (1987) have stressed. According to this stereotype, African conflicts are still considered the result of tribalism.

While it already appeared in the coverage of the Biafra crisis, Africans have since then been regarded as a massive crowd of silent and passive sufferers. They are presented as eternal victims who cannot live without foreign support, as if their fate deserved less attention, thus questioning the way the media report on suffering according to the ethnic victims' background:

> [T]here has been only a limited amount of news space and time devoted to the coverage of Third World countries in the Western media, especially in the United States. Of the limited amount of news coverage, critics charged, the Western news media tend to treat Third World nations in a negative manner, thus reinforcing stereotypes against those countries. (Chang et al., 1987: 397)

Such a framing was widespread in the 1960s, during a period of big conflicts relating to decolonialization. During the Biafra crisis, the explosion of violence between the Ibos and Nigerians would trigger discussion on the prerogative of fury among African tribes, as *Time* underlines by title 'On Tribalism as the Black Man's Burden' (August 23, 1968: 1819). 25 years later, this postcolonialist perspective is still not completely absent when *Newsweek* publishes a special issue on 'Africa: The Curse of Tribal Wars', linking 'Africa's wild profusion of languages, religions and ethnic groups' to an 'unparalleled cultural diversity' that 'brings with it a constant risk of conflict and bloodshed' (June 21, 1993: cover). From the French doctors acting as lonely heroes in the Biafra famine to Marines providing shelters and rice bags to those in the beaches of Mogadishu, it seems that Africa is trapped in passivity and plagued with a history of tribal rivalry, in contrast to Europe, where violence was thought to have been erased.

The 'Topic of Sentiment': Toward a Typology of Victims and Emotions

In her study on the 'discourse of global compassion', Birgitta Höijer points out the existence of a certain 'ideal victim', whereby 'some victims are "better" than others' (Höijer, 2004: 516). As we have outlined early on, there is a clear difference in the geographical origin of victims;

the closer they are to Europe, the better chances they have to solicit a response from the western publics and its pity. There is also a defined hierarchy in the sociology of the victim; age and gender play an important role. Men are usually taken as potential combatants and are rarely used in pictures used to illustrate civilian casualties. Women have less opportunity to fight and therefore embody the female incarnation of softness, motherhood and fragility. Weakness is also an attribute of old people, their tired bodies appealing to the cameras. But as Brauman (1993) comments, purity is deeply connected with victimology. Thus, who can be purer or more innocent than a child? 'This iconicity means that in war reporting, images of children are critical sites on which narratives about the legitimacy, justification and outcomes of war are inscribed' (Wells, 2007: 55).

Because of this, Biafra offers an interesting case study. As the first massively covered African famine, it is because of the appearance of iconic images of starving African children and their associated attributes, such as swollen bellies, blond hair due to kwashiorkor and skeletal bodies. They embody the slow 'agony' of the innocents and the 'living-dead' at the height of the famine in August 1968 ('Martyrdom and Birth of a Nation', *Le Nouvel Observateur*, August 26, 1968: 18–9). Depicted as a 'children's war' ('Agony in Biafra', *Time*, August 2, 1968: 19), the conflict in Biafra called upon the will of western citizens to endure this tragedy and maybe act to put an end to the injustice. As Wells (2007) argued,

> Representations of children have a very specific place in the iconography of war. Unlike images of adults that are inscribed into discourses of moral blame and political calculation, images of children may be fitted into a universalizing discourse. In such a discourse, 'the world's children' should be protected from the conflicts of adults (extending from parental conflict through to international conflict), and deserve the care and concern of any adult, regardless of their national or political allegiances. (Wells, 2007: 66)

A similar media representation is decisive for conflicts in Europe. At the beginning of 1982, *Time* had published a special issue on the case of 'Children of War' (January 11, 1982: 16–39), its correspondents having visited war-torn countries such as Cambodia, Ireland and Lebanon to meet more than 30 children and their living conditions. Perfect apolitical incarnations, these children at the same time embody the future of a nation: 'Children are a synecdoche for a country's future, for the political and social well-being of a culture' (Moeller, 2002: 39).

As a consequence, when Operation Peace of the Galilee started in June 1982, *Time* was tempted to track down those Lebanese children who were used in its first report in January, to illustrate their lives under a siege: 'The hope was to find these children alive after three weeks of war; if not to meet them face to face, then at least to learn of their whereabouts' ('Seven Days in a Small War', July 19, 1982: 14–9).

The result was a six-page report, written as a diary, which on a daily basis followed the lives of four children in a ruined city, boys and girls, some grieving their dead parents, others playing soldier, one of them being wounded. Through this individualization, their tragedies in fact personify the future of every child trapped in a situation of violence and act on western viewers at an emotional level. In order to do so, the media choose 'to position children's injuries as an exceptional, unforeseen and certainly unintended outcome of war. While the agents of "our side's" military violence are routinely erased in representations of war, "our" agency in rescuing the child from these unintended consequences is highlighted in more or less dramatic ways' (Wells, 2007: 66).

The choice to write this war report as a diary is quite interesting; more than simply an external account by a journalist-witness, it offers a very specific focus on individualization, thus enhancing the readers' capacity to get to the very heart of the story and questioning the moral justification of a war: 'the human presence of the sufferer [...] ranges from an undifferentiated mass of "miserable", [...] to an individual with a personal biography and a cultural history' (Chouliaraki, 2008: 383).

The same result was produced by the story of the 'Child of Srebrenica' in May 1993. The boy, called Sead Bekric, was photographed as blinded, covered in blood, lying on a stretcher. The picture was widely broadcast and made the front cover in publications such as *Newsweek* (May 10, 1993: cover). The boy became a sort of icon, an innocent target of adults' savagery. In discussing his story, *L'Express* explained the necessity of showing such pictures (May 6, 1993: 5) by remaking the whole circle from the 'bombed child, the blinded child, the saved child' to 'the exhibited child', as if the focus on an individual's tragedy would be the perfect alibi for refusing such tragedies on a larger scale: 'Some people fear that this image will trivialize the unbearable. On the contrary, it shows it, and writes it into collective memory. And, without the picture of the wounded child, Srebrenica would have risked being erased.'[21]

Yet such an increasing focus on the figures of innocence embodied by children must not suppress the fact that civilians, no matter how old they are, are regular targets in armed conflicts:

> The de facto hierarchy is expressed in how the media report on war crimes, for example. Crowned by the most innocent, the hierarchy begins with infants and then includes, in descending order, children up to the age of 12, pregnant women, teenage girls, elderly women, all other women, teenage boys, and all other men. (Moeller, 2002: 49)

Lebanon consecrated the framing of civilians as the first casualties in war, trapped in a city siege under bombardment and taken as the 'spoils of war' (*Time*, June 28, 1982: cover) or 'as hostages' ('The Dark Days of Yasser Arafat', *Le Nouvel Observateur*, July 3, 1982: 34–6). This *mise-en-scène* was even strengthened by pictures of complete destruction, old women crying in the midst of the ruins of the buildings. The story of Beirut later influenced the story of the Sarajevo siege during the Bosnian War, something quite obvious when one compares the covers from French and US newsmagazines in 1982–83 and with those in 1992–95.[22] A corresponding recurrence can be seen in the use of language, with the increase in religious semantics during the Bosnian War and the famine in Somalia: civilians are being 'crucified' and 'sacrificed' ('With the Sacrificed in Sarajevo', *Le Nouvel Observateur*, June 25, 1992: 52–8) or 'possessed' ('The Possessed in Mogadishu', *Le Nouvel Observateur*, September 3, 1992: 48–9), mutilated in an 'inferno' ('A Taste of the Inferno', *Newsweek*, September 14, 1992: 14–5), carrying their dead children such as this 'Pieta of Baidoa' ('Landscape of Death', *Time*, December 14, 1992: 30–3).

Contemplating other people's suffering implies a distance separating those regarding and those regarded, 'us' and 'them':

> The display of a politics of pity then supposes two classes of men, unequal, not with respect to merit, like in a justice issue, but only with respect to happiness. These two classes must be, on the other hand, in touch enough so that happy people can contemplate, directly or indirectly, the suffering of the unfortunates, however distant or unconcerned enough, so that their experiences and their actions can remain clearly separated. (Boltanski, 1993: 18)[23]

There is a clear difference in the media coverage of victims in a western country compared with that of victims in the Third World, as we have already emphasized. The paradigm of distance and proximity is particularly relevant here and could be seen from our analysis. If the wars in Lebanon and Bosnia were more extensively covered in our sample, the media discourses also called for an immediate denunciation and ending of the slaughter of civilians. This was less in evidence in the Biafra or the Somalia Wars:

> The more remote or exotic the place, the more likely we are to have full frontal views of the dead and dying. [...] These sights carry a double message. They show a suffering that is outrageous, unjust, and should be repaired. They confirm that this is the sort of thing which happens in that place. (Sontag, 2002: 63f)

But the focus on local victims rapidly comes to an end as soon as western countries intervene in a conflict and suffer their first losses, as was the case in Lebanon and Somalia. Right after the suicide attacks on buildings sheltering US and French troops in October 1983, which resulted in the death of 256 Marines and 58 French soldiers, the reports concentrated entirely on the dead soldiers and the call for retaliation.[24] Pictures of sobbing civilians in the ruins and wounded children in hospitals were replaced by soldiers carrying the bodies of their dead buddies, on shocking covers all framed in red and black.

The coverage was even more extreme in Somalia following the crash of two US helicopters in October 1993. The usual situation of Americans watching Africans starve was suddenly reversed; Americans were then contemplating 'one' of their soldiers, the lynched body of a white male being tortured by a savage crowd. Somali militiamen held one of the survivors, the pilot Michael Durant, as a prisoner and broadcast videos of his detention. The new victims became 'our' own dead, and the main focus, particularly in the US media, was on putting an end both to the detention of Durant and the military intervention in Somalia.

It seemed as if all of a sudden the glorious humanitarian intervention had turned into a military fiasco, raising doubts about the US ability to maintain peace.

'Trapped in Somalia', 'Bloodbath: What Went Wrong?', 'The Making of a Fiasco', 'Confronting Chaos', 'Anatomy of a Disaster': such is the litany of titles in *Newsweek*'s and *Time*'s reports on the aftermath (October 18, 1993). Victims were no longer taken as moral justification for humanitarian or military actions; only the safe return of 'our troops', framed with several polls that questioned the rightfulness of the intervention in Somalia ('Do you approve of having US troops in Somalia?', 'What should be the main goal of the US in Somalia?'), was now considered in the media discourse, as if the slaughter of civilians had never really taken place.

Discussion

In this empirical, comparative study of the media representation of humanitarian crises in two different cultural spheres, we noticed similarities and some differences in how the international news is covered and framed. We must underline, however, that this was only an exploratory analysis that would require a more systematic application of more extensive data, for example, by multiplying the comparison of wars over time and space. Moreover, while this study was made using 'framing mechanisms', it limited itself to the most obvious semiotic signs in media representations (i.e., pictures, titles, headlines and quotations).

A further investigation could be conducted with in-depth discourse analyses. This would help to identify at a more precise level whether the effects that have been observed at a first framing level, that is, one imposed by the impact of images, by titles written in huge letters, and by highlighted quotations, may also be found in the argumentation used in the articles:

The familiarity of certain photographs builds our sense of the present and immediate past. Photographs lay down routes of reference, and serve as totems of causes: sentiment is more likely to crystallize around a photograph than around a verbal slogan. (Sontag, 2002: 76)

Nonetheless, this analysis does raise a series of thought-provoking issues. The use of a historical perspective in media analysis allows us to consider the persistence of schemes of representation in different discourses. The majority of studies on the coverage of contemporary international conflicts is limited in time and space, thus, for example, the studies on the wars of the 1990s (Pieterse, 1997; Moeller, 1999). Despite this, we need to broaden our media understanding to encompass a longer period, one corresponding to the history of conflicts in the twentieth century. Media representations are, more than anything else, those of the journalists, and they cannot be separated from the more general context of social representations that are promoted on the basis of how they describe and perceive the world. These social representations often evolve over an extended period of time, some events suddenly crystallizing as absolute reference points in collective memory, as Mesnard (2002) has shown for World War II, Biafra and Vietnam.

Consequently, in the four newsmagazines chosen for this study, we have found a recurrence of cultural, traditional codes for western societies, both in pictures and in terms of semantics. These codes function at several levels; first, they act as classification categories, in particular by defining what is a 'massacre' or what is 'genocide'. Second, they indicate a gradation in the distinctiveness and scale of the event and do so by the extensive use of a connoted vocabulary, which makes use of references to the Judeo-Christian roots of western societies and the religious semantics (charity) of modern humanitarianism. Finally, they label a crisis by choosing quick shortcuts to past events, thus acting as simplifying summaries: 'Formulaic coverage of similar types of crises makes us feel that we really have seen this story before. We've seen the same pictures, heard about the same victims, heroes and villains, read the same morality play' (Moeller, 1999: 13). As Moeller has emphasized, this simplifying scheme often functions by using an archaic triangular relation between the victim ('the good one'), the persecutor ('the bad one') and the hero ('the savior').

The limit of sensibility in the West has developed strongly since the beginning of the twentieth century, revealing new concerns for justice and the well-being of mankind. It is related to what the English sociologist Geoffrey Gorer (1955) has called 'the pornography of death' or the unbearable witness of 'the pornography of pain' (Halttunen, 1995). The rise of 'victim status' can also be explained by the fact that civilians have become the principal casualties in conflicts since World War II, though a trivialization with regard to certain situations has led to 'compassion fatigue' (Moeller, 1999).

Nonetheless, the victim remains an undefined element. It changes depending on the type of crisis involved: while the focus was largely on children during the Biafra crisis, they appear alongside old women in Lebanon and Bosnia and combine with a crowd of all ages in Somalia.

How can we explain a particular focus on a certain kind of victim at a given time? There are still few answers to this question, although some hypotheses can be put forward. Focusing on an individual's career, instead of on an anonymous crowd, emphasizes the 'propositions of commitment' made by the reader (Boltanski, 1993: 215). Thus, they allow identification with, or even indignation concerning, their poor condition. We can see this, for example, in an article of *Newsweek* published during the Bosnian War in which a multitude of refugees are drowned in the same anonymous voice: 'All we can do is suffer: the plight of Yugoslavia's 1.5 million refugees' (May 25, 1992: 10–1).

How do I make the suffering of a people mine? How do I confront an individual's tragedy with which I can identify? This approach differs radically from the *Time* article 'Children of War' or the story of the 'Child from Srebrenica'. This seems to be a privileged angle in the media representations of very recent conflicts, as we saw in the case of the war in Gaza, at that moment in the media coverage when the conflict had ended, when it seemed there was only place for laments of the innocent and for rebuilding lives that had been torn apart.

In spite of the ethnic differences and their impact on the visibility of victims, this type of framing is quite often chosen in media representations of humanitarian crises as soon as the lives of civilians are at stake, when the international community is called upon because of trampling of fundamental human rights: meanwhile, the fate of the victim (or victims) hangs in the balance. The categorical status of the victim, as Brauman (1993: 150–7) points out, is instrumental in the construction of an 'international event' that would command the attention of a mediated public. The ideal, authentic victim is pure inasmuch as he or she has been deprived of their basic rights and meaningful agency.

Moreover, the victim is public insofar as the conditions of his or her existence have become an object of discourse (DeChaine, 2002: 362). The more victims are deprived of their rights, the more their innocence is affected, the more they call out for an injustice to be corrected. By headlining 'Belgrade's injured innocence' (June 22, 1992: 12–3), *Newsweek* chose a metaphor that includes a city and all of its inhabitants, who were trapped in a fury beyond understanding, while the story was illustrated with the picture of a woman ripped open, as all of the ethnic cleansing, local nationalisms and atrocities on all sides[25] could be embodied in this hopeless victim.

Such stories focus on a feeling that the international community had neglected the civilians and its own ideals of liberty, democracy, security and peace: 'How Dare You Leave Us Alone to Die!' (*Le Nouvel Observateur*, December 9, 1993: 76–8). This feeling is even heightened when children are depicted, victims of men's fury and adults' abandonment:

> Key themes of the discourse of childhood, including the family as the ideal site of childhood, converge so that the image of the lone child symbolizes abandonment. Cutting out of the frame the adults and other children who surround the child places the viewer of the image in the role of these missing carers. Children on their own are abstracted from their culture and society. [...] Rather, if lone children are not rescued then they will be abandoned to their fate. (Wells, 2007: 63–4)

The focus of victims' representations involves imbalances, but it reveals a social imagery concerned with the relief of suffering, based on universally shared values, at the risk of falling into reductive schemes. NGOs have been attacking some of the media, accusing them of sensationalism and trivialization. Such criticism was largely initiated by MSF, though it had itself used media hype in its spectacular humanitarian operations at the end of the 1970s.[26] Despite this, MSF has recently been appealing to the Seven Agency, a renowned photographic agency of famous war photographers, in order to inform people about the forgotten crisis in Congo.[27] One result of this was a photo exhibition called 'Democratic Republic of the Congo: forgotten war', with endless pitiful scenes in black and white, close-ups of skeletal bodies and mothers watching over their dying children.

It shows that the imagery of the victim, which can act both as a mobilizing tool and as a reductive one, is far from being outdated and demands that we redefine how we view and categorize others.

Key Points

- Framing mechanisms
- Victimization
- War
- Compassion
- Spectacle of suffering
- Social representations
- Collective memory
- Newsmagazines

Study Questions

1. Victimization has been defined as a tendency to induce a hierarchy in the typology of victims. Choose a case study (e.g., a two-week sample of media coverage of a given conflict) and then define the types of victims represented. What is the preferred gender/age of the victims? Are these victims given the right to speak, and if so, who among them? Is there a tendency to use personification in media discourses (i.e., to focus on individuals in a story)?
2. Media framings of humanitarian crises are made understandable for the public by reference to collective memories. Try to spot these historical parallels in media discourses: Is there any mention of past events? Do the journalists use a particular semantics such as a biblical one?
3. Framing mechanisms often function using the 'double' language of pictures and words. Using a small sample (such as an illustrated report from a newsmagazine) taken from a humanitarian emergency that resulted from an armed conflict, evaluate the use of pictures compared with words. Do you notice a similar framing in the photographs, titles and captions? Do you observe a narrative based on pictures? If so, do these pictures insist on a particular type of framing (emotional, denunciatory etc.)?

Further Reading

Allen, Tim and Jean Seaton (1999) *The Media of Conflict. War Reporting and Representations of Ethnic Violence*. London; New York: Zed Books.

Banks, Anna (1994) 'Images Trapped in Two Discourses: Photojournalism Codes and the International News Flow', *Journal of Communication Inquiry* 18(1): 118–34.

Domke, David, David Perlmutter and Meg Spratt (2002) 'The Primes of Our Times? An Examination of the "Power" of Visual Images', *Journalism* 3(2): 131–59.

Griffin, Michael (2004) 'Picturing America's "War on Terrorism" in Afghanistan and Iraq: Photographic Motifs as News Frames', *Journalism* 5(4): 381–402.

Howe, Peter (2002) *Shooting Under Fire. The World of the War Photographer*. New York: Artisan.

Kenney, Keith R. (1994) 'Images of Africa in News Magazines: Is There a Black Perspective?', *International Communication Gazette* 54(1): 61–85.

Newton, Julianne H. (2001) *The Burden of Visual Truth. The Role of Photojournalism in Mediating Reality*. Mahwah, NJ: Lawrence Erlbaum.

Rose, Gillian (2002) *Visual Methodologies. An Introduction to the Interpretation of Visual Materials*. London; Thousand Oaks, CA: Sage.

Rotberg, Robert I. and Thomas G. Weiss (eds) (1996) *From Massacres to Genocide. The Media, Public Policy, and Humanitarian Crises*. Washington, DC: Brookings Institution.

Shaw, Martin (1996) *Civil Society and Media in Global Crisis. Representing Distant Violence*. London: Pinter.

Weissman, Fabrice (ed.) (2004) *In the Shadow of 'Just Wars'. Violence, Politics, and Humanitarian Action*. Ithaca, NY: Cornell University Press.

Williams, Christopher R. (2008) 'Compassion, Suffering and the Self: A Moral Psychology of Social Justice', *Current Sociology* 56(1): 5–24.

Websites

International Committee of the Red Cross: 'Our world. Your move': www.ourworld-yourmove.org.

VII Photo Agency website: www.viiphoto.com.

United Nations Disaster Management Training Program: The News Media and Humanitarian Action: http://iaemeuropa.terapad.com/resources/8959/assets/documents/UN%20DMTP%20-%20News%20Media%20%20&%20Humanitarian%20Action.pdf.

References

Berrington, Eileen and Ann Jemphrey (2003) 'Pressures on the Press. Reflections on Reporting Tragedy', *Journalism* 4(2): 225–48.

Boltanski, Luc (1993) *La Souffrance À Distance. Morale Humanitaire, Médias Et Politique*. Paris: Editions Métailié; Diffusion Seuil.

Brauman, Rony (1993) 'When Suffering Makes a Good Story', pp. 149–58 in François Jean (ed.) *Life, Death and Aid. The Médecins Sans Frontières Report on World Crisis Intervention*. London: Routledge.

Brauman, Rony and René Backmann (1996) *Les Médias Et l'Humanitaire*. Paris: CFPJ.

Chang, T.-K., P. J. Shoemaker and N. Brendlinger (1987) 'Determinants of International News Coverage in the U.S. Media', *Communication Research* 14(4): 396–414.

Chouliaraki, Lilie (2008) 'The Mediation of Suffering and the Vision of a Cosmopolitan Public', *Global Media and Communication* 9(5): 371–91.

DeChaine, Robert (2002) 'Humanitarian Space and the Social Imaginary. Medecins Sans Frontieres/Doctors Without Borders and the Rhetoric of Global Community', *Journal of Communication Inquiry* 26(4): 354–69.

Ghanem, Salma (1996) 'Media Coverage of Crime and Public Opinion. An Exploration of the Second Level Agenda Setting', Dissertation, Austin, University of Texas.

Gorer, Geoffrey (1955) 'The Pornography of Pain', *Encounter* 5(4): 49–52.

Halttunen, Karen (1995) 'Humanitarianism and the Pornography of Pain in Anglo-American Culture', *The American Historical Review* 100(2): 303–34.

Höijer, Birgitta (2004) 'The Discourse of Global Compassion. The Audience and Media Reporting of Human Suffering', *Media, Culture & Society* 26(4): 513–31.

Mesnard, Philippe (2002) *La Victime Ècran. La Représentation Humanitaire En Question*. Paris: Textuel.

Minear, Larry, Colin Scott and Thomas George Weiss (1996) *The News Media, Civil War, and Humanitarian Action*. Boulder, CO: L. Rienner.

Moeller, Susan D. (1999) *Compassion Fatigue. How the Media Sell Disease, Famine, War, and Death*. New York: Routledge.

——— (2002) 'A Hierarchy of Innocence. The Media's Use of Children in the Telling of International News', *The Harvard International Journal of Press/Politics* 7(1): 36–56.

Pieterse, Jan Nederveen (1997) 'Sociology of Humanitarian Intervention. Bosnia, Rwanda and Somalia Compared', *International Political Science Review* 18(1): 71–93.

Price, Monroe E. and Mark Thompson (2002) *Forging Peace. Intervention, Human Rights and the Management of Media Space*. Edinburgh: Edinburgh University Press.

Reese, Stephen (2003) 'Framing Public Life. A Bridging Model for Media Research', pp. 7–32 in Stephen D. Reese, Oscar H. Gandy and August E. Grant (eds) *Framing Public Life. Perspectives on Media and Our Understanding of the Social World*. Mahwah, NJ: Lawrence Erlbaum.

Robinson, Piers (2001) 'Theorizing the Influence of Media on World Politics. Models of Media Influence on Foreign Policy', *European Journal of Communication* 16(4): 523–44.

Sontag, Susan (2002) *Regarding the Pain of Others*. New York: Farrar, Straus and Giroux.

Wells, Karen (2007) 'Narratives of Liberation and Narratives of Innocent Suffering. The Rhetorical Uses of Images of Iraqi Children in the British Press', *Visual Communication* 6(1): 55–71.

Zelizer, Barbie (1998) *Remembering to Forget. Holocaust Memory through the Camera's Eye*. Chicago: University of Chicago Press.

Notes

1 Called Operation Cast Lead, the Gaza War started on December 27, 2008 and ended on January 18, 2009, with a unilateral cease-fire.

2 Egypt and Israel have had limited access to Gaza since November 2008. Even if the Israeli Supreme Court ruled on December 29, 2008 that foreign journalists should be granted access to Gaza when the border was opened by the military, the IDF refused to comply.

3 These were journalists who were in Gaza before the military operation started. They were mainly reporters for international broadcast television stations, such as Al Jazeera and the

BBC, and for international news organizations. General access for foreign correspondents was only granted on January18, 2009, when the cease-fire was declared.

4 The article relies mainly on the story of Abed Rabu, a father who had two daughters who were wounded and a third one who was shot dead during the war.

5 For example, several charity organizations involved in helping war orphans were founded immediately after 1918, such as the Save the Children Fund (1919).

6 Also called Doctors without Borders.

7 Translated by the author from the original French text: '[Les médias insistent sur] le niveau symbolique du 'statut de la victime' […], celle-ci ne prenant véritablement corps qu'à la condition de pouvoir être vue comme une effigie de la souffrance injuste, de l'innocence meurtrie. Victime d'une nature cruelle, d'une guerre absurde – les guerres des autres sont toujours absurdes -, de bandes armées impitoyables, ou d'un dictateur sanguinaire, mais victime pure, non participante.'

8 Also known as the Nigerian Civil War, this conflict was the result of an attempted secession of the southern provinces of Nigeria, which are mainly inhabited by the Ibos tribe.

9 Also known as the First Lebanon War, it started with the IDF invasion of southern Lebanon after violence erupted between the Palestine Liberation Organisation and Israel.

10 It started after the breakup of the former Yugoslavia into independent republics, the rise of nationalisms in the former country and the increase in ethnic tensions.

11 It started after the ousting of President Siad Barre, resulting in instability among local warlords.

12 In this chapter, we choose to consider Lebanon as a westernized country. Although it is situated in Middle East, its history, culture and civilization have deep ties with the West, especially the country that colonized it, France (a large percentage of the population speak French). Moreover, the results of this study have shown that Lebanese society and its citizens are included in the same media framings as people of European background. As a result, the media seem to disfavor geographical perspective when it is a matter of establishing a connection between the cities and white citizens of the Middle East who live according to western standards and European societies and their citizens.

13 Translated by the author from the original French text: 'L'action n'est pas dissociable de la représentation, au point que celle-ci est un des déterminants de celle-là. Secourir une victime, ou, plus modestement, donner pour que des vies soient sauves, ou bien recourir aux médias pour dénoncer ce que des civils subissent, me demandent de convoquer au seuil de l'action, avant de l'entamer, puis durant son déroulement, un ensemble de représentations – y compris de représentations de moi-même – qui étayent ma décision, guident ma pratique et fournissent à celle-ci la présence nécessaire à sa reconnaissance, à mes yeux comme à ceux des autres.'

14 Translated by the author from the original French text: 'Le spectateur est, par rapport aux médias, dans la position […] de celui à qui est faite une proposition d'engagement. Un autre spectateur, qui lui rapporte une histoire et peut se présenter comme un reporter […] transmet des énoncés et des images […]. Ces énoncés et ces images ne sont pas n'importe quoi. [Ils mêlent] une description de la souffrance et l'expression d'une façon particulière d'en être concerné, ils proposent au spectateur un mode défini d'engagement émotionnel, langagier et conatif.'

15   This is particularly the case for the United States, where the protest movements against the Vietnam War were at their highest level between 1967 and 1969. As for France, May 1968 saw the mobilization of French youth's conscience concerning Third World issues and imperialism.

16   The picture was taken by Nick Ut (AP) in Saigon in 1972.

17   Under the term of UNIFIL, this coalition was placed under the command of the French army. The US army reenforced the coalition in 1982.

18   Translated by the author from the original French text: 'Nous n'avons même plus la force de regarder en face les images d'une 'purification ethnique' qu'en d'autres temps le monde entier – ou presque – combattit.'

19   This was mainly covered in French news magazines; see 'With Mitterand in Sarajevo', *Le Nouvel Observateur* special report, July 2, 1992 and 'Yugoslavia: The Limits of Humanitarian Action', L'Express special report, August 28, 1992.

20   Called Operation Restore Hope, it was conducted by the United Task Force until May 1993.

21   Translated by the author from the original French text: 'D'aucuns craignent que l'image ne banalise l'insoutenable. A l'inverse, elle le montre, et l'inscrit dans les mémoires collectives. Et, sans l'image de l'enfant blessé, Srebrenica risquait d'être massacre.'

22   For example, see 'Lebanon's Legacy', *Time* special report, August 23, 1982; 'Lebanon's Partition', *L'Express* special report, May 5, 1983; 'Hate Thy Neighbor', *Newsweek* special report on Bosnia, January 4, 1993.

23   Translated by the author from the original French text: 'Le déploiement d'une politique de la pitié suppose donc deux classes d'hommes, inégaux, non sous le rapport du mérite, comme dans une problématique de la justice, mais uniquement sous celui du bonheur. Ces deux classes doivent être, d'autre part, suffisamment en contact pour que les gens heureux puissent observer, directement ou indirectement, la misère des malheureux, mais pourtant suffisamment distantes ou détachées pour que leurs expériences et leurs actions puissent demeurer nettement séparées.'

24   For example, see 'Carnage in Beirut', *Time*, October 31, 1983; or 'Beirut: Who?', *L'Express*, November 4, 1983.

25   Although media coverage largely focused on Serbian atrocities during the conflict, later on they also reported on atrocities being committed by the Croatian and Bosnian-Herzegovinian sides.

26   One of them was the launch of an operation to save boat people in 1978.

27   The photographers involved were James Nachtway, Ron Haviv, Gary Knight, Antonin Kratochvil and Joachim Ladefoged. A glimpse of it can be seen on the Seven Agency website: www.viiphoto.com.

Women, the Media and War

The Representation of Women in German Broadsheets between 1980 and 2000

Romy Fröhlich

Summary

Our social consciousness reserves the role of the fighter solely for men. Women are not considered as being authoritative or decisive actors in the context of war and violence. They are instead viewed as more peaceful beings who are naturally opposing war and violent conflict. Consequently, during armed conflicts or other violent crises, female subjects seem to be virtually absent from the public (i.e., media) stage – a place where they are underrepresented even under normal circumstances. One could therefore assert that gender-stereotypical war coverage essentially reduces the experiences of women during war to the emotionalizing, stereotypical role of women, who are in turn supposed to give war coverage an 'affective impulse'. But because there is a significant lack of longitudinal quantitative studies on the media coverage of women during wartime, we do not really have much empirical evidence to support this view. To correct this balance, a framing analysis of quality German newspapers' war coverage between 1980 and 2000 has been conducted using a census of all content. It is the first longitudinal gender-specific content analysis of war coverage ever – not only in Germany. Before presenting the main results from this content analysis, the present contribution will provide a rough description of some of the historical and present-day challenges women face in their careers as war correspondents.

Introduction

Since the dominant model of womanhood demands neither technological competence nor courage nor physical strength, war, technology and manliness are perceived as a combination that apparently excludes women. Furthermore and in accordance with the traditional images of gender, men are even seen as promoters of war. By contrast, women are viewed as more placid beings whose feelings, thoughts and actions tend to be peaceful and who, therefore, almost naturally oppose war, warlike acts and violent conflicts. Women are supposed to resist and suffer and to be peace loving. This is our accepted model of womanhood. Thus, it would seem to be immediately obvious that it is only the role of victim that is left over for women to assume in times of war.

It is no wonder then that the image of the peaceful yet powerless female in need of protection, on the one hand, and the generally war-loving, powerful male who protects women, children and the elderly, on the other, continues to be nurtured especially and quite deliberately by warmongering forces all over the world. Research shows that the media coverage of war adopts these differentiating gender principles. However, the topic of 'women, the media and war' not only addresses the issue of how women are portrayed in the media's war coverage but also involves the issue of how women are represented among the professional content providers responsible for the production of war coverage by the media – that is, war correspondents, journalists and reporters. It is assumed here that both aspects are closely related to each other.

One of the first content analyses of German war coverage – conducted in 1998 (Fröhlich, 2002a, 2002b) – showed that only 9 percent of the analyzed articles had been written by female journalists. This confirms the impression that the press coverage of war remains a decidedly male domain. As a result, the 'particular qualities of the female gaze' that the communication scientist Irene Neverla (cited in Gernhuber, 1996: 20) ascribes to female war correspondents does not play a significant role in the war coverage of daily newspapers in Germany. Until now, however, this question has not been investigated empirically in a really broad and representative way anywhere in the world.

Hence, this chapter presents results from the first and so far only longitudinal (1989–2000) content analysis that has attempted to generate reliable empirical data from a gender perspective on the basis of a census of all content. The 'Female War Correspondents' section briefly describes some historical and present-day challenges women face in their careers as war correspondents. 'The Media Content of War Coverage' section provides a brief overview of German and American research on the representation of women in war coverage. The 'Research Question and Methodology' section presents the research question of our project and provides information about the most important methodological fundamentals, and the 'Results' section then analyzes a selection of results. To conclude, a short summary and a discussion of the prospects for additional research are provided.

Female War Correspondents

Almost everywhere in the world, journalism – especially in high-ranking echelons – remains a male business. This particularly applies to the area of war reporting. Only very few women make it in this specific area of news reporting. In the United States, there are, however, far greater numbers of female war correspondents than in Germany, and this can be traced back through history. As early as the 1840s, the *New York Herald Tribune* had a female foreign correspondent in Europe – Margaret Fuller – who reported on the ins and outs of the revolution for the establishment of a Roman Republic in 1849. During the American Civil War, Jane Swisshelm reported on the events of the war for several newspapers, and the female journalist Anna Benjamin was a correspondent during the Spanish-American War.

Without question one of the most important American pioneers in this domain was Peggy Hull, who was accredited as the first official female war correspondent in the United States by the US Department of War on September 17, 1918 and was also active worldwide as a war correspondent during World War II. In fact, World War II offered quite a wide range of female American journalists new career opportunities. In 1945, 127 female journalists and press photographers were officially accredited by the military as war reporters for the United States. The majority of them even possessed a so-called 'frontline assignment', which allowed them to work within the frontlines of battles.[1] During the period between the end of the war and the early 1950s, most of the female reporters lost their jobs – they were forced to make room for the men returning from war, who were especially to be reintegrated into the workforce. This explains why, for example, in 1968 the United States had far fewer female foreign and war correspondents than during World War II.

In Germany, female war correspondents – in fact, female foreign correspondents in general – do not have near as long a history as in the United States. The audience initially witnessed female journalists in war and crisis-hit areas during the fighting in the former Yugoslavia. Among those female international journalists who brought to our attention the devastating images and information from this nearby war-torn territory were four Germans: Renate Flottau, Susanne Gelhard,[2] Sonja Mikich[3] and Arianne Vučković.

When talking about the occupation of a war reporter, a considerable number of myths exist: the male-dominated image of the war correspondent as an adventurous type, an undaunted hero who risks life and limb to bring the telling images of the war to the world, still prevails. Arianne Vučković writes on this subject:

> I don't believe in the myth of the 'war reporter'. He [sic!] is not a hero; he is far better off than the suffering population. The journalist has money, food, bulletproof vests, helmets and armored cars. And most importantly: he can always leave the war zone and return to his own life. [...] [W]e always only suffer a fraction of what the population has to during war. I want to tell their stories; that's why every human being in the film has a name and not just the male [sic!] politician, who is usually guilty himself. (Vučković, 1996: 14)

The individualization of media coverage cited here is possibly responsible for the creation of a feeling of closeness among the audience. Individualization, however, has to be banned from the context of war reporting, since the major objective is to demonstrate that larger groups of people, the entire population, or whole ethnic communities, and not individuals are involved, as is the case in other violent and aggressive crisis situations. Nevertheless, it seems that female journalists manage to get 'closer' to the actual war through reports and features that aim to be non-anonymous. This proximity is created through their apparent closeness to the victims, on the one hand, and rather surprisingly, to the perpetrators, on the other – as the example of Sonia Mikich shows. One thing that their male colleagues apparently cannot manage to achieve was nicely put by Maria von Welser: 'Women tell stories about people, not frontlines' (cited in Gernhuber, 1996: 21).

How much of a difference it can make under certain circumstances whether a male or female journalist is researching an issue is illustrated in the following extract by

Peter Sartorius, leading editor of the *Süddeutsche Zeitung* and war correspondent in the Balkans for over four years:

> During my travels to the war-torn regions of Bosnia and Croatia, I, just like most of my colleagues, quite frequently met women who told us about the martyrdom they and others had to endure. They were Muslim women. They told us that on the Serbian side there were carefully planned and perfectly executed rape camps. But could we or were we allowed to believe that? Where was, one might rather cynically ask, the proof of these incidents? Was what we were told perhaps only a horrible illusion in tortured minds, the understandable result of exuberant fear? Was the flow of information controlled by propagandists who were only interested in discrediting the Serbs as a barbarous power who carried out dreadful acts of violence […]? One undergoes a learning process during a war in which it is constantly hammered home that no one can be believed and that even tears have no credence. That is why we treated the reports of the women with caution until all the facts were in. […] However, following intensive research especially by the female German journalist Alexandra Stiglmayer and the American Roy Gutman which confirmed the presumptions, I regretted that I had not denounced the crimes when I first heard about them. (Sartorius, 1996: 15)

A further example may indicate how much of a difference it can make if the journalist working on a story is male or female. Regarding her experiences with the 'rape camps', Alexandra Stiglmayer writes, 'The ones who stayed on the story and who produced longer contributions – they were exclusively women. Indeed, I don't know a single male editor whose interest went beyond this "lusty" sensation for our paper' (cited in Gernhuber, 1996: 20).

It is this often asserted proximity to the events of war from the perspective of the victims that makes news coverage nearly always the starting point for political decisions regarding war and peace. And it is exactly this aspect that implies an inherent danger – the danger of utilizing this form of media coverage for military purposes, as was demonstrated by the media coverage of mass rapes in the former Yugoslavia and of the topic of 'violence toward women and children' in recent years.

In this respect, one should also not forget the press conference the day before US bombs were dropped over Iraq during the second Gulf War in 1990–91: acting on the orders of the Kuwaiti government, one of the largest PR agencies in the world – Hill & Knowlton – organized for the invited international press the 'eyewitness account' of a Kuwaiti girl who had supposedly seen rapes in Kuwait city and told how Iraqi soldiers had snatched prematurely born babies from their incubators. It was only discovered at a later stage that the eyewitness account was a fake; the girl presented at the press conference was the daughter of the Kuwaiti Ambassador to the United States.

But PR and war is another highly fascinating topic that deserves intensive research. In any case, it has to be asserted that the media coverage of war(s) in particular offers numerous examples of how women and the fates of women (similar to children and their fates) are interpreted according to the values of the dominating male power elite and utilized or abused for their purposes when decisions are made on war and peace. In the context of such processes, terms such as 'military humanism', 'humanitarian intervention' and 'humanitarian warfare' have been created.

Myths not only play a large part as far as the image of the war correspondent is concerned but also in terms of the content of the war coverage itself. It can be assumed that the image of men and women in war that is created by the media – and indeed by the military too – is determined by cultural myths. For the time being though, it seems valid to assume that the dominating image of women presented in the mass media is characterized by annihilation, trivialization and marginalization. The media content relating to war is no exception here. On the contrary, it is apparent that the annihilation, trivialization and marginalization of women in the media coverage of war is especially explicit.

This annihilation, trivialization and marginalization of women is surely further enhanced by the previously described myth of the peaceful and weak female who is in need of protection and of the warmongering and strong male who protects women. This myth obscures the experiences of women in and about war, thus denying them access to media coverage. It is also the reason behind the presentation of women and their daily life during war as a marginal social problem. In doing so, the experiences of women in war are reduced to an emotionalizing role that is supposed to give war coverage an affective 'kick'.

Hence the most important role of women in war remains that of victims – selected, described and interpreted by male journalists. Women therefore remain without a voice. This process of being silenced is further enhanced by the fact that war victims are usually portrayed as an anonymous mass. We know them mostly from pictures on television that are accompanied by comments from predominantly male journalists. The still very small percentage of female foreign and war correspondents – incidentally far lower than the percentage of women in journalism in general – cannot yet make a difference in this respect.

A further dilemma relating to the mostly male-dominated media coverage arises from the emotionalizing function of women's experiences implied in their reduction to the role of victims in media coverage during wars. This is a dilemma that Peter Sartorius' account of his experiences (described above) illustrates: what lies behind his description? Women – especially in the role of the victim – cannot be trusted at first, since they are too emotional. The life and experiences of women in war are therefore not only marginalized by their being portrayed as victims; they are at the same time trivialized by being reduced to a simple emotionalizing role, since the emphasis on their supposed emotionality apparently reduces their credibility and rationality. This vicious circle is sustained by the argument that 'women are too emotional'. This is probably the basis of the numerous decisions – by let's call them media managers – to not send female journalists as reporters into war.

The argument of emotionality has probably also played a role in the attempt by Alexandra Stiglmayer to offer her report on the rape camps to the German media. Just two days before the report was shown on German television – in the women's magazine *MonaLisa* – she tried to sell her story to leading German political magazines. No one was interested. However, immediately after the report by Stiglmayer was shown on *MonaLisa*, the news magazine *Stern* called the female journalist in Zagreb and offered her a contract for the report that had been declined initially.

The political magazine *Der Spiegel* also started reporting on the topic and, following the contribution to *MonaLisa*, they signed up Cheryl Bernard and Edit Schlafer for a project in which the two internationally renowned sociologists were to report on both rape in general and during war in particular. In addition to this, the account is also an indicator of the enormous significance that television possesses as a leading medium in the journalistic system.

The Media Content of War Coverage

Gender is a socially constructed category that determines the distribution of power between men and women. This principle operates together with, or possibly in opposition to, other principles of differentiation such as class, nationality or ethnic origin. We assume here that gender roles and concepts are, *inter alia*, constructed with the aid of the mass media. Theoretical and empirical research, however, accuses the media of promoting the annihilation, trivialization, marginalization and instrumentalization of women in their coverage of war and violence. This coverage gives the impression that women and their daily lives during war are to be treated largely as a social borderline problem or, at best, presented relatively prominently for the purpose of legitimizing war – especially since, in the media, the role of the victim is generally assigned to females (see del Zotto, 2002; Elsthain, 1982; Enloe, 1994, 2000a, 2000b; Fröhlich, 2000, 2002a, 2002b).

Furthermore, theoretical and empirical research reasons that war coverage portrays men in accordance with traditional gender images and, as a result, predominantly depicts them as active participants in war (or even as advocates of war), while women, on the other hand, are portrayed as 'subjects' who disapprove of military and violent confrontation, who act peacefully, and who are made to suffer in the event of war[4] (see Cloud, 1994; Elsthain, 1987; Enloe, 1994, 2000a, 2000b; Rabinovitz, 1994; Wiegman, 1994). Other researchers claim that gender-stereotypical war coverage essentially reduces the experiences of women during war to their emotionalizing role: women are supposed to give war coverage an 'affective impulse' (see del Zotto, 2002; Klaus et al., 2002; Stabile and Kumar, 2005; Tuchman, 1979).[5]

Taking into consideration the described professional background, we can assume that violence and war are topics that make it especially difficult for women to be perceived as acting subjects. Instead, we expect the principal role of women in war coverage to be that of an 'affected object'. This assumption also seems to be reasonable, since it is still the exception throughout the world for women to play an active role in military operations[6] or on the corresponding political stage. Consequently, the most prominent role of women during wartime seems to be that of victims – politically or militarily instrumentalized, as well as selected, described and interpreted mainly by male journalists, and hence almost always lacking an individual voice.

Nonetheless, one can assume that this 'female silencing' is also enhanced by the fact that most war victims are portrayed as an anonymous and amorphous mass. As a result, especially during armed conflicts or other violent crises, women are inevitably absent from the public stage – a place where they are underrepresented even under normal circumstances. It would seem only reasonable to assume that gender-stereotypical media reporting has become particularly recognizable in war coverage and that definite differences in the framing of male and female actors in this regard have become quite apparent (see Turpin and Lorentzen, 1998: 15).

But until now this question has not been investigated empirically in a broad and representative way. Although Anglo-American communication science has conducted several content analyses of war coverage during the first and second Gulf Wars, the Falkland crisis or the military confrontation between Palestinians and Israelis (see, for example, Aulich, 1992; Bennet and Paletz, 1994; Nohrstedt and Ottosen, 2000; Zelizer, 1992), gender-specific issues were not part of the research agenda.[7]

As a result, we have conducted the first and so far only content analysis worldwide that has attempted to generate – among other aspects – reliable empirical data in (a) a gender perspective, (b) on a broad longitudinal basis and (c) on the basis of a census of all content.

Research Question and Methodology

The gender-specific data presented here stem from a content analysis funded by the German Research Foundation (DFG).[8] The object of the research was German newspaper coverage of international wars as well as coverage of the German federal security and defense policy that was published between January 1, 1989 and December 31, 2000. Security and defense policy has been included as part of the research design because these two issues are very closely linked to war coverage and thus receive special media attention in times of crisis and war.

It was an explicit aim of the research to analyze the respective coverage over a longer time period and independently of any specific war event or theater of war. The focus of the gender-related part of the research project was on the quantitative aspects of the depiction of women. The main purpose was to empirically scrutinize the popular and prevailing assumptions about women in wartime as reflected in German coverage. The longitudinal approach was chosen in an attempt to investigate whether there has been any change in the representation of women in war coverage since the major geopolitical change that took place in Europe, namely, the German reunification.

Our content analysis is founded on the following definition of 'war':

- War is a conflict that at least once within the given research period meets all of the following criteria: (a) a mass conflict that is settled by at least two armed forces (official/regular troops, no paramilitary units or police forces) (b) at gunpoint, in the course of which the respective violence must be more than just sporadic, spontaneous or isolated.

For 'German security and defense policy', the following definition was developed:

- German federal security and defense policy includes the following measures for the protection of German citizens: all measures related to (a) the military in the (b) national sphere, within the scope of (c) international alliances, organizations and any systems of mutual collective security, including activities of (d) peacekeeping and measures taken to cope with crises and to prevent conflicts. It also includes activities of (e) total defense as they relate to the (f) official German armed forces.

The news material looked at came from the politics sections of Germany's two most respected daily newspapers, the *Frankfurter Allgemeine Zeitung* (*FAZ*) and the *Süddeutsche Zeitung* (*SZ*). In total, we identified and analyzed 10,104 articles on international wars and 3,193 articles on German federal security and defense policy (*N* = 13,279 articles).[9]

In addition to the categories that measure the thematic framing of German war coverage in general, we also set up categories that measured the framing of the 'protagonists' who were mentioned within the particular coverage. As 'protagonists', we considered individual persons as well as anonymous groups of people. The category 'protagonists' allowed for two additional specifications: (1) 'actor(s)' and (2) 'affected person(s)/victim(s)'. For each actor and each affected person/victim, the respective gender,[10] nationality and the actual performing role[11] were determined.

We also determined the specific type of war[12] involved and the region[13] where the respective war took place. The analysis also ascertained whether and how the respective protagonists were explicitly portrayed in the descriptions that went beyond simple demographic information. We conducted three tests of intercoder reliability.[14] The mean of the intercoder reliability was 0.91, which represents a very good result.

Results

Only 2 percent of the actors and 1 percent of the victims in the media coverage analyzed by us were women/girls. Among the men/boys, 50 percent were actors and 31 percent were persons affected. At least at this broader level, the general assumption that women are marginalized in war coverage is confirmed for the present day. But, on the whole, this content analysis hardly found any evidence to support the hypothesis that females are mainly portrayed as victims. In light of this rather general result, separate analyses seem useful here, since the results relating to war topics could be different from those relating to security and defense policy (see Table 1).

Compared with the proportion of women who were actors in the war-related contributions (1 percent), women were (with 3 percent) slightly more likely to feature as actors in articles dealing with security and defense policy. Similarly, this also applies to the comparison between the proportions of women affected in articles related to war and in those related to

Table 1: Gender Terms in *FAZ* and *SZ* from 1989–2000 (Proportions)

Proportions[a]	All topics		Topics related to war		Topics related to security/defense policy	
	Actors (*n* = 12,435) %	Affected (*n* = 9,601) %	Actors (*n* = 9,544) %	Affected (*n* = 7,493) %	Actors (*n* = 2,891) %	Affected (*n* = 2,108) %
Man, Boy	50	31	46	30	62	34
Woman, Girl	2	1	1	1	3	2
Explicitly both sexes	x	x	x	1	x	x
Generic gender/ neutral	48	68	52	69	34	64
Total	100	100	100	100	100	100

Note: Due to the sampling design, which includes all possible cases, no significance tests were conducted.

Basis: All topics that deal with an actor or victim.

[a]Cases in which no definite actor/person affected could be identified are not included.

x = Less than 0.5 percent.

security and defense policy (1 and 2 percent, respectively). In general, these proportions are too low for any clear conclusions to be drawn.[15] In view of this, for once there are (until further clarification) doubts regarding the current theses that proclaim that in the media coverage of people affected by war and victims of war, women are most likely to be mentioned. Moreover, the results also show that a linguistic presentation that identifies both sexes (e.g., 'the male and female soldiers' or 'the men and women in the refugee camps') has not yet become standard in the German coverage that was analyzed.

As shown below, a longitudinal perspective was adopted, that is, gender terms between 1989 and 2000 are analyzed in greater detail. Table 2 shows the annual proportions of gender terms for war-related topics.

Generic gender/neutral terms prevail in the group of 'actors' as well as in the group of the 'affected'. However, there are two exceptions to this rule: in 1993, generic gender/neutral terms have the lowest share overall in both groups, which clearly favor explicit male descriptions. Since 56 percent of all topics in the war coverage analyzed here of that year (1993) had to do with the wars in the former Yugoslavia; this striking and deviant result may be taken as an indicator of a larger increase in the personalization of the media coverage of these particular wars. Another deviant result involving the general domination of generic gender/neutral terms becomes apparent for 1999: within the actors group, the proportion of generic gender/neutral terms also lies significantly below the usual level, while here again the proportion of explicitly male terms was on the rise.

Other data from our analysis show that in 1999 the war in Kosovo dominated German war coverage. The two military confrontations in 1993 and 1999 in which the Federal

Table 2: Annual Proportions of Gender Terms in Topics Related to War in *FAZ* and *SZ* from 1989–2000 (Line Percentages)

	Actors (line percentages)			Affected (line percentages)		
Proportions	**Man, Boy** **($n = 4,441$)** **%**	**Woman, Girl** **($n = 135$) %**	**Generic** **gender/neutral** **($n = 4,988$) %**	**Man, Boy** **($n = 2,216$)** **%**	**Woman,** **Girl** **($n = 78$) %**	**Generic** **gender/neutral** **($n = 5,160$) %**
1989	33	x	67	18	–	82
1990	45	1	55	21	1	78
1991	42	1	57	18	x	82
1992	34	1	65	23	2	74
1993	69	1	30	47	1	52
1994	48	2	50	32	2	66
1995	40	1	59	24	1	75
1996	43	1	55	29	1	70
1997	46	3	51	38	1	61
1998	43	2	55	30	1	69
1999	52	2	46	32	1	66
2000	45	3	52	35	1	63

Note: (1) Due to the sampling design, which includes all possible cases, no significance tests were conducted.

(2) Due to the low numbers for 'explicitly both sexes' per year, the category was excluded here.

Basis: All war-related topics related that deal with an actor/person affected.

x = Less than 0.5 percent.

Republic of Germany actively intervened obviously reveal a more individualized portrayal in the media coverage of the subjects involved. Both the perpetrators and the victims receive an identifiable (male!) face. Here, journalists report on individual human beings rather than on anonymous masses through 'episodic framing' (Iyengar, 1991) or through *Fallbeispiele* (case-based coverage) (Daschmann, 2001).

Both editorial strategies are more effective in convincing the news recipient and elicit a greater amount of emotional involvement on his or her part, which in turn can lead to a greater acceptance of the military intervention on the part of the news recipients. Therefore, it is certainly rather surprising that in the years 1999 and 1993 hardly any changes occurred in the group of female persons affected. We must not forget that up until now it has always been argued that particularly in the war proceedings in the former Yugoslavia, female victims were explicitly instrumentalized in order to legitimize the entry of NATO and the European Community into this war (see Kassel, 2002; Klaus and Kassel, 2008: 273–74). Table 3 details the respective results for the topics relating to security and defense policy.

In the coverage of security and defense policy, generic gender/neutral as opposed to gender-specific terms only dominated among the persons affected. Among the actors, obviously the greater possibilities for personalization in conjunction with the news factor

Table 3: Annual Proportions of Gender Terms in Topics Related to Security and Defense Policy in *FAZ* and *SZ* from 1989–2000 (Line Percentages)

	Actors (line percentages)			Affected (line percentages)		
Proportions	**Man, Boy** $(n = 1,804)$ %	**Woman, Girl** $(n = 88)$ %	**Generic gender/neutral** $(n = 993)$ %	**Man, Boy** $(n = 725)$ %	**Woman, Girl** $(n = 37)$ %	**Generic gender/neutral** $(n = 1,345)$ %
1989	53	1	46	14	1	85
1990	66	–	34	29	1	70
1991	50	4	47	14	–	86
1992	50	1	50	12	1	87
1993	69	2	29	46	x	54
1994	65	2	33	39	2	59
1995		x	37	34	–	66
1996	63	6	31	39	5	57
1997	59	3	37	46	2	53
1998	65	4	30	37	3	60
1999	68	3	29	38	3	59
2000	62	9	29	36	3	60

Note: (1) Due to the sampling design, which includes all possible cases, no significance tests were conducted.

(2) Due to the low numbers for 'explicitly both sexes' per year, the category was excluded here.

Basis: All topics related to security and defence policy that deal with an actor/person affected.

x = Less than 0.5 percent.

'elite person' take full effect and lead to gender-specific coverage being dominated by male actors. In general, however, the proportion of generic gender/neutral terms clearly declines in favor of gender-specific terms as the time frame being studied progresses. Accordingly, we find a definite increase in female gender-specific terms as well. The increasing general importance of gender-specific terms in the media coverage of security and defense policy may perhaps be attributed to the greater mediatic personalization or to the increasingly personalized PR activities of the respective (male and female) actors and the institutions they stem from or work for.

The increase in the number of female actors, however, may reflect a factual development: in the period studied, there are an increasing number of women present on the political stage. In any case, through the media we obtain more information about women who are politically active or hold significant mandates, offices or positions within the larger domain of security and defense. This applies to international diplomacy as well as to foreign policy. Women such as the former US Secretary of State Madeleine Albright, the UN special correspondent for Bosnia Linda Chavez, the Austrian Foreign Minister Benita Ferrero-Waldner and the Commissioner for the Armed Forces of the German Bundestag, Claire Marienfeld, are representative of such a development.

Table 4: Gender Terms in Topics Related to Security and Defense Policy in *FAZ* and *SZ* from 1989–2000 (Proportions)

Proportions[a]	Abstracta[b] %	International		National				
		UN %	Others %	Politicians %	Army %	Rebels %	Civilians %	Others %
Actors	(*n* = 2)	(*n* = 87)	(*n* = 106)	(*n* = 1,964)	(*n* = 504)	(*n* = 19)	(*n* = 27)	(*n* = 175)
Man, Boy	–	51	22	69	63	47	15	30
Woman, Girl	–	1	2	4	1	–	4	2
Both sexes	–	–	–	x	x	–	–	–
Generic gender/ neutral	100	48	76	27	36	53	82	67
Total	100	100	100	100	100	100	101	99
Affected/ Victims	(*n* = 10)	(*n* = 70)	(*n* = 92)	(*n* = 596)	(*n* = 1,057)	(*n* = 10)	(*n* = 137)	(*n* = 122)
Man, Boy	–	40	13	50	33	56	42	38
Woman, Girl	–	–	1	2	2	–	–	2
Both sexes	–	–	–	–	–	–	–	–
Generic gender/ neutral	100	60	86	49	65	44	58	60
Total	100	100	100	100	100	100	100	100

Note: Due to the sampling design, which includes all possible cases, no significance tests were conducted.

Basis: All topics related to security and defence policy that deal with an actor/person affected.

[a]Cases in which no definite actor/person affected could be identified are not included.

[b]For example 'peoples of the world' etc.

x = Less than 0.5 percent.

Against this background, we should take a closer look at the topic 'security and defense policy' to examine more closely the impression that the increase in female actors may mainly be attributed to female politicians and diplomats. As Table 4 shows, the data certainly support this impression.

Actually, the proportion of female actors in the coverage of security and defense policy is comparatively high as far as politicians are concerned (1 percent 'United Nations' and 4 percent 'politicians, national'). Interestingly enough, terms that refer to both sexes equally hardly occur at all, and if they do (less than 0.5 percent), they can only be found in the groups 'acting politicians' and 'acting army'. The increase in the number of female politicians (and army members) in fact obviously causes journalists to explicitly mention both sexes in mixed gender groups.

Table 5 shows the results for gender terms and actual roles in articles related to war. Here, women, if at all, feature in the role of acting politicians (3 percent 'United Nations'

Table 5: Gender Terms in Topics Related to War in *FAZ* and *SZ* from 1989–2000 (Proportions)

	International			National				
	Abstracta	UN	Others	Politicians	Army	Rebels	Civilians	Others
Proportions[a]	%	%	%	%	%	%	%	%
Actors	(*n* = 114)	(*n* = 779)	(*n* = 652)	(*n* = 3,368)	(*n* = 1,876)	(*n* = 1,081)	(*n* = 374)	(*n* = 12)
Man, Boy	26	40	28	60	46	37	6	39
Women, Girl	–	3	1	2	x	x	2	1
Both sexes	–	–	–	x	–	x	1	x
Generic gender/ neutral	74	57	71	38	54	63	91	60
Total	100	100	100	100	100	100	100	100
Affected/ Victims	(*n* = 168)	(*n* = 358)	(*n* = 191)	(*n* = 2,107)	(*n* = 1,280)	(*n* = 865)	(*n* = 1,616)	(*n* = 253)
Man, Boy	17	33	19	43	41	32	5	28
Woman, Girl	2	1	–	2	x	x	2	x
Both sexes	1	x	–	–	–	x	2	x
Generic gender/ neutral	80	66	81	56	59	67	91	71
Total	100	100	100	100	100	100	100	100

Note: Due to the sampling design, which includes all possible cases, no significance tests were conducted.

Basis: All topics related to war that deal with an actor/person affected.

[a]Cases in which no definite actor/person affected could be identified are not included.

x = Less than 0.5 percent.

and 2 percent 'politicians, national'). In view of the aforementioned changes in the access of women to the armed forces, it is also surprising that in the war-related coverage, women as actors and as affected persons are even less likely to be mentioned as members of the army than in the security and defense policy coverage. One might previously have assumed that their 'exotic status' in the army would have given them a certain news value. And what is even more surprising, even the war-related coverage does not contain a significant share of female victims/persons affected.

One might draw the qualified conclusion that the news coverage analyzed in this project does not show any sign of an instrumentalization of female victims in the legitimization of war – simply because there is hardly any coverage of female victims of war. Furthermore, in the war-related coverage analyzed in this project, generic gender/neutral terms are by far used most frequently to apply to civilians – this means actors as well as victims (91 percent each).

This allows for the conclusion that *FAZ* and *SZ* mention civilians generally as an 'amorphous mass'. Obviously, not even the war coverage of specific war events permits one to break down the on the whole rather anonymous and minor individualized portrayal of civilians. In fact completely the opposite is true: compared with the media coverage of security and defense issues, the proportion of generic gender/neutral terms in the war-related media coverage even increases, which results in a decrease in the number of gender-specific, and mostly male, terms, as a kind of zero-sum game.

Further explanations could be provided by the characterizations that were coded for the specific subjects explicitly recognizable in the respective news coverage (Table 6). At first glance, the 'prime role' of females is revealed here: that of victim as a particular form of affected person (77 percent).

Table 6: Characterization of Actors and Persons Affected in All Topics in *FAZ* and *SZ* from 1989–2000 (Proportions)

Proportions[a]	Man, boy		Woman, girl	
	Actors (n = 1,116) %	Affected (n = 706) %	Actors (n = 191) %	Affected (n = 31) %
Perpetrator, of which …	29	28	3	7
… Beast	5	5	–	–
… Aggressor (male/female)	18	5	3	3
… War criminal	5	17	–	3
Victim, of which …	5	36	6	77
… Dead (male/female)	3	20	–	26
… Displaced (male/female)	x	2	–	7
… Raped (male/female)	–	–	3	35
War-related characteristic, of which …	26	13	25	3
… Peacemaker (male/female)	6	2	16	–
… Diplomat (male/female)	10	1	6	–
Nation, Religion (patriot, fanatic …)	6	6	3	–
Politics, State (statesman, hardliner, doer …)	15	9	19	10
Power (imperialist, world policeman, powerful person …)	7	7	–	–
Conscience (doubter, moralist, pacifist …)	9	1	25	–
Help (humanitarian helper, savior …)	4	2	19	3
Total	100	100	100	100

Note: Due to the sampling design, which includes all possible cases, no significance tests were conducted.

Basis: All topics that deal with an actor/person affected.

[a]Cases in which no definite actor/person affected could be identified are not included.

x = Less than 0.5 percent.

However – and this again puts the results into perspective – characterization as a victim is also the single most dominant characteristic of male persons affected (36 percent). Moreover, it should be pointed out once more that 'female persons affected' constitutes a significant minority compared with the absolute number of female actors ($n = 31$ vs. $n = 191$). Against this background, the 'prime roles' of females are the peacemaker and diplomat (25 percent) as well as the doubter, moralist and pacifist (25 percent) – as particular forms of the actor.

Summary, Discussion and Future Prospects

The results of this study have only partially confirmed the assertions that existed up until now with regard to the role and portrayal of women in war coverage. The frequently made claim that women are mainly portrayed in the role of the victim in war coverage cannot be fully substantiated by this study. Actually, female persons affected constitute a significant minority compared with female actors. This is partly due to the fact that the majority of victims of war in media coverage are mostly discussed and portrayed as an anonymous and amorphous mass.

The general marginalization of women is even more pronounced in war coverage than in the coverage of security and defense policy. If at all, the acting female politician or diplomat as well as the acting doubter, moralist and pacifist remain the predominant roles of women in war coverage. In the final year of the study's observation period, there is a pronounced peak in the naming of female actors in relation to security and defense policy topics. No wonder: from the news value perspective, the new women in this field 'enjoy' high status (compared with ordinary people as victims of war) and thus constitute an important news factor for journalists.

Another interesting result shows that the breadth of alternatives for prime roles and characterizations of women affected is significantly narrower than for men affected. Conversely, the results of this study allow for the cautious conclusion that this breadth of alternatives is significantly greater for female than for male actors (see Table 6).

The divergent results of this study can first be attributed to the fact that this content analysis only examined daily newspapers, and the thesis concerning the (supposedly) dominant victim frame was established predominantly with respect to television and coverage in political magazines. Second, the results of this content analysis must also be associated with the fact that quality newspapers (broadsheets) rather than tabloids have been analyzed. Third – and this seems to be the most important factor – the 'participation' of women in war differs depending on the circumstances; it depends on when a war occurs and on the culturally determined values and norms of a society that affect the active participation of women in war (e.g., as soldiers with or without arms).

In any case, it may be assumed that the role of women in wartime – as civilians, politicians, diplomats or even as relatives of the fighting troops – will be decisively related to the status and the role that a woman is accorded in society as a whole, that is, including during peacetime. The media as part of that society will reflect this principle in their coverage of wars and other violent crises. Our conclusion is that more internationally and culturally comparative content analysis of this topic is needed.

The general dramatic marginalization of women in war coverage could have a simple reason: gendered 'unofficial/official' news source dichotomy. As del Zotto (2002: 148) wrote in her study of media representations of the war in Kosovo, 'the "unofficial/official" news source dichotomy is gendered because so much of women's political agency is conducted through "non-official" channels'.

In any case, this marginalization has an unpleasant side effect on research: as long as the number of female actors and victims continues to remain (very) low, quantitative data analyses that work with comparatively small samples remain a problem. Basically, all quantitative content analytical studies of the portrayal of women in war coverage will most likely have to face this general problem. Hence, quantitative content analytical studies about the portrayal of women in war coverage should be carried out on the basis of a census of all content (as was the case with this study).

In addition, we need more detailed and comparative qualitative content analysis. The latter should also investigate – beyond other specific aspects – the accusation that the media coverage of war overemphasizes another dominant frame for women and their wartime experiences: that of women as a reproductive force, for example, through the depiction of women as 'nurses'. This 'reproductive force' frame, however, also becomes apparent when one takes into account the subject of sexual relationships with enemy soldiers, as, for example, the post-Vietnam or post-Cambodian media coverage and the coverage of German soldiers and prostitutes in Kosovo in 2000–01 illustrate.[16]

Key Points

- Almost everywhere in the world, war coverage remains a male business. Only very few women make it in this specific area of news reporting. As a result, the particular characteristics of the female gaze that female war correspondents might have are unable to play a significant role in war coverage by the media.
- The regular annihilation, trivialization and marginalization of women in the media is further enhanced in war coverage by the myth of the peaceful and weak female who is in need of protection, on the one hand, and the war-eager and strong male who protects women, on the other. These myths obscure the experiences of women in and concerning war, thus denying them access to media coverage.
- The proximity of war correspondents to the actual war and to the victims of war often makes news coverage the starting point for political decisions on war and peace. It is exactly this aspect that represents an inherent risk – the risk of exploiting dramatic war coverage for military purposes.

- The frequently made claim that women are mainly portrayed in the role of victims in war coverage could not be fully confirmed by our study. Actually, female persons affected remain a small minority compared with the number of female actors cited in the coverage. According to our results, the dramatic marginalization of female victims in war coverage results from the fact that (female) victims of war in media coverage are mostly discussed and portrayed as an anonymous and amorphous mass.
- The 'participation' of women in the war coverage of the media depends on when a war occurs and on the culturally determined values and norms of a society that affect the active participation of women in war (e.g., as soldiers with or without arms). In any case, it can be assumed that the role of women in wartime – as civilians, politicians, diplomats or even as relatives of the fighting troops – will be decisively related to the status and the role that a woman is accorded in society as a whole, that is, including in peacetime.

Study Questions

1. What are the disadvantages, challenges and the perils of gender-balanced and victim-oriented war coverage. What are the advantages?
2. How could the risks of exploiting victim-oriented war coverage for military and for legitimizing purposes be effectively countered?
3. War coverage is increasingly dependent on official and institutionalized news sources (military and political PR, embedded journalism etc.). How could unofficial news sources attract more attention and thus become more easily accessible to war correspondents?

Further Reading

Chambers, Deborah, Linda Steiner and Carole Fleming (2004) *Women and Journalism*. London; New York: Routledge.

Goldstein, Joshua S. (2003) *War and Gender. How Gender Shapes the War System and Vice Versa*. New York; Melbourne; Madrid: Cambridge University Press.

Gourley, Catherine (2003) *War, Women, and the News. How Female Journalists Won the Battle to Cover World War II*. New York: Atheneum Books for Young Readers.

Regis, Margaret (2008) *When Our Mothers Went to War. An Illustrated History of Women in World War II*. Bellingham, WA: NavPub.

Websites

Female correspondents changing war coverage: www.womensenews.org/article.cfm?aid=1074.

Women covering war – female correspondents recall their historic role reporting from Vietnam: www.post-gazette.com/magazine/20000330namwomen2.asp.

References

Aulich, James (1992) *Framing the Falklands War. Nationhood, Culture, and Identity*. Milton Keynes; Philadelphia: Open University Press.

Bennett, Lance W. and David L. Paletz (eds) (1994) *Taken by Storm. The Media, Public Opinion, and U.S. Foreign Policy in the Gulf War*. Chicago: University of Chicago Press.

Cloud, Dana (1994) 'Operation Desert Comfort', pp. 155–70 in Susan Jeffords and Lauren Rabinovitz (eds) *Seeing Through the Media. The Persian Gulf War*. New Brunwick, NJ: Rutgers University Press.

Daschmann, Gregor (2001) *Der Einfluss von Fallbeispielen auf Leserurteile. Experimentelle Untersuchungen zur Medienwirkung*. Konstanz: UVK.

del Zotto, Augusta C. (2002) 'Weeping Women, Wringing Hands. How the Mainstream Media Stereotyped Women's Experiences in Kosovo', *Journal of Gender Studies* 11(2): 141–50.

Elsthain, Jean B. (1982) 'On Beautiful Souls, Just Warriors and Feminist Consciousness', *Women's Studies International Forum* 5(3/4): 341–48.

—— (1987) *Women and War*. New York: Littlefield.

Enloe, Cynthia (1994) 'The Gendered Gulf', pp. 211–28 in Susan Jeffords and Lauren Rabinovitz (eds) *Seeing Through the Media. The Persian Gulf War*. New Brunwick, NJ: Rutgers University Press.

Enloe, Cynthia H. (2000a) *Bananas, Beaches and Bases. Making Feminist Sense of International Politics*. Berkeley, CA; London: University of California Press.

—— (2000b) *Maneuvers. The International Politics of Militarizing Women's Lives*. Berkeley: University of California Press.

Fröhlich, Romy (2000) *Virgins, Vamps, and Lack of Reality. A Content Analysis of Crime Coverage in German Local Newspapers*, Paper presented at the Conference of the International Association of Mass Communication Research, Sydney.

—— (2002a) 'Die mediale Wahrnehmung von Frauen im Krieg. Kriegsberichterstatterinnen und Kriegsberichterstattung aus Sicht der Kommunikationswissenschaft', pp. 182–93 in Ulrich Albrecht and Jörg Becker (eds) *Medien zwischen Krieg und Frieden*. Baden-Baden: Nomos.

—— (2002b) *Women, Media, and War: The Representation of Women in the Mass Media*, Paper presented at the International Communication Association (ICA), Seoul.

Gernhuber, Susanne (1996) 'Weibliche Sichtweise', *Journalist* 47(1): 20–1.

Iyengar, Shanto (1991) *Is Anyone Responsible? How Television Frames Political Issues*. Chicago: University of Chicago Press.

Jaeger, Susanne (1998) 'Propaganda mit Frauenschicksalen? Die deutsche Presseberichterstattung über Vergewaltigung im Krieg in Bosnien-Herzegowina', pp. 75–88 in Wilhelm F. Kempf and Irena Schmidt-Regener (eds) *Krieg, Nationalismus, Rassismus und die Medien*. Münster: Lit.

—— (2002) 'Mediale Wahrnehmungsfilter. Nationalität, Ethnie', pp. 194–204 in Ulrich Albrecht and Jörg Becker (eds) *Medien zwischen Krieg und Frieden*. Baden-Baden: Nomos.

—— (2002) 'Wie Medien Geschlechterstereotype zur Kriegslegitimation nutzen. "Schöne Flüchtlingsmädchen und Vergewaltigungslager"', *Wissenschaft & Frieden* 2: 19–21.

Klaus, Elisabeth and Susanne Kassel (2008) 'Frauenrechte als Kriegslegitimation in den Medien', pp. 266–80 in Johanna Dorer and Brigitte K. R. Geiger (eds) *Medien – Politik – Geschlecht. Feministische Befunde zur politischen Kommunikationsforschung.* Wiesbaden: VS.

Klaus, Elisabeth, Kerstin Goldbeck and Susanne Kassel (2002) 'Fremd- und Selbstbilder in der Berichterstattung der deutschen Medien während des Kosovokrieges – am Beispiel des Spiegel', pp. 285–305 in K. Imhof, O. Jarren and R. Blum (eds) *Integration und Medien.* Wiesbaden: Westdeutscher Verlag.

Nohrstedt, Stig and Rune Ottosen (2000) *Journalism and the New World Order. Gulf War, National News Discourse and Globalization.* Göteborg: Nordicom.

Pater, Monika (1993) 'Die militarisierte Männlichkeit. Geschlechterverhältnisse – Medien – Krieg', pp. 97–108 in Martin Löffelholz (ed.) *Grundlagen und Perspektiven der Krisenkommunikation.* Opladen: Westdeutscher Verlag.

Rabinovitz, Lauren (1994) 'Soap Opera Woes. Genre, Gender and the Persian Gulf War', pp. 189–204 in Susan Jeffords and Lauren Rabinovitz (eds) *Seeing Through the Media. The Persian Gulf War.* New Brunswick, NJ: Rutgers University Press.

Sartorius, Peter (1996) 'Grenzen der Profession', *Journalist* 47(1): 15–6.

Stabile, Carol A. and Deepa Kumar (2005) 'Unveiling Imperialism. Media, Gender and the War on Afghanistan', *Media, Culture & Society* 27(5): 765–82.

Tuchman, Gay (1979) 'Women's Depiction by the Mass Media', *Signs* 4(3): 528–42.

Turpin, Jennifer E. and Lois Ann Lorentzen (1998) *The Women and War Reader.* New York: New York University Press.

Vučković, Ariane (1996) 'Menschen mit Namen', *Journalist* 47(1): 14–5.

Weimann, Gabriel and Gideon Fishman (1988) 'Attribution of Responsibility. Sex-Based Bias in Press Reports on Crime', *European Journal of Communication* 3(4): 415–30.

Wiegman, Robyn (1994) 'Missiles and Melodrama (Masculinity and the Televisual War)', pp. 171–87 in Susan Jeffords and Lauren Rabinovitz (eds) *Seeing Through the Media. The Persian Gulf War.* New Brunswick, NJ: Rutgers University Press.

Zelizer, Barbie (1992) 'CNN, the Gulf War, and Journalistic Practice', *Journal of Communication* 42(1): 66–81.

Zur, Ofer and Andrea Morrison (1989) 'Gender and War. Reexamining Attitudes', *American Journal of Orthopsychiatry* 59(4): 528–33.

Notes

1 Among the most prominent female American journalists 'at the frontier' were Marvin Breckinridge Patterson (1905–2002), Clare Boothe (1903–87), Esther Bubley (1921–98), Janet Flanner (1892–1978), May Craig (1889–1975), Therese Bonney (1894–1978) and Toni Frissell (1907–88).

2 Susanne Gelhard's TV news and especially the accompanying horrendous pictures of war corpses on camera that she selected for her stories quickly became the focus of a hot debate concerning what kind of images depicting war scenes should be allowed to be shown on television and which should not. I am convinced that this discussion was only

carried on – or perhaps only carried on so *heatedly* – because the images and reports in question were produced by a woman.

3   During her time as foreign TV correspondent and head of the ARD-Studio in Moscow, she became famous for being the only western journalist to be granted an interview with the Chechenian rebel leader Dschochar Dudajev. Until then, Dudajev had not let any western correspondents or journalists get near him. Just 24 hours after Mikich's interview, Dudajev was killed during a Russian air strike on April 22, 1996.

4   Incidentally, Zur and Morrison (1989: 532) refute this assumption in empirical studies as a sort of myth: 'The belief that war is a male institution which has no appeal to women is important because it implies that it is man's responsibility to prevent wars from occurring. The myth which views women as peaceful but powerless, and men as warlike and powerful does not acknowledge the interdependent relationship of men and women in the making of war. [...] wars do not simply exist through male advocacy, they also stem from the influence of a complex cultural system.'

5   For different and opposing results, see Weimann and Fishman (1988).

6   In the 1990s, women were continually granted easier entry into the armed forces (not only in the United States). In Germany, the legislation was changed at the end of the 1990s, and women thus were granted the right to participate in military service. It would seem plausible that this is reflected in the coverage of security and defense policy in a terminology that equally includes both sexes as 'male and female soldiers'.

7   This is also true for research in Europe. For Germany, compare, for example, the theoretical examination of the topic in Pater (1993) and Kassel (2002), and the empirical case analyzes of Fröhlich (2002a, 2002b) and Jaeger (1998, 2002).

8   A two-year project (summer 2001–summer 2003) in cooperation with Helmut Scherer from the Institute for Communication Research in Hannover (DFG reference number: FR 976/7-1).

9   We did not construct samples; therefore, statistical significance tests are unnecessary.

10   Besides 'male' and 'female' (i.e., gender specific), also 'generic gender/neutral' (e.g., 'the firemen' or 'the fire brigade', 'the policemen' or 'the police', 'the troops' etc.) as well as 'explicitly both sexes' (e.g., 'men and women', 'actors and actresses', 'business(wo)men', 'male and female soldiers' etc.). In the German language, terms explicitly mentioning both sexes are much easier to build than in English (e.g., 'soldiers': 'Soldaten und Soldatinnen'; politicians: 'Politiker und Politikerinnen'; teachers: 'Lehrer und Lehrerinnen' etc.).

11   International: 'United Nations', 'other than United Nations'. National: 'politician(s)', 'army', 'rebel(s)' and 'civilian(s)'.

12   Autonomy, interstate, anti-regime.

13   The Balkans, the Middle and Far East, Africa, Asia, South America; according to our definition of 'war' (see above), the Balkans was the only region in Europe where war took place within the defined research period. The armed conflicts in Northern Ireland and in the Basque provinces of Spain were not defined as wars within the scope of our definition.

14   The test included all formal variables as well as an appropriate selection of content-related variables.

15   Actors and persons affected did not have to be mentioned in one article at the same time. Therefore, for example, an actor could be portrayed without there being a direct reference to the person affected. Thus, from a data analysis viewpoint, the proportion of actors and affected persons cannot be directly compared.

16   The media made a scandal out of whether German KFOR (Kosovo Force) soldiers were customers of local brothels in Kosovo in 2000/01. See, for example, www.spiegel.de/ politik/deutschland/0,1518,108469,00.html (August 28, 2009); www.welt.de/print-wams/ article618841/Bordell_der_verlorenen_Maedchen.html (August 28, 2009).

'Something Has Changed'

International Relations and the Media after the 'Cold War'

Josef Seethaler and Gabriele Melischek

Summary

In media and communication studies, there are generally two opposing approaches to studying the role of the media in international relations. For decades, politics and the media have been assumed to go hand in hand, with the media expected either to parallel or 'index' the government's news agenda and viewpoints. On the other hand, inventions in communication technologies have led to the so-called 'CNN effect' hypothesis that claims that media coverage may affect the conduct of foreign policy, particularly in times of (armed) conflicts, just because of nonstop, real-time television footage from around the world. This trend toward a more powerful media coincided with the end of the Cold War and the increasing problem of dealing with a more fluid and uncertain international order. However, in the aftermath of 9/11, and as a corollary of the so-called War on Terror, the notion of a more powerful media seems to have lost ground and the 'indexing' hypothesis appears to have regained momentum. In the light of these multiple changes, this chapter suggests a new approach to examining the role of the media in international relations, which have become increasingly varied and ambiguous over the past decades, making it harder to deal with conflicts between states. The proposed approach is based on constructivist international theory and focuses on in-group and out-group frames of states as conveyed by the mass news media. It is argued that these frames play a crucial role in identity formation and, therefore, in defining the constraints of foreign policy-making. Based on this assumption, media analysis may contribute to public diplomacy efforts because knowing the public perception of each other is one of the most important prerequisites for successfully intervening in or dealing with conflicts.

Introduction

Since the end of the Cold War, not only the political world order has changed dramatically but with it also the character of relations between states. However, unlike previous major breakdowns, after which a new order and a new balance of forces had always emerged, the end of the Cold War has brought a new complexity and a 'new uncertainty' (Habermas, 1985) to the foreign policy landscape. The dissolution of the Soviet Union in 1991 and the end of the bipolar structure of power has not only been followed by new confrontations whose structures no longer obey the traditional patterns but also revealed the increasing difficulty of basing international relations on consensual principles.

In the face of new forms of conflict and cooperation, and a dearth in any convincing definition of 'national interests', relationships between states have become more subject to changing views. The different interpretations of the new geopolitical situation and its threats, the uncertainty about the viability of multilateral shared values and the incertitude about the acceptance of foreign policy concepts have moved foreign policy decision making out of the arcane and into public discussion. Yet despite these enormous changes, a recent overview of the current state of research on the role of media in international relations reveals areas of significant deficits in political communication research (Tenscher and Viehrig, 2007). On the one hand, international relations has emerged as a subdiscipline of political science during recent decades, dealing with the economic, cultural and political relations between nations and other actors in the international system as well as with the operation of international organizations. It still does not give, however, adequate attention to the role of the media and public opinion. Although, in recent times, communication studies has increasingly dealt with various aspects of this field on a wider scale, the formation of a theoretical, well-grounded subdiscipline of international communication is still in its infancy (Melischek et al., 2008).

The Role of the Media in International Relations

According to Wilke (1993), mass media are both a factor in and the object of foreign policy. Media appear to be a factor in international relations, as they report both on their own country and its foreign relations and on other countries and their external relations. In this respect, the media's indirect impact on politics via its influencing of public opinion has to be distinguished from direct effects on political action, for the media are increasingly becoming important sources of information even for foreign policy actors. Compared to this 'passive-receptive' use of the media by political actors, Wilke refers to an 'active-instrumentalizing' use of the media as a means of propaganda and public diplomacy. In this case, media are the object of foreign policy. (Furthermore, media may become an object of politics if they are both directly or indirectly affected by national or supranational regulations.)

Since issues of international relations are – more than any other policy field – inaccessible to personal experience, the assumption is justified that the agenda setting and news interpretation power of the media plays an important role in shaping the public perception of other countries, the relationship between them and the structures of the 'mental maps' of our world that exist in people's minds (Rosengren and Windahl, 1989). Thus the media contribute significantly to the definition of those conditions that are outlined by public opinion and represent the constraints under which foreign policy has to be accomplished. An early milestone in this research on country images conveyed by the world's media is the 'Foreign Images' study (Sreberny-Mohammedi et al., 1985), which was commissioned by UNESCO in 1979 in the wake of the discussion on a 'new world information order' (MacBride, 1980).

Research has focused more specifically on this function of the mass media since the end of the Cold War because numerous international (armed) conflicts could not be explained by the traditional East-West logic anymore. This newly arisen interest in the long underestimated role of media in international politics is impressively documented in a growing number of comparative research studies (e.g., Wasburn, 2002; Wolfsfeld, 2004; Seib, 2005; Shlapentokh et al., 2005; Balabanova, 2007; Hammond, 2007; Spencer, 2008; Gilboa and Inbar, 2010), but also in several extensive anthologies (e.g., Bennett and Paletz, 1994; Malek, 1997; Malek and Kavoori, 2000; Nacos et al., 2000; Gilboa, 2002). Most recently, several studies have been conducted in an effort to investigate media coverage of the attacks by internationally active terrorist groups and the so-called War on Terror proclaimed by former US President George W. Bush (Nacos, 2007; Norris et al., 2003).

In contrast to former findings, which had suggested that politics and the media 'have gone hand in hand' (Malek, 2003: 23), since the end of the Cold War, there is increasing evidence that the tide has turned in favor of a more powerful media (Entman, 2000). Most scholars agree that the setting of the Cold War gave the government the advantage of directing public opinion because the media were supposed to parallel or to 'index' the government's position (Bennett, 1990; Iyengar and Simon, 1993; Zaller and Chiu, 2000). Only in the case of significant dissension among political elites in supporting the government were the media encouraged to reflect these different viewpoints (Hallin, 1984). According to the 'manufacturing consent' thesis (Herman and Chomsky, 1988), this agreement is due to policy-makers' use of the media for foreign news management, which coincides with the purely commercial orientation of news organizations. This profit orientation means they minimize economic risks and are willing to distort their reporting to favor government, on which they depend as one of their primary news sources. Another reading of the situation prior to 1989 suggests that the clear-cut Cold War polarities had given the public a heuristic shortcut for understanding foreign affairs and thereby some advantage in constraining, if not influencing, the direction of foreign policy (Shapiro and Jacobs, 2002). Without this frame, however, policy-makers may even have greater opportunity to manipulate fluctuating, unsettled public opinion, especially when journalists fail to offer critical analysis (Mermin, 1999). In both perspectives, the role of the media is understood as more or less conveying government (or, at least, elite) policies.

In contrast, studies of post-Cold War crises turned this picture upside down. Above all, inventions in communication technologies, which enabled real-time news coverage 24-hours-a-day from around the world, are supposed to have led to the so-called 'CNN effect'. This claims that media not only accelerate the pace of international communication but may also affect the conduct of foreign policy by compelling and gripping visual storytelling (e.g., Robinson, 2002; Volkmer, 2004; Bahador, 2007). While the 'CNN effect' refers to a more complex and challenging information environment, which became strikingly apparent in CNN's coverage of the first Persian Gulf War in 1991, the 'CNN effect (plus)' draws attention to the new possibilities, provided by mobile phones, of filing and distributing video reports that have become a major source of information during highly volatile conflicts when journalists are not allowed to be on site (Livingston, 2003). Another more general extension of this approach, the 'Al Jazeera effect', deals with the explosive growth of new media – from satellite TV to the blogosphere – and its use 'as tools in every aspect of global affairs, ranging from democratization to terrorism and including the concept of "virtual states"' (Seib, 2008: x). Even those studies that do not adhere to these rather heuristic concepts reveal a less clear pattern of media behavior in the post-Cold War era (e.g., Goodman, 1999; Zaller and Chiu, 2000; Melischek and Seethaler, 2008), for example, by considering the conditions under which otherwise marginalized groups are able to prevent media supporting the government's policy or at least the elite's view (Wolfsfeld, 1997). However, this notion of a more powerful media seems to have lost ground in the aftermath of 9/11 and as a corollary of the War on Terror, and the 'indexing' hypothesis would appear to have regained momentum (Bennett et al., 2006; Nacos, 2007).

Following an extensive overview of research on the triangle of foreign policy, the media and public opinion in liberal democracies (Nacos et al., 2000), both a top-down and a bottom-up model seem to be too simplistic. Rarely are public attitudes on foreign affairs manipulated by the elites with the help of convergent media coverage, and rarely does public opinion, incited by the media, directly affect policy decisions. Nevertheless, the lowest common denominator of most studies can be summarized as follows: 'something has changed' (Zaller and Chiu, 2000: 81). If these changes can be interpreted as indicating a more independent approach by the media in international relations reporting, and if public opinion can be considered as being able to set 'broad and unspecified limits to the foreign policy choices' that define 'the range of options available for implementing policy goals' (Risse-Kappen, 1991: 510), then the role of the media should be reflected in light of the system changes induced by the end of the Cold War (Page, 2000).

As Entman (2008) has recently pointed out, this changing role of the media has also been acknowledged by public diplomacy. After first emerging in the 1970s (Davison, 1974), in the 1990s 'public diplomacy', as a new approach to the 'instrumentalizing use' of the media by political actors, gained acceptance as a tool for influencing public opinion in other countries more effectively, but the exertion of this influence was less obtrusive than former propaganda techniques. In particular, the deteriorating image of the United States in several parts of the world had increased the interest in questions concerning the role of mass media in international diplomacy. While traditional diplomacy refers to relationships on the level of governments, 'public diplomacy' (which borrows some ideas from public relations research) refers to the relationship between government and another country's people or between peoples (Manheim, 1994; Melissen, 2005). In the latter – and more recently introduced – case, the relationship is enabled or facilitated by governmental actions. The main task of public diplomacy is to deal with conflicts in such a way as to maximize agreement between societies and to minimize disagreement. Based on the assumption that people do have an increasing influence on the positions and attitudes of their governments, it aims to create a receptive public environment in the target country for one's own foreign policy goals (thus preventing conflicts or taking countermeasures against them). However, public diplomacy tries to get countries to change their policies toward others by transforming people's consciousness of a certain conflict. In short, building relationships, eradicating the barriers that separate societies and facilitating negotiations and agreements in order to settle disputes are among its most important functions. Obviously, the success of strategies for coping with conflicts with others and for intervening in conflicts between others depends a great deal on knowing how people in other countries perceive one's own country. Appropriate tools are needed for measuring the long underrated subjective dimension of foreign policy – tools that are able to grasp the complexity of, and the changes in, country images in a world with less predictable international relations than ever before.

Media Framing of International Relations Issues

Given the assumption that the role of public opinion in international relations can best be characterized as 'constraining' rather than 'controlling' policy-makers, with the media potentially limiting the ways in which the public perceive foreign policy issues, in this chapter we propose an approach for analyzing the role of the media in international relations, inspired by the concept of framing (Reese et al., 2001; Shah et al., 2009). In Goffman's (1974) seminal work, framing denotes a process through which people structure social reality by drawing on culturally, socially and individually available knowledge so as to be able to perceive, interpret and evaluate phenomena, and to act accordingly. Obviously, the media play an important role in emphasizing certain frames of reference while neglecting others – particularly with regard to those topics in which most people have little or no personal experience (which is especially true for the area of foreign policy). As salience transfer from the media to the public is greatest in the case of 'unobtrusive issues' such as these (Zucker, 1978), it is possible for a particular framing of these issues in news reports to have an influence on the constructs that people connect with them, if these constructs are not only applicable but also accessible (McCombs, 2004).

In the case of foreign policy coverage, we assume that the widely shared perceptions of other states as friends or rivals (or even as enemies) can be viewed as the most relevant constraints on policy-making. This assumption is based on the thinking behind constructivist international relations theory, as advanced by Alexander Wendt (1999). Contrary to 'classical' theories of international relations such as realism or liberalism, which focus on international power relations and the notion of a 'national interest' (with liberalism, at least, paying some attention to societal interest formation),[1] social constructivism argues that foreign policy is, at its most basic, a process of defining in-groups and out-groups in the modern state system. Thus, it draws attention to the ways that collective images and identities are formed and related to other collectivities (Seethaler and Melischek, 2011). As social identification can be conceived as a *dynamic* process of (re)considering and (re)negotiating the self in relation to others, it is closely related to the public sphere that represents the arena in which identities are evolved. However, information about other states' policies are beyond the scope of most people's direct experience, and therefore it can be argued that the media's framing of who we are and who we are not (or even whom we are against) does have an impact on shaping these public perceptions of self and others (Rivenburgh, 1997; Gamson, 2001: x). These frames (like the former 'Cold War frame') function as cognitive shortcuts for in-group and out-group affiliation, legitimating the adoption of cooperative policies toward states that are believed to share the same values, the same concept of legitimate domestic order and the same kind of threats to this order, while justifying competitive (or even hostile) behavior directed at 'out-group' states. Construction of in-groups and out-groups can be considered to be at the core of foreign policy, which decides on cooperation and conflict.

Applying this framing approach to media analysis, it should be possible to explore the changing role of the media in the political process more openly. In operationalizing in-group and out-group frames, attribution theory can be drawn on as one of the most powerful concepts in explaining different understandings of social reality. Concerned with how people make explanations for their own and other people's behavior (Weiner, 1986), it suggests that success and failure (or, more broadly, favorably and unfavorably perceived behavior) can be attributed, on the one hand, either to factors within the person ('internal') or to factors within the environment ('external') and, on the other hand, to factors that endure over time ('stable') or to changeable ones ('unstable'). Based on this four-fold classification, extensive research has shown that attributions may serve a self-esteem function to the extent that they are, basically, internal-stable for success and internal-unstable or external for failure (Zuckerman, 1979). This 'self-serving bias' has been extended to intergroup contexts, where group members take credit for their group's successes by attributing them to attitudes, competencies and aptitudes (i.e., internal-stable causes). In contrast, they try to deny or to explain away responsibility for the failures of their group by attributing them to external circumstances or to unstable and therefore changing or changeable causes (like luck and efforts). The opposite, of course, holds for out-groups: their successes are mainly characterized as situational, while failures are viewed as dispositional. As Kowert (1998) argues, the attributional pattern of this widely researched 'group serving bias' (Hewstone, 1989, 1990) also works at the level of nation states. In the political realm, issue positions and personal traits, representing terminal and instrumental values, can be regarded as internal and stable attributions, whereas strategies and performance (such as the past or expected 'handling' of an issue) represent internal-unstable attributions. External attributions usually relate to situational factors and societal developments (such as demographic changes) as well as to the influence of other actors, such as politicians from rival parties.

In the following, this approach is exemplified by a case study examining the differences within the transatlantic alliance over the Iraq War as conveyed by the media (particularly, by leading newspapers) in some of the involved countries, allies and opponents.

Content Analysis of Media Frames

Content analysis of media coverage was carried out at two levels. On the first level, all articles referring to the political actors of interest in the headline, the lead or the first paragraph, and/or in the picture, located on the front page, on the upper half of the pages in the front section of the newspaper as well as on opinion and op-ed pages, were coded in order to measure the attention newspapers paid to the various actors. Columns of short news, news without headlines and letters to the editor were not coded.

On the second level, coding units are those statements that refer to the previously coded political actors and include the following:

(a) Definitions of political issues related to the respective actor
(b) Evaluations of issue-related behavior of the actor (usually of policies and political outcomes)[2]
(c) Causal explanations of these evaluations[3]

Usually, statements including explanations are connected with statements including evaluations with the word 'because', or at least, it should be possible to connect them with the word 'because'. This coding procedure is in line with Entman's (2007) definition, according to which a news frame not only encompasses problem definition, evaluation and causal interpretation as its central elements[4] but also connects them in such a way as to promote a particular interpretation (in this case, an in-group or out-group affiliation).

Case Study: The Transatlantic Conflict over the Iraq War

In the case study presented, the described approach is applied to a comparative analysis of European press coverage of the United States during the 2004 presidential campaign, that is, during a period of differences within the transatlantic alliance, and also within the European Union, which emerged in the course of the last Iraq War. This topic was chosen because the approach adopted here should prove useful in the analysis of any kind of international relationship and, therefore and in particular, for small-scale conflicts which may prove harder for the public to grasp through discourse than is the case with large-scale conflicts. Considering that the main task of public diplomacy is to deal with conflicts in such a way as to maximize agreement between societies and to minimize disagreement, media analysis should help to determine the scope for foreign policy-makers in taking action to reconcile the differences. An overwhelmingly negative media coverage of the United States in countries opposing the war would have fueled critical attitudes toward strengthening the alliance once again, whereas a more positive treatment would have induced a more consensus-oriented foreign policy (Beaudoin and Thorson, 2002).

The starting point of the analysis was the absence of a consensus on the nature of the differences between the United States and Europe over the Iraq War. While some political analysts argued that in spite of all these case-specific differences, the values and global interests on both sides of the Atlantic remained very similar (Gordon and Shapiro, 2004), to others the value gap had increased so quickly that the survival of the transatlantic alliance was called into question (Kagan, 2004). This increase was mainly attributed to an intensified, traditionally French and German-led European integration.

The study examined coverage of US politics during the 2004 presidential campaign (encompassing the 'hot phase' from Labor Day to Election Day, that is, from September 6 to November 2, 2004) in eight leading newspapers from two European allies of the United States in the Iraq War (Poland and the United Kingdom) and from two countries opposing the war (France and Germany). One right-leaning and one left-leaning newspaper from each of these four countries was selected (conservative: *The Daily Telegraph, Le Figaro, Frankfurter Allgemeine Zeitung, Rzeszpospolita*; liberal: *Gazeta Wyborcza, The Guardian, Le Monde, Süddeutsche Zeitung*). The presidential election campaign was chosen because it was expected that a wide range of political issues had been addressed during the campaign, thus revealing the role the Iraq War had played in the perception of US policies as a whole. Content analysis focuses on the perception of the then President George W. Bush and his challenger, Senator John Kerry. On average, 98 articles per newspaper were coded; more than 60 percent of the articles included frames.

With regard to the overall picture of US policies, non-allied countries tended to apply out-group frames to the United States, while newspapers in allied countries were more likely to apply in-group frames (Figure 1). To specify this general relationship, a logistic regression analysis was carried out with the in-group or out-group frame as the dependent variable, the Iraq policy of the various countries and the editorial line of the newspapers as the two

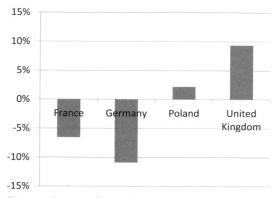

Figure 1: Framing of US Policies in European Newspapers.

Note: Differences of percentages of in-group and out-group frames; $N = 899$ attributions.

Table 1: Determinants of In-group Framing of US Policies in European Newspapers, 2004

Predictor variables	B	Wald (df)	Exp(B) = odds ratio
Iraq policy (0 = non-allied, 1 = allied)	.276	4.126* (1)	1.318
Editorial line (0 = conservative, 1 = liberal)	−.264	3.551 (1)	.768
Candidate (0 = Bush, 1 = Kerry)	.011	.006 (1)	1.011
Issue area (categorial)		5.293 (4)	
Foreign policy issues	−.014	.017 (1)	.986
Domestic policy issues	−.161	.833 (1)	.851
Economic policy issues	.411	4.769* (1)	1.509
General political issues	−.193	1.317 (1)	.824
Constant	−.019	.003 (1)	.981
R^2 (Nagelkerke)		.200	

Logistic regression analysis; N = 899 attributions; B: +/− increase/decrease of in-group framing; *p < .05; all Hosmer & Lemeshow tests not significant. In order not to let newspapers with a lot of attributions dominate the sample, each newspaper is given equal weight in the average of ratios of attributions given by the eight newspapers.

main predictors and additionally controlling for candidate references and various policy issue areas.[5] A framing of US policies in line with the respective government's position on the Iraq War would indicate the ongoing validity of the 'indexing' hypothesis. The editorial line of the newspapers was included as a crucial factor for media framing (Scheufele, 1999) and as a possible obstacle to 'indexing' the government's position because of its commitment to different viewpoints (Zaller, 1992).

As the results show, the Iraq policy turns out to be the only important factor significantly influencing the kind of framing the eight newspapers applied on US policies (Table 1). Newspapers in allied countries framed the United States more often in terms of an in-group affiliation than newspapers in non-allied countries – or in mathematical terms, the odds of a frame applied by a newspaper in an allied country demonstrating an in-group serving bias are 1.3 times higher than those of a newspaper in a non-allied country.[6] No clear evidence was found for a more independent role of the media in international relations coverage. There is a certain tendency of the newspapers to follow their editorial line in terms of the traditional liberal-conservative cleavage (when comparing the regression coefficients of both main predictors), but it is not statistically significant.[7] Moreover, the challenger's foreign policy proposals received only marginal attention.[8] All things considered, this is strong confirmation that the 'indexing' assumption is still valid in the post-Cold War era. At least in times of international conflict, governments are capable of spreading 'top-down' frames (Entman, 2004). The only slight difference concerns economic policy. Although the impact of issue areas as a whole is *not* significant, economic issues are different to the rest as they (unsurprisingly) foster in-group feelings regardless of differences elsewhere. Apart from this, the chosen kind of measurement supports the 'value gap' assumption – concerning the relationship between France and Germany on the one side and the United States on the other – as policy failures are attributed to terminal and instrumental values.

Following our theoretical considerations, the negative French and German media coverage of US policies must be expected to reinforce critical attitudes toward efforts to pour oil on the troubled waters of the transatlantic alliance. However, according to Wendt (1999: 306), identification with others and out-group devaluation are 'rarely total', and there may be different perceptions of the 'other' simultaneously, producing tensions between respective levels of group identification. In relations between states, for example, it is important to distinguish different perceptions of government and people. To prove this distinction, the perception of American people was operationalized in the sense of 'perceived public opinion' (Entman, 2000), that is, how newspapers framed the reported attitudes of the people toward US policies (as represented by the two candidates).

Again, there is a noticeable 'indexing' effect: newspapers in allied countries depict the Americans as being more in line with US policies than newspapers in non-allied countries (Table 2). However, this effect is accompanied – and that is somewhat surprising – by depicting the Americans as generally more critical of their own country's foreign policy and by displaying domestic and general political issues (such as the overall political program of the candidates) as primarily responsible for the identification of the Americans with their political leaders. As there are no significant differences between the candidates, the newspapers gave a rather balanced view of the American people, regardless of their respective editorial line. Obviously, these multifaceted frames applied to the reporting

Table 2: Determinants of In-group Framing of Perceived US Public Opinion in European Newspapers, 2004

Predictor variables	*B*	Wald (df)	Exp(*B*) = odds ratio
Iraq policy (0 = non-allied, 1 = allied)	+.321	5.466* (1)	1.379
Editorial line (0 = conservative, 1 = liberal)	−.147	1.074 (1)	.864
Candidate (0 = Bush, 1 = Kerry)	−.285	3.775 (1)	.752
Issue area (categorial)		27.020*** (4)	
Foreign policy issues	−.288	6.441* (1)	1.117
Domestic policy issues	+.342	6.138* (1)	1.407
Economic policy issues	.100	.237 (1)	.905
General political issues	+.446*	10.068** (1)	1.561
Constant	.280	.833 (1)	.940
R^2 (Nagelkerke)		.450	

Logistic regression analysis; N = 977 attributions; B: +/− increase/decrease of in-group framing; *p < .05; **p < .01; ***p < .001; all Hosmer & Lemeshow tests not significant. In order not to let newspapers with a lot of attributions dominate the sample, each newspaper is given equal weight in the average of ratios of attributions given by the eight newspapers.

US public opinion represent an important change in framing foreign countries in comparison with the clear-cut Cold War frame, and they have to be interpreted as weakening the support for the assumption of a value gap between the United States and 'Old' Europe (to quote former US Defense Secretary Donald Rumsfeld) as found in examining the influences on the European media framing of US official policies. Less devaluation means less competitiveness directed at the out-group and, therefore, less intergroup conflict potential, enabling a more consensus-oriented foreign policy.

This also becomes apparent when looking at public opinion data. According to an international PEW Research Center survey at the beginning of 2005, people in the United Kingdom and in Poland had a much more favorable opinion of the United States than people in Germany and France, which can be seen as in accordance with the media framing of US policies. However, they all held similarly favorable views of the American people – as our results have suggested (Figure 2). By revealing different frames in covering government and people, our approach allows for some implications for public diplomacy efforts. If people do have an influence on their governments through determining the scope of viable foreign policy options, then knowing the distinction between the perception of official policies and the people of one's own country in other countries might play an essential role in creating a receptive public environment in the target country for one's own policy goals, thus preventing conflicts or settling crises between states. Public diplomacy should also pay more attention to the analysis of media framing as an appropriate tool for continuously observing the societal environment in which policy-makers operate and citizens make their decisions.

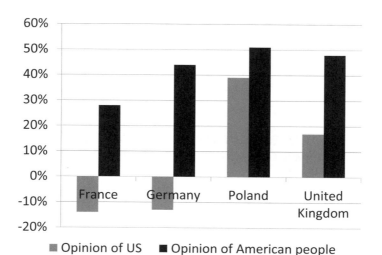

Figure 2: Opinion of the United States and of American People in Four European Countries.

Note: Differences of percentages of favorable and unfavorable ratings.

Source: PEW Research Center, Global Attitudes Survey, April–May 2005.

Key Points

- While during the Cold War the media were supposed to communicate the government's position ('indexing'), in the post-Cold War era and in the face of a growing incertitude about the acceptance of foreign policy concepts, the media are gaining more autonomy in international relations reporting.
- Social constructivism argues that foreign policy is, at its most basic, a process of defining in-groups and out-groups in the modern state system.
- Considering that public opinion primarily functions as one of the constraints of intergovernmental cooperation and conflict, the media's images of who are 'we' and 'they' are supposed to have an impact on shaping the public perceptions of self and others.
- Based on attribution theory, an analysis of in-group and out-group frames in European newspaper coverage of US politics during the Iraq War reveals different perceptions of the US government and the American people.
- This distinction can be considered as an important factor in international diplomacy as it may help to create a receptive public environment in other countries for one's own policy goals, thus preventing conflicts or making it possible to take countermeasures against them.

Research Questions

1. In foreign policy coverage, the widely shared perceptions of other states as friends or rivals (or even as enemies) can be viewed as constraining foreign policy-making. Can you describe the role of the media in this process during and after the Cold War?
2. People tend to take credits for their successes and deny responsibilities for their failures. Can you think of some examples?

Further Reading

Gorman, Lynn and David McLean (2009) 'Media, War, and International Relations' pp. 208-29 in *Media and Society. A Historical Introduction.* 2nd ed. Malden, MA; Oxford; Chichester: Wiley-Blackwell.

Oppermann, Kai and Henrike Viehrig (2011) *Issue Salience in International Politics.* London; New York: Routledge.

Websites

Details about the transatlantic crisis over the Iraq War: Gordon, Phillip H. and Jeremy Shapiro (2004) *Allies at War. America, Europe, and the Crisis over Iraq.* New York;

London: McGraw-Hill: users.telenet.be/sbruyneel/McGraw.Hill.Allies.At.War.America.
Europe.and.the.Crisis.Over.Iraq%20.pdf.

Information on US public diplomacy: publicdiplomacy.org/pages/index.php?page=about-public-diplomacy.

References

Bahador, Babak (2007) *The CNN Effect in Action. How the News Media Pushed the West Toward War in Kosovo*. Basingstoke: Palgrave Macmillan.

Balabanova, Ekaterina (2007) *Media, Wars and Politics. Comparing the Incomparable in Western and Eastern Europe*. Aldershot: Ashgate.

Beaudoin, Christopher E. and Esther Thorson (2002) 'Spiral of Violence? Conflict and Conflict Resolution in International News', pp. 45–64 in Eytan Gilboa (ed.) *Media and Conflict. Framing Issues, Making Policy, Shaping Opinions*. Ardsley, NY: Transnational Publishers.

Bennett, W. L. (1990) 'Toward a Theory of Press–State Relations in the United States', *Journal of Communication* 40(2): 103–27.

Bennett, W. L. and David L. Paletz (eds) (1994) *Taken by Storm. The Media, Public Opinion, and US Foreign Policy in the Gulf War*. Chicago; London: University of Chicago Press.

Bennett, W. L., Regina G. Lawrence and Steven Livingston (2006) 'None Dare Call It Torture. Indexing and the Limits of Press Independence in the Abu Ghraib Scandal', *Journal of Communication* 56(3): 467–85.

Davison, Walter P. (1974) *Mass Communication and Conflict Resolution. The Role of the Information Media in the Advancement of International Understanding*. New York: Praeger.

Entman, Robert M. (1993) 'Framing. Toward Clarification of a fractured paradigm', *Journal of Communication* 43(1): 51–8.

——— (2000) 'Declarations of Independence. The Growth of Media Power after the Cold War', pp. 11–26 in Brigitte L. Nacos, Robert Y. Shapiro and Pierangelo Isernia (eds) *Decisionmaking in a Glass House. Mass Media, Public Opinion, and American and European Foreign Policy in the 21st Century*. Lanhan MD: Rowman & Littlefield.

——— (2004) *Projections of Power. Framing News, Public Opinion, and US Foreign Policy*. Chicago: University of Chicago Press.

——— (2007) 'Framing Bias', *Journal of Communication* 57(1): 163–73.

——— (2008) 'Theorizing Mediated Public Diplomacy: The U.S. Case', *The International Journal of Press/Politics* 13(2): 87–102.

Gamson, William A. (2001) 'Foreword', pp. ix–x in Stephen D. Reese, Oscar H. Gandy Jr. and August E. Grant (eds) *Framing Public Life. Perspectives on Media and Our Understanding of the Social World*. Mahwah, NJ; London: Lawrence Erlbaum.

Gilboa, Eytan (2002) *Media and Conflict. Framing Issues, Making Policy, Shaping Opinions*. Ardsley, NY: Transnational Publishers.

Gilboa, Eytan and Efraim Inbar (eds) (2009) *Israeli Relations in a New Era. Issues and Challenges after 9/11*. London; New York: Routledge.

Goffman, Erving (1974) *Frame Analysis. An Essay on the Organization of Experience.* New York: Harper & Row.

Goodman, Robyn S. (1999) 'Prestige Press Coverage of US–China Policy during the Cold War's Collapse and Post-Cold War Years', *Gazette* 61(5): 391–410.

Gordon, Phillip H. and Jeremy Shapiro (2004) *Allies at War. America, Europe, and the Crisis over Iraq.* New York; London: McGraw-Hill.

Habermas, Jürgen (1985) *Die neue Unübersichtlichkeit. Kleine politische Schriften V.* Frankfurt am Main: Suhrkamp.

Hallin, Daniel C. (1984) 'The Media, the War in Vietnam, and Political Support. A Critique of the Thesis of the Oppositional Media', *Journal of Politics* 46(1): 2–24.

Hammond, Phil (2007) *Framing Post-Cold War Conflicts. The Media and International Intervention.* Manchester: Manchester University Press.

Herman, Edward S. and Noam Chomsky (1988) *Manufacturing Consent. The Political Economy of the Mass Media.* New York: Pantheon Books.

Hewstone, Miles (1989) *Causal Attribution. From Cognitive Processes to Collective Beliefs.* Oxford: Basil Blackwell.

———— (1990) 'The "Ultimate Attribution Error". A Review of Literature on Intergroup Causal Attribution', *European Journal of Social Psychology* 20(4): 311–35.

Iyengar, Shanto and Adam Simon (1993) 'News Coverage of the Gulf Crisis and Public Opinion', *Communication Research* 20(3): 365–83.

Jäger, Thomas, and Henrike Viehrig, H. (2005) *Gesellschaftliche Bedrohungswahrnehmung und Elitenkonsens. Eine Analyse der europäischen Haltung zum Irakkrieg 2003.* Arbeitspapiere zur Internationalen Politik 1. Cologne: University of Cologne.

Kagan, Robert (2004) *Of Paradise and Power. America and Europe in the New World Order.* New York: Vintage Books.

Kowert, Paul (1998) 'Agent versus Structure in the Construction of National Identity', pp. 101–22 in Vendulka Kubalkova, Nicholas Onuf and Paul Kowert (eds) *International Relations in a Constructed World.* Armonk, NY: M. E. Sharpe.

Livingston, Steven (2003) 'Diplomacy in the New Information Environment', *Georgetown Journal of International Affairs* 4(2): 111–16.

Malek, Abbas (2003) 'Foreign Policy and the Media. Studies in International News Coverage and News Agenda', pp. 23–9 in Daniel Johnston (ed.) *Encyclopedia of International Media and Communications.* Amsterdam: Elsevier.

Malek, Abbas (ed.) (1997) *News Media and Foreign Relations. A Multifaceted Perspective.* Norwood, NJ: Ablex.

Malek, Abbas and Anandam P. Kavoori (eds) (2000) *The Global Dynamics of News. Studies in International News Coverage and News Agenda.* Stamford, CT: Ablex.

Manheim, Jarol B. (1994) *Strategic Public Diplomacy and American Foreign Policy. The Evolution of Influence.* New York; Oxford: Oxford University Press.

McBride, Seán (ed.) (1980) *Many Voices, One World. Communication and Society – Today and Tomorrow. Towards a New More Just and More Efficient World Information and Communication Order.* London: Kogan Page.

McCombs, Maxwell (2004) *Setting the Agenda. The Mass Media and Public Opinion*. Malden: Blackwell.

Melischek, Gabriele and Josef Seethaler (2008) 'Media and International Relations. An Attributional Analysis of In-Group and Out-Group Perceptions in European Press Coverage of the 2004 US Election', *American Journal of Media Psychology* 1(1–2): 103–24.

Melischek, Gabriele, Josef Seethaler and Jürgen Wilke (eds) (2008) *Medien & Kommunikationsforschung im Vergleich. Grundlagen, Gegenstandsbereiche, Verfahrensweisen*. Wiesbaden: VS Verlag für Sozialwissenschaften.

Melissen, Jan (ed.) (2005) *The New Public Diplomacy. Soft Power in International Relations*. Basingstoke: Palgrave Macmillan.

Mermin, Jonathan (1999) *Debating War and Peace. Media Coverage of US Intervention in the Post-Vietnam Era*. Princeton, NJ; Chichester: Princeton University Press.

Nacos, Brigitte L. (2007) *Mass-Mediated Terrorism. The Central Role of the Media in Terrorism and Counterterrorism*. Lanham, MD: Rowman & Littlefield.

Nacos, Brigitte L., Robert Y. Shapiro and Pierangelo Isernia (eds) (2000) *Decisionmaking in a Glass House. Mass Media, Public Opinion, and American and European Foreign Policy in the 21st Century*. Lanhan MD: Rowman & Littlefield.

Norris, Pippa, Montague Kern and Marion R. Just (2003) *Framing Terrorism. The News Media, the Government, and the Public*. New York; London: Routledge.

Osgood, Charles E. (1959) 'The Representational Model and Relevant Research Methods', pp. 33–88 in Ithiel de Sola Pool (ed.) *Trends in Content Analysis*. Urbana: University of Illinois Press.

Page, Benjamin I. (2000) 'Toward General Theories of the Media, Public Opinion, and Foreign Policy', pp. 85–91 in Brigitte L. Nacos, Robert Y. Shapiro and Pierangelo Isernia (eds) *Decisionmaking in a Glass House. Mass Media, Public Opinion, and American and European Foreign Policy in the 21st Century*. Lanhan, MD: Rowman & Littlefield.

Reese, Stephen D., Oscar H. Gandy Jr. and August E. Grant (eds) (2001) *Framing Public Life. Perspectives on Media and Our Understanding of the Social World*. Mahwah, NJ; London: Lawrence Erlbaum.

Risse-Kappen, Thomas (1991) 'Public Opinion, Domestic Structure, and Foreign Policy in Liberal Democracies', *World Politics* 43(4): 479–512.

Rivenburgh (1997) 'Social Identification and Media Coverage of Foreign Relations', pp. 79–91 in Abbas Malek (ed.) *News Media and Foreign Relations. A Multifaceted Perspective*. Norwood, NJ: Ablex.

Robinson, Piers (2002) *The CNN Effect. The Myth of News, Foreign Policy and Intervention*. London: Routledge.

Rosengren, Karl E. and Sven Windahl (1989) *Media Matter. TV Use in Childhood and Adolescence*. Norwood, NJ: Ablex.

Scheufele, Dietram A. (1999) 'Framing as a Theory of Media Effects', *Journal of Communication* 49(1): 103–22.

Seethaler, Josef and Gabriele Melischek (2011) 'Integrating Salience and Interpretation. A Constructivist Approach to Media Framing in the Post-Cold War Era', pp. 99–117 in Kai

Oppermann and Henrike Viehrig (eds) *Issue Salience in International Politics*. New York, NY; London: Routledge.

Seib, Philip M. (ed.) (2005) *Media and Conflict in the Twenty-First Century*. New York: Palgrave Macmillan.

Seib, Philip M. (2008) *The Al Jazeera Effect. How the New Global Media Are Reshaping World Politics*. Washington, DC: Potomac Books.

Shah, Dhavan V., Douglas M. McLeod, Melissa R. Gotlieb and Nam-Jin Lee (2009) 'Framing and Agenda Setting', pp. 69–82 in Robin L. Nabi and Mary B. Oliver (eds) *The Sage Handbook of Media Processes and Effects*. Los Angeles: Sage.

Shapiro, Robert Y. and Lawrence R. Jacobs (2002) 'Public Opinion, Foreign Policy, and Democracy. How Presidents Use Public Opinion', pp. 184–200 in Jeff Manza, Fay L. Cook and Benjamin J. Page (eds) *Navigating Public Opinion. Polls, Policy, and the Future of American Democracy*. Oxford: Oxford University Press.

Shlapentokh, Vladimir, Joshua Woods and Eric Shiraev (eds) (2005) *America. Sovereign Defender or Cowboy Nation?* Aldershot: Ashgate.

Spencer, Graham (2008) *The Media and Peace. From Vietnam to the ‚'War on Terror'*. Basingstoke: Palgrave.

Sreberny-Mohammadi, Annabelle (1985) *Foreign News in the Media. International Reporting in 29 Countries*. Paris: UNESCO.

Tenscher, Jens and Henrike Viehrig (eds) (2007) *Internationale Politische Kommunikation. Annäherungen an eine transdisziplinäre Forschungsperspektive*. Berlin: LIT Verlag.

Volkmer, Ingrid (2004) *News in the Global Sphere. A Study of CNN and Its Impact on Global Communications*. Luton, Bedfordshire: University of Luton Press.

Wasburn, Philo C. (2002) *The Social Construction of International News. We're Talking About Them, They're Talking About Us*. Westport, CT: Praeger.

Weiner, Bernard (1986) *An Attributional Theory of Motivation and Emotion*. New York: Springer-Verlag.

Wendt, Alexander (1999) *Social Theory of International Politics*. Cambridge: Cambridge University Press.

Wilke, Jürgen (1993) 'Internationale Beziehungen und Massenmedien', pp. 175–91 in Heinz Bonfadelli and Werner A. Meier (eds) *Krieg, Aids, Katastrophen. Gegenwartsprobleme als Herausforderung für die Publizistikwissenschaft. Festschrift für Ulrich Saxer*. Konstanz: Universitätsverlag.

Wolfsfeld, Gadi (1997) *Media and Political Conflict. News from the Middle East*. Cambridge: Cambridge University Press.

——— (2004) *Media and the Path to Peace*. Cambridge: Cambridge University Press.

Zaller, John R. (1992) *The Nature and Origins of Mass Opinion*. Cambridge: Cambridge University Press.

Zaller, John R. and Dennis Chiu (2000) 'Government's Little Helper. US Press Coverage of Foreign Policy Crises, 1945–1999', pp. 61–84 in Brigitte L. Nacos, Robert Y. Shapiro and Pierangelo Isernia (eds) *Decisionmaking in a Glass House. Mass Media, Public Opinion, and American and European Foreign Policy in the 21st Century*. Lanhan, MD: Rowman & Littlefield.

Zucker, Harold G. (1978) 'The Variable Nature of News Media Influence', pp. 154–72 in Brent D. Ruben (ed.) *Communication Yearbook 2*. New Brunswick, NJ: Transaction Books.

Zuckerman, Miron (1979) 'Attribution of Success and Failure Revisited, or: The Motivational Bias Is Alive and Well in Attribution Theory', *Journal of Personality* 47: 245–87.

Notes

1   See 'Surging Beyond Realism: How the US Media Promote War Again and Again' chapter by Robert M. Entman in this book.

2   Evaluations of past or fictional situations (usually used to compare with the actual situation) were not coded.

3   According to Osgood's (1959) 'evaluative assertion analysis', all sentences in which attitude objects appear were transformed into the following statement form: attitude object (referring to the actor of interest)/verbal connector/meaning term (referring to issues, evaluations of issue-related behavior or explanations of these evaluations).

4   According to Entman (1993), treatment recommendation has to be considered as a fourth element of news frames.

5   Foreign policy, domestic policy, enonomic policy, general political issues/overall approvals, campaign issues.

6   In logistic regression analysis, the unstandardized regression coefficient (B coefficient) represents the change in the logit of the dependent variable resulting from a unit change in the predictor variable (with plus indicating an increase and minus a decrease). The logit of the dependent variable is the natural logarithm of the odds of this change occurring. Therefore, in addition to the B coefficient, the value of the odds ratio – $\exp(B)$ – is provided, which is an indicator of the change in odds resulting from a unit change in the predictor variable (holding all other independent variables constant). A value greater than 1 indicates that as the predictor increases, the odds of the outcome occurring increases. Conversely, a value less than 1 indicates that as the predictor increases, the odds of the outcome occurring decreases.

7   The example of Italy shows that the journalists' willingness to join or 'index' their government's position is to a greater extent intertwined with the media's tendency to follow their editorial line, if there is – as Hallin (1984) has argued – no consensus among political elites (Melischek and Seethaler, 2008). In Italy, the degree of consensus among political elites regarding the Iraq War was among the lowest in Europe (Jaeger and Viehrig, 2005).

8   Only an average of about 27 percent of all articles on US politics in the eight newspapers under study dealt with Senator Kerry (compared to 40 percent dealing with President Bush).

Surging Beyond Realism

How the US Media Promote War Again and Again

Robert M. Entman

Summary

This chapter[1] considers the possible role of distortion in the American public sphere with respect to the foreign policies of the United States. The distortion resides in this: military definitions of problems and military solutions become the default, the automatic and dominant way of thinking in the United States about international relations. This framework renders American foreign policy unrealistic in both the common and theoretical senses of the word. That is, the content of the public sphere fails sufficiently to reflect what history teaches and what current information strongly suggests are important and indisputable realities. Beyond this, US foreign policy fails to conform to realist or neorealist theories of international relations, which assume the state is a rational power- or security-maximizing actor. In fact, arguably, no theory of international relations adequately explains the US government's many self-defeating or excessively costly defense policies from Vietnam through Afghanistan. Instead, American foreign policy intellectuals, policy-makers and journalists appear caught in a syndrome that discourages (without entirely preventing) all from realistically assessing either the lessons of the past or current facts on the ground to applying them in pursuit of US power or security. A major reason for the theoretical shortfall in understanding this situation is that none of the major international relations theories fully incorporate the influence of mediated communication on elite calculations about domestic public opinion and political feasibility. This chapter attempts to fill that vacuum by suggesting a way to incorporate media influence into theories of foreign policy-making and international relations, using aspects of US war policies in Afghanistan and Iraq as illustrations.

Surging Beyond Realism

The ability to understand a question from all sides meant one was totally unfit for action. Fanatical enthusiasm was the mark of the real man. [...] Any who planned beforehand in order that no [war] measures should be necessary was a 'subverter of the party' and was accused of being intimidated by the opposition. (Thucydides, *The Peloponnesian War*, Book 3:82–3:83: Civil War in Corcyra)

Attended by many of the United States' leading defense policy intellectuals, the concluding session of the Triangle Institute of Security Studies Conference on 'American Grand

Strategy After War' (February 25–27, 2009) covered the strategic lessons of the Iraq War. At the session, the following claim went unchallenged: President Obama had no choice at the onset of his administration but to escalate US troop levels in Afghanistan. Why? To avoid being blamed for a future terrorist attack on the United States. As long as the United States acts forcefully in Afghanistan, went the reasoning as articulated by the Council of Foreign Relations expert Stephen Biddle, it will reduce the danger of being held politically responsible for not doing enough to prevent a future assault. The assembled experts at the conference appeared to agree that the political risk of being blamed, however groundlessly, for a terrorist attack outweighed the risk in doing what Thucydides recommended, that is, try 'to understand from all sides' and plan to avoid war. Influential *Time* magazine columnist Joe Klein essentially ratified this reading of the Washington defense elites' conventional wisdom in an essay published the next week (Klein, 2009).[2]

How could American policy be driven by political logic to increased military action in utter disregard of substantive illogic, and what are the theoretical implications? This chapter offers some answers by considering the possible role of distortion in the American public sphere with respect to US foreign policy. The distortion resides in this: military definitions of problems and military solutions become the default, the automatic and dominant way of thinking about international relations. This framework renders American foreign policy unrealistic in both the common and theoretical senses of the word. That is, the content of the public sphere fails sufficiently to reflect what history teaches and what current information strongly suggests are important and indisputable realities.

Beyond this, US foreign policy fails to conform to realist or neorealist theories of international relations, which assume the state is a rational power- or security-maximizing actor.[3] In fact, arguably, no theory of international relations adequately explains the US government's many self-defeating or excessively costly defense policies from Vietnam through Afghanistan. Instead, American foreign policy intellectuals, policy-makers and journalists appear caught in a syndrome that discourages (without entirely preventing) all from realistically assessing either the lessons of the past or current facts on the ground to applying them in pursuit of US power or security. A major reason for the theoretical shortfall in understanding this situation is that none of the major international relations theories[4] fully incorporates the heavy influence of mediated communication on elite calculations about domestic public opinion and political feasibility.

The communication media's role is shaped by their intense pro-military bias, that is, predictable patterns of reporting and editorializing (see Entman, 2007, on bias) that support the military framing of problems and solutions. This cognitive configuration makes it politically dangerous for politicians to fundamentally dissent from viewing international relations first and foremost through a military prism. Also, the militaristic bias of the media constitutes a primary reason for the divorce of American policy-making from expectations embodied in realist theories of foreign policy-making.

In other words, the media create incentives for elites not to realistically assimilate the lessons of history and thus to repeat their past mistakes of overestimating the effectiveness or underestimating the costs of war (see Van Evera, 2001: Chapter 2). After all, central to realist and neorealist doctrine is the assumption that states are rational actors. If rationality means anything, it means taking into account, even if imperfectly, lessons of the past and data from the present (see Neustadt and May, 1988, on the misuse of historical analogies) in plotting strategy for dealing with problems. The argument here is that the operations of the communication media undermine (though they do not entirely prevent) the inclinations and abilities of elites to act in that manner.[5]

Furthermore, we know there is an intimate relationship between media texts and elites' public talk (Hallin, 1986; Bennett, 1990; Mermin, 1999). In the context here, that means a self-reinforcing spiral exists: in part because elites generally either fail to see or fear for political reasons to fully apply lessons of history that counsel against military action; their public discourse is historically impoverished. That means journalists have little continuing basis to take account of history – even very recent history – in their reports. The dependence on elite words and deeds to shape today's news is so strong that it appears all but impossible for news organizations themselves to avoid repeating yesterday's mistakes – further perpetuating elites' incentives to neglect history (on event-driven news, see Entman, 2008; Entman et al., 2009; Livingston and Bennett, 2003).

Academia seems to play a critical role here. Academics have more impact on America's practice of international relations – think of Henry Kissinger, Paul Wolfowitz, MacGeorge Bundy, Madeleine Albright – and also more influence over media discourse than is true in most areas of public policy-making (see Snyder, 2004). Academic experts on crime do not head the FBI, nor do professors usually head the treasury or health departments. Yet the academic influence on foreign policy-making may come at the cost of self-censorship and constraints on the way they frame problems and solutions. The defense-oriented intellectuals – the ones on whom journalists rely heavily for quotable expertize – are subsidized to a far greater extent by military funding directly and indirectly through think tanks than those promoting peace, just as the Pentagon's budget dwarfs that of the State Department and the US Institute of Peace. Moreover, Washington journalists, policy-makers and foreign policy academic experts interact within the same, arguably conformist, social milieu, as discussed insightfully in Bennett, Lawrence and Livingston's *When the Press Fails* (2007).

Thus, the militaristic media bias is reinforced by journalists' relationships to a military-academic complex that concentrates its intellectual energies on military problems and solutions. Implicit in most academic writings on US national security is that the core policy objective must be maintaining American power, by which is apparently meant its ability to do what it wants and compel others to acquiesce. Although most writings acknowledge that nonmilitary factors influence the degree of American power, they tend explicitly or implicitly to downplay them (Nye, 2004, is an exception).

For instance, in Brooks and Wohlworth's (2008) account, US 'primacy' in the world system remains; indeed, the United States enjoys 'historically unprecedented advantages in the scales of world power' (Brooks and Wohlworth, 2008: 1) and a 'concentration of power resources [that] renders inoperative the constraining effects' of the international system (Brooks and Wohlworth, 2008: 3). The ultimate basis for this argument appears to be (a) a narrow equation of security with invulnerability to military conquest of the national territory and (b) a belief that the United States possesses an ability to impose its will in order to protect more broadly conceived security interests to a greater degree than any other individual state or combination of nations.

Given the conspicuous failure during the first decade of the twenty-first century of the United States to impose its will in defeating the Taliban and al-Qaeda, inducing China to revalue its currency to right the crippling trade imbalance, compelling Saudi Arabia and other putative allies (let alone enemies) to stop supporting terrorism, stabilizing Pakistan, bringing the Israel–Palestine conflict to peaceful resolution, curbing Iranian nuclear ambitions, controlling Russian power assertions, cleaning up the drug wars in Mexico and Colombia, controlling illegal immigration to the United States, doing anything serious about climate change or reducing its dependence on oil – not to mention its incapacity to prevent a costly global economic decline starting in 2008 – this seems a somewhat problematic argument. Problematic, that is, unless one's underlying assumption is that what power ultimately means is the ability to beat up any threatening kid on the block – as long as that kid fights fair, by means of conventional symmetric warfare. Yet that capability seems not to have done the United States much good since it became the alleged lone superpower after the collapse of the Soviet Union (see Johnson, 2004).

Research grants and ties to military and related government bureaucracies and private interests constrain discourse to heavy reliance on military means, to conceptualizing problems for US interests as military problems first and foremost. For example, perhaps the most visible debate in recent years among those who study domestic influences on US foreign policy has been over how tolerant the public is to American casualties (Brooks and Wohlworth, 2008: 5; see also Feaver and Gelpi, 2005). The assumption that heavily inflects this debate is that intolerance of casualties is a bad thing because it unduly constrains America's foreign policy options – a cornerstone of the realist disdain for public opinion.

The Media and Realism

This chapter briefly explores two recent and compelling empirical examples of the American media's inability to learn either from history itself or from their own organizational histories and explores the implications for US foreign policy-making. The examples come from my forthcoming book written with Sean Aday and Steve Livingston tentatively entitled *Framing Failure*.

The first suggests that the Bush administration used al-Qaeda in Iraq (AQI) and its purported leader Abu Musab al-Zarqawi as a replacement for the nonexistent weapons of mass destruction (WMD) in justifying its war policy once the WMD problem was debunked. All the well-known mistakes American journalists made in covering WMD were recapitulated in covering AQI and Zarqawi. So, after admitting and apologizing for their poor performance during the run-up to the Iraq War during 2002–03, the US media have largely performed in almost identical ways ever since, repeating their mistakes. The effect was to encourage US policy-makers to maintain (or refrain from criticizing) demonstrably failing war policies between 2004 and 2006, and to sustain the US occupation after that.

The second case analyzes media treatment of the Afghanistan problem during and since the 2008 presidential campaign – treatment that lay behind the reasoning that introduced this chapter, the idea that President Obama had no choice but to escalate the war in Afghanistan. In other words, Obama must repeat the Iraq mistake: sending an insufficient number of troops to perform an implausible (or impossible), financially costly and strategically murky mission of democratic nation-building in a hostile, tribally divided Muslim country that has no cultural basis for a quick transition to western-style democracy – or even to self-identity as a single nation state. And Obama does so with very little in the way of balancing potential benefits against a realistic accounting of costs for using military force.

Zarqawi as the New WMD

Let us recall the widely acknowledged traits characterizing pre-war media coverage of the WMD problem in Iraq and the media's general support for the military solution (see Bennett et al., 2007; Isikoff and Corn, 2006):

- Relying on administration sources for most information while neglecting readily available contrary information and dissenting experts and elites – and even failing to read their own news organizations' contrary reports, usually buried on page 18
- Granting credibility to dubious intelligence claims and self-serving communication strategies of the Pentagon
- Hyping a threat that turned out to be far smaller than the US government claimed
- Going along with exaggerated claims of success in combating the threat, seizing on any morsel of good news or information that seemed to confirm the administration line
- Virtually ignoring the overall strategic implications of the threats, remedies and alleged successes

These traits were on ample display in the coverage of Abu Musab al-Zarqawi. He was a Jordanian who inserted himself into an internal Kurdish political struggle by affiliating with a Sunni Kurdish insurgent group that opposed both Osama bin Laden and Saddam Hussein. Later Zarqawi loosely linked up with Osama bin Laden's al-Qaeda and renamed the group he led al-Qaeda in Iraq or Mesopotamia (AQI), we must assume largely for marketing reasons. Although this group was surely violent and much of its activity no doubt pleased

Osama bin Laden, we know that the vast majority of the insurgent violence in Iraq was not caused by AQI or Zarqawi, nor was it controlled by Osama bin Laden.

One measure of media repetition of the very mistakes they had so recently apologized for is the heavy reliance on government and military officials for stories about him. For instance, in analyzing every *New York Times* story that referred to him, Aday, Livingston and Raina (2009) found Zarqawi was less likely to get in the lead of a story when he admitted to an attack than he was if US military or government officials mentioned him, even if he had not actually committed any acts warranting attention. In other words, government propaganda statements about Zarqawi were treated as substantially more newsworthy than alleged actions by Zarqawi.

We also believe (although have not yet confirmed) that the media – as in Vietnam – accepted US government body counts when it came to numbers of 'enemies' killed and to labeling the identity of those enemies. As in Vietnam deaths were often attributed to North Vietnamese Army aggression that might have been caused by South Vietnamese guerillas, so in Iraq we suspect news reports strikingly overestimated the amount of violence caused by AQI as opposed to other insurgents.

One way to illustrate the filling of the vacuum left when the WMD rationale collapsed by using AQI and Zarqawi is by comparing the media's treatment of the good news when Zarqawi was killed in June 2006 to the coverage of the deeply discouraging bad news embedded in the US National Intelligence Estimate (NIE) on Iraq in February 2007. *Time* magazine put Zarqawi on its cover, and *Newsweek* featured Zarqawi prominently on its website, displaying a gallery of seventeen pictures relating to him, including a close-up death image that appeared in most major news outlets, and both magazines featured lengthy diagrams detailing the US forces' dramatic execution of Zarqawi.

Although both also contained passages warning that its success would not end the bloodletting in Iraq – President Bush admitted as much – these caveats were belied by the enormous visual attention. And the cautious words were outweighed by careful dissections of, as Fareed Zakaria (editor of *Newsweek International*) wrote, 'political signs' that gave reason for 'hope'. The killing offered visually compelling images, symbolized much-desired progress, and above all, offered emotionally gratifying victory against a personalized enemy. In the event, insurgent and militia violence shot up dramatically after Zarqawi's death.

Compare the fuss about this purported indicator of military progress to treatment of the February 2, 2007, release of the NIE, the consensus view of sixteen US intelligence agencies indicating the remote likelihood of strategic success in Iraq. The typical media response to this negative report was apparently boredom. A search of the 39 US newspapers in the LexisNexis Major Papers library reveals just six newspapers mentioning the NIE report on the front page and seventeen covering it on inside pages (average page number = 11). Just three of the papers published unsigned editorials on the report.

Time did not mention the NIE at all, according to a Nexis search. *Newsweek* devoted seven sentences to it in a total of three different stories. CBS and NBC each did broadcast 350- to 400-word stories that accurately summarized the report's 'dark new assessment'

(NBC *Nightly News*, February 2, 2007), whereas *ABC* apparently ignored it. In contrast, *ABC*'s *World News* devoted about 4,000 words to Zarqawi's death in just its first two days of coverage, and CBS and NBC offered similarly extensive treatment.

The disparity in media reactions reveals news organizations' apparent proclivities to convey the administration's orchestrations of news that promotes its military problem definition and remedy, such as the Zarqawi death, while allocating comparatively little attention to news, such as the NIE report, that fundamentally challenges the underlying military justifications and remedies of the administration policy. Journalists might have regarded the NIE report as 'old news', in that its pessimism did not radically differ from that of the Iraq Study Group (ISG) headed by James Baker and Lee Hamilton a few months earlier. But whereas the ISG was produced by a bipartisan group of foreign policy 'realists' no longer serving in government, the NIE represented a consensus of sixteen intelligence agencies led by the Bush administration's own appointees. Aside from its importance to assessing policy, this story might therefore have been expected to generate more attention for its 'man-bites-dog' quality.

The kind of coverage illustrated by these examples may help explain the course of public opinion between mid-2004 and mid-2006, which established a political environment that discouraged elite dissent from Bush's military solution. After a drop coinciding roughly with the Abu Ghraib scandal and the first anniversary of the war, in spring 2004, many indicators of public opinion stabilized. Perhaps, more important than this apparent stability in surveyed public opinion was its disorganization.

This trait is illustrated by an August 2006 *New York Times* and CBS poll showing 55 percent approving President Bush's handling of the campaign against terrorism, even while 60 percent disapproved his 'handling of the Iraq situation'. It was Bush himself who said Iraq was the main front in the 'War on Terror'; yet substantial majorities simultaneously opposed his Iraq policy and endorsed his conduct of that 'War on Terror'. A majority of voters also gave him and his Congressional party victories in the 2004 presidential and congressional elections.

The absence of a clear trend toward a crystallized majority opposed to the president's Iraq policy sent ambiguous political signals to leaders, discouraging elite opponents to war from active dissent. Until at least the November 2006 elections, no large and consistent majority opinion for policy change was apparent – no unambiguous pressure or encouragement from polls showing a majority seeking rapid termination of the war.

Our research suggests that the two-year period of stability and contradiction in indicators of public opinion reflects, to some extent, the press's incapacity to consistently narrate the shortcomings of the war policy – that is, to clearly portray the Bush administration's incompetence in conception and execution of its military solution at least through 2006, a judgment that virtually every expert and politician across the ideological spectrum agreed on by 2007.

Instead, although they certainly provided many episodic reports of bad news in Iraq, they remained consistently responsive to government's military frame. Thus the polls offered disorganized, difficult-to-interpret information to elites, reflecting the weakness and disorganization of the oppositional frame in the media even as it reinforced the disincentives for elites to invest political capital in organizing such an opposing narrative. Indeed, throughout 2007 and 2008, anxiety about a public backlash for 'losing' Iraq apparently kept the Democratic majority in Congress from using all the tools at its disposal to force troop withdrawals. Thus was the government's persistence in Iraq War policy bolstered, lessons of history notwithstanding. The relationships look something like this adaptation of Entman's (2004) cascading network activation model (Figure 1):

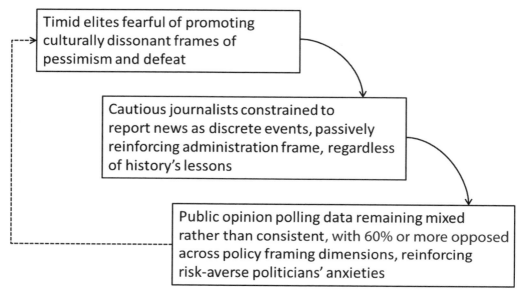

Figure 1: Explaining the Limits of Elite and Media Opposition, or Why (US) Journalists Are Doomed to Repeat.

Without going into detail, it is worth noting that despite the repudiation of the ruling Republican Party in the 2006 election, the policy response was actually to escalate the war in the form of the so-called 'surge'. Our data suggest that media coverage early on favored the surge. Although it became much more negative later on, media treatment of the surge later turned heavily positive as elites from Obama to John McCain pronounced it a 'success' – a judgment that except in military terms was highly premature (Aday et al., forthcoming). I might add that Obama's praise for the surge is yet another example of elite fear of speaking up against military framing for fear of the media's militaristic bias, just as was his decision to escalate in Afghanistan.

Obama's Treatment of the Afghanistan Problem

Turning now to Afghanistan coverage, we analyzed every Page 1 story in the *New York Times* from January 1, 2008, through February 25, 2009, on the assumption that America's most prestigious, influential newspaper would offer the most rigorous test of our argument. We found 36 front-page stories referencing Afghanistan. We also did a separate and quite limited analysis of 54 newspapers' treatment of Obama's February 17, 2009, decision to escalate the war. These analyses both support our argument.

In the 36 front-page *New York Times* stories, fully fifteen mentioned *only* military solutions, whereas one focused exclusively on diplomatic solutions and one only on nation-building. Four others mentioned both the military solution and a review of Afghanistan policy conducted during the early weeks of the Obama administration. Aside from three stories that mentioned no solution, the rest of the stories, numbering twelve, covered some combination of solutions, and of them, ten at least included the military option in the mix.

Thus a focus on the military dimension overwhelmed all others. One combination story mentioned both the troop increase and the option of total withdrawal from Afghanistan – and this was the only story of the 36 mentioning military withdrawal at all.

To provide another test of media recapitulating history, we looked at the 53 US newspapers included in the Press Display database plus the *New York Times* for the two days following Obama's decision (February 18 and 19). We found just eight put the story on Page 1, with four of them including a picture (which conveys the story's importance and encourages readership).[6] Five papers published editorials on the decision (albeit all critical) on February 18 or 19. Not only does this minimal coverage of a major policy shift echo the treatment of the NIE report in 2007, but it also recapitulates what happened during Vietnam when President Johnson decided on a major escalation that went barely noted by the press.

Discussion and Conclusion

What explains the media's militaristic bias? In brief, professional norms interacting with commercial, cultural and political pressures come together to create a vicious spiral of elite silence. These interactions are explored at greater length in the forthcoming book (Aday et al., forthcoming).

America's non-utility maximizing, if not irrational, approach to the pursuit of US interests has dire consequences for the entire world. The distorting effect of the American media's militaristic bias and journalists' inability to learn from their own mistakes covering past wars or even from mistakes made early on when covering wars that last for many years influences the entire international system. There are exceptions to this tendency, mainly involving what we might call the 'Nixon in China' syndrome; that is, when the normally more bellicose Republican Party favors diplomacy over force, or favors non-involvement, the media treatment becomes far less militaristic (see Entman, 2004). However, such periods are rare.

Let us end on a deliberately provocative note: perhaps the international system would be better off if indeed US foreign policy conformed to realist theory rather than so often pursuing military options that either undermine America's own interests or impose on the United States itself costs far in excess of any benefits. If that is ever to happen, major media organizations would have to alter their practices. Although calls for journalism reform are virtually always useless, it seems to me not inconceivable that journalists could use a realist frame that constantly asks 'How does this policy serve America's self-interest?' despite all the pressure from elites and citizens as well to treat unwavering support of military solutions as the only path to patriotism.

Key Points

- Military definitions of problems and military solutions become the default, the automatic and the dominant way of thinking in the foreign policy-making process of the United States, the most powerful country in the international system.
- The media's role is underappreciated by conventional theories of international relations. Perhaps the most important gap in theory is its neglect of the way the US media's standard operating procedures discourage American policy-makers and defense intellectuals from realistically assessing either the lessons of the past or current facts on the ground and applying them in pursuit of US power or security.
- This suggests the need to modify existing theories of international relations to take account of the possibility that domestic media considerations reduce the applicability of realist, neorealist and liberal internationalist theories to actual behavior by nation states, at least in the case of the United States.
- Illustrating this point, contrary to conventional wisdom, is the fact that US journalistic shortcomings in covering Iraq between 2002 and 2009 were not limited to the pre-war period, during which dubious claims about the intentions, past actions and capabilities of Saddam Hussein's government were accepted without much questioning. But these shortcomings continued throughout the war in Afghanistan and apply just as much to the coverage of it.

Study Questions

1. Compare the incentives and disincentives that the dominant newsmaking practices of European and US media create for those making defense policies in the respective countries.
2. Construct a new theory of international relations that takes into account the important role of mediated political communication, or modify one of the major existing theories so that it incorporates the influence of the media on policy-making and public opinion.
3. Imagine a new set of media practices – a set of procedures for making international news that could actually be implemented by the American media – that might reduce the militaristic bias that, according to the author, distorts the foreign and defense policies of the United States.

Further Reading

Bennett, Lance W., Regina G. Lawrence and Steven Livingston (2007) *When the Press Fails. Political Power and the News Media from Iraq to Katrina*. Chicago, IL: University of Chicago Press.

Entman, Robert M. (2004) *Projections of Power. Framing News, Public Opinion, and U.S. Foreign Policy*. Chicago, IL: University of Chicago Press.

Nacos, Brigitte L., Robert Y. Shapiro and Pierangelo Isernia (eds) (2000) *Decisionmaking in a Glass House. Mass Media, Public Opinion, and American and European Foreign Policy in the 21st Century*. Lanham: Rowman & Littlefield.

Websites

Nieman Watch Dog Journalism Project: www.niemanwatchdog.org.

Open Democracy: www.opendemocracy.net.

PEW Research Center's Project for Excellence in Journalism – Annual Report on American Journalism: www.stateofthemedia.org.

References

Aday, Sean, Steven Livingston and P. Raina (2009) *The Current Wars in Iraq*, Paper Presented at the International Studies Association Conference, New York.

Aday, Sean, Steven Livingston and Robert M. Entman (forthcoming) *Framing Failure*.

Bennett, Lance W. (1990) 'Toward a Theory of Press–State Relations in the United States', *Journal of Communication* 40(2): 103–27.

Bennett, Lance W., Regina G. Lawrence and Steven Livingston (2007) *When the Press Fails. Political Power and the News Media from Iraq to Katrina*. Chicago, IL: University of Chicago Press.

Brooks, Stephen G. and William Curti Wohlforth (2008) *World Out of Balance. International Relations and the Challenge of American Primacy*. Princeton, NJ: Princeton University Press.

Entman, Robert M. (2004) *Projections of Power. Framing News, Public Opinion, and U.S. Foreign Policy*. Chicago, IL: University of Chicago Press.

—— (2007) 'Framing Bias. Media in the Distribution of Power', *Journal of Communication* 57(1): 163–73.

—— (2008) 'Theorizing Mediated Public Diplomacy. The U.S. Case', *The International Journal of Press/Politics* 13(2): 87–102.

Entman, Robert M., Steven Livingston and Jennie Kim (2009) 'Doomed to Repeat. Iraq News, 2002–2007', *American Behavioral Scientist* 52(5): 689–708.

Feaver, Peter and Christopher Gelpi (2005) *Choosing Your Battles. American Civil–Military Relations and the Use of Force*. Princeton, NJ; Oxford: Princeton University Press.

Hallin, Daniel C. (1986) *The 'Uncensored War'. The Media and Vietnam*. New York; Oxford: Oxford University Press.

Isikoff, Michael and David Corn (2006) *Hubris. The Inside Story of Spin, Scandal, and the Selling of the Iraq War*. New York: Crown.

Jervis, Robert (2002) 'Theories of War in an Era of Leading-Power Peace', *American Political Science Review* 96(1): 1–14.

Johnson, Chalmers A. (2004) *The Sorrows of Empire*. New York: Metropolitan Books.

Keohane, Robert O. (1986) *Neorealism and Its Critics*. New York: Columbia University Press.

Klein, Joe (2009) 'Afghanistan: Can Obama Avoid a Quagmire?', *Time*, March 5.

Livingston, Steven and Lance W. Bennett (2003) 'Gatekeeping, Indexing, and Live-Event News. Is Technology Altering the Construction of News?', *Political Communication* 20(4): 363–80.

McDonald, Matt (2008) 'Securitization and the Construction of Security', *European Journal of International Relations* 14(4): 563–87.

Mermin, Jonathan (1999) *Debating War and Peace. Media Coverage of US Intervention in the Post-Vietnam Era*. Princeton, NJ: Princeton University Press.

Neustadt, Richard E. and Ernest R. May (1988) *Thinking in Time. The Uses of History for Decision-Makers*. New York: The Free Press.

Nye, Joseph S. (2004) *Soft Power. The Means to Success in World Politics*. New York: Public Affairs.

Page, Benjamin I. and Marshall M. Bouton (2006) *The Foreign Policy Disconnect. What Americans Want from Our Leaders but Don't Get*. Chicago, IL: University of Chicago Press.

Reus-Smit, Christian and Duncan Snidal (2008) *The Oxford Handbook of International Relations*. Oxford; New York: Oxford University Press.

Snyder, Jack (2004) 'One World, Rival Theories', *Foreign Policy* 145: 52–62.

Van Evera, Stephen (2001) *Causes of War. Power and the Roots of Conflict*. Ithaca: Cornell University Press.

Williams, Michael C. (2003) 'Words, Images, Enemies. Securitization and International Politics', *International Studies Quarterly* 47(4): 511–31.

Notes

1　This chapter draws heavily on Entman et al. (2009).

2　Wrote Klein, 'Taken together, the emerging Pakistan and Afghanistan policies sound … impossible, but unavoidable' (ellipsis in original).

3　Realist theory stresses the primary goal of states is power, neorealist that the chief aim is security (Van Evera, 2001: 15, Note 11; see also Keohane, 1986). An approachable summary of the other two major schools of thought, liberalism and constructivism, is Snyder (2004).

4　These also include liberal internationalism and constructivism and many variants and combinations (see Jervis, 2002; Reus-Smit and Snidal, 2008; Snyder, 2004). A recent addition, securitization (also called the Copenhagen School; see, for example, McDonald, 2008), does include political communication as a central component though without much attention to the role of mediated communication (Williams, 2003, is a partial exception).

5   It is worth noting that the normative stance within realism itself is to dismiss public opinion and domestic political considerations as a distraction and potential detriment to rational power-maximizing. Perhaps this is one reason the empirical theory neglects the role not merely of public opinion but of the communication media that shape elite perceptions of their domestic political options and opportunities in making foreign policy decisions (see Entman, 2004, on the role of media in shaping perceived and anticipated public opinion; see also Page and Bouton, 2006).

6   *USA Today, Los Angeles Times, Baltimore Sun, Houston Chronicle, The Washington Post, New York Times, San Francisco Chronicle, Spokane Spokesman.*

PART III

Globalization and the 'Postmodern' War of Images

The Coverage of Terrorism and the Iraq War in the 'Issue-Attention Cycle'

Stephan Russ-Mohl

Summary

The study summarizes research results on US coverage of terrorism, the 2003 Iraq War and the following occupation, showing how an economic theory of journalism can provide a clearer understanding of its complexities by viewing a familiar subject of investigation from a new angle. From an 'attention economic' perspective, besides the customary area of circulation where goods and services are exchanged, a second area of circulation becomes even more decisive, where information is exchanged for attention. This unusual perspective reveals an issue-attention cycle in media coverage and leads to the conclusion that most of the factors that endanger the progress to a more peaceful world can be traced back to the personal interests of those involved, and thus to economic roots.

Two Models of War Coverage

War and terrorism, as humanists have argued, are irrational per se. Realists, following Clausewitz's formula that war is 'a continuation of politics by other means', have drawn a different lesson from history, and cynics tend to side with them, pointing out that frequently the 'winner takes all' (Frank and Cook, 1996).

Economists approach these basic questions differently, attempting to first clarify under which circumstances war and terrorism 'pay', which systems of incentives they promote and what kinds of group behaviors they reenforce.

Modern warfare takes place in two interrelated realms. Generally, in an 'attention economy', besides the customary area of circulation where goods and services are exchanged for money, a secondary area of circulation kicks in, where information is exchanged for attention (Franck, 1998; Davenport and Beck, 2001; Fengler and Russ-Mohl, 2005). As a result, during a war, a media conflict appears in tandem with the military conflict. 'The media are missiles', says Karmasin (2009). Media outlets serve as artillery and their messages become bullets. In a globalized world linked by media networks, this becomes even more decisive in determining the outcome of a war, particularly in situations in which the warring parties depend upon the approval of a democratic public.

If journalists adopted the role assigned to them in journalism textbooks – that of objective, thoughtful and independent observers according to Model A (see Figure 1) – then democracies would rarely become involved in wars.

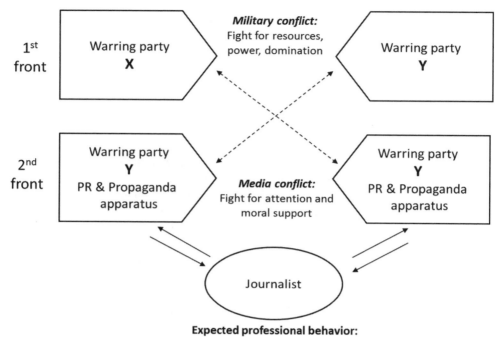

Figure 1: Model A: The War Reporter as an Observer Striving for Independence and Objectivity.

Essentially, journalists are always 'embedded' at all times – not necessarily with military troops, to be sure, but definitely within their societies or 'hemispheres'. Thus, Al Jazeera shows a far different picture of the Iraq War than CNN. The personal interests of war reporters, bureau chiefs, editors and publishers (and other ideological factors) ensure that most of them engage in herd behavior.

The problems posed by information asymmetries in 'principal/agent' relationships have real consequences for journalism (Höhne and Russ-Mohl, 2004; Fengler and Russ-Mohl, 2005b, 2008). When two actors are involved in a market transaction and both are interested in making a 'deal', usually they are not equally well informed about the conditions of the 'sale'. The 'agent', in most cases the subordinate or seller, possesses more information about the goods or services to be provided than the 'principal', who is usually the boss or client. This imbalance may lead to distrust.

Similar information asymmetries characterize many other media transactions, although there exists no formal contract relationship between journalists and their sources. When starting an investigation, journalists can be seen as 'principals' depending on information that is made accessible to them by PR 'agents' or other sources. At the same time, journalists act in reversed roles as 'agents' for their audiences. This twofold role as 'principals' and 'agents' makes it difficult – if not virtually impossible – for journalists to admit to their audience that they themselves are, in fact, frequently not the well-informed 'information and news professionals' they like to appear.

Many other 'principal/agent' relationships also influence the process of news production – some of them working in a cascade-like fashion one behind the other. Each of them may contribute to the partial distortion of news content, to under- and over-reporting as well as to the nondisclosure of facts. The 'blind spots' of media coverage are not merely accidental. They are, most frequently, the result of self-interested behavior.

During the Iraq invasion of 2003, the majority of American correspondents were placed alongside the troops, and this 'embedding' tended to shape their perception of events (Lewis, 2003; Wells, 2003; Cooke, 2007) – their very location forcing war reporters into the role of 'principals' being fed selectively with information by their 'agents', the military.

In the patriotic upsurge prompted by the initial phase of the invasion, bureau chiefs and in-house editors (now the 'principals' of war reporters) stuck unpleasant news reported by their own correspondents ('agents') on the back pages of their newspapers. They responded to the national mood, adjusted their coverage to accord with what their competitors were reporting, and reserved the front pages for Bush administration spin (Broder, 2008). Accordingly, Model A becomes implausible; the cumulative 'rationales' of the parties involved culminate, instead, in Model B (Figure 2).

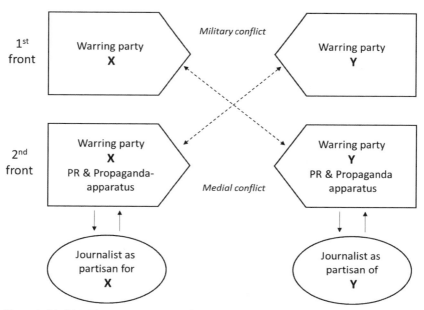

Figure 2: Model B: The War Reporter Is and Will Continue to Be Integrated into Her or His Culture and Community – And Is Biased Accordingly.

This has another effect, one that is probably as old as war reporting itself: both warring parties (now in the role of audiences and thus 'principals' of the media) mistrust media outlets beyond their direct control and perceive their reports as hostile. Vallone et al. (1985) identified this 'hostile media phenomenon' using the example of a massacre that occurred in Beirut.

The Three Major Phases of an Issue-Attention Cycle

Given the limited space available here, it does not make much sense to analyze the coverage of terrorism and the Iraq War separately. The Iraq War would probably never even have taken place without the terrorist attacks on the World Trade Center and the Pentagon. And the war brought its own kind of terror: in this respect, the American torturers of Abu Ghraib and Guantánamo do not differ much from the suicide bombers of the Taliban and al-Qaeda. During the Iraq invasion of 2003, the Bush administration had unprecedented success in controlling the flow of information via a highly professional system of news management (Robertson, 2005). The administration claimed that the Iraq War was part of the struggle against terrorism, and in doing so became 'victims of groupthink' (Janis, 1972), not even realizing that its own policies boosted the recruiting efforts of the al-Qaeda terror network (Bennett et al., 2007: ix).

The debacle has been subject to much analysis, but most of this is published in books, scholarly articles, and the back pages of elite publications rather than in the mass media outlets that reach the majority of Americans (see Kamalipour and Snow, 2004; Isikoff and Corn, 2006; Rich, 2006; Bennett et al., 2007; Cooke, 2007).

There are three distinguishing elements involved in the coverage of the Iraq War. First, a long process of framing and agenda-setting, which can, in retrospect, be seen unquestionably as a phase of herd behavior and as a collective failure of journalistic professionalism. After September 11, 2001, the media largely promoted the propaganda of the Bush administration. Later, there was a brief period of backpedalling, self-criticism and examining errors, but it focused on renouncing past mistakes rather than on charting a new direction. Since mid-2007, the media's attention has shifted elsewhere.

Phase One: The Government's Exploitation of the American Media

In the first phase, the American government perpetuated the idea that Saddam Hussein possessed weapons of mass destruction and was also closely allied with the al-Qaeda terror network. There were few influential journalists who questioned the administration's propaganda-style presentations or provided in-depth analysis of their veracity. The terrorist threat induced a kind of paralysis that resulted in near de facto cooperation between the government and the mainstream media.[1] The few who questioned the prevailing wisdom were quickly branded as 'unpatriotic' and bowed to the climate of opinion, ensuring that there was little chance of a critical viewpoint taking hold.

Despite the freedom of the press principle, antiwar voices are rarely heard in a nation involved in conflict. An investigation shows that in India and China, antiwar coverage constituted 35 and 40 percent, respectively, of the total coverage of the Iraq War in 2003, the first year of the war – despite vastly different media systems (one characterized by censorship, the other by freedom of the press), while in the United States only 8 percent of the coverage was antiwar (Yang, 2008). But why was this so?

In democratic societies, a necessary condition for war is the development of a 'patriotic consensus' among the public that becomes a part of reality and reduces the war to a single compelling plot: the defense of national values.[2] In the initial phase of a military confrontation, there is an elite consensus – or at least the effect of a 'spiral of silence' – among the elites to stifle those who oppose the war.

Researchers identified more than 900 instances in which President Bush and his government lied to the public, especially regarding Iraq's possession of weapons of mass destruction, his regime's alleged links to al-Qaeda and Iraq's attempt to procure uranium supplies from Africa.[3]

Philip Taubman (2008), senior editor of the *New York Times* and former head of the paper's Washington, DC bureau, confirmed from a journalist's perspective what had already been disclosed by former Bush spokesman and administration insider Scott McClellan (2008): the White House and the Pentagon engaged in brazen manipulation of the media. To mention just one more example, Vice President Dick Cheney hoodwinked the *New York Times* by having his minions make 'off the record' leaks to the paper asserting that intelligence reports indicated that Iraq had acquired the necessary equipment for uranium enrichment. On the day when this 'exclusive' was published, Cheney and National Security Advisor Condoleezza Rice referred explicitly to the *Times* article – even though it had been planted by Cheney's own staff (McManus, 2009). This reminds cynics of Karl Kraus' famous saying: 'How is the world ruled and how do wars start? Diplomats tell lies to journalists, and then believe what they read' (see Isikoff and Corn, 2006).

During the first days of the invasion, reporters embedded with the US army provided reports of fighting at close quarters. However, the television reports were subject to all the advantages and disadvantages of the embedding system, in which correspondents limited themselves to reporting only what they had seen themselves.[4]

There is some comfort in knowing that the leaders of two main publications focusing on journalism and the media have formulated a different standard of what constitutes a 'patriotic' journalist. In 2003, *American Journalism Review*'s managing editor Rem Rieder recalled the invaluable role played by journalists at the end of the Vietnam War: 'Some of the best journalism in my memory was the work of the young reporters in Vietnam', he says, citing the work of David Halberstam, Neil Sheehan, Malcolm Browne and Peter Arnett. Rieder's colleague at *Editor & Publisher*, Greg Mitchell, faults newsroom leaders for shortchanging 'the biggest political and moral issue of our time' (cited in Ricchiardi, 2008).

Phase Two: Self-Reflection and Explanation

Later, there was a period of self-flagellating clarification as to how the mass media were systematically misled by the Bush administration (Massing, 2004; Isikoff and Corn, 2006; Rich, 2006; Bennett et al., 2007; Mitchell and Springsteen, 2008). This marked a turning point in the coverage of the war and occupation of Iraq.

It is surely no coincidence that the beginning of this period in 2004 coincided with the publication of images of the torture scandal at Abu Ghraib, which were broadcast around the world and further discredited the American military engagement in Iraq. Seymour Hersh, who had exposed the My Lai massacre during the Vietnam War, once again played a key role in uncovering the scandal. He contributed an in-depth investigative article to *The New Yorker*, thus providing background and giving meaning to the images of the torture scenes that had earlier circulated widely on television, particularly on the Arabic, Qatar-based television station Al Jazeera (Hersh, 2004).

Both the *New York Times* and *The Washington Post* issued apologies to their readers for their failings. The *Times* published an extensive editor's note, which between the lines included an acknowledgement of how difficult it is for newsroom directors to admit failure in cases as sensitive as this (*New York Times*, 2004), a point reiterated by the *Times*' ombudsman Daniel Okrent (2004). The *Post* published a lengthy piece by their media critic Howard Kurtz, which the paper's chief editor Leonard Downie did not get to read in advance (Mitchell, 2004; Strupp, 2004).

However, to the best of our knowledge, none of the leading media outlets ever discussed the extent to which they were – like it or not – economic beneficiaries of both the war and terrorism. The idea that the media have a 'symbiotic' relationship with belligerent governments as well as with terrorists (Frey, 2004; Rohner and Frey, 2007) is understandably taboo, but it is nevertheless difficult to deny. Among the early critics of the coverage of the Iraq War in the mainstream media was Michael Getler.[5] As ombudsman of *The Washington Post*, he documented approximately 25 lapses of journalistic professionalism in his Sunday column. One must look closely, he argues, because the editors had in different ways failed to meet their own standards. In the case of *The Washington Post*, the problem was that they had 'buried' many important stories in their back pages. The *New York Times*, however, published misleading front-page articles, placing trust in reporter Judith Miller, who faithfully reproduced the propaganda of the Bush administration and Iraqi spin doctors.

This assessment is confirmed by David Broder (2008), a veteran reporter and a prominent foreign policy expert at *The Washington Post*. According to him, the Bush administration had no whistle-blowers along the lines of Deep Throat, the informant who disclosed the details of the Watergate case to Bob Woodward and Carl Bernstein.

The most notable scoop in the reassessment of the Iraq debacle was contributed by the *New York Times*' David Barstow. He disclosed how the Pentagon controlled coverage of the war and terrorism on American television through dozens of commentators who appeared repeatedly on different TV channels as 'independent' military experts, including ten retired generals. In fact, they were consulting contractors linked to the military-industrial complex, including lobbyists and managers from a total of 150 Pentagon affiliates. They were also regularly briefed and provided with information to assist them in their television appearances (Barstow, 2008).

However, even as self-criticism prevailed in the second phase of the Iraq War coverage, the Bush administration managed to spin the issue of torture, keeping it low key and maintaining that the problem was confined to a few individual cases. Instead of using the term 'torture', officials strategically opted to speak of 'abuse' – a term adopted by most of the media as well.[6]

Phase Three: Slipping from the Media's Radar

In early 2007, the attention given to the incipient presidential campaign and the race for the nomination supplanted coverage of the war. Reporting on events in Iraq and the political debate about the local military involvement constituted only around 12 percent of the news coverage. The media – and with them most likely the majority of Americans – simply lost interest in the Iraq War.

The media had allowed 'the third-longest war in American history to slip off the radar screen' as Sherry Ricchiardi wrote in the *American Journalism Review* (2008). Armando Acuna, ombudsman of the *Sacramento Bee*, pointed out that the conflict that costs taxpayers about US$12.5 billion a month (nearly US$5,000 a second) had all but disappeared from front-page news. Acuna calculated a 70 percent decline in Iraq-related articles on the front page of the *Bee*. The Associated Press news agency, which has asked researchers to chart the daily reporting from 65 US newspapers, found similar results. In September 2007 there were 457 front-page reports on Iraq, but in the months that followed the number dwindled to less than 50 (quoted in Ricchiardi, 2008).

The Project for Excellence in Journalism (2008) revealed that by 2008 the Iraq War had essentially vanished from evening television news. During the first ten weeks of 2007, Iraq remained a hot topic, claiming 23 percent of news broadcasts. One year later, Iraq-related stories constituted only 3 percent of the total broadcasts. Cable channels showed the figure drop from 24 percent to a meager 1 percent. During the first half of 2008, the three main networks (CBS, ABC and NBC) combined devoted a total of 181 minutes to Iraq, compared with 1,157 minutes for the entire previous year. Mainstream media collectively turned away from the war. CBS no longer maintained a single correspondent in Iraq, where 150,000 US soldiers remained deployed in 2008. In Afghanistan, no US broadcaster employed a permanent correspondent (Stelter, 2008).

It was becoming increasingly difficult for foreign correspondents – particularly those based in the war zones of Afghanistan and Iraq – to have stories featured on the evening news. Lara Logan, chief correspondent for CBS News, mischievously described strategies used to negotiate with news headquarters. 'Generally what I say is: "I'm holding this armor-piercing RPG"', referring to the acronym for rocket propelled grenade. 'It's aimed at the bureau chief, and if you do not put my story on the air, I'm going to pull the trigger' (Stelter, 2008). Logan's dark anecdote is amusing, though the issue it confronts is no laughing matter. Thus far, a lack of media attention has yet to lead US correspondents to attempted bombings.

The displacement of the war from the nation's front pages is not solely the fault of the media: according to Terry McCarthy, ABC's Iraq correspondent, bringing up Baghdad at a dinner party 'is like a conversation killer' (Stelter, 2008). Bill Keller, the editor-in-chief of the *New York Times*, offers another variation on the theme: 'There is a cold and sad calculation that readers and viewers are not that interested in the war, whether because they are preoccupied with paying four dollars for a gallon of gas and avoiding foreclosure, or because they have Iraq fatigue' (quoted in Carr, 2008).

Yet to assume a society would engage with a crisis that is left unreported is simply absurd. The local emphasis of the American mass media works against in-depth war coverage. Even on Memorial Day, an occasion calling for the war to return to front pages, luring the conflict's many consequences back into the spotlight, the main focus remained a local one. The *Los Angeles Times* dedicated its front page to soldiers from California who died in Afghanistan and Iraq, and *The Washington Post* personalized the war with a series called 'Faces of the Fallen' (Carr, 2008).

In the spring of 2008 – the fifth anniversary of the war's onset – the media commemorated the 4,000 US deaths. Apart from that, according to Hayes and Myers (2008) of Ohio State University, war casualties became victims of hyper-local reporting, as media attention was primarily bestowed upon coffins buried in local cemeteries. When Lt. Col. Billy Hall – one of the highest ranking officers killed in Iraq – was buried in Arlington Cemetery, his family agreed to grant media access to the ceremony. The military, however, took pains to ensure that journalists were kept away from the funeral. According to Dana Milbank of *The Washington Post*, the de facto ban on media at Arlington funerals fits in neatly with White House efforts to sanitize the war in Iraq (Ricchiardi, 2008).

The war is far away and much less present in the collective consciousness than the Vietnam War was to the earlier generation. The old formula – according to which an increasing number of casualties diminish public support for a war – seems no longer to apply. In Vietnam, however, three times as many soldiers were in action than in Iraq.[7] By the middle of 2009 more than 4,200 American soldiers had been killed in Iraq, against 58,000 in Vietnam.

Above all, the military acted on a commitment to avoid the mistakes associated with the Vietnam quagmire. As the draft is no longer a requirement in the United States, the army can now avoid the public spotlight more effectively.[8]

The Costs of War Reporting

The previously discussed developments are not simply due to the particular dynamics of issue-attention cycles (Downs, 1972). They can also be attributed to changes in the media's own policies governing its operations. Safety risks and economic factors are more likely to explain the withdrawal of reporters from Iraq. Under the present circumstances, correspondents jet and parachute from crisis to crisis. Maintaining a long-term presence of reporters is no longer affordable, beginning with the insurance costs for operations in war and disaster areas. 'They are prohibitive' says Matthew Stannard, an experienced foreign reporter with the *San Francisco Chronicle*.[9] This leads to outsourcing.

An increasing number of freelance journalists – either inexperienced 25-year-olds or native stringers – are at the front lines. Some of them may fall short of providing reliable levels of professionalism, but the concerns about insurance costs are significantly reduced. The notion that the life of an Iraqi is not worth as much as the life of an American outrages moralists and human rights activists, but in economic terms it is true. In plain figures expressed as insurance risks, a human life in Third World countries is worth just a few thousand dollars, while in the United States a life may be worth ten million dollars – a figure in line with rising premiums.

Even more shocking is the fact that the *New York Times* spends three million dollars a year to maintain its office in Iraq. And the number excludes the salaries of journalists, instead covering fees for rent, guards and electric generators! Disclosed in the *Columbia Journalism Review* in 2007, these figures raise questions about how we are to be informed about war and terror, and the extent to which it is reasonable to expect private media companies to inherit the cost. The journal's editorial celebrates maintaining this level of coverage as an act of commitment to democracy. Less euphorically put, however, it shows at least a high degree of corporate social responsibility that is rarely found among private media companies and frequently not even in government-funded media.

Most competitors will make a different assessment, partly because of the influence of their investors on Wall Street. A few months earlier, the *American Journalism Review* (Ricchiardi, 2007) had already reported that many media companies were ordering their correspondents back from the front in light of escalating threats to foreigners in Iraq and the astronomical cost of security. Paul Friedman, Senior Vice President of CBS, said that attempts to share the immense costs and security risks with other broadcasters failed because of logistical issues (Stelter, 2008).

High Risks for Journalists Remaining in Iraq

Reporters on the ground 'struggle mightily to cut through the fog and spin' (Ricchiardi, 2007), but the mobility of correspondents is extremely limited. When they attempt to gather material to verify statements made by the military or the Pentagon, reporters place themselves in life-threatening situations. In Fallujah (a city 43 miles west of Baghdad and the site of two major assaults by the Americans in 2004), or in certain neighborhoods of Baghdad, they may not venture out at all. According to Ricchiardi (2007),

Before they go out on assignments, correspondents work through a litany of questions: Where is it? What time is it? How can I get there? How can I get back? Who can I talk to?

Who controls the neighborhood? Who guards the checkpoints? Is there enough fuel in the car and plenty of air in the tires? Is this story worth the risk? […] To blend in, female journalists often don an abaya, a long robe worn by Muslim women, and a head scarf. Some male reporters with dark features grow mustaches and beards and try to emulate the attire of Iraqi men. Some blondes dye their hair black. Many operate on the 15-minute rule: they never stay longer in any one place for fear that someone with a cell phone will alert assassins of the soft target. Even the smallest of details can be giveaways, for instance wearing a seatbelt in a car, as Iraqis rarely use them.

Iraq differs from other wars in another respect: in the fight for media attention, journalists themselves have become targets. Samantha Appleton, a photographer who worked for *Time* and *The New Yorker* in Iraq, said that in 2003 it was still possible to move about with relative freedom. Four years later, it was customary to travel with at least two cars and three to five armed bodyguards. Moreover, for the few remaining reporters, the military makes their work more difficult (Carr, 2008).

Of the 123 journalists detained for their work in 2007, only three were based in Iraq. However, according to Reporters without Borders (2007), 46 (more than half) of the 83 journalists who died while working in 2007 perished in Iraq. Relatives of the victims likely found little consolation in the notion of their loved ones having acted on faith in democracy or furthering the freedom of the press. However, these 46 murders still undoubtedly received much more media attention than most of the other casualties in the war. This again raises a question posed years ago by the economist Frey (2004): to what extent do the media become an accomplice of the terrorists by reporting on their attacks – in this case, writing about and overexposing the murders of their colleagues?

For the few remaining reporters, the military makes their work more difficult (Stelter, 2008). This leads to elements of war reporting that despite examination by a number of experts have failed to penetrate public consciousness. Because today's media report on war differently than was the case in Vietnam, the Bush administration was able to wage its war in Iraq relatively undisturbed. Long-term questions remained unexamined. What will happen to Iraq if the Americans pull out? The fact that this could still be a *Time* cover story in 2007, four years after the start of the war, speaks volumes.

The Social Costs of Insufficient War and Terror Coverage

What are the social costs if the media lack sufficient capacity to effectively monitor a very powerful government and to adequately inform the public about what is going on in the world? (McManus, 2009). The war in Iraq provides some preliminary answers. American journalism is in a state of crisis because it has lost not only much of its resource base but also much of its moral authority.

The near-perfect control of the news cycle by the military and the US government also explains the American public's ignorance regarding the amateurish manner in which the Bush administration's Coalition Provisional Authority arranged a transitional government after the invasion. As Rajiv Chandrasekaran (2007, 2008), former head of *The Washington Post*'s bureau in Baghdad, documented, 'expert personnel sent to the country proved to be clueless Republican party hacks who had never worked outside of the United States and had little or no linguistic, political, and cultural knowledge to contribute to efforts to ensure peace, democracy, and reconstruction'. The author also points out that not a single American congressman had anything but a rudimentary knowledge of what has been actually going on in Iraq. Only one US senator visited Iraq approximately 70 times and at least occasionally left the controlled environment of US military bases (Chandrasekaran, 2008).

A truly dangerous mix of traditional and new factors influencing the media's war and terror coverage helped create the distortions, herd behavior and finally the ignorance and negligence described, which inevitably affects decision making elsewhere in society, in particular in the political system.

Conclusions: Endangering Progress Toward a More Peaceful World

In light of the above argumentation, it is possible to conclude the following:

- Media wars tend to become the subject of one or even several issue-attention cycles with an upturn, a turnaround and a downturn phase.
- Government spin and efforts by official sources (military, government, industry, political parties and nonprofit organizations) to control the media agenda are increasing. Institutions spend a great amount of resources on shaping public attention.
- The resource base for financing investigative war and terrorism reporting is shrinking. The public's willingness to pay for journalism, and thus for news and adequate information, is decreasing, and it becomes less likely that journalism can be financed adequately by advertising. Also the movement toward placing want ads online rather than in the pages of newspapers has meant a decline in the amount of revenue available to newspapers in general.
- War reporting in itself seems to have become more dangerous, as reporters more frequently become targets of the warring parties. Media outlets perhaps pay too much attention to this aspect of war coverage, and thus encourage terrorist attacks on journalists because of the guaranteed media attention.
- However, the mainstream media's generally introspective and self-critical analysis of war coverage was insufficient and all too brief – which may have been partially compensated by new forms of media criticism, particularly in the 'blogosphere'.

- Rational decisions by individual media users, spin doctors, war reporters, editors and publishers collectively produce the lies, half-truths and disinformation that promote war and endanger any political progress toward conflict resolution – and, thus, a more peaceful world.
- Most of these factors can be traced back to the personal interests of those involved and thus to economic roots. Some of the information that has been withheld can be traced back to principal/agent relationships between the sources, journalists and their audiences. They should therefore be more thoroughly analyzed by an economic theory of journalism that is in need of being further developed (Meyer, 2008; Fengler and Russ-Mohl, 2005, 2008a, 2008b) and that would incorporate the insights of behavioral economics (Ariely, 2008; Harford, 2008; Heuser, 2008; Shermer, 2008).

Key Points

- Two models of war reporting can be identified. The first ideal-typical model refers to journalists striving for independence and objectivity. In the second model, the journalists remain embedded in their culture and their community – and are biased accordingly.
- Three major phases in the issue-attention cycle of the US media coverage of the Iraq War can be observed. The first phase of herd behavior, which implies a collective failure of journalistic professionalism, was followed by a short period of self-reflection and examination. Finally, the media simply lost interest in the Iraq War.

Study Questions

1. 'Principal/agent' relationships lead to information asymmetries that have real consequences for the process of news production. Can you think of examples of these relationships? What kind of consequences would you expect?
2. Besides the dynamics of issue-attention cycles, which other factors can be taken into account to explain the withdrawal of reporters from Iraq?
3. Discuss some of the reasons why, in today's society, investigative journalism is shrinking. What consequences do you expect?

Further Reading

Fengler, Susanne and Stephan Russ-Mohl (2008a) 'The Crumbling Hidden Wall: Towards an Economic Theory of Journalism', *Kyklos* 61(4): 520–42.

——— (2008b) 'Journalists and the Information-Attention Markets: Towards an Economic Theory of Journalism', *Journalism* 9(6): 667–90.

Websites

American Journalism Review: www.ajr.org/.

New York Times' Iraq coverage: topics.nytimes.com/top/news/international/countriesandterritories/iraq/index.html?ref=topics.

References

Ariely, Dan (2008) *Predictably Irrational. The Hidden Forces that Shape Our Decisions*. New York: Harper.

Barstow, David (2008) 'Behind TV Analysts: Pentagon's Hidden Hand', *New York Times*, April 20.

Bennett, Lance W., Regina G. Lawrence and Steven Livingston (2007) *When the Press Fails. Political Power and the News Media from Iraq to Katrina*. Chicago, IL: University of Chicago Press.

Broder, David (2008) *The US Presidential Race 2008*, Presentation at Stanford University, April 3, 2008. Standford, CA.

Carr, David (2008) 'The War We Choose to Ignore', *New York Times*, May 26, 2008.

Center for Public Integrity (2008) 'Center Documents 935 False Statements by Top Administration Officials to Justify Iraq War', Press Release, January 23, 2008, www.publicintegrity.org/news/entry/189 (May 1, 2009).

Chandrasekaran, Rajiv (2007) *Imperial Life in the Emerald City. Inside Iraq's Green Zone*. New York: Vintage Books.

——— (2008) *Inside Iraq's Green Zone*, Presentation at Stanford University, May 19, 2008. Stanford, CA.

Cooke, John B. (2007) *Reporting the War. Freedom of the Press from the American Revolution to the War on Terrorism*. New York: Palgrave Macmillan.

Davenport, Thomas H. and John C. Beck (2001) *The Attention Economy. Understanding the New Currency of Business*. Boston, MA: Harvard Business School Press.

Downs, Anthony (1972) 'Up and Down with Ecology – the "Issue-Attention Cycle', *Public Interest* 28: 38–50.

Fengler, Susanne and Stephan Russ-Mohl (2005) *Der Journalist als 'Homo oeconomicus'*. Konstanz: UVK.

——— (2008a) 'The Crumbling Hidden Wall. Towards an Economic Theory of Journalism', *Kyklos* 61(4): 520–42.

——— (2008b) 'Journalists and the Information-Attention Markets. Towards an Economic Theory of Journalism', *Journalism* 9(6): 667–90.

Franck, Georg (1998) *Ökonomie der Aufmerksamkeit. Ein Entwurf*. München: Hanser.

Frank, Robert H. and Philip J. Cook (1996) *The Winner-Take-All Society. Why the Few at the Top Get So Much More than the Rest of Us*. New York: Penguin Books.

Frey, Bruno S. (op. 2004) *Dealing with Terrorism – Stick or Carrot?* Cheltenham, UK; Northhampton, MA: Edward Elgar.

Harford, Tim (2008) *The Logic of Life. The Rational Economics of an Irrational World*. New York: Random House.

Hayes, Andrew and Teresa A. Myers (2008) *Testing the 'Proximate Casualties' Hypothesis: Local Troop Loss, Attention to News, and Support for Military Intervention*, Presentation at the Annual International Communication Association (ICA) conference, May 22–26, 2008. Montreal, Canada.

Hersh, Seymour (2004) 'Torture at Abu Ghraib', *The New Yorker*, May.

Heuser, Uwe J. (2008) *Humanomics. Die Entdeckung des Menschen in der Wirtschaft*. Frankfurt am Main; New York: Campus.

Höhne, Andrea and Stephan Russ-Mohl (2004) 'Zur Ökonomik und Ethik der Kriegsberichterstattung', *Zeitschrift für Kommunikationsökologie* 1: 11–23.

Isikoff, Michael and David Corn (2006) *Hubris. The Inside Story of Spin, Scandal, and the Selling of the Iraq War*. New York: Crown.

Janis, Irving L. (1972) *Victims of Groupthink. A Psychological Study of Foreign-Policy Decisions and Fiascoes*. Boston: Houghton, Mifflin.

Kamalipour, Yahya R. and Nancy Snow (2004) *War, Media, and Propaganda. A Global Perspective*. Lanham, MD: Rowman & Littlefield.

Karmasin, Matthias (2009) *Wars and Public Spheres*, Paper Presented at the Symposion 'War, Media, and the Public Sphere', March 6–7, 2009. Vienna.

Lewis, Justin (2003) 'Facts in the Line of Fire', *The Guardian*, November 6, 2003.

Massing, Michael (2004) 'Now They Tell Us', *New York Review of Books* 51(3): 26.

McClellan, Scott (2008) *What Happened. Inside the Bush White House and Washington's Culture of Deception*. New York: Public Affairs.

McManus, John H. (2009) *Detecting Bull. How to Identify Bias and Junk Journalism in Print, Broadcast and on the Wild Web*. Sunnyvale, CA: Unvarnished Press.

Meyer, Philip (2008) *Raising the Ante Again*, Presentation at University of North Carolina, March 28, 2008. Chapel Hill.

Mitchell, Greg (2004) 'Washington Post Says Iraq Coverage Was Flawed', *Editor & Publisher*, August 12, 2004.

Mitchell, Greg and Bruce Springsteen (2008) *So Wrong for So Long. How the Press, the Pundits – and the President – Failed on Iraq*. New York: Union Square Press/Sterling.

Okrent, Daniel (2004) 'The Public Editor. Weapons of Mass Destruction or Mass Distraction?' *New York Times*, May 30, 2004.

Project for Excellence in Journalism (2008) *The State of the News Media 2008. An Annual Report on American Journalism*, www.stateofthenewsmedia.org/2008 (May 1, 2009).

Reporters without Borders (2007) *Worldwide Press Freedom Index*, www.rsf.org (May 1, 2009).

Ricchiardi, Sherry (2007) 'Obstructed View', *American Journalism Review*, www.ajr.org/article.asp?id=4301 (May 1, 2009).

——— (2008) 'Whatever Happened to Iraq?', *American Journalism Review*, www.ajr.org/article.asp?id=4515 (May 1, 2009).

Rich, Frank (2006) *The Greatest Story Ever Sold. The Decline and Fall of Truth in Bush's America*. New York: Penguin Books.

Robertson, Lori (2005) 'In Control', *American Journalism Review*, www.ajr.org/article.asp?id=3812 (May 1, 2009).

Rohner, Dominic and Bruno Frey (2007) 'Blood and Ink! The Common-Interest-Game between Terrorists and the Media', *Public Choice* 133: 129–45.

Shermer, Michael (2008) *The Mind of the Market. Compassionate Apes, Competitive Humans, and Other Tales from Evolutionary Economics*. New York: Times Books.

Stelter, Brian (2008) 'Reporters Say Networks Put Wars on the Back Burner', *New York Times*, June 23, 2008.

Strupp, Joe (2004) 'Kurtz Explains His Critique of Washington Post Iraq Coverage', *Editor & Publisher*, August 12, 2004.

Taubman, Philip (2008) Presentation at the Center for International Security and Cooperation, Stanford University, May 19, 2008. Stanford, CA.

Vallone, Robert P., Lee Ross and Mark R. Lepper (1985) 'The Hostile Media Phenomenon. Biased Perception and Perceptions of Media Bias in Coverage of the Beirut Massacre', *Journal of Personality and Social Psychology* 49(3): 577–85.

Wells, Matt (2003) 'Embedded Reporters "Sanitised" Iraq War', *The Guardian*, November 6, 2003.

Yang, Jin (2008) *One War, Three Pictures. A Cross-Country Analysis of the 2003 Iraq War*, Presentation at the International Communication Association Conference, May 22–26, 2008. Montreal.

Notes

1 See 'Delivering War to the Public: Shaping the Public Sphere' chapter by Philip Seib in this book.

2 See 'Surging Beyond Realism: How the US Media Promote War Again and Again' chapter by Robert M. Entman in this book.

3 Center Documents 935: 'False Statements by Top Administration Officials to Justify Iraq War', press release, January 23, 2008, www.publicintegrity.org (May 1, 2009).

4 See 'Delivering War to the Public: Shaping the Public Sphere' chapter by Philip Seib in this book.

5 Interview with the author, Washington DC, April 13, 2008.

6 See 'Mass-Mediated Debate about Torture in Post-9/11 America' chapter by Brigitte L. Nacos in this book.

7 See 'Between Reporting and Propaganda: Power, Culture and War Reporting' chapter by Daniel C. Hallin in this book.

8 Interview with the author, Washington DC, April 13, 2008.

9 Interview with the author, Stanford University, May 6, 2008.

The Media and Humanitarian Intervention

Philip Hammond

Summary

This chapter addresses the role of the media in relation to post-Cold War humanitarian intervention. The first part of the chapter briefly outlines the contemporary debate about humanitarian intervention, arguing that this discussion is often confused and lacks critical perspective. The second part of the chapter then attempts to develop such a critical framework, examining the practical and in-principle problems with humanitarian intervention and suggesting an alternative way to understand it as an ideological response to the major political shift of the end of the Cold War. The final section focuses more closely on the role of the media, examining both how governments have paid close attention to image and presentation, and how journalists themselves have responded to their new role as advocates for intervention.

The chapter argues that post-Cold War humanitarian intervention has been driven by a search for meaning and purpose on the part of western elites. Media presentation has taken on a disproportionate importance because intervention is essentially narcissistic, concerned with producing the 'right' image. Yet often the problems with media coverage have derived as much from journalists' own spontaneous efforts as they have joined in with the search for meaning, as from official misinformation and manipulation of the media.

The Contemporary Debate

The context for the emergence of contemporary ideas about humanitarian intervention is the new era that began with the fall of the Berlin Wall in 1989. The ending of the Cold War was widely understood to have given the United Nations Security Council a new lease of life, since it would no longer be thwarted by the Soviet Union's power of veto, and to have freed western foreign policy from the necessity of countering the Soviet threat. This, it was hoped, would mean that more principled, ethical policies could be adopted, since it was no longer necessary to support repressive regimes because of the demands of Cold War politics. The new direction – and the new importance of humanitarian considerations – was soon evident in the aftermath of the 1991 Gulf War when, having already achieved the explicit aim of driving Iraqi forces out of Kuwait, the US-led coalition intervened in Iraq further in order to set up 'safe havens' for Kurds and other minorities. This was the first of a number of humanitarian military interventions in the early 1990s – in Somalia,

Bosnia and Haiti – which seemed to bear out the claim that western governments were increasingly acting on ethical concerns.

From the start, it appeared for too many analysts that the media had an important role to play. It was even suggested that news coverage might be setting the foreign policy agenda of western states – the so-called 'CNN effect'. Pointing to the Kurdish refugee crisis and Somalia, former US Defense Secretary James Schlesinger wrote in 1992 that 'policies seem increasingly subject, especially in democracies, to the images flickering across the television screen' (Livingston, 1997: 1). Even if they were not actually dictating policy, the media were surely able, it was claimed, to play a positive role in facilitating and promoting humanitarian action by drawing attention to suffering and abuse (Minear et al., 1996). Like post-Cold War foreign policy itself, it was sometimes argued that the media could further an ethical approach to international affairs and promote cosmopolitan values. British international relations professor Martin Shaw (1996: 123), for example, describes the 1991 Kurdish refugee crisis as 'the media's finest hour'. By encouraging and endorsing western military action for humanitarian ends, he maintains, the media were acting as advocates for 'the globally vulnerable' and thereby aiding the emergence of a 'global civil society' (Shaw, 1996: 178).

This is an exceedingly idealized picture. Former aid worker Conor Foley, for instance, who visited the Kurdish 'safe haven' established in northern Iraq by the victorious Gulf War coalition, describes it as a 'hellhole'. One refugee told him that being there was 'like living in the world's biggest concentration camp' (Foley, 2008: 45–6). Back in the United Kingdom, however, Foley found that no one was interested in his story of what the 'safe haven' was really like, since a NATO ally, Turkey, was the main cause of the refugees' ongoing suffering. It is also doubtful that media coverage had much direct influence on the initial decision to intervene: Piers Robinson, in his study of the CNN effect, suggests that the key factor was the US government's desire to allow Turkey, which had supported the Gulf War, to contain the problem of Kurdish refugees who laid claim to Turkish territory as well as to part of Iraq (Robinson, 2002: 69–71). Indeed, academic research into the CNN effect has generally warned against overestimating the power and influence of the media: studies have shown that in Somalia and other cases news coverage followed interest on the part of political leaders rather than leading it (Livingston, 1997; Livingston and Eachus, 1995; Mermin, 1999).

Even if we were to push these awkward facts aside and fix our gaze on the idealized realm of 'global civil society', it is questionable whether there is anything positive about the media promoting humanitarian intervention. In the case of Iraq, by taking part of the country's territory and airspace out of its control (as designated 'safe havens' and 'no-fly zones' policed by the western military), the idea became established that it was acceptable to violate the principles of equality among sovereign states and noninterference in a state's internal affairs, which had underpinned the post-1945 UN system. By legitimizing the idea that, in the name of humanitarianism, the 'international community' could regulate and interfere in Iraq as it saw fit, the postwar humanitarian intervention, even more than the Gulf War itself, paved the way for more than a decade of punitive international sanctions and repeated Anglo-American bombing of Iraq, culminating in the 2003 invasion of the country.

No doubt an advocate of global civil society like Shaw (who opposed the 2003 Iraq War) would recoil from such a suggestion, and indeed even to this day humanitarian intervention is routinely seen in a positive light.

It is often assumed that there is a radical discontinuity between the humanitarian interventions of the 1990s and the 'War on Terror' that followed the 9/11 terror attacks in 2001. Even before President Barack Obama assumed office in 2009, observers started to talk of a possible 'return to' or 'revival of' humanitarian intervention once the administration of George W. Bush was consigned to the history books. In a *Newsweek* cover story titled 'How to Fix the World' (December 8, 2008), for example, Fareed Zakaria argued that, with Obama's election to the presidency, 'there is a unique opportunity to use American power to reshape the world'. *The Economist's* November 13, 2008 editorial argued that Obama had 'a chance to restore America's moral leadership' and urged that 'America's president-elect needs to remake the case for humanitarian intervention abroad'.

Similarly, the prominent human rights lawyer Geoffrey Robertson lambasted the Bush administration's disregard for international law, but took heart from the fact that 'human rights experts' on Obama's team were complaining of 'the UN's reluctance to intervene in the domestic affairs of its members' and were floating the idea that 'a new international organization is required, not as an alternative to the UN but as an association of democratic nations' (*Daily Telegraph*, December 7, 2008). Just as commentators hoped that Obama's election might signal a return of 1990s-style ethical interventionism, so after 9/11 they had worried that it might recede: 'Since the end of the cold war, human rights has become the dominant moral vocabulary in foreign affairs', observed Michael Ignatieff, wondering whether 'after September 11 [...] the era of human rights has come and gone' (*New York Times*, February 5, 2002).

In fact, however, there was considerable continuity in policy between the liberal interventionism of the 1990s and the neoconservatives' 'War on Terror'. It is striking, for example, that Irwin Stelzer's collection of essays expounding the ideas of neoconservatism includes as an exemplar of the outlook a speech that British Prime Minister Tony Blair gave during the 1999 Kosovo conflict setting out his 'doctrine of international community' (Stelzer, 2004). Indeed, the key objections raised by critics of the Iraq War – that it was conducted illegally, outside the authority of the United Nations, by a 'coalition of the willing' against a state that was committing no act of international aggression and that presented no threat to the West – were all equally applicable to NATO's Kosovo campaign. Yet the Kosovo War – the high point of armed humanitarianism – was widely excused as illegal but moral. A postwar British parliamentary inquiry, for example, argued that while the bombing may have been of 'dubious legality', it was 'justified on moral grounds' (UK Foreign Affairs Select Committee, 2000).

Similarly, the Independent International Commission on Kosovo (IICK) concluded that while 'the intervention was [...] not legal', humanitarian considerations meant that it was nevertheless 'legitimate' (IICK, 2000: 289). In the UK media, 'humanitarian' justifications offered for war in 1999 tended to be accepted at face value, while similar arguments made for intervention after 9/11 in Afghanistan and, particularly, Iraq were more often viewed with skepticism (Hammond, 2007). It is not immediately obvious, however, why this might be the case: the rhetoric and arguments developed to justify the 'War on Terror' were strikingly similar to those used in relation to earlier humanitarian interventions.

The idea that Obama should 'use American power to reshape the world', in Zakaria's phrase, for example, is strongly reminiscent of Blair's promise in the wake of 9/11 to 're-order this world around us' (Blair, 2001). Indeed, in their immediate reactions to the 9/11 attacks, both British and American leaders characterized the conflict in which they were engaged as a fight for values, emphasizing ethical and humanitarian themes. Addressing the US Congress in September 2001, President Bush said, 'This is the world's fight. This is civilization's fight. This is the fight of all who believe in progress and pluralism, tolerance and freedom.' Declaring that 'we have found our mission and our moment', he described the conflict not in terms of the narrow pursuit of national self-interest, but as a broader 'fight for our principles' (Bush, 2001).

It is difficult to see much difference between Bush's understanding of the 'War on Terror' as a war between '[f]reedom and fear, justice and cruelty', and Blair's explanation of NATO's 1999 Kosovo campaign as 'a battle of good against evil' (*The Sun*, April 5, 1999) or as a 'battle for the values of civilization and democracy everywhere' (*The Independent*, May 24, 1999). Speaking in October 2001, Blair also understood the West's response to 9/11 in terms of a 'fight for freedom' which could 'bring [...] values of democracy and freedom to people round the world'. With respect to the then imminent bombing of Afghanistan, he said he wanted the 'world community' to show 'as much its capacity for compassion as for force', promising to 'assemble a humanitarian coalition alongside the military coalition so that inside and outside Afghanistan, the refugees [...] are given shelter, food and help' (Blair, 2001).

Similar claims were again made by Bush and Blair in 2003 when they presented disarmament and liberation as twin objectives of the invasion of Iraq. Bush said he had 'a strategy to free the Iraqi people from Saddam Hussein and rid his country of weapons of mass destruction' (*The Independent*, March 25, 2003), for example, and Blair said that 'Iraq will be disarmed of weapons of mass destruction and the people of Iraq will be free' (*The Independent*, March 28, 2003).

Despite the unpopularity of the Iraq War, critics of the conflict sometimes indicated their ongoing support for humanitarian intervention. Internationally, the war gave rise to divisions as the French and German governments dissented from the aggressive stance adopted by the United States and Great Britain. Yet both France and Germany countered Anglo-American bellicosity with their own plans for a humanitarian invasion, proposing to make Iraq an international protectorate policed by thousands of UN troops (Hume, 2003). Similarly, domestic critics of the war maintained their faith in the potential for the British and US governments to act ethically in the international arena.

In Britain, for example, *The Independent* opposed the invasion of Iraq but at the same time welcomed the fact that 'the world's superpower is throwing its weight around for the benefit of Africa', arguing that American pressure on Zimbabwean President Robert Mugabe to step down showed that the United States could 'still be a power for good' ('Editorial', *The Independent*, May 2, 2003). Similarly, some American activists simultaneously called for an end to intervention in Iraq while demanding an intervention in the Darfur region of Sudan, adopting the slogan 'Out of Iraq, into Darfur' (Mamdani, 2007). Celebrity campaigner Mia Farrow even held a meeting with the private security firm Blackwater to explore the possibility of a freelance mission to beef-up the African Union force in Darfur, despite what ABC News (August 20, 2008) described as the company's 'controversial history and allegations of murdering civilians in Iraq'.

The fact that it now seems possible to be both 'antiwar' and simultaneously to advocate armed western intervention points to the confusion that surrounds questions of war and conflict today. In relation to the Iraq War, much debate seemed to boil down to a question of personal conscience, whereby leaders such as Blair said they had to invade because it was 'the right thing to do', while critics called back 'not in my name'. Distrusting the ethical claims of Bush and Blair, critics preferred their own ethical agenda that called on western leaders to send troops somewhere else. This is cause for concern, since it suggests that we lack a clear critical vocabulary to discuss (humanitarian) military intervention and its media treatment. Certainly many academics continue to push the idea that the news media should advocate and facilitate intervention (Chouliaraki, 2008; Shaw, 2007). Yet the history of 'ethical' intervention since the end of the Cold War has not been a happy one. There are both practical and in-principle reasons to doubt its supposedly positive character.

A Critical Framework

The record of humanitarian intervention offers few examples of success and many cases of failure. The first fully fledged humanitarian military intervention of the post-Cold War era was the US-led UN mission to Somalia in 1992, which ended in disaster. For the United States, the intervention came to an ignominious conclusion with a hasty withdrawal after the deaths of eighteen US personnel in clashes with local militia. For the Somalis, the intense international attention left their country in an even greater state of chaos, and instability has continued to this day. While the mission was in progress, UN troops committed various abuses against Somalis, including rape, torture and detention without trial, and in some instances indiscriminately killed civilians (African Rights, 1993; de Waal, 1998). The number of Somali casualties remains uncertain, but seems to have been in the thousands; at the upper end, Noam Chomsky (1999: 69) cites a CIA estimate of 7,000–10,000 killed. Yet there has been little critical commentary on the fact that a 'humanitarian' mission resulted in the killing and abuse of large numbers of those it was supposedly helping.

It is notable that while there was great public interest in the graphic details of torture of suspected 'enemy combatants' at the US detention facility in Guantánamo Bay, Cuba, and of suspected 'insurgents' at Abu Ghraib prison in Iraq, similar abuses in Somalia – carried out by a blue-helmeted, multilateral peacekeeping force – attracted far less censure either at the time or since. Perhaps because, like the Kosovo campaign, it was seen as basically 'moral' and well-intentioned, the catastrophic mission to Somalia instead spurred calls for further intervention: critics complained that failure in Somalia had made the United States reluctant to act elsewhere, particularly in Bosnia and Rwanda (Livingston and Eachus, 2000).

Yet the problem is not simply one of intentions. Even if we were to accept that the intentions behind international intervention were entirely good, the very fact of powerful outside sponsors picking sides in local conflicts tends to make matters worse by prolonging conflict and discouraging compromise. Perhaps the clearest example of this is Bosnia, where international involvement had a devastating impact. Although there were economic and political developments within Yugoslavia in the late 1980s and early 1990s that encouraged the rise of nationalist and separatist politics, the decisive factor in aggravating these tensions into bloody civil war was western support for Bosnian independence. As Susan Woodward (1995: 198) argues, 'Western intervention [...] provided the irreversible turning point in [the] escalation toward [...] war.'

With European (especially German and Austrian) recognition of Slovenian and Croatian independence in 1991, and US-led recognition of Bosnia in 1992, the secessionist leaders of these republics had no incentive to reach a compromise or negotiated solution with the federal Yugoslav state. This damaging diplomatic intervention was driven not so much by events on the ground but rather by rivalries between the leading European powers and the United States, each attempting to assert its international authority in the new and uncertain post-Cold War order. Although western policy was presented at the time as a way of resolving conflict, in reality it had the opposite effect, since the status of ethnic minorities within the borders of these republics had not been settled prior to independence.

Once war was underway, western involvement continued to make matters worse: the United States encouraged the Bosnian Muslims to reject peace agreements negotiated by the Europeans, for example in Lisbon in 1992 (a proposed settlement similar to the one that was eventually adopted in 1995) and in Geneva in 1993 (Chandler, 2000: 24; Woodward, 1995: 243–44). Moreover, as Woodward argues, the US policy of encouraging the prosecution of war crimes via the International Criminal Tribunal for the former Yugoslavia, even at points in the conflict when the Serbs were seeking to negotiate an end to hostilities, 'required a conspiracy of silence about atrocities committed by parties who were not considered aggressors' (Woodward, 1995: 323). As discussed further below, many journalists proved all too willing to adapt their reporting to accommodate this selective silence.

A similar pattern of misrepresentation and destructive international interference was evident in later efforts to encourage a western humanitarian intervention in Darfur. As Alex de Waal has noted, the 'first international outcry' over Darfur in 2004 came at a point when the level of violence was falling, but regardless of the changing dynamics of the conflict, the campaigners' constant refrain was that 'things are getting worse' (de Waal, 2008). In September 2006, for example, Hollywood activist George Clooney told the UN Security Council, 'My job is to come here today and to beg you on behalf of the millions of people who will die – and make no mistake, they will die – for you to take real and effective measures to put an end to this.' This apocalyptic assessment did not match what was happening in Darfur at the time. As de Waal points out,

> What actually happened was that the Sudan army dispatched a battalion of recent conscripts, stiffened by a few experienced regulars and some militia, into the middle of rebel-held north Darfur. On 11 September, the Janjaweed vanished and the [rebels] attacked, annihilating the well dug-in but inexperienced army unit. Perhaps 400 soldiers died in less than an hour. (de Waal, 2007: 9)

By 2007, aid agencies had begun to worry about the apparent ability of 'Save Darfur' campaigners to influence policy-makers, given the likely impact of the humanitarian intervention that activists demanded. In response to an advertising campaign calling for tough western action, the head of the InterAction coalition of aid groups, Sam Worthington, condemned the 'inability of Save Darfur to be informed by the realities on the ground and to understand the consequences of [its] proposed actions'. According to Worthington, the sort of aggressive intervention advocated by the campaigners 'could easily result in the deaths of hundreds of thousands of individuals' (*New York Times*, June 2, 2007). Similarly, Action Against Hunger warned that 'a non-negotiated intervention [...] could have disastrous consequences that risk triggering a further escalation of violence while jeopardizing the provision of vital humanitarian assistance to millions of people' (Action Against Hunger, 2007). Given the record of international humanitarian intervention, such fears were well founded.

The problem is not only the poor track record and results. There is also a serious in-principle objection to humanitarian or otherwise ethical interventionism. As indicated above, in the post-Cold War era humanitarianism has provided the rationale for a dramatic break from the principles of sovereign equality and noninterference established under the UN system after the World War II, institutionalizing a system of sovereign inequality, in which powerful states are seen as having the right, even the duty, to interfere in the internal affairs of weaker countries. Of course, the Cold War was hardly an era of peace in the Third World, but the overall trend was toward independence and self-determination for the former colonies.

This trend was reversed in the 1990s, when conflicts that were concerned with national self-determination ended instead with the establishment of international protectorates, first in Bosnia and later in Kosovo. From the outset, media commentators were clearly well aware of the fact that new rules of international relations were being established. At the time of the mission to Somalia, for example, newspaper editorials noted that the intervention marked 'a radical departure in international law' (*Times*, December 1, 1992) and set 'an important precedent' (*The Independent*, December 23, 1992). But this development was seen as entirely positive: the *Times* advocated 'putting Somalia under temporary trusteeship', while *The Independent* advised 'imposing formal and continuing UN mandates on once-sovereign states' under a 'benign imperium' (*The Independent*, December 1, 1992).

Such calls for a return to the days of imperialism reached a peak at the time of the 1999 Kosovo bombing. The American writer David Rieff called for a 'recolonization of part of the world' under a system of 'liberal imperialism' (Rieff, 1999: 10), and Bernard Kouchner, the founder of Médecins Sans Frontières who was appointed as the first governor of postwar Kosovo, argued that 'as part of the emergent world order, a new morality can be codified in the right to intervention' (*Los Angeles Times*, October 18, 1999).

In subsequent years, as British international relations theorist David Chandler observes, the rhetorical emphasis has shifted away from a confrontational 'right to intervene' toward the less provocative idea of a 'responsibility to protect' (2006: 31), as developed by the International Commission on Intervention and State Sovereignty (2001). The idea is that states have responsibilities to the international community as well as to their own citizens, and that the international community has a duty to intervene if states cannot or will not meet these responsibilities. Yet the redefinition of sovereignty as 'responsibility' effectively means the end of sovereignty. The non-western state is no longer understood as sovereign – as accountable to no higher power than its own citizens – but as necessarily held to account from above by international actors.

This approach to international relations resembles the 'might is right' approach of an earlier era – but in the twenty-first century it is no longer 'legitimised by a conservative elite, on the basis of racial superiority and an imperial mission, but by a liberal elite, on the basis of ethical superiority and a human rights mission' (Chandler, 2005: 156).

If the redefinition of sovereignty as 'responsibility' effectively means the end of sovereign equality, it also means the end of international law, argues Chandler: 'By the mid-1990s, the UN's role had been transformed from an institutional attempt to provide a collective security system towards one where open-ended resolutions "authorized" unilateral military interventions which were then retrospectively validated' (2005: 250). When a 'coalition of the willing' bypassed the UN Security Council and legitimized military intervention on ethical, humanitarian grounds in Kosovo in 1999, it opened the way for the projects for 'regime change' in Afghanistan and Iraq a few years later. Indeed, while there were many objections to the Bush administration's willingness to use preemptive force against Iraq, this idea had been advocated as part of the West's 'right to intervene' for humanitarian or human rights reasons: Kouchner, for example, argued after the Kosovo conflict that it was 'necessary to take the further step of using the right to intervention as a preventive measure to stop wars before they start and to stop murderers before they kill' (*Los Angeles Times*, October 18, 1999). As Chandler observes,

> The new rights of intervention – whether cast in terms of a new right of humanitarian intervention or an extended right of self-defence, which includes the right of prevention or pre-emption – cannot be available to any but a select few. These are the rights of Great Power hegemony, not the rights of legal equality. (2005: 250)

These practical and principled objections to humanitarian intervention ought to be at the center of any consideration of 'ethical' foreign policies or 'moral' intervention.

The alternative is to engage in a subjective game of trying to guess which declared ethical motives are sincere (Somalia? Kosovo?), and which are not (Afghanistan? Iraq?) – as if all that mattered were good intentions. It is worth recalling that although it is often associated with left-of-center figures such as the former British Minister Tony Blair, former US President William J. Clinton or the former German Chancellor Gerhard Schroeder, it was archconservative Ronald Reagan who, in a December 1992 speech, first articulated the idea that humanitarian intervention could offer a new framework for western foreign policy after the end of the Cold War. Noting that the 'end of communist tyranny' had 'robbed much of the West of its uplifting, common purpose', Reagan asked,

[M]ight we not now unite to impose civilised standards of behaviour on those who flout every measure of human decency? Are we not nearing a point in world history where civilised nations can in unison stand up to the most immoral and deadly excesses against humanity, such as those now defacing Somalia and Bosnia?

[...] the world's democracies must enforce stricter humanitarian standards of international conduct. What I propose is a humanitarianism velvet glove backed by a steel fist of military force. (*The Sunday Times*, December 6, 1992)

Reagan delivered this speech on the day that the idea was being put into practice by his successor and former Vice President George Bush Senior launching the humanitarian intervention in Somalia.

Perhaps the most striking thing about Reagan's remarks is his explicit proposal that humanitarianism could make good the loss of an 'uplifting, common purpose' following the defeat of the Soviet enemy. As French international relations theorist Zaki Laïdi has observed, today 'war is no longer a continuation of politics by other means [...] [but the] initial expression of forms of activity or organization in search of meaning' (Laïdi, 1998: 95). In this way, he suggests, war, intervention and other forms of international activism may be understood as attempts to offset the 'crisis of meaning' precipitated by the end of the Cold War. The collapse of the politics of Left and Right both domestically and internationally has left us, according to Laïdi, in 'a world without meaning'.

In these circumstances, 'war becomes not the ultimate means to achieve an objective, but the most "efficient" way of finding one' (Laïdi, 1998: 95). Military action – including humanitarian intervention and, for that matter, the 'War on Terror' – has in other words been driven by a search for meaning and purpose in our post-ideological era. It is the emptiness of the public sphere – manifested in a crisis of authority, of institutions, of public and political disengagement – that drives an elite search for purpose and meaning elsewhere. In that sense, regardless of the altruism or good intentions of particular individuals, the ostensibly other-directed foreign policy of humanitarian intervention is essentially narcissistic. As Ignatieff – an advocate of humanitarian intervention – has acknowledged, western policy in Bosnia was 'often driven by narcissism':

We intervened not only to save others, but to save ourselves, or rather an image of ourselves as defenders of universal decencies. We wanted to know that the West 'meant' something. This imaginary West, this narcissistic image of ourselves, we believed was incarnated in the myth of a multiethnic, multiconfessional Bosnia. [...] Bosnia became the latest bel espoir of a generation that had tried ecology, socialism, and civil rights only to watch all these lose their romantic momentum. (Ignatieff, 1998: 95)

The desire to 'save' Bosnia was a desire to restore meaning to western societies: whereas the Cold War 'made sense of the world for us', Ignatieff (1998: 98) argues, now we have 'lost our narrative'.

This narcissistic drive to draw meaning from international intervention has continued long after the war in Bosnia ended. Contemplating the ongoing conflicts in Afghanistan and Iraq in 2006, for example, Blair described them as 'a battle utterly decisive in whether the values we believe in triumph or fail', and pointed to elections there as a 'symbol of hope, and of belief in the values we too hold dear' (2006b). The struggle of Afghans and Iraqis, in other words, was understood as helping the West to overcome its own lack of confidence and cohesion: 'The fact of their courage', argued Blair, 'should give us courage; their determination should lend us strength; their embrace of democratic values [...] should reinforce our own confidence in those values' (2006a). Similarly, pondering the damage done to US credibility by the Bush administration, former State Department spokesman James Rubin wondered what it would take to restore America's 'moral authority': 'Frankly, I don't think we'll be able to do it until some new event happens, some new humanitarian crisis, [like] Bosnia, or Kosovo or Somalia, and then we can come in and help. And that, that's the kind of thing that can help' (BBC Radio 4, December 3, 2007).

Rubin's idea that another Bosnia or a new Kosovo would help to restore authority and purpose to US foreign policy recalls the way that neocons at the Project for the New American Century argued that their ambitions for military reform and enhanced US 'global leadership' were unlikely to be realized quickly, 'absent some catastrophic and catalyzing event – like a new Pearl Harbor' (PNAC, 2000: 51). The hope is that the West will be able to overcome internal problems through confronting an external threat or disaster that could be thought to embody them. It is particularly telling that such responses are envisaged in advance, before the wished-for threat or catastrophe has actually materialized.

The Role of the Media

The fact that intervention is geared up to creating a sense of meaning and purpose has two major consequences for the role of the media. The first is that image and presentation become hugely, disproportionately important. This has been particularly obvious in the 'War on Terror' interventions, where the official desire to produce the 'right' image led the military to lay on photo opportunities and to stage spectacles for the media or for their own camera crews. Early in the post-9/11 campaign in Afghanistan, for example, international TV news programs screened video footage of US Special Forces staging a nighttime raid on Kandahar. The film, taken by the US forces themselves, had some propaganda value since it demonstrated their ability to put forces on the ground in the heart of Taliban-held territory. But the mission appeared to have no military significance in itself: as Seymour Hersh reported in *The New Yorker* (November 5, 2001), a different special forces team had gone in beforehand to make sure the area was secure for the second, camera-toting team.

Similar moments of manufactured drama characterized the Iraq campaign, from the videotaped rescue of Private Jessica Lynch from al-Nasiriyah; through the evacuation of 'Little Ali', a boy who had his arms blown off by the coalition missile that killed his family; to the choreographed toppling of Saddam Hussein's statue outside the hotel housing international journalists. These attempts to produce a defining image showing the western military in a positive light were rarely successful precisely because they were so obviously contrived, although journalists did sometimes join in with the effort.

At the beginning of the Afghan War, for example, *The Economist* offered some advice on how to achieve 'success in the propaganda war', noting that 'humanitarian aid to Afghan refugees, and demonstrable care about civilian casualties there, will play an important role' (*The Economist*, October 4, 2001). As these comments suggest, the 'humanitarian' aspect of contemporary military action is often key to producing positive images.

Indeed, the same official attention to media presentation characterized the humanitarian interventions of the 1990s. When the troops sent by President Bush on Operation Restore Hope arrived in Somalia in 1992, for instance, they were not confronted by an armed enemy but by journalists attempting to interview them. Bewildered soldiers tried to evade the reporters, and later complained that the TV lights and camera flashbulbs had interfered with their night-vision equipment, but the media had been invited to be there by the Pentagon, which had 'made little effort to disguise the fact that the dawn landing had been set up in much the same way as a sporting event' (*Times*, December 10, 1992).

Similarly, Greg Philo et al. observe that US aerial aid drops to the massive refugee camps that developed on Rwanda's borders in the wake of the mass killings of 1994 were 'a classic example of a publicity stunt which contributed nothing to resolving a crisis'. Philo et al. suggest that the air drop was not really necessary, since aid was already arriving by road, and in any case much of the 'aid' was useless: the parcels contained 'dirty clothes, gruyere cheese (labeled "perishable needs refrigeration"), ski-mittens, biscuits (labeled "do not drop"), chocolate and [supermarket] flour' (1999: 224–25). They also note that aid agencies on the ground seemed equally publicity-conscious, eager 'to help orphaned and abandoned children [...] [but less] interested in digging latrines', even though it was that latter, less glamorous, activity that would have been of greatest practical help in the midst of a cholera epidemic (Philo et al., 1999: 224–25).

The media's response to humanitarian stunts has often appeared contradictory, both criticizing and distancing themselves from official attempts to generate good publicity, but simultaneously endorsing an interventionist stance and joining in with the effort to produce feel-good images and sound bites. One brief cause célèbre during the Bosnian War, for example, was the plight of an injured five-year-old girl, dubbed 'Little Irma' by the British tabloids. Two newspapers, *The Sun* and the *Daily Mail*, each attempted to mount its own rescue mission, but they were warned off by the UK government, which wanted to ensure that it got all the good publicity for evacuating Irma from Sarajevo to a London hospital.

The quality press was less impressed by what *The Guardian*'s Maggie O'Kane disparaged as a 'cheap publicity stunt' (*The Guardian*, August 10, 1993). Yet while a broadsheet paper such as *The Guardian* distanced itself from official stunts that tabloids sought to emulate, this did not imply any more fundamental questioning of western involvement in Bosnia. O'Kane could see that there was 'a chilling cynicism' in the government's publicity-seeking mercy mission for Little Irma, but her main complaint was that it was 'distracting attention from the central issue of military intervention'.

Similarly, although reports of the staged beach landings in Somalia in December 1992 often took a wry view of the military's clumsy attempt to look impressive, journalists were also complicit in creating the image of a country that needed to be saved from itself. Western journalists deliberately emphasized the most appalling images of suffering, asking aid workers where they could find some 'stick action' – emaciated infants who could be photographed at the point of death (Carruthers, 2000: 240) – and in one incident they reportedly 'trampled starving children [...] in their desperation to obtain the best photographs' (*The Guardian*, December 16, 1992). As Michael Maren notes, such imagery was misleading and one-sided: the impact of famine was localized but 'there was very little reporting that let people know that most of Somalia was fine' (Maren, 1997: 211). Instead, the media produced what Rakiya Omaar and Alex de Waal described as 'disaster pornography', the effect of which could only be to bolster the argument for humanitarian military intervention (*Los Angeles Times*, December 10, 1992).

The second consequence of the pursuit of war and intervention as a means to shore up a sense of meaning and purpose for western societies is that media reporting of crises tends to become detached from mundane reality and instead interprets events in terms of a Manichean clash of good and evil. The attempt to make intervention appear meaningful, in other words, results in public discussion of conflicts and crises becoming distorted as events are removed from their local context, and presented in terms of a titanic struggle in which the intervening powers demonstrate their own importance and 'values'. Rony Brauman, the former president of Médecins Sans Frontières, has perceptively described this phenomenon, objecting to the increasingly common 'perception of armed conflicts as "genocides" (the Former Yugoslavia, Sudan, and undoubtedly more to come)'. As Brauman argues,

> To qualify a war as genocidal is to leave the terrain of politics, of its relations of force, of its compromises and contingencies, in order to situate oneself in some metaphysical beyond in which the only conflict is between Good and Evil: fanatics versus moderates, bloodthirsty hordes versus innocent civilians. (Brauman, 2008)

Indeed, over the past 20 years our understanding of genocide has been transformed: from being understood as an exceptional event, it is now seen as an almost everyday occurrence. The term 'genocide' was used in news coverage to describe the situation in Darfur, Iraq, Kosovo, Rwanda, Bosnia and even civil conflict in Somalia (Hammond, 2007). Without exception, the tendency to interpret contemporary conflicts through parallels with the Nazi era has distorted understanding of events. As the veteran BBC foreign correspondent John Simpson later observed about the reporting of Bosnia, 'A climate was created in which it was very hard to understand what was really going on, because everything came to be seen through the filter of the Holocaust' (Simpson, 1998: 444–45).

Yet the same misleading framework was soon reproduced wholesale in the coverage of Kosovo. On the same day (April 1, 1999) that the *Mirror* newspaper reported 'Nazi style terror' in Kosovo, *The Sun* detected 'chilling echoes of the Holocaust', *The Guardian* reported 'grim new echoes of Nazi horrors', *The Times* described 'genocidal operations in Kosovo', and in *The Independent* David Aaronovitch said that 'when you examine the views of the man and woman on the Belgrade tram, it is easier to see how so many Germans in the Thirties bought the Joseph Goebbels version of the world'.

As this last example suggests, the parallel with the Nazis was a powerful way to demonize the enemy and justify NATO bombing. It is also notable that Aaronovitch's comments explicitly vilify the Serbian people as a whole, rather than only their leaders – an approach also adopted by others. The *Telegraph*'s Patrick Bishop suggested that 'Serb' is a synonym for 'barbarian' (*Daily Telegraph*, March 26, 1999), for example; *The Sun* said they should be 'shot like wild dogs' (*The Sun*, April 14, 1999); and in the left-wing *New Statesman* magazine Steve Crawshaw claimed that 'many millions of Serbs' had 'become liars on a grand scale or gone mad, or both' (*New Statesman*, May 31, 1999).

These vituperative attacks in newspaper comment sections were ostensibly borne out by reports of atrocities in the news pages: as one BBC journalist put it, 'for the Western allies, the steadily accumulating evidence of atrocities will be confirmation that this was a just war' ('Newsnight', BBC2, June 14, 1999). Yet the evidence did not bear out NATO claims that 10,000 or 100,000 or even more had been killed. The actual figure appears to be closer to 5,000 – a number that includes combatants as well as civilians, Serbs as well as ethnic Albanians (United Nations Mission in Kosovo, 2003). Moreover, even had all the atrocity stories been true, this could hardly have been held to justify the war, since the allegations related to the period when NATO was already bombing. Journalists conveniently 'forgot' that there had been no refugee crisis or humanitarian disaster until after NATO had started bombing. One reporter explained that 'NATO went to war so the refugees could come back to Kosovo' (BBC, June 16, 1999); another acclaimed 'the success of the US policy', on the grounds that 'the President fought this war so that these people could go home in peace' (Channel 4, June 22, 1999).

Even in the most apparently clear-cut case – the mass killings and atrocities in Rwanda in 1994 – it is questionable whether labeling the violence as 'genocide' really aided understanding, since the concept tended to be used in a simplistic fashion, abstracting the violence from its immediate context of civil war, often deliberately. The American author and journalist Philip Gourevitch, for example, voiced the consensus view that 'although the genocide coincided with the war, its organization and implementation were quite distinct from the war effort' (Gourevitch, 2000: 98). The reason for treating the mass killings of April–June 1994 as a distinct and separate event is to place them in the sort of abstract moral context described above by Brauman (2008), rather than in the historical context of the civil war between government forces and the Rwandan Patriotic Front (RPF).

Yet the consequences of the war – a rapid expansion of the armed forces, successive waves of internally displaced refugees and international diplomatic intervention to secure a flawed power-sharing agreement – must logically have contributed directly to the terrible violence of 1994 (see Mamdani, 2001). Through bracketing out the recent context of civil war – and thereby also closing off important questions about the impact of prior western interference – the only possible explanation for the appalling violence becomes the idea that its Hutu perpetrators were slaves to a genocidal ideology. Many commentators rejected the idea (which was often present in early news reporting) that the violence was the spontaneous product of innate 'tribal hatreds'; yet the supposedly more 'moral' alternative explanation, seeing the violence as premeditated and systematic genocide, did not produce any greater understanding when it was taken up in media coverage. While it is true that some early reports of 'tribal massacres' naturalized supposed differences between Hutu and Tutsi, later reporting of 'genocidal massacres' presented the whole country, and indeed the wider region, as defined by its difference, inherently prone to explosive violence and permanently on the verge of a further descent into evil.

Similar problems can be seen in the more recent use of the term 'genocide' to characterize the conflict in Darfur. As Deborah Murphy notes in her study of US media coverage, 'In general, Darfur was removed from the Sudanese context [...] most of the articles reviewed were not really about Darfur itself' (Murphy, 2007: 320–21). The most obvious point of comparison for explaining Darfur was the decades-long war in southern Sudan, but this 'compelling analogy' was 'largely ignored'. Instead, parallels were drawn with the Holocaust, Cambodia, Bosnia, Kosovo and, most frequently, Rwanda.

The point of the comparisons, as Murphy observes, was 'to urge US intervention'. Back in 1994, US officials avoided using the term 'genocide' publicly to describe the killing in Rwanda – despite reportedly characterizing it as such in internal discussions (Peterson, 2000: 295). Advocates of intervention became convinced that if only western leaders would recognize the violence as genocide they would then be bound to intervene. The falsity of this assumption was revealed in 2004, when then Secretary of State Colin Powell declared that 'genocide has been committed in Darfur and [...] may still be occurring', but then said that 'no new action is dictated by this determination'. Again it is questionable whether using the term 'genocide' helped to explain the nature of the violence. As Brauman asks,

How is one to understand the fact that two million Darfuris have sought refuge around the principal army garrisons of their province? How is one to understand the fact that one million of them live in Khartoum, where they have never been bothered during the entire course of the war? (Brauman, 2008)

Yet the preference of activists, campaigners – and campaigning journalists – for the 'genocide' framework derived less from a desire to understand events and more from an urge to influence them. According to de Waal, 'activists who campaigned […] for the US government to declare Darfur "genocide" did so because they wanted an intervention' (de Waal, 2007: 8).

The tendency for political leaders (as in Kosovo) or campaigners (as in Darfur) to portray international intervention in local conflicts in terms of an epic confrontation between good and evil serves the direct purpose of justifying action as a response to exceptional circumstances. Yet it is also indicative of the wider attempt to use war and intervention in order to create a sense of political purpose and meaning, and it is generally this second consideration that is most important in understanding the role of the media. There have, of course, been instances of deliberate deception and concerted propaganda campaigns – most notably in the cases of Kosovo and Iraq. Yet in many crises and conflicts since the end of the Cold War, the problems with media coverage have been caused less by official manipulation of the media and more by journalists' own unprompted attempts to encourage intervention by adopting a style of reporting that rejects objectivity in favor of moral engagement and seeks to influence western public opinion and policy.

In Britain, the best-known supporter of this approach is the former BBC war correspondent Martin Bell, who coined the term 'journalism of attachment' to describe the new style of advocacy journalism. This is an approach that, in Bell's words, 'cares as well as knows' and which 'will not stand neutrally between good and evil, right and wrong, the victim and the oppressor' (Bell, 1998: 16–18). In the United States, CNN reporter Christiane Amanpour has advanced a similar argument, declaring that '[i]n certain situations, the classic definition of objectivity can mean neutrality, and neutrality can mean you are an accomplice to all sorts of evil' (Ricchiardi, 1996). As Mick Hume (1997) suggests, in the Bosnian War advocacy reporting provided 'a twisted sort of therapy, through which foreign reporters [could] discover some sense of purpose – first for themselves, and then for their audience back home', as journalists undertook a 'moral mission on behalf of a demoralized society' (Hume, 1997: 18). In effect, journalists have joined in with the narcissistic search for meaning described above.

Although it is often presented as a critical or oppositional stance, advocacy journalism promotes a moralistic humanitarian discourse, echoing and encouraging the development of similar themes by powerful western governments. In adopting this approach, reporters have frequently played down or ignored facts that did not fit a simplistic, good versus evil portrayal of conflict, have excused or even celebrated violence against 'unworthy' victims and have uncritically welcomed western military action. In the Balkans, for example, international support for the secession of Slovenia, Croatia and Bosnia inevitably cast the Serbs as the villains. Phillip Corwin, who served as the United Nations' Chief Political Officer in Sarajevo, describes a 'juggernaut of pro-Bosnian, anti-Serb sentiment in the international community' for which the western media constituted 'a powerful public relations arm' (Corwin, 1999: 38). For 'attached' journalists, it seems that this PR work extended to ignoring facts that did not fit the black-and-white picture of Bosnia that they wanted to promote. As John Simpson recalls, for example,

> Once, when I was in Sarajevo, the UN discovered that Muslim troops were holding a couple of dozen Serbs in a section of drainage pipe three feet high. They opened the front of the pipe once a day to throw food into the darkness inside. The journalists, many of them committed to the principle of not standing neutrally between victim and oppressor, showed no interest at all in this story. It was inconvenient and, as far as I know, was not reported. (*The Sunday Telegraph*, September 14, 1997)

For all its professions of morality and concern for victims, this approach to journalism deliberately made some victims invisible.

In both Bosnia and Rwanda, killings and atrocities that were carried out with the diplomatic and military support of the United States and its allies were welcomed by advocacy journalists. When the Croats forcibly expelled around 200,000 Serbs from the Krajina in 1995, killing an estimated 2,500 in the process, *The Guardian*'s Martin Woollacott wrote that the attack was 'to be welcomed', describing the slaughter of civilians as 'a hold on Serbian aggression' (*The Guardian*, August 5, 1995), while *The Independent*'s editorialist said it was 'tempting to feel euphoric' (*Independent*, August 7, 1995). NATO airstrikes against the Bosnian Serbs were also encouraged and celebrated by journalists, with few questions asked about the pretext for such action. Bell describes the reaction of international reporters to NATO bombing in 1995, for example: 'through the jaded press corps [...] there spread a feeling new to all of us – a sense of awe and wonderment' (Bell, 1996: 281).

This reaction was not the product of traditional patriotic or militaristic attitudes, but arose from the outlook of 'caring' advocacy journalism. There was a similar sequel to the Rwanda tragedy. As the good Tutsi/evil Hutu framework became entrenched in the months following RPF victory, journalists grew increasingly critical of the provision of relief to Hutu refugees and regretted their initial sympathy for the tens of thousands of cholera victims who died in refugee camps on Rwanda's borders. As Gourevitch puts it, humanitarian aid workers were 'openly exploited as caterers to what was probably the single largest society of fugitive criminals against humanity ever assembled' (Gourevitch, 2000: 267). So when the RPF invaded Zaire in 1996, attacking the camps and massacring refugees, journalists saw this as a positive development. Nik Gowing's interviews with humanitarian workers and journalists reveal how the mass killings of Hutu refugees were justified and legitimized by reporters who viewed events through a 'lens of sympathy' (Gowing, 1998: 41). Many were 'readily pro-Tutsi to the exclusion of what one journalist accepted was "any other more balanced possibility"', says Gowing, while 'all Hutus were often implicitly written off as "killers" or "extremists"' (Gowing, 1998: 40–1). Oxfam's Director of Emergencies, Nick Stockton, described how journalists helped condone the attacks: 'some of the best

British correspondents who knew the region and its politics rapidly promoted a consensus that here, at last, was the chance to deal with an entirely murderous group [the Hutu] who had been foolishly succoured by aid' (Gowing, 1998: 36).

Another of Gowing's interviewees, an aid worker, noted that '[m]ost journalists had committed themselves to the idea that the camps were full of genocidal Hutu maniacs, and that they had to be repatriated' (Gowing, 1998: 24). When Mugunga camp was shelled for six hours on November 15, 1996 with heavy mortar and artillery, for example, *The Independent* welcomed this as 'some good news from Africa', describing it as 'the outcome everyone wished for' (*The Independent*, November 16, 1996).

Conclusions

Despite the fact that, in the years since the 2003 invasion of Iraq, the mood in western societies appears to have become more antiwar, this has done little to disturb the consensus established in the 1990s in favor of humanitarian intervention. The role of the media in relation to such intervention has most often been discussed in terms of the potential for news coverage to influence policy, based on the underlying assumption that intervention for humanitarian ends is a positive thing. Whether media coverage actually did pressure governments to adopt policies of humanitarian intervention in the 1990s, it is certainly the case that many journalists began to understand their role in these terms: one of the most striking features of media coverage of post-Cold War crises has been the emergence of a 'journalism of attachment' advocating tough military intervention for 'ethical' reasons.

In adopting this style of reporting, journalists effectively joined the western elite's narcissistic search for meaning, in which it was hoped that humanitarian military intervention could offer a new sense of purpose for the post-Cold War world. Image and presentation have been all-important in interventions and wars justified on humanitarian grounds, since the goal has been to demonstrate western 'values' at the expense of weaker states. The media have frequently drawn attention to suffering and atrocity, but by depicting events according to a simplistic narrative of 'good and evil', they have also distorted them. Journalists have been less concerned about the suffering of those deemed to be 'unworthy' victims, and have rarely asked fundamental questions about the actions of western governments and their local allies, even though the sovereignty of weak countries has been violated by the powerful time and again in the name of humanitarianism.

Key Points

- Post-Cold War humanitarian intervention has been driven by a search for meaning and purpose on the part of western elites.
- Media presentation is disproportionately important because humanitarian intervention is essentially narcissistic, concerned with producing the 'right' image.

- The problems with media coverage derive not only from official manipulation of the media but also from journalists' own spontaneous efforts as they join in with the narcissistic search for meaning and chose or construct sides of good and evil.

Study Questions

1. What might be the problems with an 'attached' style of journalism in wartime? Is it better or worse than 'objective' reporting?
2. What factors led to the rise of humanitarian intervention after 1989? Is there any evidence that media reporting influenced western policy?

Further Reading

Chandler, David (ed.) (2002) *Rethinking Human Rights. Critical Approaches to International Politics*. Houndmills; Basingstoke; Hampshire; New York: Palgrave Macmillan.
Coker, Christopher (2001) *Humane Warfare*. London; New York: Routledge.
Hammond, Philip (2007) *Media, War and Postmodernity*. Abingdon: Routledge.
Hammond, Philip and Edward S. Herman (eds) (2000) *Degraded Capability. The Media and the Kosovo Crisis*. London; Sterling, VA: Pluto Press.
Keeble, Richard (1997) *Secret State, Silent Press. New Militarism, the Gulf and the Modern Image of Warfare*. Luton, Bedfordshire, UK: University of Luton Press.

References

Action Against Hunger (2007) *A Political Solution Is Essential to Achieving Security in Darfur*, www.actionagainsthunger.org (May 18, 2007).
African Rights (1993) *Human Rights Abuses by the United Nations Forces*, web.peacelink.it/afrights/reports.htm (March 2, 2010).
Bell, Martin (1996) *In Harm's Way*. New York: Penguin Books.
——— (1998) 'The Journalism of Attachment', pp. 15–22 in Matthew Kieran (ed.) *Media Ethics*. London; New York: Routledge.
Blair, Tony (2001) *Speech to the Labour Party Conference*, October 2, 2001.
——— (2006a) *Foreign Policy Speech I*, March 21, 2006.
——— (2006b) *Foreign Policy Speech II*, March 27, 2006.
Braumann, R. (2008) *The ICC's Bashir Indictment. Law against Peace*, www.worldpoliticsreview.com/ (July 23, 2008).
Bush, George W. (2001) *Address to a Joint Session of Congress and the American People*, September 20, 2001, georgewbush-whitehouse.archives.gov/news/releases/2001/09/20010920-8.html (December 19, 2011).

Carruthers, Susan L. (2000) *The Media at War. Communication and Conflict in the Twentieth Century*. Basingstoke; London; New York: Macmillan; St Martin's Press.

Chandler, David (2000) 'Western Intervention and the Disintegration of Yugoslavia, 1989–1999', pp. 19–30 in Phil Hammond and Edward S. Herman (eds) *Degraded Capability. The Media and the Kosovo Crisis*. London; Sterling, VA: Pluto Press.

——— (2005) *From Kosovo to Kabul. Human Rights and International Intervention*. London; Ann Arbor, MI: Pluto Press.

——— (2006) *Empire in Denial. The Politics of State-Building*. London: Pluto Press.

Chomsky, Noam (1999) *The New Military Humanism. Lessons from Kosovo*. Monroe, ME: Common Courage Press.

Chouliaraki, Lilie (2008) 'The Media as Moral Education. Mediation and Action', *Media, Culture & Society* 30(6): 831–52.

Corwin, Phillip (1999) *Dubious Mandate. A Memoir of the UN in Bosnia, Summer 1995*. Durham, NC: Duke University Press.

de Waal, Alexander (1998) 'US War Crimes in Somalia', *New Left Review* 230: 131–44.

——— (2007) 'War Games', *Index on Censorship* 36(4): 6–11.

——— (2008) 'Darfur Activism. The Debate Continues', *Making Sense of Darfur Blog*, January 8, 2008, http://www.ssrc.org/blogs/darfur/category/darfur/ (December 19, 2011).

Foley, Conor (2008) *The Thin Blue Line. How Humanitarianism Went to War*. London: Verso.

Gourevitch, Philip (2000) *We Wish to Inform You that Tomorrow We Will Be Killed with Our Families. Stories from Rwanda*. London: Picador.

Gowing, Nik (1998) *New Challenges and Problems for Information Management in Complex Emergencies*, Background Paper to 'Dispatches from Disaster Zones. The Reporting of Humanitarian Emergencies', Conference, May 28, 1998. Westminster, London.

Hammond, Philip (2007) *Framing Post-Cold War Conflicts. The Media and International Intervention*. Manchester; New York: Manchester University Press.

Hume, Mick (1997) *Whose War Is It Anyway? The Dangers of the Journalism of Attachment*. London: BM InformInc.

——— (2003) *Euro-Occupation Plan for Iraq. The Franco-German Alternative to War Is a 'Peaceful Invasion'*, www.spiked-online.com/Printable/00000006DC48.htm (February 10, 2003).

Ignatieff, Michael (1998) *The Warrior's Honor. Ethnic War and the Modern Conscience*. London: Chatto & Windus.

Independent International Commission on Kosovo (IICK) (2000) *The Kosovo Report. Conflict, International Response, Lessons Learned*. Oxford; New York: Oxford University Press.

International Commission on Intervention and State Sovereignty (2001) *The Responsibility to Protect*, http://www.idrc.ca (January 21, 2011).

Laïdi, Zaki (1998) *A World without Meaning. The Crisis of Meaning in International Politics*. London; New York: Routledge.

Livingston, Steven (1997) *Clarifying the CNN Effect. An Examination of Media Effects According to Type of Military Intervention*, Research Paper R-18, Joan Shorenstein Center on the Press, Politics and Public Policy, Harvard University, tamilnation.co/media/CNNeffect.pdf (March 2, 2010).

Livingston, Steven and Todd Eachus (1995) 'Humanitarian Crises and U.S. Foreign Policy: Somalia and the CNN Effect Reconsidered', *Political Communication* 12(4): 413–29.

—— (2000) 'Rwanda: US Policy and Television Coverage', pp. 209–30 in Howard Adelman and Astri Suhrke (eds) *The Path of a Genocide. The Rwanda Crisis from Uganda to Zaire.* London: Transaction Publishers.

Mamdani, Mahmood (2001) *When Victims Become Killers. Colonialism, Nativism, and the Genocide in Rwanda.* Princeton, NJ: Princeton University Press.

—— (2007) 'The Politics of Naming: Genocide, Civil War, Insurgency', *London Review of Books* 29(5): 5–7.

Maren, Michael (1997) *The Road to Hell. The Ravaging Effects of Foreign Aid and International Charity.* New York: Free Press.

Mermin, Jonathan (1999) *Debating War and Peace. Media Coverage of U.S. Intervention in the Post-Vietnam Era.* Princeton, NJ: Princeton University Press.

Minear, Larry, Colin Scott and Thomas George Weiss (1996) *The News Media, Civil War, and Humanitarian Action.* Boulder, CO: L. Rienner.

Murphy, Deborah (2007) 'Narrating Darfur. Darfur in the U.S. Press, March–September 2004', pp. 314–36 in Alexander de Waal (ed.) *War in Darfur and the Search for Peace.* Cambridge, MA: Harvard University.

Peterson, Scott (2000) *Me against My Brother. At War in Somalia, Sudan, and Rwanda: A Journalist Reports from the Battlefields of Africa.* London: Routledge.

Philo, Greg, L. Hilsum, L. Beattie and R. Holliman (1999) 'The Media and the Rwanda Crisis', pp. 211–229 in Greg Philo (ed.) *Message Received.* Harlow, England; New York: Longman.

Project for the New American Century (PNAC) (2000) *Rebuilding America's Defenses,* www. newamericancentury.org/ (December 19, 2011).

Ricchiardi, Sherry (1996) '"Over the Line?" (Journalists as Advocates in the Bosnian War)', *American Journalism Review* 18(7): 24–31.

Rieff, David (1999) 'A New Age of Liberal Imperialism?', *World Policy Journal* 16(2): 1–10.

Robinson, Piers (2002) *The CNN Effect. The Myth of News, Foreign Policy, and Intervention.* London; New York: Routledge.

Shaw, Ibrahim S. (2007) 'Historical Frames and the Politics of Humanitarian Intervention. From Ethiopia, Somalia to Rwanda', *Globalisation, Societies and Education* 5(3): 351–71.

Shaw, Martin (1996) *Civil Society and Media in Global Crisis. Representing Distant Violence.* London: Pinter.

Simpson, John (1998) *Strange Places, Questionable People.* London: Macmillan.

Stelzer, Irwin M. (ed.) (2004) *Neo-Conservatism.* London: Atlantic.

UK Foreign Affairs Select Committee (2000) *Fourth Report,* www.publications.parliament.uk/ pa/cm199900/cmselect/cmfaff/28/2802.htm (December 19, 2011).

United Nations Mission in Kosovo (UNMIK) (2003) *Office of Missing Persons and Forensics Press Release,* www.eulex-kosovo.eu/en/justice/office-on-missing-persons-and-forensics.php (December 19, 2011).

Woodward, Susan L. (1995) *Balkan Tragedy. Chaos and Dissolution After the Cold War.* Washington, D.C.: Brookings Institution.

Shifting Frames in a Deadlocked Conflict?

News Coverage of the Israeli-Palestinian Conflict

Nel Ruigrok, Wouter van Atteveldt and Janet Takens

Summary

International news coverage of the Israeli–Palestinian conflict is as complex and dynamic as the conflict itself. This chapter demonstrates how a combination of techniques can yield a thorough understanding of the foreign perception of this conflict by showing both long-term trends and in-depth details. Specifically, an automatic, keyword-based co-occurrence analysis of ten years of Dutch, American and British newspaper coverage is conducted using a technique called 'associative framing'. This is combined with a manual semantic network analysis of both Dutch newspaper coverage and open survey questions of a specific event in this conflict, namely, the Gaza War of 2008/09. The automatic analysis reveals that overall attention is increasing but is strongly centered on key events. These key events are also responsible for shifts in the frames used in the newspapers. On the whole, coverage is mainly episodic and conflict related. In contrast to the Palestinians, Israel also receives attention in contexts other than their mutual conflict. The manual analysis confirms the episodic nature of the coverage, and shows a balance in the expert and journalistic evaluation of both sides of the Gaza conflict. By contrast, public opinion is also interested in the religious and diplomatic aspects of the conflict, and is mainly critical of Israel.

Introduction

The conflict between Israel and the Palestinians is a regional conflict with a global impact (see Box 2 for a timeline of the conflict). Many battles have been fought in the twentieth century between the Arab nations and Israel, most recently the Gaza conflict at the end of December 2008. The international community, especially the western countries, plays an important secondary role in this conflict. They traditionally support the state of Israel, supply humanitarian aid and infrastructure support to the Palestinians, and act as mediators. This is illustrated, for example, by the role of the United States in forging the Camp David accords and by the recent appointment of Tony Blair as a special envoy of the 'quartet' of the United States, the European Union, the United Nations and Russia.

As the policy of the western democracies is relevant to the Middle East conflict, it is interesting to consider the news coverage of the conflict in those countries. For the majority of the population around the globe, this information is the only source they have about the events in the Middle East. Especially during a sudden, dramatic event, people depend on these journalistic choices to form an opinion about the event. It is commonly understood that the presentation of events in news coverage has a considerable impact on how the audience feel about the particular event being described, and how we interpret the event and other related issues (Pan and Kosicki, 2003). Overall, studies show that major dramatic events increase the amount of media coverage to a great extent (Lawrence and Bennett, 2000; Vasterman, 2005). Besides the increased attention paid to it, the event might also change the way in which the issue is portrayed in the media. These key events can be seen as 'critical discourse moments' in which the media can reframe the event and the related issues (Gamson, 1992).

In this chapter, we focus on how major events within the conflict, but also on a global level, had an impact on the framing of the conflict between the Israelis and the Palestinians. This yields the following overarching research question (RQ):

How is the Israeli–Palestinian conflict framed in western newspapers, and how does this relate to western public opinion?

We study this question by combining two techniques. The first is a longitudinal automated content analysis of a large number of articles in three countries, aimed at exploring the general trends and events in the news coverage over the past decade. This is complemented by a case study of the recent Gaza conflict, for which we manually analyze articles from a shorter time period for one country, and link these results to a manual content analysis of the responses to open survey questions concerning this conflict. The case study allows us to investigate in detail the specific frames used in the newspaper coverage and their relation with public opinion. The longitudinal study allows us to select a case study and its scope in an informed manner, and helps us to put the detailed findings in a larger perspective.

Framing News Coverage

The study of framing has gained an important place in the field of communication research in recent years. One of the most common definitions of framing is provided by Entman (1993), who describes framing as selecting 'some aspects of a perceived reality and make them more salient in a communicating text, in such a way as to promote a particular problem definition, causal interpretation, moral evaluation, and/or treatment recommendation for the item described'. Within framing literature, we see a distinction between those studies that examine media frames and that type of research that focuses on audience frames (Cappella and Jamieson, 1997; Entman, 1993; Scheufele, 1999). The former branch of research focuses on how issues are presented in the news (Norris, 1995; Patterson, 1993; Semetko and Valkenburg, 2000).

Within this branch of research, two forms may be distinguished: 'Equivalency frames' present an issue in different ways with 'the use of different, but logically equivalent, words or phrases' (Druckman, 2001: 228), thus causing a major change in audience preference when the same problem is presented in different wordings, such as 'rescuing some' versus 'sacrificing others' (Quattrone and Tversky, 1988; Tversky and Kahneman, 1981).

Other researchers focus on 'issue framing' (Druckman, 2004). In line with Entman's definition, 'issue framing' can be defined as a process of selecting and emphasizing certain aspects of an issue on the basis of which the audience can evaluate the issue described or the protagonists associated with the issues. Examples are 'strategic' or 'game' frames, which are often found in coverage of political campaigns (Patterson, 1993). Other examples of news frames are 'conflict' and personalization frames (Price and Tewksbury, 1997) or episodic versus thematic frames, such as they have been distinguished by Iyengar (1991).

The second branch of research focuses on how individuals perceive and interpret issues presented to them. Some researchers consider framing to be a linear transfer of the salience process, straight from the sender to the audience (Eagley and Chaiken, 1998; Zaller, 1992, 1994). Other researchers, however, consider the framing process to be an interaction between message content and the interpreter's social knowledge. This interaction process leads to a construction of a mental model as a resulting form of interpretation (Rhee, 1997). Besides the creation of these mental models, the framing process can trigger a mental model or frame that already exists within the recipient's perception. Snow and Benford (1988) state in this respect that media frames and audience frames interact through 'frame alignment' and 'frame resonance' (see also Snow et al., 1986).

Within the complex discussion of framing, we see a common denominator in the fact that many studies base the idea of a frame on associations, either between concepts, or between concepts and attributes, or on more complex networks of concepts. In this study, therefore, we will focus on what we call 'associative framing' (Ruigrok and van Atteveldt, 2007). Associative frames consist of associations between concepts and other concepts, where 'concepts' is a general term that can denote actors, issues and attributes. From the point of view of the cognitive perspective, these frames refer to schemata of interpretation (Goffman, 1974), and the main associations in a message can be seen as its 'central organizing idea' (Gamson and Modigliani, 1987).

Conflicts in the News: Context and Representation

A news item must be meaningful for the audience before it becomes news. This is also true of conflicts. Galtung and Ruge (1965) point out in their seminal study on news values that the spectacle of a conflict makes such an event more meaningful for news media audiences. Moreover, researchers found that proximity may affect news selection as well as the coverage and framing of news items (Entman, 1991; Kaid et al., 1993). Proximity in this respect includes both geographical as well as cultural proximity. Meyers et al. (1996) showed clearly that while the conflict in Bosnia (1992–95) was covered extensively in the western press, the conflict in Rwanda, which took place at the same time, received far less coverage. This consideration yields the first research question:

- RQ 1: To what extent is the conflict between Israel and the Palestinians covered in the news, and which protagonist is mentioned more often?

In order to really understand a conflict, it is important to have an overview of not only the protagonists but also the background of the conflict and the context in which incidents within a long-lasting conflict occur. As research shows, news coverage of conflict is often more episodic than thematic, focusing heavily on events instead of background and context (Papacharissi and Oliveira, 2008). Moreover, it is often very shallow and reduced to simplified, stereotyped images (Meyers et al., 1996; Ruigrok, 2005). The Bosnian War is a clear example where news coverage rarely focused on the complexity of the conflict, and most of the news coverage was reduced to a simplistic picture of evil Serbs murdering innocent Muslims (Nederlands Instituut voor Oorlogsdocumentatie, 2002).

The lack of references to the context in which particular reported conflicts occur leaves audiences with little knowledge about the conflict. The same holds true for the conflict in the Middle East, which is characterized by numerous violent actions from both the Israeli and the Palestinian side. In their research into news coverage of the conflict and the effect of this news coverage on the British public, Philo and Berry (2004) conclude that mentioning terms without providing context leads to confusion within the public because 'the Israeli presence is not described as a military occupation and the significance of this is not explained, it was not clear what the word "occupation" actually meant' (Philo and Berry, 2004: 118). Researchers at the Loughborough University Communications Research Centre (2006) looked into news coverage on the BBC website and in current affairs programs. They conclude that the events journalists write about are rarely related to historical events. Talking about the settlements, they fail to mention the fact that since 1967 Israel has been occupying these territories. The coverage also lacks references to the war and peace processes.

When looking at the terms used to describe protagonists, researchers found different terms for Israeli versus Palestinian actions. When talking about Israeli actions, journalists use terms such as 'military operations' against 'terrorist targets', 'directed attacks' or 'retaliations' (Fisk, 2005: 555, 612; Korn, 2004: 256). When Israeli action causes victims on the Palestinian side, these casualties are often labeled as 'clashes', 'confrontations' or 'incidents' (Ackerman, 2001: 65; Zelizer et al., 2002: 290; Korn, 2004: 255). Philo et al. (2003) found similar results for the television media in the United Kingdom while studying news coverage after the Second Intifada (see also Philo and Berry, 2004).

This difference in how the protagonists are portrayed also becomes clear when one looks at the sources quoted in the news. For the most part, the interpretation of the facts by Israel is described in the coverage while the Palestinian point of view is largely disregarded. Ackerman (2001), for example, found that the American media focus heavily on the disturbances in the

West Bank or in Gaza and disregard the fact that the Israelis have occupied these territories. Also, with respect to the casualties on both sides, differences may clearly be seen in the news coverage. Rinnawi (2007) in her research into the Israeli media and the Second Intifada shows that coverage of Palestinian victims is minimized while it is stressed that the Israelis are the victims of the conflict. The western media as well place greater emphasis on Israeli victims than on Palestinian victims. According to Philo and Berry (2004), thirteen times as many Palestinian deaths could be counted compared with the number of Israeli victims, but in the news coverage the Israeli victims are greatly overrepresented.

Finally, Zelizer et al. (2002) focused on the portrayal of Palestinians after the Second Intifada in American newspapers. The researchers conclude that Palestinians are described not from a Palestinian point of view – as martyrs – but only from an Israeli point of view – as suicide bombers or terrorists. Fisk (2005: 554) concluded that for the international media these terms had become commonplace. He states that if Palestinians kill Israelis, they are called terrorists, while when Israelis kill Palestinians they are called 'crazy Jewish colonists' or 'underground Jewish fighters'. This overview shows how differently the protagonists are portrayed and therefore yields the following research question, which is divided into five sub-questions:

- RQ 2: How do newspapers frame the conflict?
  - RQ 2a: To what extent is the coverage episodic/thematic and how does this change over time?
  - RQ 2b: What substantive frames are used in covering the conflict and how do they change over time?
  - RQ 2c: Who is portrayed as victims and who as culprits in the news?
  - RQ 2d: Who gets to speak in the news?
  - RQ 2e: Who is to blame for the conflict?

Differences between Newspapers

According to Goldfarb (2001), the representation of the conflict and the protagonists differs in the European and American press. Whereas the European news coverage tends to cover both sides of the conflict, the American media seem less eager to cover Palestinian perspectives in the coverage because of their long-lasting friendship with the state of Israel. Moreover, the European countries have a longer history of dealing with the conflict, having had interest in the region as early as the beginning of the twentieth century, while the United States only became involved in the conflict after the World War II. Therefore, we are interested in the following question:

- RQ 3: To what extent can the coverage in some newspapers be said to be more favorable to one side in the conflict?

Public Opinion

Agenda-setting research shows that journalistic choices have significant effects on the issues people are concerned about. McCombs and Shaw (1972) showed this effect when studying the American elections of 1968, and subsequent studies have found similar results ever since (Dearing and Rogers, 1996). Besides an agenda-setting effect, studies also found that the way the media cover politics influences public perception of the performance of candidates and parties, and consequently also their voting behavior (Kiousis et al., 2006; Kleinnijenhuis et al., 2007; Farnsworth and Lichter, 2006). In this respect, priming theory states that a certain amount of media attention is sufficient in influencing political attitudes because it alters the standards by which people make evaluations (see Iyengar et al., 1982; Miller and Krosnick, 1996).

With respect to conflict coverage, Findahl's (1998) study provides a striking example of the effects on public opinion of enduring news depicting 'good guys' and 'bad guys'. He studied the news audience in the Swedish town of Umeå and questioned them about a massacre that had been committed by Croatian armed forces in autumn 1993, a massacre that was front-page news for several days. One year later, most people still remembered the vivid pictures of the massacre. Yet their interpretation of the pictures had changed. Whereas, in 1993, they said that Croatian forces had committed the atrocities, one year later, Serbs had replaced the Croats and the Croatian massacre had become a Serb massacre. The pictures remained the same, but the context had changed in keeping with the general image of the Bosnian War that was presented in the international media. The Serbs were the 'bad guys', the Muslims the victims. Findahl concludes, 'In this way the history, or one's memory of the history, can be influenced by the news, especially when the audience does not have relevant knowledge and experience of their own on which they can rely' (Findahl, 1998: 123). With these considerations in mind, we are interested in the following research question:

- RQ 4: To what extent is public opinion similar to the news coverage?

Method

As we said before, our study is two-pronged, meaning we have used two different methods, a method for the automated content analysis and another for our manual content analysis.

Automated Content Analysis

In this part of our study, we included three main newspapers from the United States (US), the United Kingdom (UK), and the Netherlands (NL). In each of these countries we analyzed one quality newspaper. For the United States, this was *The Washington Post*, for the United

Table 1: Total Number of Articles on Israelis and/or Palestinians

Abbreviation	Country	Newspaper	Articles
US	United States	*Washington Post*	22,097
UK	United Kingdom	*Guardian*	17,254
NL	Netherlands	*NRC Handelsblad*	11,878

Kingdom, *The Guardian*, and for the Netherlands, the *NRC Handelsblad*. From these newspapers, we analyzed all articles containing either the word 'Israel/Israelis' or 'Palestine/Palestinians'. The newspapers were searched from September 1, 1997 to September 1, 2007, and samples were taken when one of these words was mentioned. Table 1 lists the number of articles.

In order to answer our research questions, we defined a number of concepts and related keywords for which we measured the frequency and the associations with Israel and Palestine (see Table 2) by using the AmCAT program for measuring frequency and associative framing as described by van Atteveldt (2008: chapters 5 and 10).

Table 2: Keywords Used for Frequencies

Actors	Dutch	English
Israel	Israel*	Israel*
Palestine	Palest*	Palest*
Only Israel	Israel* NOT Palest*	Israel* NOT Palest*
Only Palestine	Palest* NOT Israel*	Palest* NOT Israel*
Both (conflict)	Israel* AND Palest*	Israel* AND Palest*
Issues		
Economy	econo* export* import* handel* bedrij* bnp bbp werkloos* werkgelegen* banen	econo* export* import* trade* trading business* gdp gnp unemploy* job*
Politics	politic* politiek* verkiezing* referend*	politic* election* referend*
Conflict	conflict* OR oorlog* OR vrede* OR onderhandel* OR bemiddel* OR aanslag* OR terror* OR terreur* OR bom* OR beschiet* OR invasie*	conflict* war* peace* negotia* mediat* attack* terror* bomb* shoot* invasion*
Culture	sport* olymp* songfest* wetensch* universi* educ*	sport* olymp* 'song festival' scien* universit* cultu* educa*
Word use: Territories		
Occupied	'bezet* gebied*'	'occup* territ*'
Palestinian	'palest* gebied*'	'palest* territ*'

(Continued)

267

Table 2: (*Continued*)

Actors	Dutch	English
Episodic vs. Thematic		
Episodic	slachtoffer* aanslag* aanval* bom* vandaag gister* vanmorgen beschiet* demonstr* opstand schermuts* 'eerste Intifada'	victim* attack* bomb* today yesterday 'this morning' shoot* demonstr* upris* 'first Intifada'
Thematic	holocaust naqba 'yom kippur' zesdaags* syri* jordan* iran irak vn 'recht terugke*'~4 vluchteling* armoe* uitzichtlo*	holocaust naqba 'yom kippur' 'six day war' syri* jordan* iran iraq un 'right return'~4 refugee* povert* hopeless*
Word use: the Wall		
Total	apartheidshek* apartheidsmuur apartheidsbarriere segregatiehek segregatiemuur segregatiebarriere barriere hek* vredeshek* vredesmuur vredesbarrière	wall fence barrier
Apartheid	apartheidshek* apartheidsmuur apartheidsbarriere segregatiehek segregatiemuur segregatiebarriere	'apartheid fence' 'apartheid wall' 'apartheid barrier' 'racial segregation wall'
Fence	barriere hek* afscheiding*	barrier fence 'separation wall' 'separation barrier'
Security	veiligheidshek* veiligheidsmuur veiligheidsbarriere anti-terrorismehek* anti-terrorismemuur anti-terrorismebarriere verdedigingshek* verdedigingsmuur verdedigingsbarriere	'security fence' 'security wall' 'security barrier' 'anti-terrorist fence' 'anti-terrorist wall' 'anti-terrorist barrier' 'defense fence' 'defense wall' 'defense barrier'
Wall	Muur	Wall
Substantive Frames		
Terror	terreur* terror* aanslag* bomaanslag* zelfmoordaan*	terror* 'suicide attack*'
Fight	gevecht* vecht* oorlog* aanval* tank* soldat* beschiet* bombar*	fight* war* attack* tank* soldier* shoot* bombar*
Law	recht rechten mensenrecht* wet wettel* wettig* vn 'internationaal gerechtshof'	law* justic* legal* un icj 'international court justice'~5
Suffering	slachtoffer* ziekenhui* gewond*	suffer* victim* wound* hospital*
Religion	jood* islam* moslim* religi* christ* orthodox*	jew* islam* muslim* religi* christ* orthodox*
Peace	vrede* onderha* bemiddel* akkoor* verdrag*	peace* negotia* media* accor* treaty treaties

Visibility, Co-occurrence and Symbolic Associations

The core notion of our framework is that a document, in our case an article, mentions a number of concepts with a certain frequency. For the purposes of calculation, we converted this frequency into a number between 0 and 1 – called the (reading) probability of the concept – using Formula 1 (see Box 1) below. The association between the two concepts A and B is defined as the probability of reading about B given that one has read about A in a randomly chosen article, in other words, the conditional probability of encountering B given that one has already encountered A. This probability is calculated using Formula 2 (see Box 1).

Although this measure is related to more traditional measures of association such as cosine distance, correlation and χ^2 values, it has two important advantages. First, this is a deliberately asymmetric measure, since, for example, Hamas might be strongly associated with terrorism while terrorism is more strongly associated with other concepts such as al-Qaeda. Second, we are not interested in associations compared with what one would predict based on an independent distribution but rather in the associations themselves. If all articles are framed in a dominant frame, for instance a patriotic frame, this still means that the individual articles are also framed that way.

Apart from these desirable substantive features, using this asymmetric measure has the convenient methodological advantage whereby all associations of a concept may be calculated based only on the articles in which that concept occurs, while symmetric measures such as correlation would also require all articles containing the concepts with which the first concept might co-occur.

Box 1: Formula of Reading Probability and Association

Formula 1: Reading chance $p(c \mid m)$ of concept c in massage m as a function of frequency $count(c,m)$ of that concept in that article and the parameter b (set to 4 in this study)

$$p(c \mid m) = 1 - \left(1 - \frac{1}{b}\right)^{count(c,m)}$$

Formula 2: Association $ass(c_b \rightarrow c_t)$ of concepts cb and ct as the conditional reading probability defined as a function of massage weight $p(m)$ and reading chance $p(c \mid m)$ (Formula 1)

$$ass(c_b \longrightarrow c_t) = \frac{\sum m \, p(m) \cdot p(c_b \mid m) \cdot p(c_t \mid m)}{\sum_m p(m) p(c \mid m)}$$

See Van Atteveldt (2008: chapter 5) for an illustrated and more detailed explanation of this method.

Box 2:   Timeline of the Israeli–Palestinian Conflict 1998–2009

Time Line of the Israeli-Palestinian Conflict 1998–2009:

- October 1998: PLO Chairman Arafat and Israeli Prime Minister Netanyahu sign the Wye Memorandum, which aimed to implement the 1995 Israeli Palestinian Interim Agreement.
- May 1999: Israel elects Labor party leader and Former General Barak as Prime Minister.
- July 2000: US President Clinton initiates the Camp David summit between Palestinian President Arafat and Israeli Prime Minister Barak; they fail to reach an agreement.
- September 2000: Israeli opposition leader Sharon visits the Temple Mount in Jerusalem; his controversial visit is followed by riots, and marks the start of the Second Intifada, a period of intensified violence between the two protagonists.
- February 2001: Right-wing Likud leader Sharon is elected Prime Minister in Israel, replacing Barak.
- 2002: Different states start off peace initiatives, such as the Road Map to Peace initiated by the European Union, Russia, the United Nations and the US, or the Arab Peace Initiative convened by Saudi Arabia.
- March–May 2002: Israel conducts operation Defensive Shield in the West Bank, following a large number of Palestinian suicide attacks on civilian targets.
- January 2003: elections in Israel give wide margin (40 seats) to right wing Likud party, returning PM Sharon for another term.
- July 2004: the International Court of Justice (ICJ) rules that the Israeli security barrier violates international law and must be torn down.
- November 2004: Palestinian Authority President Arafat dies.
- January 2005: Abbas is elected President of the Palestinian National Authority.
- August 2005: Israel unilaterally removes settlements and military posts from Gaza and the Northern West Bank; the Disengagement plan is initiated by Israeli Prime Minister Sharon.
- August 2006: Israel starts the Second Lebanon War after attacks of Hezbollah in July 2006.
- December 27, 2008: Israel starts a three week military operation called Operation Cast Lead in Gaza.

Manual Content Analysis

For the second part of the study, the coding of the articles was conducted using the NET (Network of Evaluative Texts) method, a semantic network analysis method, stemming from Evaluative Assertion Analysis (Osgood, 1956) and developed by van Cuilenburg et al.

(1988). The NET method divides a text into a number of so-called 'nuclear statements' that describe the relations between objects such as actors and issues in the following form:

Source: Subject/Predicate/Direction of the predicate/Object

The 'source' is the source of the news, the actor that gets to speak. The 'subject' is the actor or issue from whom (from which) the action or energy stems, and the 'object' is the actor or issue that the action/energy is directed to. The list of actors and issues is established beforehand and is hierarchically ordered, making it possible for coders to code very specific relations between actors and issues while we use more general concepts in the analysis phase.

The term 'knowledge objects' is used as an overarching concept for those political and societal actors, in addition to issues, that are frequently encountered in the news. For instance, the hierarchy of actors and issues describes that Olmert is a prime minister, which is an executive politician, which is an 'actor'. Similarly, throwing stones is considered violence, which is an 'issue'. Different statements may be found, for example, statements expressing violent acts such as 'Israel is bombing Gaza', which is coded as a negative action between Israel and Gaza, while a sentence such as 'Abbas clashes with Olmert' yields two statements, one with a negative affinitive relation between Abbas and Olmert and one negative affinitive relation between Olmert and Abbas.

Moreover, causal relations between issues or between actors and issues are coded, such as 'the Gaza conflict makes people homeless'. For purely evaluative statements, there is a special object called the 'ideal', which represents the positive ideal. Thus, a sentence such as 'Israeli violence is excessive' is coded as a nuclear statement dissociating Israel from the ideal. Another special object, 'reality', is used when something happens without a specified cause. Thus, 'Upsurge of violence in Gaza' would be coded as 'reality' causing 'violence'. News items such as newspaper articles often contain literal or paraphrased quotes from actors. In NET, all statements contain one or more (nested) sources. If no explicit source is found, the newspaper itself is considered the source.

For this specific research, we used all articles about the conflict from December 26, 2008 to January 24, 2009 in the main Dutch newspapers (*de Volkskrant, NRC Handelsblad, Trouw, De Telegraaf, Algemeen Dagblad, Spits* and *Metro*). We found a total of 854 relevant articles. The coding of the articles yielded 5,706 statements.

Operationalization

The coded statements form a total network of actors and issues that can be used for different analyses of different aspects of the news. First of all, it was used to measure the total amount of articles and the support or criticism that is stated by other actors toward the protagonists of the conflict. Besides these analyses, we looked at the role in which the actors appear. Are they portrayed as the culprit or the victim of the conflict? Moreover, who gets to speak in the news? Finally, we also considered the evaluative statements of the editorial boards when talking about Israeli or Palestinian actors.

Public Opinion

Besides the news coverage, we also looked at Dutch public opinion right after the Gaza conflict. We asked 507 respondents to give their opinions on the conflict and to indicate who was to blame for the conflict. Half of the respondents were men, half were women. Almost 70 percent of the respondents read a newspaper and followed the news about the Gaza conflict to some extent. In order to compare the answers with the content analysis of the newspapers, we coded the answers the same way we coded the news articles. This yielded 2,627 statements.

Results

In this section, we will discuss the results of our study following the research questions as formulated above.

The Conflict in the Middle East: 1999–2009

First of all, regarding the frequency of the articles that were found over time, Figure 1 shows the relative attention paid to the topic in the newspaper articles over time presented as percentage of the total amount of news in a newspaper.

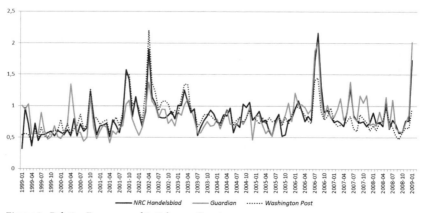

Figure 1: Relative Frequency of Articles per Quarter.

Table 3: Relative Attention Paid to Protagonists and Issues in the Three Countries

	US	UK	NL
Palestinians	8.5%	10.8%	10.3%
Israel	51.8%	47.4%	45.4%
Both	39.8%	41.8%	44.3%
N (articles)	**22.097**	**17.254**	**11.878**

Clear peaks can be seen for all three newspapers. The first peak in the second quarter of 2002 deals with Operation Defensive Shield, a military operation by Israel in Ramallah, which was followed by incursions into the six largest cities in the West Bank and their surrounding localities as well as the house arrest of Arafat. The second peak in the news is the war with Lebanon in the summer of 2006. Minor peaks in the news consist of 9/11 and the Second Intifada in October 2000. The small peak in the summer of 2005 has to do with the news about Israel removing all Jewish settlements and military equipment from the Gaza Strip.

With respect to RQ 1, Table 3 lists the relative frequencies of articles mentioning either Palestine/Palestinians or Israel/Israelis, or both. The table shows that Israelis are more often mentioned without mentioning Palestinians rather than the other way around. Only in 8–11 percent of all articles are Palestinians mentioned without referring to Israelis, while in about half of the articles Israel or its inhabitants are mentioned without referring to Palestine or the Palestinians. The differences between the newspapers show that this is especially true of the American newspaper but less so for the UK and the NL ones.

Framing the Conflict

If we define conflict articles as those articles mentioning both Israel and Palestine, we obtain the sample of articles listed in Table 4. For all news sources, around 40–45 percent of the articles are included.

In our study, we distinguish between episodic and thematic framing based on an association at the paragraph level of Israel/Palestine with words indicating thematic (historical, causal

Table 4: Number of Conflict Articles Mentioning both Israel and Palestine, Absolute and as a Percentage of the Total Number of Articles

	US	UK	NL
Total	22,097	17,254	11,878
Included	8,786	7,216	5,263
Percentage	**40%**	**42%**	**44%**

Table 5: Association of the Protagonists with Episodic and Thematic Concepts

	US	UK	NL
Episodic	0.16	0.15	0.18
Thematic	0.08	0.09	0.10

and international references) and episodic framing (time indicators, attacks). In Table 5, we present the ratio of associations of the two protagonists with episodic terms and the association of the two protagonists with terms dealing with thematic words (see Table 2 for a list of the key words indicating thematic and episodic news coverage).

In all newspapers, there is substantially more episodic than thematic framing, giving a straight answer to RQ 2a. Figure 2 shows the ratio of episodic framing to the total amount of thematic plus episodic framing over time. From 1999 to the Second Intifada, episodic and thematic framing occur with roughly the same frequency. With the start of the Second Intifada, episodic framing rises to around 80 percent. This slowly declines again until reaching parity again around 2006. With the tensions rising in 2008, the amount of episodic news coverage increases again. Thus, the answer to RQ 2b is relatively complex. It seems that with the increase of violence in the conflict, the episodic coverage increases as well. However, more detailed analyses are needed to answer this RQ more specifically.

In order to answer RQ 2b, we investigate to what extent articles are framed using one of the substantive frames listed in Table 6.

As listed in Table 6, in all of the newspapers we examined, 'fight' and 'peace' frames were used most often to describe the conflict. These frames are operationalized as the association

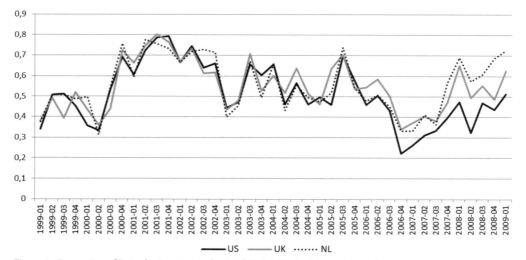

Figure 2: Proportion of Episodic Framing to the Total (Episodic plus Thematic) per Quarter.

Table 6: Substantive Frames Used in Conflict Articles

	US	UK	NL
Fight	0.18	0.15	0.11
Law	0.03	0.04	0.05
Religion	0.10	0.10	0.12
Suffering	0.03	0.03	0.03
Terrorism	0.05	0.04	0.09
Peace	0.15	0.11	0.12

between the protagonists and words such as 'war' and 'fighting' (fight) and 'treaties' and 'mediation' (peace), respectively. The 'fight' frame is most frequent in the United States, followed by the United Kingdom and the Netherlands, while for the 'peace' frame the ranking of the Netherlands and the United Kingdom are reversed. 'Religion' is also most frequent in the NL coverage, followed by the United States and the United Kingdom. Similarly to 'peace', 'terrorism' is most frequently used in the United States and the Netherlands and less so in UK coverage. 'Law' and 'suffering' frames are both used less frequently.

Figure 3 shows the development of four of these frames over time. In 3a, all papers show the same pattern: the 'fight' frame increases with the start of the Second Intifada and remains high until after Defensive Shield, after which it declines gradually before peaking with the Lebanese War.

Figure 3b shows the 'terrorism' frame. This frame is very infrequent when the Second Intifada breaks out, but increases sharply in 2001, peaking during the 9/11 attacks. This can be especially seen in the Dutch news coverage. With the conflict flaring up again in 2008, the 'terrorism' frame shows an increase, especially in the Dutch newspaper. Figure 3c shows the 'peace' frame. The use of this frame is high before the Second Intifada, when negotiations were providing hope for a peaceful solution to the conflict. The frame drops sharply when the Second Intifada quashes the hopes of the Oslo accords in 2000. Although it increases again with the Powell mission to the Middle East and the Road Map to Peace in 2002, these increases are temporary and the use of the frame remains low. Finally, 3d shows the 'suffering' frame. In this frame, the three papers diverge: in the United Kingdom, the frame remains constant at around 0.02. In the Netherlands, the frame increases after the start of the Second Intifada, but it soon decreases to the same level as the United States and United Kingdom. In the US news coverage, different peaks can be seen, for example in 2004, when attention was paid to the suffering of the population when the wall was built.

We can see that especially the start of the Second Intifada is an important event: the proportion of conflict articles increases, Palestinians are mentioned more often compared with Israelis, framing becomes more episodic, and 'fighting' and 'suffering' increases, while 'peace' decreases. In all cases, the effect wears off very slowly, taking five years or more to reach pre-Intifada levels. This is especially interesting given that the start of the Second

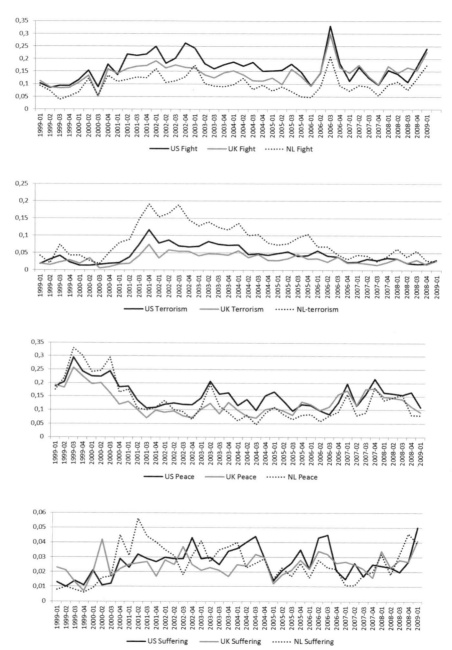

Figure 3: Substantive Framing per Quarter. (a) Fight, (b) Terrorism, (c) Peace and (d) Suffering (from Top to Bottom).

Intifada did not lead to a strong increase in coverage, so it appears that frequency shifts and frame shifts can be orthogonal.

Consistent with our earlier work (Ruigrok and van Atteveldt, 2007), 9/11 was the key event in increasing the 'terrorism' frame, but for the other frames it did not cause a shift. This shows that different key events can affect different aspects of framing of the same conflict. The second most important event is Operation Defensive Shield and the house arrest of Arafat, which often showed a decrease in the shifts caused by the start of the Intifada. Finally, the Lebanon War showed a markedly different framing of the news about the conflict, when suddenly the Israeli–Palestinian conflict became a sideshow rather than the main event, but this effect was not lasting. Thus, it can be seen that certain key events lead to certain frame shifts, although it is not immediately clear why they lead to these changes.

Somewhat unsurprisingly, the local conflict event of the Second Intifada leads to more conflict-oriented framing, while the global terror event 9/11 leads to more terrorism-oriented framing. However, 9/11 did not cause more thematic framing, even though conceivably the Israeli–Palestinian conflict could now be reported on through the lens of the War on Terror. Moreover, the local conflict event of Operation Defensive Shield caused a decrease rather than an increase in the most conflict-oriented frames, possibly because it became obvious that the conflict was more nuanced and long-winded than previously thought.

Word Use for Disputed Concepts

RQ 3 asked who is portrayed as a victim and who as a culprit in the news coverage. In order to measure this, we looked at the preferred terms used in the news coverage when talking about disputed concepts, in particular for the occupied or Palestinian territories and the West Bank wall or security fence. If we consider the two terms 'occupied territories' and 'Palestinian territories', we can define the ratio of the former to the total use of the two terms as a measure of the relative frequency of the charged term 'occupied territories'.

Figure 4 shows this ratio over time for the three main sources. In the United Kingdom, the ratio remains fairly constant at around 0.7/0.8. In the United States and the Netherlands, however, the ratio is in general lower than that of the United Kingdom, with the United States having a ratio of around 0.4 and the NL news coverage a slightly higher one of 0.5. In other words, the answer to RQ 3 is dependent on the newspaper being investigated.

Table 7 shows the frequency of the four names that we investigated for the wall/fence. 'Apartheid' includes names such as 'apartheid wall' and 'racial segregation wall' that stress the supposed negative effects of the wall. 'Fence' contains words such as 'barrier' or 'fence' that do not invoke connotations of the Berlin Wall but also do not stress the supposed positive effects such as security or antiterrorism. 'Security' contains words that do stress these supposed positive effects. Finally, 'wall' contains simply the word 'wall', which invokes connotations of the Berlin Wall.

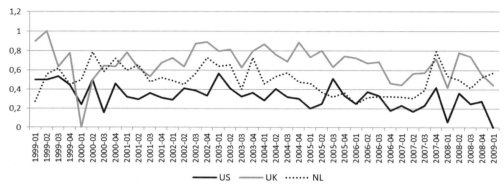

Figure 4: Proportion of 'Occupied Territories' to the Total (Occupied plus Palestinian), per Quarter.

Looking at the table, it becomes immediately clear that although the relatively neutral names 'wall' and 'fence' are most frequent, the positive name 'security' (fence) is much more frequent than 'apartheid' (wall), the latter hardly being used at all. This answers RQ 3 in that the Israeli side is more often portrayed as the victim than is the Palestinian side.

Similarly, we can define the ratio of euphemistic terms ('fence' or 'security' fence) to the total number of mentions. Figure 5 shows this ratio over time for the three news sources.

As far as the United States and the United Kingdom are concerned, it can clearly be seen that as the wall/fence becomes more controversial because of the UN resolution and International Court of Justice (ICJ) verdict in 2004, the framing shifts from 'wall' to 'fence' before gradually shifting back once the attention has decreased. In the NL coverage, the framing starts out with almost 0.8 for 'wall', but this quickly drops to the same level as for the United Kingdom and the United States and subsequently follows the same pattern. Overall, the answer to RQ 3 is a fairly complicated one: journalists prefer the euphemistic terms as the wall/fence becomes controversial and shift back to the charged term as soon as the attention decreases again, although for the Netherlands it is more difficult to interpret the graph.

To answer RQ 3, we can try to interpret the differences between the newspapers in all the analyses presented above. In the NL news, the overall reporting on Israel and on conflict issues in the news about Palestine is stronger than in the other newspapers. The United

Table 7: Frequency of Four Terms for the West Bank Wall/Fence

	US		UK		NL	
Apartheid	4	0%	23	0.6%	6	0.2%
Fence	1,992	41.2%	1,704	42.9%	1,115	46.3%
Security	230	4.8%	282	7.1%	168	7%
Wall	2,610	54%	1,967	49.5%	1,118	46.4%

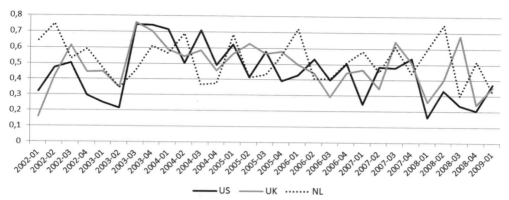

Figure 5: Proportion of Euphemistic Terms (Barrier/Fence plus Security) to the Total Number of Mentions, per Quarter.

Kingdom was least inclined to switch from the charged term 'occupied territories' to the more neutral 'Palestinian territories', and the news on the wall/fence showed no clear difference in this respect. The Netherlands was most inclined to use episodic framing, which may be seen as favorable toward Israel in that it is generally more difficult to understand the actions and motives of the culturally more remote Palestinians than it is to understand the Israelis. In the substantive framing, the United Kingdom was least likely to use a terrorism framing – the terrorism framing being more negative toward the Palestinians – and the Netherlands and the United States were about equal. Thus, the answer to RQ 3 is that the United Kingdom covers the conflict in a more balanced way than the United States, but the same cannot be said for the NL coverage. Obviously, more newspapers should be investigated besides the three used in our study in order to be able to generalize these differences between newspapers as differences between cultures or news cultures.

The Gaza Conflict in Dutch Newspapers

In this section, we will focus in more detail on the conflict and consider the news coverage of the most recent clash in the conflict, the war in Gaza 2008-09. We look at different frames and how the protagonists are portrayed in the news coverage of Dutch newspapers and compare these findings with how the Dutch public sees the conflict and its participants.

Substantive Frames in the News

In line with the automated content analysis, we look at substantive frames in the news coverage. Here we look at the 'war frame', the 'other actors about war frame', the 'diplomatic

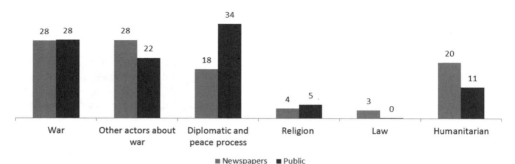

Figure 6: Substantive Frames in Newspapers and among the Public (in Percentages).

frame', the 'religious frame', the 'law frame' and the 'humanitarian frame'. The newspapers do not show any significant differences as far as the coverage of sub-issues is concerned. The main part of the coverage considered the war and the opinion of participating actors and experts. The international legal and religious aspects of the conflict are hardly mentioned (see Figure 6). This is in line with the international news coverage we discussed in previous sections. The suffering of people and the road to peace are also important issues in the news.

The way the public views the conflict shows similarities with the news coverage. Also, the public mentions the actual war and the opinion of protagonists and experts as being the main topics. However, differences may be found with respect to the religious and diplomatic aspects of the conflict. The public mentions these topics more often. Last but not least, whereas the newspapers mention international law from time to time in their coverage, this topic is not mentioned at all by the public.

Support and Criticism

One aspect of the manual coded news coverage has to do with the support and criticism directed at the protagonists in the conflict. These statements are shown in Table 8. In the columns we present the actor who is supporting or criticizing, while in the rows those actors are mentioned at whom the support or criticism is directed. Besides the number of statements (N), we also give the average direction of the statements running from -1 (extremely critical) to $+1$ (extremely supporting) (Q).

In the news coverage, Israeli actors are twice as often portrayed as attacking Palestinians than the other way around. In our definition, both verbal statements as well as actions are taken into account in this analysis. The result can be interpreted as portraying Israel as the aggressor. In addition to the Palestinians, who are cited in 140 statements, the international community criticizes Israel for its deeds in 124 statements. These countries indicate even some support for

Table 8: Support and Criticism Among Protagonists in the Gaza Conflict

	Israelis		Palest-inians		Interna-tional actors		CDA		PvdA		Christian Union		Right opposi-tion		Left opposi-tion		Total	
	N	Q	N	Q	N	Q	N	Q	N	Q	N	Q	N	Q	N	Q	N	Q
Israel	64	0.1	140	−0.8	124	−0.4	28	0.5	11	−0.6	4	1	14	1	18	−0.9	403	−0.4
Palestine	340	−0.7	92	−0.2	80	0.2	10	−0.8	2	0	2	−0.5	2	−1	8	1	536	−0.4
Total	404	−0.6	232	−0.5	204	−0.2	38	0.2	13	−0.5	6	0.5	16	0.8	26	−0.3	939	−0.4

the Palestinians in the coverage. Dutch politicians and even the Dutch government are divided over the issue. The Christian Democrats (CDA) support Israel and criticize the Palestinians, while their partner in the coalition, the Social Democrats (PvdA), criticize Israel. The opposition is divided between left and right-wing parties, with the left-wing parties criticizing Israel and supporting the Palestinians, while for the right-wing parties the opposite is true.

Victims in the Conflict

In an effort to provide context to the conflict, one aspect to be considered is who is being portrayed as the victim or culprit in the conflict. Normally, the underdog can count on more support than the aggressor. In Table 9, we see that the newspapers focus more heavily on the suffering of Palestinians than on the suffering of Israeli citizens. Also, the emphasis is more negative for the Palestinians than for the Israelis. For our analysis, this means that the suffering being depicted is couched in more extreme terms.

The only exception here is *De Telegraaf*. This newspaper pays slightly more attention to the suffering of the Palestinians, but the emphasis on the suffering of Israelis is greater.

Table 9: Factual Statements About Israelis and Palestinians

	Israeli		Palestinians		Total	
	N	Q	N	Q	N	Q
de Volkskrant	23	−0.8	44	−0.8	67	−0.8
NRC Handelsblad	31	−0.4	49	−0.6	80	−0.5
De Telegraaf	19	−0.4	23	−0.3	42	−0.4
Trouw	40	−0.4	95	−0.6	135	−0.5
Algemeen Dagblad	14	−0.6	42	−0.6	56	−0.6
Spits	16	0.1	25	−0.7	41	−0.4
Metro	12	−0.3	33	−0.6	45	−0.5
Total	**155**	**−0.4**	**311**	**−0.6**	**466**	**−0.5**

Besides *Trouw, Metro, AD* and *de Volkskrant* also pay more attention to the suffering of the Palestinians than to that of the Israelis.

Sources

During the media war, the belligerent parties try to get their story into the news. Being quoted in the news offers one the opportunity to frame the news in favor of your own position or party. Especially during a war it is important to be able to give your own opinion in the news coverage. In Figure 7, we show what sources are used in all the newspapers, whether Israeli or Palestinian. Almost all the newspapers include more Israeli sources in their news than Palestinian ones. Especially in *De Telegraaf*, the Israeli sources are given far more space to tell their story than the Palestinians. By contrast, *Trouw* is an exception in that it gives Palestinian sources more room.

Evaluations

We are better off without Israel.

(Column in *Spits*, January 9, 2009)

Israel has the right to protect itself.

(Column in *Trouw*, January 13, 2009)

A special form of statements found in the news coverage is the evaluative statement that can be attributed to the newspapers themselves. In their editorials or op-ed pieces, journalists can put forward their own opinion concerning the different protagonists. The quotes above are examples of such statements.

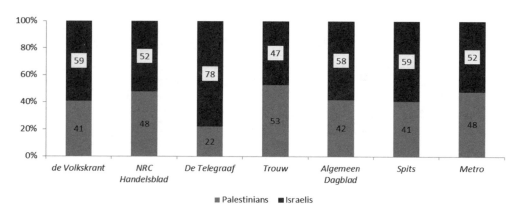

Figure 7: Sources in the News.

Table 10: Evaluative Statements About Israelis and Palestinians

	Israeli		Palestinians	
	N	*Q*	*N*	*Q*
de Volkskrant	24	−0.6	10	−0.6
NRC Handelsblad	12	−0.4	6	−0.2
De Telegraaf	7	−0.4	1	−1.0
Trouw	24	−0.5	11	−0.5
Algemeen Dagblad	10	−0.6	5	0.2
Spits	4	−0.3	3	0
Metro	4	0	4	−1.0
Total	**85**	**−0.5**	**40**	**−0.4**
Public	**160**	**−0.5**	**188**	**−0.1**

In general, Israel is criticized more often and more harshly than the Palestinians (see Table 10). *De Volkskrant, Trouw, NRC Handelsblad* and *Algemeen Dagblad* show more evaluative statements in their news and are more negative toward Israel than toward the Palestinians. The other newspapers show such low numbers of evaluations that it is difficult to determine their point of view toward both of the belligerent parties.

When looking at the public's responses, we see the same pattern as in the news coverage. Especially Israel is more often criticized and more harshly (160 times, −0.5), while more sympathy is given to the Palestinians.

Conclusions

This chapter investigated the coverage of the Israel–Palestinian conflict in western newspapers. Specifically, we conducted an automated longitudinal content analysis of a decade of news in one Dutch, one British and one US newspaper and examined long-term trends in attention and framing. This was combined with an in-depth manual semantic network analysis of Dutch news coverage and open survey questions about the 2008-09 Gaza conflict.

In the longitudinal analysis, using frequency analysis and associative framing analysis, we were able to show a number of interesting developments in the time frame as far as the occurrence and framing of different concepts are concerned. The overall attention being paid to the conflict shows a gradual increase culminating in a strong peak in 2002 around the time of the Israeli Operation Defensive Shield and surrounding events. After that, attention remains fairly high before another peak is reached with the Lebanon War in 2006. In all the newspapers, although articles mentioning both protagonists are most frequent, there are more articles that mention the Israelis alone rather than the opposite, namely, the Palestinians.

We looked at the word use for disputed concepts, in particular the terms 'West Bank wall' or 'fence' and the 'Palestinian' or 'occupied territories'. We found that strong terms such as 'wall' were used less frequently than the more neutral 'fence', especially when the wall/fence was most controversial. For the territories, the British coverage consistently used the charged term 'occupied territories', while the Dutch and American press tended to use the more neutral 'Palestinian territories'. Overall, we found more evidence of episodic than of thematic framing, especially after the start of the Second Intifada. Following this, we also found an increase in the use of 'conflict' and 'suffering' frames and a decrease in the number of 'peace' frames. The 'terrorism' frame also increased but especially after 9/11 this frame really peaked.

The automated analysis shows a number of interesting trends, but it fails to answer some key questions having to do with valence and framing. For that purpose, we conducted a manual semantic network analysis of the news coverage of the 2008 Gaza conflict in seven different Dutch newspapers, and compared this with a similar analysis of an open survey question about the conflict. We found that in both the media and in public opinion the most attention was paid to factual developments in the war and to expert opinions, but the public focuses more on the religious and diplomatic aspects than do the newspapers, while at the same time it tends to ignore the international legal aspects of the conflict. The newspapers show the Israelis as attackers and the Palestinians as victims. Dutch political actors are divided along the left–right axis, with the left favoring more the Palestinians and the right favoring more the Israelis. In the direct evaluations given by journalists, both Israel and the Palestinians are evaluated negatively. Public opinion is mainly critical of Israel.

This chapter shows how information gathered from different sources and using different techniques can be combined to paint a more complete picture of a complex problem. Using only the automated analysis would have left crucial questions concerning valence and framing unanswered, while using only the manual analysis would have given a detailed picture of a very short period without the possibility of putting that period into perspective.

But manual and automated content analyses each have their own problems. Automated analysis can be skewed by a bad choice of keywords, thus producing results that are based on 'noise' rather than on data and without showing symptoms such as low reliability, which would signal that something is going wrong in the analysis. Moreover, the associations found by co-occurrence analysis can be difficult to interpret, as one then only knows that *something* is going on, but not *what* is going on. Manual analysis can validate the automatic findings and help in interpreting the associations and other findings. If the relations are relatively stable, a small manual analysis can suffice to interpret the longitudinal analysis, rendering the data from the second type of analysis more valuable. Manual analysis is expensive and therefore restricted to limited time periods or samples. It is often difficult to determine an appropriate time period or newspaper selection beforehand.

As a result, automated analysis may be used to guide this process. Moreover, if one detects a pattern in the automated analysis, it is possible to formulate certain proxies or necessary conditions based on the automatic data that can be used to extrapolate the manual data beyond the original sample. For example, if manual analysis shows an increase in the presence of a certain causal relation between two issues, once these issues stop co-occurring soon after the manual sample, we know that that causal relation no longer exists. If the co-occurrence continues to increase, this can be an indication that the trend perceived in the manual data is persisting.

This chapter showcases only some of these possibilities, and much more analytical work may be done with these datasets. However, even by telling the separate stories together one gets a better sense of the events than from one of the stories alone.

Key Points

- Automated and manual analysis can be combined for a fuller picture of (conflict) coverage.
- Automated analysis excels at showing trends and events in very large datasets, allowing the researcher to investigate longer time periods and multiple countries or newspapers.
- Manual Semantic Network Analysis can show the network of causation and evaluation in texts, allowing more detailed questions to be answered.
- Semantic network analysis can be used to analyze both media coverage and open questions, allowing uniform analysis of both sides of the communication channel.
- Substantively, the foreign coverage of the Israel–Palestine conflict is trend driven and balanced, but at the same time increasingly episodic and conflict-centered.
- Public opinion can be said to be more thematic and is, on the whole, critical of Israel.

Study Questions

1. To what degree can the differences observed between the newspapers of the different states in this study, in terms of the frames that portray the protagonists as either victims or culprits, be explained by differences in cultural proximity and by the historical relations between these states and Israel, or these states and the Palestinians/Palestinian authorities?
2. To what degree are the developments in the use of the different substantive frames as shown in Figure 3 related? Pay attention to the effect of the use of different substantive frames on each other and to the impact of international key events and important events in the Israeli–Palestinian conflict.

3. How can the changes in the ratio of episodic framing to the total amount of episodic and thematic framing be explained? Reflect on developments in substantive framing and key historical events.

Further Reading

Druckman, James N. (2001) 'The Implications of Framing Effects for Citizen Competence', *Political Behavior* 23(3): 225–56.

Entman, Robert M. (1993) 'Framing: Toward Clarification of a Fractured Paradigm', *Journal of Communication* 43(4): 51–8.

Goldfarb, Michael (2001) 'All Journalism Is Local: Reporting on the Middle East: How the U.S. and European Media Cover the Same Events Differently', *The Harvard International Journal of Press/Politics* 6(3): 110–15.

Korn, Alina (2004) 'Reporting Palestinian Casualties in the Israeli Press: The Case of Haaretz and the Intifada', *Journalism Studies* 5(2): 247–62.

Philo, Greg, Alison Gilmour, Susanna Rust, Etta Gaskell, Maureen Gilmour and Lucy West (2003) 'The Israeli–Palestinian Conflict: TV News and Public Understanding', pp. 133–48 in Daya K. Thussu and Des Freedman (eds) *War and the Media. Reporting Conflict 24/7*. London; Thousand Oaks, CA: Sage.

Ruigrok, Nel and Wouter van Atteveldt (2007) 'Global Angling with a Local Angle: How U.S., British, and Dutch Newspapers Frame Global and Local Terrorist Attacks', *The Harvard International Journal of Press/Politics* 12(1): 68–90.

Sheafer, Tamir and Shaul R. Shenhav (2009) 'Mediated Public Diplomacy in a New Era of Warfare', *The Communication Review* 12(3): 272–83.

References

Ackerman, Seth (2001) 'Al-Aqsa Intifada and the U.S. Media', *Journal of Palestine Studies* 30(2): 61–74.

Cappella, Joseph N. and Kathleen Hall Jamieson (1997) *Spiral of Cynicism. The Press and the Public Good*. New York: Oxford University Press.

Dearing, James W. and Everett M. Rogers (1996) *Agenda-Setting*. Thousand Oaks, CA: Sage.

Druckman, James N. (2001) 'The Implications of Framing Effects for Citizen Competence', *Political Behavior* 23(3): 225–56.

———— (2004) 'Political Preference Formation: Competition, Deliberation, and the (Ir)relevance of Framing Effects', *American Political Science Review* 98(4): 671–86.

Eagley, Alice H. and Shelly Chaiken (1998) 'Attitude Structure and Function', pp. 269–322 in D.T. Gilbert, S.T. Fiske and G. Lindzey (eds) *The Handbook of Social Psychology*. New York: The McGraw-Hill.

Entman, Robert M. (1991) 'Framing U.S. Coverage of International News: Contrasts in Narratives of the KAL and Iran Air Incidents', *Journal of Communication* 41(4): 6–27.

———— (1993) 'Framing: Toward Clarification of a Fractured Paradigm', *Journal of Communication* 43(4): 51–8.

Farnsworth, Stephen J. and Robert S. Lichter (2006) 'The 2004 New Hampshire Democratic Primary and Network News', *The Harvard International Journal of Press/Politics* 11(1): 53–63.

Findahl, Olle (1998) 'News in Our Minds', pp. 111–27 in Karsten Renckstorf, Dennis McQuail and Nicholas Jankowski (eds) *Television News Research. Recent European Approaches and Findings.* Berlin: Quintessenz.

Fisk, Robert (op. 2005) *De grote beschavingsoorlog.* Amsterdam, Antwerpen: Anthos; Standaard.

Galtung, Johan and Mari Holmboe Ruge (1965) 'The Structure of Foreign News: The Presentation of the Congo, Cuba and Cyprus Crises in Four Norwegian Newspapers', *Journal of Peace Research* 2(1): 64–90.

Gamson, William A. (1992) *Talking Politics.* Cambridge, UK; New York: Cambridge University Press.

Gamson, William A. and Andre Modigliani (1987) 'The Changing Culture of Affirmative Action', pp. 137–77 in Richard Braungart (ed.) *Research in Political Sociology.* Greenwich, CT: JAI Press.

Goffman, Erving (1974) *Frame Analysis. An Essay on the Organization of Experience.* Boston, MA: Northeastern University Press.

Goldfarb, Michael (2001) 'All Journalism Is Local. Reporting on the Middle East: How the U.S. and European Media Cover the Same Events Differently', *The Harvard International Journal of Press/Politics* 6(3): 110–15.

Iyengar, Shanto (1991) *Is Anyone Responsible? How Television Frames Political Issues.* Chicago: University of Chicago Press.

Iyengar, Shanto, Mark D. Peters and Donald R. Kinder (1982) 'Experimental Demonstrations of the "Not-So-Minimal" Consequences of Television News Programs', *The American Political Science Review* 76(4): 848–58.

Kaid, Lynda L., Barbara Harville, John Ballotti and Maria Wawrzyniak (1993) 'Telling the Gulf War Story: Coverage in Five Papers', pp. 86–98 in Bradley S. Greenberg and Walter Gantz (eds) *Desert Storm and the Mass Media.* Cresskill, NJ: Hampton Press.

Kiousis, Spiro, Michael Mitrook, Xu Wu and Trent Seltzer (2006) 'First- and Second-Level Agenda-Building and Agenda-Setting Effects. Exploring the Linkages Among Candidate News Releases, Media Coverage, and Public Opinion during the 2002 Florida Gubernatorial Election', *Journal of Public Relations Research* 18(3): 265–85.

Kleinnijenhuis, J., O. Scholten, W. van Atteveldt, A. van Hoof, A. Krouwel, D. Oegema, J. de Ridder, N. Ruigrok and J. Takens (2007) *Nederland Vijfstromenland. De Rol van de Media en Stemwijzers bij de Verkiezingen van 2006.* Amsterdam: Bert Bakker.

Korn, Alina (2004) 'Reporting Palestinian Casualties in the Israeli Press. The Case of Haaretz and the Intifada', *Journalism Studies* 5(2): 247–62.

Lawrence, Regina G. and W. Lance Bennett (2000) 'Civic Engagement in the Era of Big Stories', *Political Communication* 17(4): 377–82.

Loughborough University Communications Research Centre (2006) *The BBC's Reporting of the Israeli–Palestinian Conflict (August 1 2005–January 31 2006).* Loughborough University.

McCombs, Maxwell E. and Donald L. Shaw (1972) 'The Agenda-Setting Function of Mass Media', *Public Opinion Quarterly* 36(2): 176–87.

Meyers, Garth, Thomas Klak and Timothy Koehl (1996) 'The Inscription of Difference: News Coverage of the Conflicts in Rwanda and Bosnia', *Political Geography* 15(1): 21–46.

Miller, Joanne M. and Jon A. Krosnick (1996) 'News Media Impact on the Ingredients of Presidential Evaluations. A Program of Research on the Priming Hypothesis', pp. 79–99 in Diana C. Mutz, Paul M. Sniderman and Richard A. Brody (eds) *Political Persuasion and Attitude Change*. Ann Arbor: University of Michigan Press.

Nederlands Instituut voor Oorlogsdocumentatie (NIOD) (2002) *Srebrenica. Een 'Veilig' Gebied*. Amsterdam: Boom.

Norris, Pippa (1995) 'The Restless Searchlight: Network News Framing of the Post-Cold War World', *Political Communication* 12(4): 357–70.

Osgood, Charles E. (1956) 'Behavior Theory and the Social Sciences', *Behavioral Science* 1(3): 167–85.

Pan, Zhongdang and Gerald M. Kosicki (2003) 'Framing as Strategic Action in Public Deliberation', pp. 35–66 in Stephen D. Reese, Oscar H. Gandy and August E. Grant (eds) *Framing Public Life. Perspectives on Media and Our Understanding of the Social World*. Mahwah, NJ: Lawrence Erlbaum.

Papacharissi, Zizi and Maria Fatima de Oliveira (2008) 'News Frames Terrorism. A Comparative Analysis of Frames Employed in Terrorism Coverage in U.S. and U.K. Newspapers', *The International Journal of Press/Politics* 13(1): 52–74.

Patterson, Thomas E. (1993) *Out of Order*. New York: Knopf.

Philo, Greg and Mike Berry (2004) *Bad News from Israel*. London; Sterling, VA: Pluto Press.

Philo, Greg, Alison Gilmour, Susanna Rust, Etta Gaskell, Maureen Gilmour and Lucy West (2003) 'The Israeli–Palestinian Conflict: TV News and Public Understanding', pp. 133–48 in Daya K. Thussu and Des Freedman (eds) *War and the Media. Reporting Conflict 24/7*. London; Thousand Oaks, CA: Sage.

Price, Vincent and David Tewksbury (1997) 'News Values and Public Opinion: A Theoretical Account of Media Priming and Framing', pp. 173–212 in George A. Barnett and Franklin J. Boster (eds) *Progress in Communication Sciences*. Greenwich, CT: Ablex.

Quattrone, George A. and Amos Tversky (1988) 'Contrasting Rational and Psychological Analyses of Political Choice', *The American Political Science Review* 82(3): 719–36.

Rhee, June W. (1997) 'Strategy and Issue Frames in Election Campaign Coverage: A Social Cognitive Account of Framing Effects', *Journal of Communication* 47(3): 26–48.

Rinnawi, Khalil (2007) 'De-Legitimization of Media Mechanisms: Israeli Press Coverage of the Al Aqsa Intifada', *International Communication Gazette* 69(2): 149–78.

Ruigrok, Nel (2005) *Journalism of Attachment. Dutch Newspapers during the Bosnian War*. Amsterdam: Het Spinhuis.

Ruigrok, Nel and Wouter van Atteveldt (2007) 'Global Angling with a Local Angle: How U.S., British, and Dutch Newspapers Frame Global and Local Terrorist Attacks', *The Harvard International Journal of Press/Politics* 12(1): 68–90.

Scheufele, Dietram A. (1999) 'Framing as a Theory of Media Effects', *Journal of Communication* 49(1): 103–22.

Semetko, Holli A. and Patti M. Valkenburg (2000) 'Framing European Politics: A Content Analysis of Press and Television News', *Journal of Communication* 50(2): 93–109.

Snow, David A. and Robert D. Benford (1988) 'Ideology, Frame Resonance, and Participant Mobilization', *International Social Movement Research* 1(1): 197–217.

Snow, David A., Burke E. Rochford, Steven K. Worden and Robert D. Benford (1986) 'Frame Alignment Processes, Micromobilization, and Movement Participation', *American Sociological Review* 51(4): 464–81.

Tversky, Amos and Daniel Kahneman (1981) 'The Framing of Decisions and the Psychology of Choice', *Science* 211(4481): 453–58.

van Atteveldt, Wouter (2008) *Semantic Network Analysis. Techniques for Extracting, Representing and Querying Media Content.* Charleston, SC: BookSurge.

van Cuilenburg, Jan J., Jan Kleinnijenhuis and Johannes A. de Ridder (1988) *Tekst en Betoog. Naar een Computergestuurde Inhoudsanalyse van Betogende Teksten.* Muiderberg: Coutinho.

Vasterman, Peter (2005) *Mediahype.* Amsterdam: Aksant.

Zaller, John (1992) *The Nature and Origins of Mass Opinion.* Cambridge, UK; New York: Cambridge University Press.

—— (1994) 'Elite Leadership of Mass Opinion: New Evidence from the Gulf War', pp. 186–209 in Lance W. Bennett and David L. Paletz (eds) *Taken by Storm. The Media, Public Opinion, and U.S. Foreign Policy in the Gulf War.* Chicago: University of Chicago Press.

Zelizer, Barbie, David Park and David Gudelunas (2002) 'How Bias Shapes the News. Challenging the *New York Times*' Status as a Newspaper of Record on the Middle East', *Journalism* 3(3): 283–307.

Public Discourse on the Georgian War in Russia and the EU

A Content Analysis of the Coverage in Traditional Print Media and Emerging Online Media

Cordula Nitsch and Dennis Lichtenstein

Summary

This chapter focuses on public discourse in Russia and the European Union (EU) regarding the Georgian War. Armed conflicts arouse considerable interest and an increased demand for information. To form a well-founded public opinion, independent and comprehensive media coverage is a prerequisite. However, empirical research indicates that war coverage shows deficits and mainly reflects the perspective of political and economic elites. Unlike traditional mass media, the emerging online media are more autonomous. They provide an open forum that is easily accessible and can offer additional information and alternative opinions. They therefore have the potential to act as a corrective in public discourse. Using the Georgian War in 2008 as an example, a quantitative content analysis was conducted to determine the character of the public discourse in traditional print media and emerging online media. To account for the varying degree of media dependency, we examined the coverage in Russia and the EU – represented by four EU member states (Great Britain, Germany, Austria, and France). The analysis focuses on the framing of the war and on the actors who were quoted in the respective media. The findings show rather similar framing patterns in Russia and the EU and therefore fewer international differences between the public discourses than had been expected. Differences between traditional print media and the emerging online media are found in the case of Russia only. This result proves that – at least in countries with a rather restricted media system – the emerging online media provide additional and alternative input regarding the events of the Georgian War.

Introduction

In August 2008 the five-day war in the Caucasus marked a significant disturbance in the post-Cold War relationship between Russia and the western world. The countries involved were Georgia, on the one side, and Russia (together with the separatist Georgian regions of South Ossetia and Abkhazia), on the other. Western nations were indirectly involved in the incident because of the impending acceptance of Georgia as a member state of NATO. The conflict was reminiscent of the earlier antagonism between the eastern block and the western alliance and served as a touchstone for post-Cold War international relationships.

In order to form an opinion on the war, for example, on the appropriate political and military action, the public relies on unbiased media coverage. The coverage should include information on the cause of the conflict, the course of the war, the differing political views and the possible aftermath. However, research has shown that the media rarely fulfill this need for all-embracing and objective coverage (for a review, see McQuail, 2006). The media tend to side with the country where they are located or with its allies, and the news are often influenced by political propaganda and direct or indirect censorship. This applies primarily to traditional mass media, while the emerging online media seem to be less restricted. The versatile possibilities of articulation (e.g., through weblogs, social networks or Twitter) have meanwhile broken the information monopoly of the mass media. Today, a large amount of additional information is transmitted via these new media services. Generally speaking, the different types of emerging online media are open to everyone and thereby provide a forum for people who can rarely articulate their point of view in the mass media. In times of conflict and crisis, eyewitness accounts from ordinary citizens often show a different picture than mass media coverage does – particularly when the mass media are strongly influenced by the official political elites (Krempl, 2004). Applying these considerations to the Georgian War, one can assume that the war coverage differs between the respective countries and between the different types of media.

This chapter aims at analyzing public discourse in the traditional mass media and the emerging online media in Russia and the EU. It starts out with theoretical considerations on the deliberative function of the media in democracies and emphasizes the need for a critical media discourse – especially in times of war. We argue that structural factors undermine the normative function of the mass media. We will also discuss the possibility that the emerging online media might become a corrective in public discourse. By empirically examining the media coverage of the Georgian War, we attempt to uncover differences in public discourse such as it is reflected in the traditional mass media and the emerging online media. Both the Russian media and the media of the European member states (Austria, Great Britain, Germany and France) we have chosen for this study are analyzed. In a third step, an overview of the course of the Georgian War is provided. Subsequently, information on the research design is given before the results are presented. The main focus is on the comparison between the traditional mass media and the emerging online media in both Russia and the EU. The chapter concludes with a short summary and points out some aspects that need further research.

Public Discourse and the Exceptional Circumstances of Wartime

The legitimacy of political actions is closely tied to public discourse. Public discourse takes place mainly in the media, and the normative idea of a free and deliberative discourse holds that debate leads to the general acceptance of a well-founded opinion (Habermas, 1992).

Pluralism as an important element of deliberative public discourse refers to the unrestricted access to the media for all relevant public actors and the representation of all opinions concerning an issue. Thus, recent approaches to deliberative democracy (see Benhabib, 1996; Fishkin, 1995; Habermas et al., 1992) emphasize that the sovereignty of a people is not confined to the act of voting but also includes citizens' involvement in the process of democratic opinion formation. Not only the viewpoints of the elite but also the opinions of the general public have to be included in public discourse, and their voices need to be 'clear, loud, and equal' (Verba et al., 1995: 509).

The output of the deliberative process is known as 'public opinion'. It provides orientation and can also affect political decisions, since politicians realize that 'public opinion is ultimately translated into votes' (McQuail et al., 2008: 268). A well-founded public opinion is even more relevant in times of crisis and war. News coverage can cause either support or rejection with respect to a particular policy decision (Bennett and Lawrence, 2008: 255).[1] Exceptional and critical circumstances usually lead to an uncertainty as to how to assess the situation, and citizens want to be sure that their government does not wage an immoral or unnecessary war (Aday et al., 2005: 4). Consequently, the public seeks information and orientation more actively (Bilke, 2008: 139) and may resort to consulting the emerging online media in addition to the traditional mass media.

Traditional Mass Media and the Public Discourse on War

The normative idea of an all-inclusive deliberative public discourse raises rather unrealistic expectations for the media insofar as the basic rules and restrictions of the media system may impede this demand: the media have to select and condense not only certain issues but also the resulting interpretations. In doing so, the traditional mass media have primarily been criticized for focusing on political elites and disregarding the perspectives of minorities (Fraser, 1992: 120). In addition, it can be argued that social power regulates public discourse and leads to an informal censorship (Bennett and Lawrence, 2008: 250). According to Herman's and Chomsky's (2002) propaganda model, the mass media are influenced by the political and economic system and tend to follow the strategic interests of the elites. The authors identify five factors that affect news coverage:

(1) the size, concentrated ownership, owner wealth, and profit orientation of the dominant mass-media firms; (2) advertising as the primary income source of the mass media; (3) the reliance of the media on information provided by government, business, and 'experts' funded and approved by these primary sources and agents of power; (4) 'flak' as a means of disciplining the media; (5) 'anticommunism' as a national religion and control mechanism. (Herman and Chomsky, 2002: 2)

The propaganda model can decisively account for the type of news coverage that prevails in times of war (Herman and Chomsky, 2002: xxix). Since the Vietnam War, governments and the military are fully aware of the importance of controlled information management. The conflicting parties try to influence the mass media with selective information and by using a manipulative language (see Collins and Glover, 2002). Furthermore, the political and economic elites have a privileged position in enforcing their preferred 'framing' of the war (D'Angelo, 2002: 876). According to Entman (1993: 52), framing means 'to select some aspects of a perceived reality and make them more salient in a communicating text, in such a way as to promote a particular problem definition, causal interpretation, moral evaluation, and/or treatment recommendation for the item described'.

In wartime, the national political and economic elites use framing strategies and their access to the media to communicate their political and military actions to the wider public. The dominant framing strategies in post-Cold War conflicts are related to the War on Terror, which includes a demonization of the combatant. Moral rationales, such as human rights, are provided to justify military action (Bilke, 2008: 152; Hammond, 2007: 220). These allow for a clear differentiation between the belligerents and serve to categorize the countries involved according to a 'good versus evil' schema.

Furthermore, the propaganda offices of the government and the military anticipate the news selection routines of media organizations. Their information management takes the mass media's dependency on topicality and the competitive situation of the media into account. So-called 'soft' censorship became especially popular during the 2003 Iraq War, when embedded journalists were allowed to accompany the soldiers. Closeness to the soldiers resulted in a strong feeling of camaraderie on the part of journalists, a situation that has been compared with the well-known 'Stockholm Syndrome' (Krempl, 2004: 94–5). In addition, the Pentagon controlled journalistic access to the military, denying it to journalists from countries that did not support the war.[2] Tactics such as these are generally seen as more effective than the complete refusal to release any pictures and information (Luhmann, 2000: 8).

Several studies have shown that the traditional mass media rarely question the government's position in wartime (see, for example, Eilders and Lüter, 2000; Mermin, 1999; Vincent, 2000). Instead, the national media display a 'rally around the flag' mentality and do not actively seek alternative information or interpretations. Bennett's (1990) indexing thesis states that the degree of controversy about an issue in the media is tied to the homogeneity or heterogeneity of parliamentary debate. If the opposition does not challenge the government's policy, the media usually do not question the official position either. By merely reflecting parliamentary debate, the media tend to disregard their watchdog function (Bennett and Lawrence, 2008: 254). Patriotic news coverage is supported, and interpretations that are not consistent with the dominant opinion are shunned. As a consequence, the public is often denied unbiased coverage.

To sum up, various examples demonstrate that the mass media cannot be credited with an all-embracing account of the course of wars or with encouraging critical discussion of the legitimacy of armed conflicts. This shortcoming leaves a gap that might be filled by alternative information sources, such as the emerging online media.

The Emerging Online Media and the Public Discourse on War

Over the past several years, the Internet has gained more and more importance as a source of (political) information and has made it easier for the average citizen to participate in public debates (Baker, 2007: 101–2). As opposed to the traditional mass media, the emerging online media are less controlled and barely institutionalized. They provide an endless forum for a variety of opinions, thus challenging the famous dictum that 'whatever we know [...] about the world in which we live, we know through the mass media' (Luhmann, 2000: 1).

Twitter, mailing lists, social networks and weblogs are some examples of the emerging media that are 'now becoming a structural component of the media mix' (Cooper, 2011: 150). Weblogs are defined as 'first person, frequently updated online journals presented in reverse chronological order' (Hindman, 2009: 102). Blogs are a 'social genre' because they link up with other blogs and encourage readers to comment on their articles (Rettberg, 2008: 21). The authors within the blogosphere are strongly interconnected, since they mostly provide a 'blogroll' – a list of links to other blogs the author has chosen to point out to the readers – and links to articles on other blogs. Their main area of strength thus lies in collective information gathering, in comparing information and in commenting on the mass media coverage (Krempl, 2004).

Blogs can (a) dispute the frame that dominates the traditional media, (b) reframe an issue by offering additional information or (c) contextualize it by offering additional relevant facts (Cooper, 2011: 140). Blogs can be a vehicle for substantive media criticism and enrich public discourse in general. Because of the global availability of the Internet and easy and unlimited access to weblogs, bloggers can also refer to the content of foreign emerging online media and enable a transnational discourse. After 9/11, a general increase in the amount of political content was registered, and the specific genre of war blogs, which is seen as a new form of war-related communication, evolved (Bucher, 2004: 285). Especially in wartime countless eyewitness accounts from the conflict areas (articles, videos and photographs) appear on the Internet.

By enabling ordinary citizens to directly and actively participate in public debates, the emerging online media can be seen as making political discourse less exclusive (Benkler, 2006; Reynolds, 2006). Furthermore, the filters postulated by the propaganda model obviously do not apply to the emerging online media because they lack an organized and commercial structure (Krempl, 2004: 108). This allows for more independent discourse: actors from civil society can articulate their opinions with a relatively modest financial investment (i.e., access to a computer connected to the Internet), politicians do not have to adapt to the traditional mass media's selection filters, and journalists have the option of writing for the emerging online media without being limited by economic considerations.

In essence, the characteristics of the emerging online media allow the prospect of a new form of democratic participation. The structure of communication has become less hierarchical, the level of pluralism in public discourse has increased, and political debates are more democratized (Chadwick, 2006). With an optimistic eye one could hope for the fulfillment of the normative idea of a free discourse, without any gatekeepers (Williams and Carpini, 2000: 61).

In contrast to the euphoric appraisals given above, the extreme openness of the Internet has also provoked some skepticism: the high number of websites and voices might result in a fragmented public sphere in which the condensing of relevant issues for political processing becomes impossible. This endangers both a common political culture and a successful democratic process (Sunstein, 2001: 9). Other authors argue that market concentration of the Internet sector compromises its openness (Noam, 2003), or that Internet providers and governments become powerful gatekeepers by using firewalls (see Deibert et al., 2008). Although the formal barriers that keep ordinary citizens from participating in an online discourse are still lower than those in the traditional mass media, the vision of an equality of participants is misleading (Hindman, 2009: 32). Besides the digital divide (see Norris, 2001), search engines ensure that only heavily linked websites are prominently placed and become significant in public discourse. This 'winner-takes-all' scenario in the 'Googlearchy' (Hindman, 2009: 55) aggravates the inequality of opinions: 'even though there are apparently millions of self-publishing bloggers, concentration of audience attention is extreme' (Baker, 2007: 107) and possibly even higher than for newspapers.

In contrast to the more institutionalized mass media, the emerging online media cannot be characterized as exerting a continual and all-embracing monitoring of public affairs. Weblogs concentrate essentially on personal experiences and trivial observations, whereas political content still remains a 'niche market within the broader Web' (Hindman, 2009: 100). Since bloggers usually do not have the resources and patience necessary for time-consuming research (Lovink, 2007: 47), they mainly reproduce information from the traditional mass media. This often results in 'more-of-the-same' commentary instead of alternative information.

Despite the many euphoric or pessimistic statements, the relevance of the emerging online media for public discourse has not yet been fully clarified and their corrective function is still in doubt (Delhaes, 2002: 68).[3] Nonetheless, in wartime there are some examples of citizens' participation and of an enrichment of public discourse: during the Kosovo conflict in 1999, which has been labeled the first 'internet-war' (Taylor, 2000: 194), the direct online interaction of civil society reached a new level (Krempl, 2004). During this conflict the emerging online media challenged the traditional mass media (Goff, 1999: 28). Another famous example is the blog of Salam Pax. His eyewitness accounts from the Iraq War in 2003 contributed alternative aspects to the mass media coverage and received a high deal of attention (for documentation on this blog, see Pax, 2003).

A positive impact is also asserted in the study produced by Tremayne and colleagues (2006), who conclude, 'Although it is clear that many bloggers on each side choose to isolate themselves by linking only to ideological compatriots and to media supportive of their point of view, there is at least a place in the middle where ideas can be debated and, possibly, positions changed' (Tremayne et al., 2006). In order to examine these theoretical considerations, the Georgian War was chosen as an event where public discourse could be analyzed in both the traditional mass media and the emerging online media.

Cause and Course of the Georgian War

The origins of the Georgian War in 2008 date back to an earlier conflict in 1991–92 that resulted in the de facto separation of South Ossetia from Georgia and a UN peacekeeping mandate for Russia.[4] Tension increased again after Mikheil Saakashvili was elected president in 2004. His intention was to reconstitute Georgia's former territory. Furthermore, his aim was a closer relationship with the western world and possible NATO membership. South Ossetia and Abkhazia, on the contrary, were aiming to achieve independence and closer ties with Russia. The Russian government – Medvedev had just become president and his predecessor Vladimir Putin took over the powerful role of prime minister – supported their separatist efforts and issued Russian passports for the population in these regions. In addition, Russia distrusted any eastward expansion of NATO.

Evidently, the situation in this area had been tense for quite some time. The conflict eventually escalated late in the evening of August 7 – while international attention was concentrated on the Olympic Games in China. Georgia attacked its separatist region South Ossetia and the military conflict widened as Russia immediately took the side of South Ossetia, responding with swift military action. The justification of Russia's involvement in the conflict was its need to protect its ethnic minorities. Both Georgia and Russia 'hired Western PR companies to help put across their messages' ('The PR Battle for the Caucasus', BBC, October 2008[5]). The EU strongly supported Georgia's sovereignty and territorial integrity. Immediately after the outbreak of the war, French President Sarkozy, whose country held the EU presidency at that time, traveled to Georgia to present a peace agreement. Since Russia quickly dominated the armed conflict, Georgia's president Mikheil Saakashvili agreed to the signing of a cease-fire on August 15. Despite numerous western calls for a quick withdrawal, Russian troops remained in the area for about two more months. The withdrawal was finally completed when control was handed over to an EU observer mission in October 2008.

After the conflict, Georgia's NATO membership was removed from the political agenda. The western community hesitates to include countries that clearly lack stability and whose membership might impair their relationship with Russia. Currently, the situation in Georgia remains unstable and its NATO membership is a distant prospect (Bär, 2009: 37[6]). Although Russia did not officially incorporate South Ossetia into the Russian Federation, it has taken complete control of the region's security.

Hypotheses and Research Design

To analyze public discourse concerning the Georgian War, a quantitative content analysis of the media coverage in Russia and the EU was conducted. Both print and online media were analyzed. We examine therefore two dimensions of comparison: an international comparison between Russia and the EU and a comparison between the two types of media.

Based on the theoretical background, three hypotheses were tested.

- H 1: Public discourse on the Georgian War differs between Russia and the EU.

The first hypothesis refers to the international comparison. Russia is not only one of the belligerents but its media system is also characterized by a strong dependency on the political system (Pasti, 2006: 84).[7] Especially in times of conflict and war, significant parallelism can be expected between the official political position and the mass media coverage. The EU, on the contrary, is characterized by on the whole liberal and democratic media systems, and its media are therefore rather independent. Besides, the EU member states are only indirectly involved in the Georgian War and supported the Georgian position. Owing to these unequal initial positions, international differences between the European and the Russian media discourse are expected.

- H 2: Public discourse in Russia and the EU differs between the traditional mass media and the emerging online media.

Our second hypothesis takes the differences between traditional print media and the emerging online media into account. As argued above, the traditional mass media cannot be credited with achieving an all-embracing account of the course of a war. The emerging online media have the potential to compensate for this deficiency in the coverage. Because of their varying structural dependency on the political and economic system, war coverage is likely to differ between these two types of media.

- H 3: Differences between public discourse in the traditional mass media and the emerging online media are more pronounced in Russia than in the EU.

Finally, our third hypothesis is closely linked to Hypothesis 2, since we assume that with regard to the restrictive nature of the Russian media system, citizens' need to consult online media in order to express alternative opinions would be stronger in Russia than in the EU member states.

The analysis of public discourse focuses on two aspects that are both indicators of pluralistic media coverage: (1) the framing of the war and (2) the actors who are quoted in the media. A large variety of different actors and different frames implies a high level of pluralism, which is a precondition of deliberative debate. In the specific case of the Georgian

War, it is first of all important that actors from both warring parties have a chance to express their points of view. Furthermore, it is of interest which other actors have access to the media and whether they are mainly from western or from eastern regions.

To identify the frames, a qualitative content analysis of a random sample of the articles was conducted.[8] Altogether nine frames were detected. According to Entman (1993: 52), a frame contains four elements. This can be demonstrated by an example: the frame 'return of the Cold War' refers to the 'problem situation' of the competition between the western and eastern world in gaining hegemony in world politics. Within this logic, the Georgian War is only a symptom of a larger development. The 'causal interpretation' refers to Georgia's efforts to become a member of NATO, which provokes Russia, which is looking for an excuse to intervene. With respect to the 'moral evaluation', Russia's disproportionate military reaction to Georgia's attack on South Ossetia is criticized. Finally, the 'treatment recommendation' relates to de-escalating the crisis and returning to the former status quo in Georgia.

Three more frames put the situation in Georgia in a global political context. The frame 'reentrance of Russia to world politics' signifies that after the collapse of the Soviet Union, Russia now returns as a powerful agent in world politics. Unlike the frame 'return of the Cold War', it does not directly refer to a competitive situation between Russia and the western world. The frame 'new world order' highlights the complexity and difficulty of international relations in the years following the Cold War. The previous East–West division has become obsolete and countries face the need to strategically reposition themselves. The third frame – the 'assertion of Russia's might against western influence' – also refers to the dynamics of international relations. However, it does not focus on the general reorganization of the balance of power in world politics but instead stresses the eastward expansion of NATO and similar western influences. Russia obviously distrusts the actions of the West and tries by any means to maintain its traditional sphere of influence.

Three frames focus on the issue without referring to a larger context: the framing of the Georgian War as an 'ethnic conflict' highlights the heterogeneity of this region. The ethnic fragmentation is seen as the main reason for the war, and Georgia's discrimination of its minorities is emphasized. The frame 'separatism' highlights the political intention of South Ossetia and Abkhazia to become independent, and 'humanitarian catastrophe' puts the destruction and the suffering of the population into focus.

Furthermore, two frames that mainly address the financial aspects of the conflict could be identified. The frame 'costs of the conflict' stresses the resources that are spent directly on engagement in the war – for instance, human resources or the costs for the military. The frame 'economic consequences' focuses on the potential economic costs that emerge indirectly from the Georgian War, such as the impact on international trade and energy supply.

Public discourse on the Georgian War was coded in both the Russian and the European media. The European public sphere is characterized by complexity and multilingualism and lacks a homogeneous pan-European media system.[9] For this reason, the media of several member states of the EU were analyzed. Because of the potential reach of the media content being studied, EU member states were chosen that are home to the three languages most frequently spoken: Great Britain, Germany/Austria and France (European Commission, 2006: 4).[10]

For each language area (English, German, French and Russian), two weekly news publications were analyzed. The news publications studied mainly focus on political information, reach a large number of readers and are considered opinion leaders in their respective countries. For the selection of the emerging online media, we decided to adopt a user's perspective and simulated the search behavior of an Internet user looking for additional information on the Georgian War.

By using relevant keywords (e.g., Georgian War/conflict, Caucasian War/conflict), Google's respective national domains were searched. Because Google is less popular in Russia, we used the search engine Yandex for identifying the relevant Russian emerging media. The first two media results (either individual weblogs or online platforms) that included reasonable coverage of the Georgian War were chosen for the analysis.[11]

The time period under study was from mid-July to mid-September (July 14, 2008 to September 15, 2008). It includes the weeks before the escalation, the period of armed conflict and the four weeks following the signing of the cease-fire. For each country, no more than four students with country-specific language skills conducted the coding. The intercoder reliability was 0.82 for the total of all variables.

A total of 272 Russian and European articles were identified that cover the Georgian War either as a main topic or as a side topic. The basis for the analysis was 130 articles in the traditional print media and 142 articles in the emerging online media (see Table 1). Because four European countries were included, the number of articles was larger for the EU than for Russia. For each of the articles, no more than three frames were coded. Furthermore, all actors cited in the articles were coded.

Table 1: Media under Study

	Print media	**Articles**	**Online media**	**Articles**
Germany/ Austria	*Spiegel* *Profil*	28	www.spiegelfechter.com www.hannes-swoboda.at	18
Great Britain	*Observer* *Economist*	34	www.opendemocracy.net www.wired.com	32
France	*L'Express* *Le Point*	30	lecafepoliticien.blogspot.com nicolaslandru.blogspot.com	35
Europe		92		85
Russia	*Argumenti i fakty* *Itogi*	38	v-tretyakov.livejournal.com olegpanfilov2.livejournal.com	57
Total		**130**		**142**

Results

Of the 272 Russian and European articles a total of 410 frames were coded. The framing frequencies clearly differ between Russia and Europe: for Europe (n = 177 articles) the average per article is 1.7 frames, while for Russia (n = 95 articles) it is 1.1. This shows that the Russian media generally are less active in framing the war and provide fewer interpretations of how to assess the military events. Furthermore, a higher number of frames were found in the articles of the traditional print media (on average, 1.8 frames per article) than in those of the emerging online media (1.3 frames per article). Similar differences become obvious with respect to the second indicator, quoted actors: the 272 articles contain 1,137 direct or indirect quotations. Whereas the European articles on average quote 5.8 actors, the Russian articles only quote 1.1 actors. Differences are also found with regard to the types of media: on average, 5.1 actors appear in the articles of the traditional print media as opposed to an average of 3.3 in the articles of the emerging online media. For both 'framing' and 'quoted actors', the differences mainly result from the more extensive volume of the print articles – which provides more opportunities for quoting actors and framing the conflict.

In our first hypothesis, we expected differences between public discourse in Russia and in the EU. Nonetheless, as far as the framing of the Georgian War is concerned, the European and the Russian media show a high degree of consensus (r = .63, p > .05; see Table 2). The media of both Russia and the EU mostly frame the Georgian War in terms of a 'new world order' – 28.4 percent of the Russian articles and 33.9 percent of the European articles contained this frame. Media coverage thus points out the uncertainty of the future political order: Georgia aims to reorient itself, the international alliances are in flux and changes in the former relationships are to be expected. The ranking of the other frames shows only slight differences between the European and the Russian media. Only the frame 'costs of the

Table 2: Frames in the Russian and European Media – Rank Order (in Percentages)

Rank	Russian media (n = 95 articles)		European media (n = 177 articles)	
1	New World Order	28.4	New World Order	33.9
2	Return of the Cold War	14.7	Re-entrance of Russia to World Politics	28.2
3	Humanitarian Catastrophe	13.7	Return of the Cold War	27.7
4	Re-entrance of Russia to World Politics/Costs of the Conflict	11.6	Humanitarian Catastrophe	20.3
5	–	–	Separatism	16.9
6	Economic Consequences	10.5	Economic Consequences	15.8
7	Ethnic Conflict	7.4	Assertion of Russia' Might	15.3
8	Separatism	6.3	Ethnic Conflict	10.2
9	Assertion of Russia' Might	5.3	Costs of the Conflict	4.0

Table 3: Quoted Actors in the Russian and European Media (in Percentages)

Quoted Actors from ...	Russia (*n* = 109 quoted actors)	Europe (*n* = 1.028 quoted actors)
Russia/South Ossetia/Abkhazia	59.6	36.6
Georgia	11.9	24.9
Western countries	12.8	29.1
Eastern countries	8.3	3.8
Others	7.3	5.6

$\chi^2 = 35{,}11$; df = 4; $p \leq .001$***; Cramer's $V = .18$. Percentages may not total 100 due to rounding.

conflict' is ranked significantly differently. Whereas it is ranked in fourth position in Russia (occurring in 11.6 percent of the articles), it only plays a marginal role in the EU and is ranked in last position (4.0 percent of the articles). This result is not surprising, since none of the EU member states was financially involved in the war, and the events of the armed conflict did not entail any 'costs' as far as these countries were concerned.

Other than the framing, a comparison of the quoted actors in the Russian versus the European media shows obvious differences (see Table 3). The actors were aggregated into five categories that distinguish the conflicting parties: (1) Russia together with South Ossetia and Abkhazia, (2) Georgia, (3) western countries, (4) eastern countries and (5) other actors.[12] The Russian media strongly focus on actors from its own side – 59.6 percent of the quotes are from people of Russian, South Ossetian or Abkhazian origin. Georgians hardly get access to the Russian media; they only account for 11.9 percent of all cited actors. The same is true of actors from western countries that also play a subordinate role. The European media coverage is less biased when it comes to quoting actors from the conflicting parties. Nevertheless, Georgian actors are not represented as frequently as actors from the opposing side (24.9 percent vs. 36.6 percent). Furthermore, actors from western countries gain more than twice as much attention as in the Russian media and account for almost one-third of the actors.

Summing up, our first hypothesis is only partly confirmed. The Russian and the European media use a rather similar framing of the Georgian War, and public discourse is internationally dominated by the frame 'new world order'. However, one can detect remarkable differences with respect to the quoted actors in Russian and European media coverage. The strong emphasis on actors from their own side in the Russian media contrasts with the fairer balance of the parties involved in the conflict in the European media.

Hypothesis 2 and 3 referred to public discourse on the Georgian War in different types of media. We expected differences between the traditional mass media and the emerging online media in both Russia and the EU (H 2). Since the Russian media system is less independent than the media systems of the EU member states and since Russia is one of the belligerents, we also expected that the differences between the types of media would be more pronounced in Russia (H 3).

In the EU, the framing of the Georgian War shows strong parallels in the traditional print media and the emerging online media ($r = .76$; $p \le .05^*$; see Table 4). Both types of media refer to the same top-three frames that all focus on global political aspects: 'new world order', 'reentrance of Russia to world politics' and 'return of the Cold War'. This indicates that both types of media emphasize the concern of the western community about the international balance of power. European public discourse strongly focuses on the interpretation that Russia is demonstrating its power in world politics and that tensions between the eastern and western world remain. Noteworthy differences only appear for the frame 'economic consequences'. This frame is ranked in fourth position in the traditional print media (appearing in 23.9 percent of the articles) but only in the second to last position in the emerging online media (7.1 percent of the articles).

As was also the case for framing, our analysis did not reveal noteworthy differences in regard to the quoted actors in EU public discourse (see Table 5). The traditional print media and the emerging online media focus on three groups of actors: actors from Russia and its allies, actors from Georgia and actors from western countries. Actors from eastern countries play hardly any role in the public discourse of the four EU member states. In both media types, quotations from actors on the Russian side account for the largest share (35.1 percent resp. 38.6 percent). The opponents, actors from Georgia, account for around one quarter of all quotes (27.1 percent vs. 21.9 percent, respectively). European public discourse also refers to a high percentage of actors from western countries – mainly quoting statements and opinions from actors of the respective nation.

Table 4: Frames in the Traditional Print and the Emerging Online Media: EU – Rank Order (in Percentages)

Rank	Traditional print media (n = 92 articles)		Emerging online media (n = 85 articles)	
1	New World Order	38.0	New World Order	29.4
2	Re-entrance of Russia to World Politics	33.7	Return of the Cold War	28.2
3	Return of the Cold War	27.2	Re-entrance of Russia to World Politics	22.4
4	Economic Consequences	23.9	Humanitarian Catastrophe/ Separatism	20.0
5	Humanitarian Catastrophe	20.7	–	–
6	Assertion of Russia' Might	17.4	Assertion of Russia' Might	12.9
7	Separatism	14.1	Ethnic Conflict	9.4
8	Ethnic Conflict	10.9	Economic Consequences	7.1
9	Costs of the Conflict	4.3	Costs of the Conflict	3.5

Table 5: Quoted Actors in the Traditional Print and the Emerging Online Media: EU (in Percentages)

Quoted Actors from …	Traditional print media (n = 590 quoted actors)	Emerging online media (n = 438 quoted actors)
Russia/South Ossetia/Abkhazia	35.1	38.6
Georgia	27.1	21.9
Western countries	28.8	29.5
Eastern countries	4.9	2.3
Others	4.1	7.8

χ^2 = 14,28; df = 4; $p \leq .01$**; Cramer's V = .12. Percentages may not total 100 due to rounding.

Turning to the Russian media, apart from the dominant frame 'new world order', public discourse in the traditional print media and the emerging online media focuses on extremely different interpretations ($r = .18$, $p > .05$; see Table 6). The next two most frequent frames in print media coverage are 'costs of the conflict' and 'economic consequences'. The emerging online media, however, focus equally on the frames 'humanitarian catastrophe' and 'return of the Cold War'. The traditional mass media's emphasis on the financial and economic aspects of the Georgian War is in striking contrast to the treatment of these aspects in the emerging online media, which hardly refer at all to these aspects. This is especially the case for the frame 'costs of the conflict', which shows strong differences between the different

Table 6: Frames in the Traditional Print and the Emerging Online Media: Russia – Rank Order (in Percentages)

Rank	Traditional print media (n = 38 articles)		Emerging online media (n = 57 articles)	
1	New World Order	31.6	New World Order	26.3
2	Costs of the Conflict	26.3	Return of the Cold War/ Humanitarian Catastrophe	14.0
3	Economic Consequences	18.4	–	–
4	Re-entrance of Russia to World Politics/Return of the Cold War	15.8	Re-entrance of Russia to World Politics/Ethnic Conflict	8.8
5	–	–	–	–
6	Humanitarian Catastrophe	13.2	Economic Consequences/ Separatism	5.3
7	Assertion of Russia' Might	10.5	–	–
8	Separatism	7.9	Assertion of Russia' Might/ Costs of the Conflict	1.8
9	Ethnic Conflict	5.3	–	–

types of media. It is ranked in second position in the Russian print media (occurring in 26.3 percent of the articles) but only in eighth position in the emerging online media (1.8 percent of the articles).

Because Russia is one of the warring parties and therefore financially involved in the war, it is not surprising that the frames 'costs of the conflict' and 'economic consequences' play an important role in the print media. However, these aspects are seen as negligible in the blogosphere. By contrast, the blog coverage often refers to the 'humanitarian catastrophe'. This frame is only ranked in sixth position in the Russian print media, indicating that the civilian situation was seen as less important or was even deliberately omitted.

The results for Russia also show that the emerging online media provide a greater variety of actors than the traditional print media (see Table 7). Public discourse in the Russian print media is dominated by Russian actors and actors from its allies South Ossetia and Abkhazia (67.5 percent). Although actors of Russian, South Ossetian and Abkhazian origin account for the largest group in the emerging online media as well (40.6 percent), the Russian blogs far more frequently embrace people from the opposing Georgian side (28.1 percent vs. 5.2 percent in the traditional print media). Obviously, the Russian print media restrict access to actors from countries that may be counted on to express opposite opinions. This indicates a more balanced and more pluralistic discourse in the emerging online media.

To sum up, public discourse in the traditional print media and the emerging online media shows minimal differences in the EU but remarkable differences in Russia. Thus, our second hypothesis is only partly supported. This finding also implies that the third hypothesis is supported: public discourse differs more strongly among the two media types in Russia than in the EU. The rank order of the preferred frames shows little in common between the emerging online media and the traditional print media, and public discourse in the Russian print media shows a strong emphasis on Russian actors, whereas the online media account for a greater variety of actors.

Table 7: Quoted Actors in the Traditional Print and the Emerging Online Media: Russia (in Percentages)

Quoted Actors from ...	Traditional print media (n = 77 quoted actors)	Emerging online media (n = 32 quoted actors)
Russia/South Ossetia/Abkhazia	67.5	40.6
Georgia	5.2	28.1
Western countries	11.7	15.6
Eastern countries	9.1	6.3
Others	6.5	9.4

Statistical preconditions for chi-square test not fulfilled.

Conclusions

Public discourse depends on the supply of independent information concerning political processes and on the inclusion of diverse actors and opinions. Media coverage that contains a variety of actors and includes controversial views is crucial for a well-functioning public discourse.

We argued that if the traditional mass media do not allow for critical and comprehensive discourse, people will turn toward alternative sources. An important option for further political information and interpretation are the emerging online media. This source becomes especially relevant in times of war when the traditional mass media tend to carry the official positions of the country where they originate. In wartime, the public searches for orientation and looks for additional information more actively. Coverage in the emerging online media may compensate for certain deficits in the news coverage of traditional mass media.

In analyzing public discourse on the Georgian War in the Russian and in the European media, we focused on the framing patterns and on quoted actors. Open access to the media guarantees different interpretations and opinions – and therefore pluralism – and is an essential condition for a deliberative discourse. Our results indicate that the differences between public discourse in the Russian and European media are not too pronounced. Although Russia is one of the warring parties and the EU member states analyzed in our study are far less involved, both frame the Georgian War in a similar manner. Nevertheless, as far as the actors being quoted are concerned, international differences become more obvious: unsurprisingly, the Russian media strongly focus on actors from Russia, whereas the European media show a more balanced relation between actors from the two conflicting parties.

Regarding the different types of media, it can be said that differences in the framing of the traditional print media and the emerging online media could only be observed for Russia. This is consistent with the assumption that the Russian media system is highly dependent on the political system. In the traditional print media and the emerging online media, not only the rank order of the frames differs but also the percentages of the actors quoted. For the specific case of the Georgian War, these differences indicate that Russian weblogs provide additional impact and interpretation and can thus function as a corrective in public discourse. Still, it is questionable whether the emerging online media provide additional input for public discourse in those periods when routine politics dominates. Furthermore, there is no evidence indicating the number of people who turn to the Internet and the information they obtain from it. But since people tend to search actively for more information in times of crisis and war, the influence of the emerging online media on public debate and opinion should not be underestimated.

Weblogs are only one example of the emerging online media. In the past couple of years other types of emerging online media have developed and established themselves within the media landscape. Above all, social networks have given public discourse a new dimension. They became, for instance, an important communication channel during the Arabic 'Spring

Revolution' of 2011. The ongoing development of the emerging online media and their role in public discourse thus provides a rich field for further research.

Key Points

- Georgian War
- Public discourse
- International comparison
- Intermedia comparison
- Content analysis

Study Questions

1. What fundamental problems and challenges do journalists and the media face in times of war?
2. Take a closer look at the differences between the media systems of Russia and the United States (or that of any other western country) and compare their regulatory frameworks, the situation of journalists and the media content.
3. The emerging online media contribute to an increase in political participation. What arguments support or challenge this thesis?

Further Reading

Becker, Jonathan (2004) 'Lessons from Russia: A Neo-Authoritarian Media System', *European Journal of Communication* 19(2): 139–63.

Hammond, Philip (2007) *Framing Post-Cold War Conflicts. The Media and International Intervention*. Manchester; New York: Manchester University Press.

McLaughlin, Greg (2002) *The War Correspondent*. London; Sterling, VA: Pluto Press.

Schechter, Danny (2006) *When News Lies. Media Complicity and the Iraq War*. New York: SelectBooks.

Tumber, Howard and Jerry Palmer (2004) *Media at War. The Iraq Crisis*. London: Sage.

Zhou, Yuqiong and Patricia Moy (2007) 'Parsing Framing Processes: The Interplay between Online Public Opinion and Media Coverage', *Journal of Communication* 57(1): 79–98.

Websites

War Blog 1: www.blogsofwar.com.
War Blog 2: www.russiablog.org.

References

Aday, Sean, Steven Livingston and Maeve Hebert (2005) 'Embedding the Truth. A Cross-Cultural Analysis of Objectivity and Television Coverage of the Iraq War', *The Harvard International Journal of Press/Politics* 10(1): 3–21.

Baker, Edwin C. (2007) *Media Concentration and Democracy. Why Ownership Matters*. New York: Cambridge University Press.

Bär, Dorothee (2009) 'Medwedjew – Der Präsident für ein neues Russland?', *Politische Studien 424. Schwerpunktthema: Russland unter Medwedjew – eine erste Bilanz* (March/April): 30–40.

Benhabib, Seyla (1996) 'Towards the Deliberative Model of Democratic Legitimacy', pp. 67–94 in Seyla Benhabib (ed.) *Democracy and Difference. Contesting Boundaries of the Political*. Princeton, NJ: Princeton University.

Benkler, Yochai (2006) *The Wealth of Networks. How Social Production Transforms Markets and Freedom*. New Haven, CT; London: Yale University Press.

Bennett, Lance W. (1990) 'Toward a Theory of Press–State Relations in the United States', *Journal of Communication* 40(2): 103–27.

Bennett, Lance W. and Regina G. Lawrence (2008) 'Press Freedom and Democratic Accountability in a Time of War, Commercialism, and the Internet', pp. 247–67 in Doris Graber, Denis McQuail and Pippa Norris (eds) *The Politics of News. The News of Politics*. Washington, DC: CQ.

Berkel, Barbara (2006) *Konflikt als Motor europäischer Öffentlichkeit. Eine Inhaltsanalyse von Tageszeitungen in Deutschland, Frankreich, Grossbritannien und Österreich*. Wiesbaden: VS.

Bilke, Nadine (2008) *Qualität in der Krisen- und Kriegsberichterstattung. Ein Modell für einen konfliktsensitiven Journalismus*. Wiesbaden: VS.

Bucher, Hans-Jürgen (2004) 'Internet und Krieg. Informationsrisiken und Aufmerksamkeitsökonomie in der vernetzten Kriegskommunikation', pp. 275–96 in Martin Löffelholz (ed.) *Krieg als Medienereignis II. Krisenkommunikation im 21. Jahrhundert*. Opladen: Westdeutscher Verlag.

Chadwick, Andrew (2006) *Internet Politics. States, Citizens, and New Communication Technologies*. New York: Oxford University Press.

Collins, John and Ross Glover (2002) *Collateral Language. A User's Guide to America's New War*. New York; London: New York University Press.

Cooper, Stephen D. (2011) 'The Oppositional Framing of Bloggers', pp. 135–55 in Paul D'Angelo and Jim A. Kuypers (eds) *Doing News Framing Analysis. Empirical and Theoretical Perspectives*. New York; London: Routledge.

D'Angelo, Paul (2002) 'News Framing as a Multiparadigmatic Research Program: A Response to Entman', *Journal of Communication* 52(4): 870–88.

Deibert, Ronald, John Palfrey, Rafal Rohozinski and Jonathan Zittrain (eds) (2008) *Access Denied. The Practice and Policy of Global Internet Filtering*. Cambridge, MA: MIT Press.

Delhaes, Daniel (2002) *Politik und Medien. Zur Interaktionsdynamik zweier sozialer Systeme*. Wiesbaden: Westdeutscher Verlag.

Eder, Klaus and Cathleen Kantner (op. 2000) 'Transnationale Resonanzstrukturen in Europa. Eine Kritik der Rede vom Öffentlichkeitsdefizit', pp. 306–32 in Maurizio Bach (ed.) *Die Europäisierung nationaler Gesellschaften. Kölner Zeitschrift für Soziologie und Sozialpsychologie. Sonderheft 40*. Wiesbaden: Westdeutscher Verlag.

Eilders, Christiane and Albrecht Lüter (2000) 'Research Note: Germany at War. Competing Framing Strategies in German Public Discourse', *European Journal of Communication* 15(3): 415–28.

Entman, Robert M. (1993) 'Framing: Toward Clarification of a Fractured Paradigm', *Journal of Communication* 43(4): 51–8.

European Commission (2006) *Europeans and Their Language. Special Eurobarometer*, ec.europa. eu/public_opinion/archives/ebs/ebs_243_sum_en.pdf (December 19, 2011).

Fishkin, James S. (1995) *The Voice of the People. Public Opinion and Democracy*. New Haven: Yale University Press.

Forster, Christian (2009) 'Einführung', *Politische Studien 424. Schwerpunktthema: Russland unter Medwedjew – eine erste Bilanz* (March/April): 21–9.

Fraser, Nancy (1992) 'Rethinking the Public Sphere: A Contribution to the Critique of Actually Existing Democracy', pp. 109–42 in Craig J. Calhoun (ed.) *Habermas and the Public Sphere*. Cambridge, MA: MIT Press.

Goff, Peter (1999) 'Introduction', pp. 13–37 in Peter Goff and Barbara Trionfi (eds) *The Kosovo News and Propaganda War*. Vienna: International Press Institute.

Habermas, Jürgen (1992) *The Structural Transformation of the Public Sphere. An Inquiry into a Category of Bourgeois Society*. Cambridge: Polity Press.

Hammond, Philip (2007) *Framing Post-Cold War Conflicts. The Media and International Intervention*. Manchester; New York: Manchester University Press.

Herman, Edward S. and Noam Chomsky (2002) *Manufacturing Consent. The Political Economy of the Mass Media*. New York: Pantheon Books.

Hindman, Matthew (2009) *The Myth of Digital Democracy*. Oxford: Princeton University Press.

Jill, A. Edy and Patrick C. Meirick (2007) 'Wanted, Dead or Alive: Media Frames, Frame adoption, and Support for the War in Afghanistan', *Journal of Communication* 57(1): 119–141.

Krempl, Stefan (2004) *Medien, Internet, Krieg. Das Beispiel Kosovo. Ein Beitrag zur kritischen Medienanalyse*. München: Reinhard Fischer.

Lewis, Justin, Rod Brookes, Nick Mosdell and Terry Threadgold (2006) *Shoot First and Ask Questions Later. Media Coverage of the 2003 Iraq War*. New York; Washington, DC; Baltimore; Bern; Frankfurt am Main; Berlin; Brussels; Vienna; Oxford: Lang.

Lovink, Geert (2007) *Zero Comments. Blogging and Critical Internet Culture*. New York: Routledge.

Luhmann, Niklas (2000) *The Reality of the Mass Media*. Stanford, CA: Stanford University Press.

McQuail, Denis (2006) 'On the Mediatization of War. A Review Article', *International Communication Gazette* 68(2): 107–18.

McQuail, Denis, Doris Graber and Pippa Norris (2008) 'Conclusion. Contemporary Challenges in Journalism and Democracy', pp. 268–77 in Doris Graber, Denis McQuail and Pippa Norris (eds) *The Politics of News. The News of Politics*. Washington, DC: CQ.

Mermin, Jonathan (1999) *Debating War and Peace. Media Coverage of US Intervention in the Post-Vietnam Era*. Princeton, NJ: Princeton University Press.

Neuberger, Christoph, Christian Nuernbergk and Melanie Rischke (2007) 'Weblogs und Journalismus: Konkurrenz, Ergänzung oder Integration? Eine Forschungssynopse zum Wandel der Öffentlichkeit im Internet', *Media Perspektiven* (2): 96–112.

Niedermaier, Ana K. (2008) *Countdown to War in Georgia. Russia's Foreign Policy and Media Coverage of the Conflict in South Ossetia and Abkhazia.* Minneapolis, MN: East View Press.

Noam, Eli (2003) *The Internet: Still Wide Open and Competitive?* Oxford: Oxford Internet Institute, www.oii.ox.ac.uk/publications (March 2, 2011).

Norris, Pippa (2001) *Digital Divide. Civic Engagement, Information Poverty, and the Internet.* Cambridge: Cambridge University Press.

Pasti, Svetlana (2006) 'Concepts of Professional Journalism. Russia After the Collapse of Communism', pp. 72–89 in Frank Marcinkowski, Werner A. Maier and Josef Trappel (eds) *Medien und Demokratie. Europäische Erfahrungen. Media and Democracy: Experiences from Europe.* Bern: Haupt.

Pax, Salam (2003) *The Baghdad Blog.* London: Atlantic on behalf of Guardian Newspapers.

Rettberg, Jill W. (2008) *Blogging.* Cambridge, UK; Malden, MA: Polity Press.

Reynolds, Glenn H. (2006) *An Army of Davids. How Markets and Technology Empower Ordinary People to Beat Big Media, Big Government, and Other Goliaths.* Nashville, TN: Nelson Current.

Risse, Thomas and Marianne van de Steeg (2007) *The Emergence of a European Community of Communication. Insights from Empirical Research on the Europeanization of Public Spheres,* www.atasp.de (December 19, 2011).

Rutherford, Paul (2004) *Weapons of Mass Persuasion. Marketing the War against Iraq.* Toronto: University of Toronto Press.

Sunstein, Cass R. (2001) *Republic.com.* Princeton, NJ: Princeton University Press.

Taylor, Philip M. (2000) 'The World Wide Web Goes to War, Kosovo 1999', pp. 194–201 in David Gauntlett (ed.) *Web.studies. Rewiring Media Studies for the Digital Age.* London; New York: Arnold; co-published in the United States of America by Oxford University Press.

Tremayne, Mark, Nan Zheng, Jae Kook Lee and Jaekwan Jeong (2006) 'Issue Publics on the Web: Applying Network Theory to the War Blogosphere', *Journal of Computer-Mediated Communication* 12(1): 290–310.

Verba, Sidney, Kay Lehman Schlozman and Henry E. Brady (1995) *Voice and Equality. Civic Voluntarism in American Politics.* Cambridge, MA: Harvard University Press.

Vincent, Richard C. (2000) 'A Narrative Analysis of US Press Coverage of Slobodan Milosevic and the Serbs in Kosovo', *European Journal of Communication* 15(3): 321–44.

Wessler, Hartmut, Bernhard Peters, Michael Brüggemann, Katharina von Königslöw and Stefanie Sifft (2008) *Transnationalization of Public Spheres.* Basingstoke, UK; New York: Palgrave Macmillan.

Williams, Bruce A. and Michael X. Delli Carpini (2000) 'Unchained Reaction: The Collapse of Media Gatekeeping and the Clinton–Lewinsky Scandal', *Journalism* 1(1): 61–85.

Zasurskij, Ivan I. (2003) *Media and Power in Post-Soviet Russia.* New York: M. E. Sharpe.

Notes

1   TV images of conflict areas and civilian casualties usually result in an antiwar atmosphere. The impact of media coverage became strikingly apparent during the Vietnam War. As the tide of public opinion turned against the war, the American government finally had to end

its involvement. In Germany, for instance, Chancellor Schroeder's position opposing the country's participation in the Iraq War contributed greatly to his reelection in 2002.

2 A study by the Cardiff School of Journalism, Media and Cultural Studies proved the success of this strategy in achieving the desired media coverage (Lewis et al., 2006). Rutherford (2004: 7) describes the media coverage of the Iraq War as a convergence of journalism, marketing and entertainment.

3 Generally speaking, the credibility of emerging online media is ranked rather low by the public (Neuberger et al., 2007). One reason might be that antidemocratic actors who failed to attract the attention of the traditional mass media increased their presence through the online media (Sunstein, 2001).

4 For documentation on the conflicting relationship between Russia and Georgia in the past twenty years, see the press review of Niedermaier (2008).

5 See www.bbc.co.uk/worldservice/documentaries/2008/10/081029_caucases_doc.shtml (retrieved November 15, 2010).

6 See also Julia Ioffe, 'Russia and Georgia Three Years Later', August 9, 2011, www.newyorker.com/online/blogs/newsdesk/2011/08/russia-georgia-three-years-later.htm (retrieved November 15, 2011).

7 Gorbachev's policy of glasnost led to the proliferation of independent newspapers during the 1990s. However, when Putin became president, control of the media was again intensified and the freedom of the Russian press ended (Zasourskij, 2003). Today the media are highly influenced by the state, especially state television, where criticism of the government's policies is nonexistent (Forster, 2009: 23-4).

8 For this purpose, one randomly selected article for each of the sixteen media was analyzed, thus screening approximately 7 percent of the entire material.

9 Nevertheless, several studies have shown the increasing Europeanization of the public sphere, which is especially evident in times of conflict. The framing of certain incidents shows similarities throughout the national media in Europe (see Berkel, 2006; Eder and Kantner, 2000; Risse and van de Steeg, 2007; Wessler et al., 2008).

10 As a consequence, no Eastern European country is represented. This has to be taken into account when interpreting the results because a particularly critical attitude toward Russia can be expected in the Eastern European media discourse.

11 All of the analyzed emerging media concentrate on political topics and are written by ordinary citizens, journalists or politicians. For example, the weblog 'nicolaslandru.blogspot.com' is written by a freelance journalist in the Caucasus region; the author of 'www.hannes-swoboda.at' is an Austrian politician who is a member of the European Parliament, and 'www.opendemocracy.net' and 'www.wired.com' are online platforms and therefore open for everyone who wants to publish his or her opinion.

12 The category 'other actors' includes, for instance, actors from humanitarian organizations, international institutions and countries that do not fit the East–West classification.

Limitations of Journalism in War Situations

A Case Study from Georgia

Roman Hummel

Summary

H ow is reporting in international crisis situations done? In a qualitative investigation during the Georgian War in 2008, journalists and their informants were examined. The main focus was placed on the daily working routine of war correspondents and their familiarity with the region. Hypotheses concluded on the basis of the survey suggest that the quality of reporting is directly linked to the intellectual resources of journalists (understanding of local languages, background knowledge concerning the region), on one hand, and to the material resources of the media houses that dispatch them, on the other. A division into four distinctive groups (global players, special correspondents, war cowboys and background reporters) can be made. The fewer the resources they have at their disposal, the more journalists tend to resort to framing strategies: the interpretation and reporting of a given conflict is done according to concepts that were previously experienced as successful.

Introduction

The question of whether news is 'unbiased', willfully tendentious propaganda or maybe partially inaccurate because of factors beyond the intent of reporters is as old as journalism itself. Especially the coverage of wars and international conflicts by the media is discussed not only in the ranks of social scientists but even more by the general public. The debate about the trustworthiness of such information is therefore often influenced itself by propaganda and anti-propaganda.

Without a doubt, a partisan bias tends to occur in some reporting of international crises – especially by the media of those countries that are directly involved. It is also clear that journalists may involuntarily give their stories a specific spin owing to societal or cultural circumstances (for instance, because of their identification with political elites or because of an unacknowledged contempt for foreignness).

Nevertheless, the focus of this chapter is differently placed. Here the 'too often neglected' (Schudson, 2000: 175) daily routine of war correspondents is at the center of investigation. The research interest lies in the professional structures of reporting in emergency situations. Thanks to fortunate circumstances – the author had the opportunity to be in Georgia as an unpaid consultant for the United Nations High Commissioner for Refugees (UNHCR) from

September 18 to 27, 2008 – the exploration of journalism in a war situation could be done on the spot and not after the fact, when the mission had already become 'just another story of the past'. The qualitative outcome leads to the hypothesis that framing is a major factor in news production the more complex a crisis situation is and the less journalists are in a position to cover the entire range of that 'what's going on'.

The reporting of the recent war in Georgia is a good opportunity to study international crisis reporting for the following reasons: first, it was placed on the international media agenda 'out of the blue'. Therefore, the news coverage of it could not resort to common knowledge or to established stereotypes such as in long-lasting conflicts; second, the history of the incidents and also the contradictory appearance of political symbols – peacekeeping troops allowing evictions and looting by local militia, a self-declared pro-US government that still adored Stalin – complicated the work of international journalists, who were expected by their editors and the recipients of the news to explain the situation at short notice. It is assumed here that in such circumstances the structures of journalistic news gathering become more visible than in everyday situations.

This is neither the place to unfold the multifaceted history of the Caucasus region, nor am I pretending to be an expert on it. However, some facts have to be laid out simply in order for one to recognize that the Georgian conflict can honestly be understood in different ways or not at all – if one fails to dig into some factual details of the past.

Historical Background

Inhabitants with various entirely distinct languages and even more pronounced regional identities populate the country of the 'Golden Fleece' of Greek Mythology. The autochthonous four main languages, Kartwelic (Georgian), Abkhasic, Mingrelic (isolated languages) and Ossetian (an Iranian language) (Gumppenberg and Steinbach, 2008: 192ff), have nothing in common. Russian is still today's *lingua franca* – and other international languages like English are barely understood – a fact that makes reporting by international journalists often complicated. Pitfalls results also from the history of the region, which is interpretable in many different ways. The different national and international actors in this conflict are busy trying to sell their version of the past and present even with the assistance of international PR agencies.[1]

The territory claimed by today's Georgia was ruled by kings from the eleventh to the fifteenth centuries before falling apart into different principalities. They soon afterwards came under Ottoman control together with other parts of the Caucasus. From the late eighteenth century on, the Russian Empire succeeded in replacing the Turks through military actions. After the Russian Revolution of 1917, an independent Georgian Republic was declared but without the consent of the population in the territory of the actual split-away provinces of Abkhazia and Ossetia and of Ajaria in the South.

Uprisings in these regions gave the Red Army in 1921 a reason to occupy the territory and to establish the Soviet Republics of Abkhazia, Georgia, Ajaria as well as the 'Autonomous

Region of Ossetia'. Eventually in 1936 Stalin, an ethnic Georgian, decreed the incorporation of the above-mentioned territories into the 'Socialist Soviet Republic of Georgia'.

After the fall of the Soviet Union, Georgia declared its independence within the boundaries of the former constituent Soviet Republic. But so did forces in Abkhazia, Ajaria and South Ossetia (North Ossetia remained with Russia after 1991). In 1992–94 a war – of independence or secession, depending on one's interpretation – broke out, followed by massacres and ethnic cleansing. Subsequently, the Commonwealth of Independent States (CIS) obtained a UN peacekeeping mandate to secure the cease-fire, and predominantly Russian troops moved into parts of the territory of Abkhazia and South Ossetia. (Ajaria in the southwest remained under the administration of Georgia.)

During the night of the August 8, 2008, Georgian military forces took action to enter into South Ossetia but were totally defeated by the Russians, accompanied by South Ossetian *francs-tireurs*. Abkhazian militia used the opportunity to push Georgian forces out of those parts of the province's territory they were still in. As was also true of the first struggles for different forms of independence between 1992 and 1994, the fighting of 2008 resulted in the flight and expulsion of many civilians. As in the battles of 1992 and 1994, different militias with different ethnic, political and economic backgrounds and interests were again involved on both sides. The hot phase of the crisis was terminated by the signing of a cease-fire by Russia and Georgia on August 15 and 16, 2008. The decision by the Russian Parliament to acknowledge Abkhazia and South Ossetia as sovereign states led to international disputes and again brought Georgia into the headlines, but this was mostly covered from outside of the region.

The return to 'normal' political tension and, as a result, the disappearance of the conflict from the international media agenda can be dated to October 1, 2008, when the EU Monitoring Mission to Georgia became operational.

Methods and Data Set

Just before my research in Georgia began, a short questionnaire (fifteen items only) in English was designed and distributed to international journalists in the region from August 16 onward. With the help of local supporters and journalists' networks, a questionnaire was distributed electronically as well as in a printed version in different places in Georgia where foreign correspondents used to meet. The main focus of this questionnaire[2] was on the journalists' experience in crisis reporting, their familiarity with the region in question, their reflection on reliable sources, their support network in Georgia, and on their knowledge of the regional languages, including Russian.

Although the questionnaire was personally handed over or posted to at least one hundred journalists who were in Georgia at the time, the return rate was a failure (only one response). As personal interviews with correspondents[3] revealed later, the lack of confidence and the sneaking suspicion one could be named and criticized in public was the main reason for the nonresponse.

The outcome of the study is therefore based on eight directed interviews *in situ* with (a) journalists, (b) leading representatives of the UNHCR Caucasian mission who were regularly being contacted by international journalists and (c) on personal observation during my work[4] in Tbilisi, Gori, Zugdidi as well as in the Abkhazian part of the country (Gagra, Sukhumi). This small qualitative field study can only claim to be indicative and serves therefore as a means for generating hypotheses.

The Situation of Journalists

International journalists were never subject to accreditation procedures in Georgia, neither by the Georgian authorities nor by UNHCR, even though the latter took it into consideration for reasons of protection,[5] since, on the one hand, there were reports of intrusions into the privacy of displaced persons,[6] and on the other hand, the professional status and the intentions of people pretending to be journalists were not always clear. People could also travel any time without any restriction and without the need for a visa for Georgia, but they could not travel to Abkhazia or South Ossetia. This is the reason why no data about the number of journalists reporting on the Georgian crisis are available.

According to UNHCR staff,[7] who gained their experience in several crisis operations worldwide, two waves of journalistic investigations occur when crises break out. They unanimously emphasized this similarity when discussing different regional hot spots such as Kosovo, Afghanistan, Iraq and Georgia.

In the first phase, which lasts from the outbreak of violence until significant signs of de-escalation occur (such as a cease-fire), the lion's share of international media coverage is done. Most journalists leave the hot spot after the conflict subsides. Three types of journalists of differently structured backgrounds move in during this period (see also Table 1):

Table 1: The Two Waves of Journalistic Investigations after a Crisis Break Out

1st wave of conflict	Global players
	Special correspondents
	Cowboys
2nd wave of conflict	Global players
	Background reporters

- Type 1: 'Global players in journalism' (working for the BBC, CNN, AP etc.) with a huge amount of technical and intellectual resources.

  These reporters are described as professional and as personally and structurally well equipped. Most of them have already covered the region in question for a longer period;

a number of them have at least a basic command of local languages (in the case of Georgia, mostly Russian); they have solid background knowledge, and they are mostly supported by a team that assists them with concrete journalistic tasks (pre-research, seeking for competent interview partners) as well as with the technical aspects (booking of accommodations, reliable stringers, drivers, transmission facilities). Compared with their colleagues mentioned below, they also have sufficient financial resources at their disposal. On-the-ground investigation often takes place once basic desk research by the home editorial board has occurred.

- Type 2: 'Special correspondents', the greatest number of reporters in the hot phase of a conflict.

The majority of these journalists are general war or foreign policy reporters who work mostly in a stand-alone situation. Not all of them are fully employed by one media organization, and they therefore sell stories to different publishers. They have limited time and economic resources and are forced to produce stories with a minimum of expenditure. They are experienced journalists and have in most cases also covered other crises. But they have only a limited knowledge of the given conflict's background, and their command of regional languages is for the most part poor. Hence they are inclined to engage in 'self-embedding' and depend on local authorities and international organizations for transportation, interpreters, background information, accommodations and so on.

Their lack of means for carrying out in-depth research is often compensated for by recourse to seemingly clear-cut news techniques such as personalization, archetypes (helpless mothers with children, tented refugees etc.) or good versus bad dichotomies. According to the informants who were contacted in this study in Georgia, the majority of these journalists are more interested in 'human stories of misery and glory' than in in-depth background information. Similar observations are reported from the Kosovo crisis: journalists even knew in advance what they wanted to hear from the refugees they interviewed in their efforts to get a perfect touching story.[8]

- Type 3: The third group, the smallest of the three, is referred to by other journalists as 'war cowboys'.[9]

In contrast to other journalists, for the most part they do not even have contract with a media outlet but instead try to produce scoops on their own and sell the result of their investigations to anyone who is willing to pay them, from publishing houses to relief organizations but sometimes even to less reputable institutions. Their knowledge of the facts is rated as low as their professional ethics.

The second phase of a crisis – after the military operations have officially stopped (during the recent events in Georgia, this was after August 16) – attracts far fewer correspondents. The 'global players' reduce the size of their teams but remain in the region; 'special correspondents' and 'cowboys' leave when no further escalation is expected.

In this phase, the medium-sized, quality media send 'background reporters' to produce bigger background stories as long as the conflict remains sufficiently topical. These journalists are in most cases well prepared (this fact also emerged from interviews with journalists conducted after the cease-fire in Georgia), have their itinerary and budget arranged in advance, and in numerous cases also work as regional correspondents (in this case, mostly in Moscow[10]). Even though they mostly work alone, they share facilities, drivers and stringers, thus giving the impression that they are not competing for scoops. Some of them had already been to Georgia before, not only during the most recent war episode.

As the main sources for their research, they name other media such as the BBC, Reuters and AP, as well as UN organizations, the Organization for Security and Co-operation in Europe (OSCE) and the web reports of humanitarian nongovernmental organizations (such as Human Rights Watch, Memorial, the Institute for War and Peace Reporting). Special emphasis is placed on their own in-depth knowledge of the region and their skills in Russian. Nonetheless, in direct contact with locals, none of the observed journalists was able to communicate properly without a Russian-speaking interpreter.

General Observations on the Work of Journalists in Georgia

Personal observations combined with conversations and interviews with UNHCR staff and journalists in Georgia could be condensed to the following conclusions.

One main factor in the reporting done specifically in unclear and confusing situations – as a crisis mostly is – obviously consists of what Goffman (1980: 17) has called framing: an interpretation of a social situation on the basis of a previously learned concept. We try to organize our perception by defining certain situations on the basis of our earlier experiences. This factor is related to the behavioral learning theory (see Prisching, 1992: 48), that is, assuming that an activity will continue to be carried out the more it proves itself successful or the more peers act in the same way. Frames are essential for a rapid understanding of that 'what's going on', but they can easily be used for deception or result in illusions.

A striking example of framing was the journalistic coverage of the only tented camp for displaced persons in the city of Gori, which according to the UNHCR never had more than 3,000 inhabitants – a fraction of less than 2 percent of the 190,000 temporarily displaced persons. Contradictorily enough, it was also the most visited site of foreign correspondents in Georgia. Journalists, their editors and, of course, their audience too have learned from the presentations of past crises: 'real refugees' live in tents (see Figure 1).

Another reason for the media influx into the Gori camp was the fact that it was located in the periphery of a larger city and could be reached in a mere two-hour drive from the capital. The misery of other refugees who sought shelter in dilapidated former hotels (see Figure 2) was hardly of any interest to foreign reporters.

The Georgian government even had the idea of using the frame of a tented camp, thus signifying the tragedy of war, as part of their PR strategy. There were plans to construct a tent city directly beside the airport in Tbilisi to demonstrate the severity of the refugee problem

Figure 1: A Visitor in Gori Camp; Photo: R. Hummel.

Figure 2: A Refugee Sitting in the Run-Down Hall of a Former Hotel in Tbilisi; Photo: R. Hummel.

to all those people who came to Georgia. A feeling for 'journalistic framing', as Robinson (2002: 130) has pointed out, can obviously facilitate strategic 'information management' by the interested parties.

Furthermore, the Gori camp, unlike the other shelters for displaced persons, also became one of the principal meeting points for representatives of international political organizations such as members of the European Parliament. To state the matter cynically, they all saw in the camp what they expected to see in a hardship situation, but in doing so they neglected other more important aspects. Presumably, the readers and viewers of such clearly framed news might also be given the false impression that they understand better 'what's going on'.

The media's focus on the tent city in Gori seems to demonstrate that the selection of reportable events is not only determined by classic news values such as simplicity, proximity and sensation, but perhaps even more so by easy accessibility. The conflict in western Georgia, which led to the complete splitting-off of the province of Abkhazia, solicited – according to the informants interviewed for this study – less attention on the part of foreign correspondents than the conflict in central Georgia. In the latter case, the conflict is also at a less convenient distance from Tbilisi.

The presence of interested journalists in a certain place because of international attention seems to upgrade the newsworthiness of every event that occurs there. The facts that under normal conditions are not considered worthy of international coverage have an increased chance of being reported if they can be suitably framed (like a thunderstorm that caused the flooding of streets and agricultural damage in mid-September 2008[11]). Not only extraordinary events such as war attract journalists and reporting, but also the reporters who are attracted have to prove that they are worth their salary by reporting as much as they can. The presence of journalists creates news. In this respect, the reporting from international hot spots also contains some incidental elements.

One could argue that the framing of a specific situation by journalists is nothing more than the selection of newsworthy events on the basis of certain news criteria. The findings from this research in Georgia suggest, however, that news factors and framing are different but complementary forms of news selection. Each story reported by professional journalists is selected and told according to certain news factors. Framing is an additional process in news gathering, one that allows the effort required for news production to be minimized. This makes journalistic operations more cost effective but trivializes the output at the same time.

Concluding Hypotheses

- The depth of reporting from crisis regions is essentially influenced by the structure of the working conditions of journalists. This includes personal preparation as well as the time devoted to research, the budget and the organization in the field.

- One cannot speak of 'crisis journalism' as such: there is a considerable difference between at least two groups: a well-equipped one that is associated with big 'media players' and at least one other that is forced to produce without having sufficient means to do so.
- The less resources journalists have (i.e., time, money, knowledge), the more attention they pay to the general stereotypes of conflicts in general – even when those stereotypes do not help to explain the particular situation as such: dichotomies (good guys vs. bad guys), human misery ('blood in the streets', destruction) or iconographic stereotypes (tent camps). The quality of the infrastructure that journalists have at their disposal in each particular case has more influence on the coverage than the news factors of the event itself.
- The more the actual facts match situations that have been encountered in earlier reporting (learned frames), the more likely it is that they will be reported and vice versa. The specific characteristics of a crisis thus have less of a chance of being covered. An example from the Georgian conflict is the internationally rarely reported devotion

Figure 3: Red Cross Trucks in Front of the Stalin Monument in Gori; Photo: R. Hummel.

to Stalin, which means not only that more than two-thirds of the population are in favor of the still standing Stalin monuments but also that 'touristy gimmicks' such as 'Stalin wine' are sold in souvenir shops (see Figure 3).[12] The more complex a crisis situation is and the less journalists there are who can be considered prepared, the more these journalist resort to framing strategies.

- The presence of journalists creates news out of events that otherwise would hardly be noticed. This might also be true in reverse: the absence of international journalists on site means that even newsworthy incidents are left unreported, as Nick Davies of *The Guardian* has described it in his philippic on journalism (Davies, 2009: 117).

As a concept useful in the empirical examination of the above-mentioned hypotheses, professional perception must be a focus. The 'filtering of reality' by journalists obviously develops under the influence of a 'power triangle' consisting of the structure of working conditions, news values considered as an adjustment of the character of an event to the presumed interest of the public, and framing such as it results from the personal and collective learning process needed for interpreting reality.

Key Points

- War correspondence
- Framing concept
- Coverage of Georgian conflict
- Newsworthiness
- Working situation of crisis journalism

Study Questions

1. What impact does the working environment of journalists have on the quality of news?
2. How could one verify or disprove the hypotheses that have been raised here?
3. Why are journalists hesitant to discuss their working background?

Further Reading

Goffman, Erving (1974) *Frame Analysis. An Essay on the Organization of Experience.* Boston, MA: Northeastern University Press.
Preston, Paschal, Monika Metykova and Jacques Guyot (2009) *Making the News. Journalism and News Cultures in Europe.* London; New York: Routledge.

Websites

Institute for War and Peace Reporting: iwpr.net.

References

Chupick, Jason (2008) 'Russia vs Georgia PR War Continues', *PRNewser*, August 27, 2008, http://www.mediabistro.com/prnewser/russia-vs-georgia-pr-war-continues_b944 (December 19, 2011).

Davies, Nick (2009) *Flat Earth News. An Award-Winning Reporter Exposes Falsehood, Distortion and Propaganda in the Global Media*. London: Vintage Books.

Goffman, Erving (1980) *Rahmen-Analyse. Ein Versuch über die Organisation von Alltagserfahrungen*. Frankfurt am Main: Suhrkamp.

Gumppenberg, Marie-Carin von and Udo Steinbach (eds) (2008) *Der Kaukasus. Geschichte – Kultur – Politik*. München: Beck.

Hall, Peter C. and Martin Berthoud (eds) (2001) *Krieg mit Bildern. Wie Fernsehen Wirklichkeit konstruiert*. Mainz: ZDF.

Prisching, Manfred (1992) *Soziologie. Themen – Theorien – Perspektiven*. Wien; Köln; Weimar: Böhlau.

Richter, Simone (1999) *Journalisten zwischen den Fronten. Kriegsberichterstattung am Beispiel Jugoslawien*. Opladen: Westdeutscher Verlag.

Robinson, Piers (2002) *The CNN Effect. The Myth of News, Foreign Policy, and Intervention*. London; New York: Routledge.

Schudson, Michael (2000) 'The Sociology of News Production Revisited', pp. 175–200 in James Curran and Michael Gurevitch (eds) *Mass Media and Society*. London: Arnold.

Notes

1 According to Chupick (2008), Russia used the PR agencies 'GPlus Europe', and Georgia, 'Aspect Consulting', 'Orion Strategies' and 'Squire Sanders Public Advocacy'.

2 It was later used as the basic concept for the narrative interviews with journalists.

3 All the journalists interviewed in Georgia worked for European media, for print, public broadcasting as well as news agencies; as not all of them were willing to be quoted, no further specification can be given.

4 I served as a photographer for UNHCR.

5 Interview with Alessandra Morelli, head of the UNHCR Emergency Unit, Gori, September 19, 2008.

6 According to international law, the term for a person who flees within the territory of the state he or she is a citizen of is 'displaced person', not 'refugee'.

7 Interview partners were in alphabetical order: Stefano Berti, Florian Hassel, Alessandra Morelli, Melita Sunjic, Tapio Vahtola.

8 Told by Jörg Brase, a ZDF reporter: in this particular case, it was the separation of families (Hall and Berthoud, 2001: 123). Stefan Reineke, also a ZDF reporter at the time of the Kosovo crisis, recounts an unconfirmed anecdote of an American journalist bumping into a refugee camp who asks, 'anybody here speaking English and raped' (Hall and Berthoud, 2001: 121).

9 See Richter (1999: 136) about the Kosovo crisis and Hall and Berthoud (2001: 132) about Chechnya, where the increasing number of such 'war cowboys' and 'instant experts' with little journalistic proficiency is a matter of complaint.

10 Accreditation in the Russian Federation was the only way for journalists at the time to get an entry permit into Abkhazia or South Ossetia. Only UN staff were allowed to enter from the Russian and from the Georgian side.

11 RSOE Emergency and Disaster Information Service, Budapest, Hungary, 2008–09–21 17:12:01 – Flood – Georgia, EDIS CODE: FL-20080921–18601–GEO.

12 See *Georgia Times*, September 7, 2009, www.georgiatimes.info/en/news/20808.html.

Mass-Mediated Debate about Torture in Post-9/11 America

Brigitte L. Nacos

Summary

The question whether to torture captured terrorists arose in the United States soon after the terrorist attacks of September 11, 2001. Both the entertainment and the news media shaped the discourse around the treatment of so-called 'enemy combatants' and, by extension, the trade-offs between security and civil liberties/human rights. As this chapter shows, systematic quantitative and qualitative content analyzes of print and television news and an assessment of the long-running television drama *24* revealed biases in favor of torture before the actual torturing of detainees at Abu Ghraib and other US-run detention facilities abroad were revealed and before the great reluctance to use the T-word for torture in pertinent news reports emerged. Based on anecdotal evidence and public opinion trends, the author assumes links between mass media content, on the one hand, and attitudes about torture among policy-makers and the general public, on the other.

Introduction

> [A]t Abu Ghraib prison, outside of Baghdad, an Iraqi prisoner […] Manadel al-Jamadi, died during an interrogation. His head had been covered with a plastic bag, and he was shackled in a crucifixion-like pose that inhibited his ability to breathe; according to forensic pathologists who have examined the case, he asphyxiated. (Mayer, 2005)

In the fall of 2007, during his confirmation hearing before the US Senate's Judiciary Committee, attorney general designate Michael Musakey claimed to be clueless as to the nature of waterboarding. He said that he did not know whether this interrogation technique constituted torture. In a letter to the committee, he seemed to side with the administration's position that CIA interrogations of terrorists, or suspected terrorists, are exempt from anti-torture laws that the military and others must follow. He was confirmed as the highest US official to enforce the laws of the land. Once in office, Mukasey did not change his position. Instead, during an appearance before the Senate Judiciary Committee, he said that he would not rule out the use of torture in the future (Shenon, 2008).

Waterboarding has been used as a method of torture for hundreds of years. In more recent times, it has been practiced by human rights violators among state and non-state actors. According to one account, 'in some versions of the technique, prisoners are strapped to a board, their faces covered with cloth or cellophane, and water is poured over their mouths to stimulate drowning; in others, they are dunked head-first into water' (Human Rights Watch, 2006). In the past, US authorities considered this particularly gruesome interrogation method to be torture and punishable as a war crime. Thus, following World War II, 'US military commissions successfully prosecuted as war criminals several Japanese soldiers who subjected American prisoners to waterboarding. A US army officer was court-marshaled in 1968 for helping to waterboard a prisoner in Vietnam' (Human Rights Watch, 2006).

But that changed after 9/11. Waterboarding and other torture techniques were no longer off-limits in the 'war on terrorism'. While some reports about 'aggressive interrogation' methods of so-called 'enemy combatants' in US-run prisons abroad had been published earlier, most Americans learned about such gross human rights violations in the spring of 2004, when CBS News on *60 Minutes* and Seymour Hersh in *The New Yorker* revealed the torturous treatment of detainees at Abu Ghraib. Administration officials blamed the isolated incidents on rogue soldiers, but eventually evidence showed that 'harsh' interrogation practices – indeed, torture – were backed by opinions written and approved by legal experts in the White House and the Departments of Justice and Defense in express violation of the United Nations Convention against Torture, the US Constitution and the Uniformed Code of Military Justice.[1]

Referring to what administration critics called 'torture memos', Donald P. Gregg, national security advisor from 1982 to 1988 to then Vice President George H.W. Bush, wrote in 2004,

> Recent reports indicate that Bush administration lawyers, in their struggles to deal with terrorism, wrote memos in 2003 pushing aside longstanding prohibitions on the use of torture by Americans. These memos cleared the way for the horrors that have been revealed in Iraq, Afghanistan and Guantánamo and make a mockery of administration assertions that a few misguided enlisted personnel perpetrated the vile abuse of prisoners. [...] I can think of nothing that can more devastatingly undercut America's standing in the world or, more important, our view of ourselves, than these decisions. Sanctioned abuse is deeply corrosive – just ask the French, who are still seeking to eradicate the stain on their honor that resulted from the deliberate use of torture in Algeria. (Gregg, 2004)

But in spite of evidence to the contrary, the administration denied that detainees were being or had been tortured. After the US Congress adopted and the president signed a bill with anti-torture provisions in October 2006, President George W. Bush insisted in his signing statement that the new law 'will allow the Central Intelligence Agency to continue its program for questioning key terrorist leaders and operatives' (White House, News Release, October 17, 2006[2]). He claimed that it was the president's prerogative to decide what methods CIA interrogators were allowed to use. But in the same breath, he continued to tell Americans and the rest of the world that he had not authorized torture, that torture was against America's laws and values, and that the United States did not torture. Similarly, right after Vice President

Richard Cheney stated in a radio interview that the 'dunk in water' (meaning waterboarding) in the interrogation of detainees was a 'no-brainer', he added, 'We don't torture. That's not what we're involved in' (White House, News Release, October 24, 2006[3]).

The White House clung to the 'we-do-not-torture' line even after CIA director Michael V. Hayden admitted in early 2008 that waterboarding had been used during the interrogations of three leading al-Qaeda figures, Abu Zubayda, Abd al-Rahim al-Nashiri and Khalid Sheikh Mohammed. In reaction, a White House spokesperson said that President Bush would 'authorize waterboarding future terrorism suspects if certain criteria are met' (Fromkin, 2008). Vice President Cheney 'vigorously defended the use of harsh interrogation techniques on a few suspected terrorists saying that the methods made up "a tougher program, for tougher customers"' (Stout and Shane, 2008). Neither the president nor vice president considered waterboarding or 'harsh interrogation techniques' to be torture.

Not surprisingly, on March 8, 2008, President Bush announced during his regular Saturday morning radio address that he had vetoed legislation that would have prohibited the CIA from using waterboarding and other harsh interrogation tactics. He justified his veto by stating that the prohibitions 'would take away one of the most valuable tools on the war on terror'. And he added that 'this is no time for Congress to abandon practices that have a proven track record of keeping America safe' (White House, Presidential Radio Address, March 8, 2008[4]). In other words, torturing terrorists and suspected terrorists remained part of Mr. Bush's 'war on terrorism'.

Besides prohibiting torture altogether, the vetoed bill would have banned the following:

- Forcing a prisoner to be naked, perform sexual acts or pose in a sexual manner
- Placing hoods or sacks over the head of a prisoner and using duct tape over the eyes
- Waterboarding
- Using military working dogs
- Inducing hypothermia or heat injury
- Depriving a prisoner of necessary food, water or medical care

As far as the administration's 'aggressive interrogation' policies and practices were concerned, the dye was cast long before the public learned about the torturing of detainees at Abu Ghraib and elsewhere, long before torture became part of the public debate.

Mass Media, Public Opinion and Torture after 9/11

How did the media deal with the torture issue in the months and early years after the horrific terrorist attacks on September 11, 2001? After examining pertinent media content, the following chapter addresses the question whether and how the media's handling of the torture issue might have contributed to public and elite sentiments.

Did the mass-mediated torture debate after 9/11 play a part in the creation of a public climate that may have emboldened administration officials to disregard domestic and international laws against the use of torture and encourage the actual violation of detainees' human rights?

Entertainment Media

In March 2002, ABC News anchor Ted Koppel showed participants of an electronic town hall meeting on torture and curbs of civil liberties in general, a scene from the TV series *NYPD Blues* in which detective Andy Sipowicz brutally 'tuned up' a suspect (*Nightline Townhall Meeting*, ABC News, March 8, 2002). A year later, *World News Tonight with Peter Jennings* opened with a segment on 'torture or persuasion' by showing a torture scene from the motion picture *The Siege* with Bruce Willis. The clip underlined that, as Jackie Judd said, 'Hollywood's version of torture knows no limits' (ABC News, March 4, 2003). Marc McGuire, the TV/radio writer of the *Times Union* in Albany, NY, concluded, 'Today on TV, sanctioned torture and murder are condoned like never before, not only by the individual characters, but also their employers.'

This pro-torture trend in the entertainment offerings was thought to bolster the support for tough antiterrorism measures that included curbs on civil liberties and human rights values in the name of greater security. According to Robert Thompson, an expert on popular television, '[t]he federal government could not have come up with a better set of [TV] series to prepare its audience for the new order of the day' (McGuire, 2003).

For years, the Fox TV series *24* has been highest on the hit list of these especially brutal shows. According to one critic, the series' hero Jack Bauer, played by Kiefer Sutherland, 'makes torture popular' (Canadian Broadcasting Company, February 12, 2009[5]). Jane Mayer (2008) and Philippe Sands (2008) reveal that although the creation of a Hollywood writer without any expertize in intelligence or the military, *24* influenced American interrogation doctrine. Lawyers in the Bush administration who wrote legal opinions in support of 'aggressive interrogation' admired Jack Bauer, the torture scenes he presided over and the high success rate of his brutal methods. Among his early admirers was John Yoo, the author of the so-called 'torture papers'. Michael Chertoff, at the time deputy attorney general and eventually secretary of homeland security in the Bush administration, said in a panel discussion at a conservative think tank that the series 'reflects real life' (Lithwick, 2008).

Diane Beaver, the top military lawyer at Guantánamo, told Sands that in search for finding an interrogation model that worked, Jack Bauer of *24* 'gave people lots of ideas' (Mayer, 2008: 196). She revealed that while working in the Guantánamo facility, 'We saw it [*24*] on cable' and the series was 'hugely popular' (Sands, 2008: 62). Furthermore, Beaver told Sands that *24* scenes 'contributed to an environment in which those at Guantánamo were encouraged to see themselves as being on the frontline – and go further than they otherwise might' (Sands, 2008: 62). During a panel discussion on terrorism and the law in Ottawa, a Canadian judge said, 'Thankfully, security agencies in all our countries do not subscribe to the mantra "What would Jack Bauer do?". US Supreme Court Justice Anthony Scalia disagreed and argued, 'Jack Bauer saved Los Angeles [...] He saved hundreds of thousands of lives. Are you going to convict Jack Bauer? Say that criminal law is against him? Is any jury going to convict Jack Bauer? I don't think so!' (Lattman, 2007).

Rank and file soldiers, too, became fans of Jack Bauer and his deeds. In early 2007, Brigadier General Patrick Finnegan of the West Point Military Academy met producers of the show in California. He told them that promoting illegal behavior in the series was having a damaging effect on young troops (Shakir, 2007).

Research has demonstrated that heavy television viewers are affected over time by the predominant values expressed in the programs they watch regardless whether they watch entertainment or news (Shanahan and Morgan, 1999). Thus, one wonders whether the proliferation of brutality and torture in motion pictures and television entertainment in general and Jack Bauer's frequently torturous treatment of suspected terrorists in particular influenced the views and actions of legal experts and rank-and-file guards in military prisons.

The Role, Influence and Responsibility of the Press

Unlike the entertainment media, the news media have particular responsibilities in terms of their public affairs content. Although aware of the influence of entertainment media, the main focus here is on qualitative and, to a lesser extent, quantitative content analyses of print and television news and political discussion and talk programs after 9/11.

The press freedom that liberal democracies guarantee their presses, and that is close to absolutist in the United States, comes with a set of responsibilities. In Article I of its 'Statement of Principles', the American Society of Newspaper Editors (ASNE), a pioneer in articulating and promoting journalistic ethics, summarizes the most fundamental role of the press as follows, 'The American press was made free not just to inform or just to serve as a forum for debate but also to bring an independent scrutiny to bear on the forces of power in the society, including the conduct of official power at all levels of government' (American Society of Newspaper Editors, 1996).[6]

This is an affirmation of the ideal of the press as medium of information, as facilitator of public discourse and as watchdog of government, and of the most fundamental values of the democratic system – most of all that it is one of laws, not men. To torture or not to torture was one of the issues that arose after the attacks of 9/11 and related directly to America's fundamental values. Reason enough to examine how the press discharged its responsibility in this particular case.

Mass-Mediated Torture Debate Before the Abu Ghraib Revelations

While the debate about the pro and contra of torture in the 'war on terrorism' was not particularly high on the news media's agenda after 9/11 and before the Abu Ghraib revelations, the issue was not ignored either. Typically, political talk show hosts, expert guests, reporters, commentators and columnists handled this subject in a rather cavalier fashion. Stewart Taylor Jr., for example, wrote in the *National Journal*:

> Unlike the 1949 Geneva Convention regarding prisoners of war, the torture convention protects even terrorists and other 'unlawful combatants'. But its definition of torture – intentional infliction of 'severe pain or suffering, whether physical or mental' – leaves room for interpretation. It's a good bet that Khalid Sheikh Mohammed [captured al-Qaeda chief-of-operation in US custody] has felt some pain. And if that's the best chance of making him talk, it's OK by me. (Taylor, 2003)

Newsweek columnist Jonathan Alter suggested,

> Even as we continue to speak out against human-rights violations around the world, we need to keep an open mind about certain measures to fight terrorism, like court-sanctioned psychological interrogation. And we'll have to think about transferring some suspects to our less squeamish allies, even if that's hypocritical. Nobody said this was going to be pretty. (Alter, 2001)

In the *Atlantic Monthly*, Mark Bowden distinguished between hard-core torture and torture lite or what he suggested should be called 'coercion'. With respect to torture lite, he wrote, 'Although excruciating for the victim, these tactics leave no permanent marks and do no lasting physical harm' (Bowden, 2003: 53). Finally, he embraced a curious double standard:

> The Bush Administration has adopted exactly the right posture on the matter. Candor and consistency are not always public virtues. Torture is a crime against humanity, but coercion is an issue that is rightly handled with a wink, or even a touch of hypocrisy; it should be banned but also quietly practiced. (Bowden, 2003: 76)

In other words, do it, but do not admit it and do not get caught. After his article was published, Bowden was interviewed on several TV programs. The hosts and anchors seemed not uncomfortable with his views.

When opponents of torture did appear on such shows, they were typically drawn from human rights/civil liberty organizations and allotted less time to articulate their arguments than were the supporters of any form or some type of torture. While not favoring wholesale torture, Harvard law professor Alan Dershowitz did not argue in favor of wholesale torture; he suggested torture in extreme cases, when a judge can be convinced that a detainee has knowledge of an imminent terrorist attack. In such a 'ticking time bomb' scenario, he recommended torture as the only chance to get the information to prevent a terrorist strike (Dershowitz, 2002). Dershowitz published op-ed pieces that explained his view and was repeatedly interviewed on high-profile TV network programs – twice on CBS, thrice on NBC. The search words 'Alan Dershowitz' and 'torture' materialized several dozen hits in the Lexis/Nexis all-transcripts category for the two-year period from October 1, 2001 to September 30, 2003.

Harvard law professor and former Deputy Attorney General of the United States Philip Heymann rejected torture warrants as suggested by his colleague. He argued, 'Judges have deferred to the last fourteen thousand requests for national security wiretaps and they would defer here' (Heyman, 2003: 111). Unlike Dershowitz, Heymann did not get much media attention. *The Boston Globe* was a notable exception: on February 16, 2002 the newspaper published opinion pieces by Dershowitz and Heymann side by side on the op-ed page.

Some of the leading newspapers took editorial stands against torture. *The Washington Post*, for example, published two such editorials in the two years after 9/11. In one of them, the newspaper stated, 'there are certain things democracies don't do, even under duress, and torture is high on the list' ('Torture Is Not an Option', *The Washington Post*, December 27, 2002: A24). Other editorial pages rejected torture most of the time but accepted it in the context of the post-9/11 'war on terrorism'. Thus, the *Buffalo News* editorialized,

A recent story in the *Washington Post* makes clear what every American must have already suspected regarding the treatment of al-Qaeda and Taliban prisoners. Harsh treatment, perhaps to the point of torture. For the most part, we're not losing sleep over that revelation, given the facts of the last 15 months. But while aggressive interrogation techniques are both important and even, to a point, acceptable, there still must be rules and mechanisms for accountability to prevent wholesale torture. ('A Question of Torture', 2002)

Some of the media's chosen experts were enthusiastic advocates of wholesale torture and vilified the opponents of this interrogation method. These voices became more frequent and louder in the media after the capture of Khalid Sheikh Mohammed, an al-Qaeda operative thought to have organized and coordinated the 9/11 attacks. Law professor emeritus Henry Mark Holzer, for example, wrote,

There are those among us – Jimmy Carter-like pacifists and Ramsey Clark-type America haters come to mind – who would probably stand by idly and endure an atomic holocaust. But most people would doubtless opt for torture, albeit reluctantly. These realists – and I suspect they are a large majority of the American public – would be correct. In approving the use of torture – or at least accepting it – they needn't suffer even a scintilla of moral guilt. Torture of whatever kind, and no matter how brutal, in defense of human rights and legitimate self-preservation is not only not immoral; it is a moral imperative. (Holzer, 2003)

All in all, advocates of torture, torture lite, coercion, aggressive interrogation and extraordinary rendition (meaning the outsourcing of torture to states known as notorious human rights violators) were frequently represented and rarely challenged in television news and talk programs and on the op-ed pages of newspapers in the two-and-a-half years after 9/11.

The Public and Torture Before the Abu Ghraib Revelations

Some of the torture advocates claimed to have popular support on their side in that 'most people would doubtless opt for torture, albeit reluctantly' (Holzer, 2003). Such claims were not born out by actual public opinion surveys but based on what Robert Entman has called 'perceived public opinion'. According to Entman,

> [P]erceived opinion is the general sense of the public's opinions that is held by most observers, including journalists and politicians, and members of the public themselves. This is a convenient fiction observers use to characterize the comprehensive preferences of a majority of citizens [...] Polling opinion and perceived public opinion may or may not be identical, because politicians and journalists frequently ignore survey results, in part because the data are so often inconclusive and in part because neglecting polls can be strategically useful. Instead, they just declaim about what the American people allegedly believe – and they can usually find a poll somewhere to support them. (Entman, 2000: 21)

Table 1 shows that contrary to 'perceived public opinion' the American public was not in favor of torture in the months after 9/11. Instead, a majority or plurality of the public opposed torture in the few surveys conducted. It was only after the capture of Khalid Sheikh Mohammed in early March 2003 and a mass-mediated debate in which proponents of torture took strong stands that the only available survey revealed a public opinion move toward more support for torture. Taking into account the margin of error, there was a tie between supporters and opponents of torture.

Table 1: US Public Opinion on the Torture of Terrorists/Suspected Terrorists before the Abu Ghraib Revelations (in Percentages)

	Support	Oppose	Depends/don't know/ not sure
Gallup/CNN/USA TODAY October 5–6, 2001	45	53	3
Fox News/Opinion Dynamics March 12–13, 2002	41	47	12
Fox News/Opinion Dynamic March 12–13, 2003	44	42	14

The 'They' against 'Us' Divide

The most extreme advocates of torture in the mass media debate had a great deal in common with terrorists in that they used the same techniques to push the 'they' against 'us' divide that is central to terrorist rhetoric. One way to vilify 'them' and set 'them' apart is a process of moral disengagement during which the enemies 'are depersonalized and dehumanized. They are derogated to the ranks of subhuman species. Dehumanization makes it possible for the radicals to be disengaged morally and to commit atrocities without a second thought' (Sprinzak, 1990: 82).

For terrorists, part of the moral disengagement process has long been the practice of looking upon 'them' as animals, calling them 'pigs' or 'dogs'. Efforts to dehumanize terrorists or alleged terrorists were not absent from the terrorism debate before and after the Abu Ghraib revelations.

Thus, in early 2003, after the capture of Khalid Sheikh Mohammed, Jack Wheeler of the Freedom Research Foundation appeared on the Fox News' *Hannity & Colmes* program. When Alan Colmes asked, 'Tell us what you want to do to this guy', Dr. Wheeler answered, 'Whatever is necessary to extract the information that he has out of his brain. And I mean whatever is necessary'. Later in the program, the guest said in an exchange with host Sean Hannity, 'I don't care what you do to him. This man is a piece of human garbage.' Hannity's answer: 'Well I agree with that' (*Hannity & Colmes*, Fox News, March 5, 2003). Shortly after the Abu Ghraib revelations, a former CIA operative said in a discussion of interrogation methods,

> We catch an al Qaeda member, we knows [sic] he's al Qaeda, his life as he knows it has got to be over. Listen, I lived with these animals. This is a sub-human species of somehow a deviation of the human, of the true human. They care for nothing. They kill everything in their path. All bets are off. This is an animal that's unlike any we've ever faced. (*Hannity & Colmes*, Fox News, May 13, 2004)

One wonders whether the perception of real or alleged enemies in the 'war on terrorism' as 'garbage', 'animals' and 'subhuman' contributed to the attitudes of those who allowed and committed the torturing of detainees in American-controlled facilities.

One American soldier, an MP who had worked at Abu Ghraib prison, for example, testified that on one occasion one of the guards, Sergeant Ivan L. Frederick II, had pointed at two naked detainees who were forced to masturbate. 'Look what these animals do when you leave them alone for two seconds', he said. According to his sworn statement, one detainee recalled that 'they forced us to walk like dogs on our hands and knees. And we had to bark like a dog and if we didn't do that, they start hitting us hard on our face and chest with no mercy' (Danner, 2004: 245).

Such actual efforts to dehumanize prisoners were not limited to the Iraqi prison. The following entry in the interrogation log of Mohammed al-Qahtani, believed to have been the designated 20th hijacker in the 9/11 terrorist attacks and held in the Guantánamo Bay, reveals that the al-Qaeda member was considered even less than an animal: 'Told detainee that a dog is held in higher esteem [than he] because dogs know right from wrong, and know how to protect innocent people from bad people. Began teaching the detainee lessons such as stay, come, and bark to elevate his social status up to that of a dog' (Zagorin and Duffy, 2004: 33).

The vilification of 'them' was more frequently aimed at their religious beliefs and precepts. After the capture of Khalid Sheikh Mohammed (KSM), *The Washington Times* published on op-ed article that described in gruesome details the kind of torture that would make Khalid Sheikh Mohammed 'sing in an hour'. The author clearly was out to violate Mohammed's sensitivities related to his Islamic faith. He suggested the al-Qaeda terrorist should be injected with a drug that would paralyze his breathing muscles but not affect his central nervous system and his ability to think and answer questions. He should be put on a mechanical respirator without which he would suffocate and die. After these preliminaries, the interrogation should continue this way:

> Now the interrogation begins. KSM is asked a series of questions to which the answers are known [e.g., Are you a Muslim? Would you like a drink of pig grease?]. If he lies, the respirator is turned off. Few experiences are more terrifying than that of suffocation. After a sufficiently terrifying period of suffocation, the respirator is turned back on, the question is asked again, and the process repeats itself until he tells the truth [...]
>
> After all useful information has been extracted from his brain, KSM should be informed that he will now be killed after his body is smeared with pig fat, that his dead body will be handled by women, and all actions taken that prevent a Muslim from entering heaven upon death so that he dies believing he will never get the heavenly wine and virgins, but will burn in Hell instead. Upon his execution, there should be no physical remains. The body should be cremated and the ashes scattered to the winds. (Wheeler, 2003)

While these remarks were particularly extreme, there were plenty of other attacks on Islam, Muslims in general and American Muslims. The Reverend Franklin Graham, who delivered the benediction at George W. Bush's first presidential inauguration, said, for example, that 'Islam as a whole is evil', and that 'It wasn't Methodists flying into those buildings, and it wasn't Lutherans. It was an attack on this country by people of Islamic faith' (*Nightly News*, NBC, November 16, 2001). Anchor Tom Brokaw introduced the news segment that reported Graham's remarks by telling his audience that 'one of the president's close friends in the American religious establishment has had some very harsh words for the Muslim faith'. One wonders how the maligning of the whole religion of Islam could be described simply as having 'some very harsh words'.

As ABC's *World News Tonight with Peter Jennings* reported, Franklin Graham had plenty of company among leading evangelical preachers when it came to vilifying Muslims and Islam, as the following excerpts from the broadcast demonstrates:

Jerry Falwell, Televangelist: 'I think Mohammed is a terrorist.' Reverend Jerry Vines, Evangelist: 'Islam was founded by Mohammed, a demon-possessed pedophile who had 12 wives, and his last one was a nine year old girl.' Jimmy Swaggart, Televangelist: 'We ought to take, we ought to take every single Muslim student in every college in this nation and ship them back to where they came from.' (ABC News, 2002)

At the end of the segment, anchorman Jennings told his audience benignly, 'This is a delicate subject, as you know' (ABC News, 2002). Such news messages did not only disparage Muslims abroad but vilified Muslim Americans as well – sometimes even explicitly. On CNN, the Reverend Anis Shorrosh, introduced as 'a Christian theologian who has ministered in the Middle East', suggested that 'theologically a Muslim cannot be a true patriotic American citizen, because his allegiance is to Allah, the Moon [sic] God of Arabia' (*Talkback Live*, CNN, August 15, 2002[7]).

Mass Media, Public Opinion and Torture after Abu Ghraib

It may never be known whether and how these attacks and the absence of equally prominent rebuttals in the news influenced practitioners of torture and their enablers. But the investigation of the abuse, torture and death of detainees at Abu Ghraib and elsewhere uncovered patterns aimed at degrading Muslim inmates' faith and violating the well-known sensitivities of Muslims and Arabs. In his sworn testimony, one Abu Ghraib prisoner described unspeakably sadistic brutalities and the following attacks on his religion and the precepts of Islam: 'They ordered me to curse Islam and because they started to hit my broken leg, I cursed my religion. They ordered me to thank Jesus that I'm alive. And I did what they ordered me. This is against my belief. They forced me to eat pork and they put liquor in my mouth' (Danner, 2004).

Describing the human rights violations at Abu Ghraib, Seymour Hersh wrote,

Yet another photograph shows a kneeling, naked, unhooded male prisoner, head momentarily turned away from the camera, posed to make it appear that he is performing oral sex on another male prisoner, who is naked and hooded.

Hersh left no doubt about the aim and impact of these and many similar 'abuses':

Such dehumanization is unacceptable in any culture, but it is especially so in the Arab world. Homosexual acts are against Islamic law and it is humiliating for men to be naked in front of other men. Bernard Haykel, a professor of Middle Eastern Studies at New York University explained, "Being put on top of each other and forced to masturbate, being naked in front of each other – it's all a form of torture." (Hersh, 2004)

The News Media and the 'T' Word

In August 2007, the only US army officer to stand trial on charges related to the Abu Ghraib horror was acquitted of accusations that he had not properly supervised enlisted soldiers involved in the Abu Ghraib torture scandal. The *New York Times* published an article about the acquittal that mentioned 'torture' only once – in reference to what happened at Abu Ghraib during the reign of Saddam Hussein. Once in the headline and seven times in the article, the more benign terms 'abuse' or 'abused' were chosen in addition to 'brutal treatment' and 'violent techniques' (Van Zielbauer, 2007). This was no exception but the rule in the print press, in radio and in television.

Whereas the American news media had no problem to use the term 'torture' in the hypothetical debate before the Abu Ghraib revelations, members of the fourth estate were terribly reluctant to use the T-word once they had shown and the public had seen the graphic pictures of the horror in the detention facility. Anchors, correspondents and reporters themselves preferred terms like 'abuse', 'alleged abuse', 'mistreatment' and 'wrongdoing'. Here they followed the lead of the Bush administration and the political class.

Before the Abu Ghraib scandal broke, the Bush administration did not bother much to partake in the mass-mediated discussion on whether to torture captured terrorists. After the Abu Ghraib images shocked the world, administration officials and their supporters were frequent news sources that either denied that imprisoned 'enemy combatants' had been tortured or justified what they called benignly aggressive interrogation for the sake of preventing further terrorist strikes. As Susan Sontag wrote in her essay 'Regarding the Torture of Others',

> There was also the avoidance of the word 'torture' [on the part of the Bush administration]. The prisoners had possibly been the objects of 'abuse', eventually of 'humiliation' – that was the most to be admitted. 'My impression is that what has been charged thus far is abuse, which I believe technically is different from torture', Secretary of Defense Donald Rumsfeld said at a press conference. 'And therefore I'm not going to address the "torture" word.' (Sontag, 2004)

Table 2 shows that in the year following the breaking news of the Abu Ghraib scandal the three major television networks and two of the country's leading elite newspapers chose the term 'abuse' far more often than 'torture' in stories about or related to Abu Ghraib. In total, 158 pertinent stories that ABC News aired contained the term 'abuse', but only 43 mentioned the term 'torture'. And since 43 of these stories mentioned both 'abuse' and 'torture', there were a total of 115 segments mentioning only 'abuse' in the context of Abu Ghraib and none referring solely to 'torture'.

The linguistic choices were very similar at CBS News and NBC News. During the same time period, the print media, too, chose the term 'abuse' far more often than 'torture' in the context of Abu Ghraib. For example, whereas only 144 articles in the *New York Times*

Table 2: Terms in Abu Ghraib-related Reporting (May 1, 2004–April 30, 2005)

	Abuse and torture (*N*)	Abuse only (*N*)	Torture only (*N*)
ABC News	43	115	–
CBC News	42	118	13
NBC News	35	151	7
New York Times	179	508	144
Washington Post	193	380	37

N = Number of broadcast segments/newspaper stories.

mentioned 'torture' and not 'abuse', there were 508 news items containing 'abuse' and not 'torture'. Similarly, *The Washington Post* published ten times more stories that mentioned 'abuse' and not 'torture' (380) in the context of Abu Ghraib, than articles containing the term 'torture' only (37).

Equally revealing was the reluctance of the print press to use the term 'torture' in headlines above stories dealing with the Abu Ghraib case. In the year following the Abu Ghraib revelations, the *New York Times*, for example, carried 42 news items with the word 'torture' in their headlines and 'Abu Ghraib' in the full text. Of these, 24 were letters to the editor, one an editorial, another one an essay on torture by Susan Sontag and three were book reviews dealing with volumes on Abu Ghraib and torture. Thus, only thirteen news articles that mentioned Abu Ghraib in the full text used the T-word in the headlines. Conversely, of the 130 news items that mentioned 'abuse' in their headlines, twelve were letters to the editor and one was an editorial, so that 117 pertinent straight stories contained the term 'abuse' in the headlines.

While the results of the quantitative analysis are revealing, they do not tell the whole story of the media's avoidance of the T-word. Even investigative reporter Seymour Hersh was very careful in his linguistic choices when he wrote his initial Abu Ghraib story. While Hersh's article carried the headline 'Torture at Abu Ghraib', a title that was presumably picked by his editors, the author himself characterized what was done to detainees as 'wrongdoing' and 'abuse' – not torture. When the T-word was mentioned, Hersh referred to the 'torture and weekly executions' at Abu Ghraib during Saddam Hussein's reign of terror, a quote by a professor of Middle Eastern studies and the findings in General Taguba's report (Hersh, 2004). In this respect, the reporting patterns of the news media at large mirrored the trailblazing article in *The New Yorker*.

In most instances, anchors, correspondents and reporters themselves did not speak or write of 'torture' in the context of the Abu Ghraib scandal, but left this characterization to named or unnamed sources that were critical of the treatment of detainees by Americans. A case in point was the CBS Evening News on April 29, 2004: in introducing the story about the US army's response 'to documented mistreatment of Iraqi prisoners by American soldiers', Dan Rather himself spoke of 'mistreatment' and 'abuses'. In the following correspondent report, David Martin referred to 'Iraqi prisoners mistreated and humiliated by their American jailers'. He mentions the T-word only in the context of 'the Abu Ghraib Prison outside Baghdad, once infamous under Saddam Hussein as a place of torture and death'.

Or take the NBC *Nightly News* of May 7, 2004: in introducing the 'Iraqi prisoner abuse scandal', anchor Brian Williams asked, 'What were military superiors told about the abuse and when were they told?' In the following report, after speaking of 'abuses' and 'abuse', Lisa Myers mentioned that the International Red Cross warned the US government of the 'widespread abuse' of detainees 'tantamount to torture'.

Typically, broadcasts contained the term 'torture' when President George W. Bush and others in the administration denied that they approved the torturing of terrorists and enemy combatants, or when administration officials released documents that supported these denials. The following excerpt from ABC's *World News Tonight with Peter Jennings* on June 22, 2004 illustrates this pattern:

Peter Jennings: 'The White House today produced a huge number of documents for reporters about torture. The president and other members of the administration have been accused by many of their critics of condoning torture in the war against terrorism, at Abu Ghraib prison in Iraq, at Guantánamo Bay and other places less in the news. Our White House correspondent Terry Moran has been looking at the paperwork this afternoon, and there was a lot of it, Terry.'

Terry Moran: 'President Bush declared unequivocally that he has not and will not order a detainee to be tortured.'

President George W. Bush: 'I have never ordered torture. I will never order torture.'

Leading newspapers used the T-word in straight news stories mostly, when the term was mentioned in defense of the Bush administration. This was even more so with respect to headlines. Thus, of the few pertinent headlines in the *New York Times* that contained the T-word, the following were typical:

Ashcroft says the White House never authorized tactics breaking laws on torture. (June 9, 2004)
US spells out new definition curbing torture. (January 1, 2005)
Bush's counsel sought ruling about torture. (January 5, 2005)
Gonzales speaks against torture during hearing. (January 7, 2005)

However, the editorial page editors of the *New York Times* were far less reluctant to resort to the T-word in headlines of the letters-to-the-editor sections and their own opinion pieces. Shortly after the Abu Ghraib scandal broke, for example, the *New York Times* published an editorial under the headline 'The Torture Photos' that stated,

It seems gloomily possible that in years to come, when people in the Middle East recall the invasion of Iraq, they will speak not of the lost American lives or the toppling of a brutal dictator. The most enduring image of the occupation may be those pictures of grinning American soldiers torturing Iraqi prisoners. (*New York Times*, May 5, 2004: 26)

Most Americans learned from news accounts about the horrors. When asked by pollsters in the weeks after the torture story broke whether they happened to follow news reports of prisoner abuse in Iraq involving US soldiers, between 76 and 83 percent said that they had followed the story 'very closely' or 'closely'.[8]

Public Opinion after Abu Ghraib

Since the news media used the T-word sparingly to describe the treatment of Iraqi inmates at Abu Ghraib, the majority of Americans felt that what occurred in the Iraqi prison was 'abuse' rather than 'torture'. When asked a few weeks after being exposed to the Abu Ghraib visuals, 'Do you think what American soldiers did to prisoners at the Abu Ghraib prison in Baghdad amounts to torture, or do you think it was abuse, but not torture?' 60 percent said it was 'abuse but not torture', while only 29 percent felt it was 'torture' (survey conducted by ABC News/*Washington Post*, May 20–23, 2004).

Moreover, contrary to the public's reluctance to support the torturing of terrorists before the Abu Ghraib scandal broke, categorical opposition to torture declined in the years following the revelations. Thus, when asked by pollsters whether torture against suspected terrorists was justified to get important information, only a minority of Americans selected the 'never' option. Administration officials and their supporters claimed frequently that 'aggressive interrogation' methods had yielded information in some cases that helped to capture terrorists and prevent further terrorist strikes. A strong majority of the public bought into this justification and supported torture often, sometimes or rarely in order to gain information (see Table 3).

Table 3: Justification of Torture Against Suspected Terrorists to Gain Information (in Percentages)

	Often	**Sometimes**	**Rarely**	**Never**	**Don't know**
July 2004	15	28	21	32	4
March 2005	15	30	24	27	4
October 2005	15	31	17	32	5
September 2006	18	28	19	32	3
February 2008	17	31	20	30	2

Source: Pew Research Center for the People & the Press.

Conclusion

Before the Abu Ghraib revelations in the spring of 2004, advocates of 'extraordinary interrogation' methods against suspected terrorists drove the torture debate in the news media. Yet a majority or plurality of the American public rejected the torturing of so-called 'enemy combatants' in the context of the 'war on terrorism'. After the arrest of one of the masterminds of 9/11, al-Qaeda operative Khalid Sheikh Mohammed, the public was split on the torture question. It is noteworthy, that during this period, the administration and other authoritative voices did not participate much in the torture discourse.

That changed after the Abu Ghraib revelations. The administration and its supporters became very much part of the mass-mediated torture debate and either denied that Americans or surrogates in other countries were guilty of torturing detainees or justified 'aggressive interrogation' as a means to get information for the prevention of further terror attacks. Their arguments seemed to carry more weight with the American public than opposing views that the news carried as well.

One can only guess whether and how the television drama *24*, that was popular among conservatives and liberals alike (Tenenboim-Weinblatt, 2009: 382–83), affected public attitudes on the treatment of terrorists or suspected terrorists. But the shift to solid public support for torture as a means to prevent further terrorism coincided with increased brutality in the *24* scenes in the months and years after the Abu Ghraib revelations. By 2005, one TV critic concluded,

> This is not the first time torture has been featured on the show [...] But in the present season of '24' torture has gone from being an infrequent shock bid to being a main thread of the plot. At least a half-a-dozen characters have undergone interrogation under conditions that meet conventional definitions of torture. The methods portrayed have varied, and include chemical injection, electric shock and old-fashioned bone-breaking. (Green, 2005)

Officials at the highest level of the US government did not retreat from their pro-torture stands. In 2008, Supreme Court Justice Antonin Scalia told the BBC that 'it is far from clear that torture is unconstitutional and says that it may be legal to "smack [a suspect] in the face" if the suspect is concealing information which could endanger the public' (BBC News, 2008[9]). Less than two weeks into the Obama presidency, former Vice President Cheney renewed his defense of the Bush administration's interrogation methods. He said in an interview that protecting the homeland's security is 'a tough, mean, dirty, nasty business'. As for terrorists, he added, 'These are evil people. And we're not going to win this fight by turning the other cheek.' Finally, he warned that it was likely that terrorists would attempt to carry out a catastrophic nuclear or biological terrorist attack in the coming years and that he feared 'the Obama administration's policies will make it more likely the attempt will succeed' (Harris et al., 2009).

One wonders whether this warning and similar admonitions by Cheney and other defenders of human rights violations in the 'war against terrorism' before and after Obama took the oath of office impacted the early torture-related decisions of his administration. While the first executive order that the president signed prohibited coercive interrogation methods, he left in place the equally controversial extraordinary rendition program that comes down to an outsourcing of torture to countries with a tradition of gross human rights violations. Moreover, Obama's Justice Department followed the example of their predecessors as they invoked 'state secrets' in their refusal to testify in trials and thereby force the dismissal of court actions initiated by victims of extraordinary renditions and torture.

Key Points

- In periods of perceived national security threats, liberal democracies wrestle with the question whether and how to curb civil liberties and human rights for the sake of greater security for their citizens.
- In the post-9/11 United States of America, one of the more controversial issues in the mass-mediated debate concerned the treatment of captured terrorists and, more specifically, the use of torture for the purpose of obtaining information likely to prevent further terrorist attacks.
- News reporting and political talk shows, as well as entertainment (i.e., television spy and crime dramas), figure prominently in shaping the public debate on torture.
- News media and even entertainment shows tend to follow the lead of government officials, especially during national security crises, if these officials choose to participate in mass-mediated debates. This was the case with respect to reporting and entertainment (i.e., the *24* TV drama) after the torturing of detainees in Abu Ghraib and other US-controlled prisons had been revealed.
- While the US public was divided about the torture issue before the Abu Ghraib revelations, afterwards there was growing public support when the pertinent news coverage increased significantly and was tilted in favor of officials who either denied that the United States tortured or defended the practice in the name of preventing more catastrophic terrorist acts.

Study Questions

1. Why is it necessary to include the entertainment media, not simply the news content, in researching mass-mediated policy debates?
2. What is the responsibility of a free press in liberal democracies vis-à-vis the government? Did the American news media discharge this responsibility with respect to the torture debate?

3. Radical extremists tend to undergo processes of moral disengagement before resorting to violence; in what respect might America's mass-mediated torture debate have contributed to the moral disengagement of policy-makers and the actual mind-set of torturers?

Further Reading

Bennett, Lance W., Regina G. Lawrence and Steven Livingston (2007) *When the Press Fails. Political Power and the News Media from Iraq to Katrina.* Chicago, IL: University of Chicago Press.

Danner, Mark (2004) *Torture and Truth. America, Abu Ghraib, and the War on Terror.* New York: New York Review Books.

Tenenboim-Weinblatt, Keren (2009) "'Where Is Jack Bauer When You Need Him?" The Uses of Television Drama in Mediated Political Discourse', *Political Communication* 26(4): 367–87.

Websites

Human Rights Watch: www.hrw.org/en/publications.

The Pew Research Center for the People and the Press: people-press.org.

Think Progress Weblog: thinkprogress.org.

White House Briefing Room: www.whitehouse.gov/briefing-room/statements-and-releases.

References

'A Question of Torture', *Buffalo News*, December 30, 2002: B8.

Alter, Jonathan (2001) 'Time to Think About Torture', *Newsweek*, November 5, 2001.

American Society of Newspaper Editors (ASNE) (1996) *ASNE Statement of Principles*, www.asne.org/kiosk/archive/principl.htm (December 19, 2011).

Bowden, Mark (2003) 'The Dark Art of Interrogation', *Atlantic Monthly*, October 2003: 51–76.

Danner, Mark (2004) *Torture and Truth. America, Abu Ghraib, and the War on Terror.* New York: New York Review Books.

Dershowitz, Alan M. (op. 2002) *Why Terrorism Works. Understanding the Threat, Responding to the Challenge.* New Haven: Yale University Press.

Entman, Robert M. (2000) 'Declarations of Independence. The Growth of Media Power after the Cold War', pp. 11–26 in Brigitte L. Nacos, Robert Y. Shapiro and Pierangelo Isernia (eds) *Decisionmaking in a Glass House. Mass Media, Public Opinion, and American and European Foreign Policy in the 21st Century.* Lanham, MD: Rowman & Littlefield.

Fromkin, Dan (2008) 'We Tortured and We'd Do It Again', *The Washington Post*, February 6, 2008.

Green, Adam (2005) 'Normalizing Torture on "24"', *New York Times*, May 22, 2005.

Gregg, Donald P. (2004) 'After Abu Ghraib; Fight Fire with Compassion', *New York Times*, June 10, 2004.

Harris, John F., Mike Allen and Jim Vandehei (2009) 'Cheney Warns of New Attacks', *Politico Blog*, February 5, 2009, www.politico.com/news/stories/0209/18390.html (December 19, 2011).

Hersh, Seymour (2004) 'Torture at Abu Ghraib', *The New Yorker*, May 10, 2004.

Heymann, Philip B. (2003) *Terrorism, Freedom, and Security. Winning without War*. Cambridge, MA: MIT Press.

Holzer, Henry Mark (2003) 'Terrorism Interrogations and Torture', *Milwaukee Journal Sentinel*, March 16, 2003: 5J.

Human Rights Watch (2006) 'U.S.: Vice President Endorses Torture', October 26, 2006, www.hrw.org/en/news/2006/10/25/us-vice-president-endorses-torture (October 15, 2010).

Lattman, Peter (2007) 'Justice Scalia Hearts Jack Bauer', *Wall Street Journal Law Blog*, June 20, 2007, blogs.wsj.com/law/2007/06/20/justice-scalia-hearts-jack-bauer/ (February 12, 2009).

Lithwick, Dahlia (2008) 'The Fiction behind Torture Policy', *Newsweek*, July 26, 2008.

Mayer, Jane (2005) 'A Deadly Interrogation', *The New Yorker*, November 14, 2005.

—— (2008) *The Dark Side. The Inside Story of How the War on Terror Turned into a War on American Ideals*. New York: Doubleday.

McGuire, Marc (2003) 'Good Guys Are Doing Bad Things This Season', *Times Union* (Albany, NY), January 14, 2003: Section D.

Sands, Philippe (2008) *Torture Team. Rumsfeld's Memo and the Betrayal of American Values*. New York: Palgrave Macmillan.

Shakir, Faiz (2007) 'U.S. Military: Television Series "24" is Promoting Torture in the Ranks', *ThinkProgress*, February 13, 2007, thinkprogress.org/default/2007/02/13/10296/torture-on-24 (February 12, 2009).

Shanahan, James and Michael Morgan (1999) *Television and Its Viewers. Cultivation Theory and Research*. Cambridge, UK; New York: Cambridge University Press.

Shenon, Philip (2008) 'Mukasey Will Not Rule Out Waterboarding', *New York Times*, January 31, 2008.

Sontag, Susan (2004) 'Regarding the Torture of Others', *New York Times Magazine*, May 23, 2004.

Sprinzak, Ehud (1990) 'The Psychopolitical Formation of Extreme Left Terrorism in a Democracy: The Case of the Weatherman', pp. 65–85 in Walter Reich (ed.) *Origins of Terrorism*. New York: Cambridge University Press.

Stout, David and Scott Shane (2008) 'Cheney Defends the Use of Harsh Interrogation', *The Washington Post*, February 7, 2008.

Taylor, Stewart (2003) 'Is It Ever Right to Torture Suspected Terrorists?' *National Journal*, March 8, 2003.

Tenenboim-Weinblatt, Keren (2009) '"Where Is Jack Bauer When You Need Him?" The Uses of Television Drama in Mediated Political Discourse', *Political Communication* 26(4): 367–87.

Van Zielbauer, Paul (2007) 'Army Colonel Is Acquitted in Abu Ghraib Abuse Case', *New York Times*, August 29, 2007.

Wheeler, Jack (2003) 'Interrogating KSM; How to Make the al Qaeda Terrorist Sing', *The Washington Times*, March 5, 2003.

Zagorin, Adam and Michael Duffy (2004) 'Inside the Interrogation of Detainee 063', *Time*, June 20, 2004: 26–33.

Notes

1 The Eighth Amendment of the US Constitution forbids the use of 'cruel and unusual punishments', which is widely interpreted as a prohibition of the use of torture. The Uniformed Code of Military Justice forbids torture outside the United States.
2 See www.whitehouse.gov/news/releases/2006/10/20061017-1.html (December 19, 2011).
3 See www.whitehouse.gov/news/releases/2006/10/20061024-7.html (December 19, 2011).
4 See www.whitehouse.gov/news/releases/2008/03/20080308.html (March 9, 2008).
5 See www.cbc.ca/health/story/2008/11/28/bauer-torture.html?ref=rss (December 19, 2011).
6 I use the terms 'press' and 'media' interchangeably in this chapter, although they differentiate in the strict sense between the print press and the catch-all media.
7 See transcripts.cnn.com/TRANSCRIPTS/0208/15/tl.00.html (December 19, 2011).
8 Pew Research Center for the People and the Press: Surveys, conducted by Princeton Survey Associates International, June 3-13, 2004, and the Henry J. Kaiser Family Foundation/Princeton Survey Associates International, June 4-8, 2004.
9 See news.bbc.co.uk/2/hi/programmes/law in_action/7238665.stm (April 25, 2008).

Authors

Robert M. Entman is the J.B. and Maurice C. Shapiro Professor of Media & Public Affairs and International Affairs at the School of Media and Public Affairs, George Washington University, Washington D.C., United States.

Romy Fröhlich is a professor at the Department for Communication Science and Media Research Ludwig Maximilian University Munich, Germany.

Valérie Gorin is a lecturer at the Centre for Education and Research in Humanitarian Action (CERAH), University of Geneva, Switzerland.

Daniel C. Hallin is a professor at the Department of Communication, University of California San Diego, United States.

Philip Hammond is professor of media and communications at and head of the Centre for Media and Culture Research, London South Bank University, United Kingdom.

Roman Hummel is professor of journalism at the Department of Communication Science, University of Salzburg, Austria.

Matthias Karmasin is professor of media and communication science, University of Klagenfurt, Austria.

Magnus-Sebastian Kutz is a personal assistant at the State Ministry for Urban Development and Environment, Hamburg, Germany.

Diego Lazzarich is a research fellow and lecturer in History of Political Thought at the Department of Political Science "Jean Monnet", Second University of Naples, Italy.

Dennis Lichtenstein is a research assistant for media and communication studies at the Institute for Social Science, University of Düsseldorf, Germany.

Gabriele Melischek is a consultant at the Austrian Academy of Sciences, Comparative Media and Communication Studies, Vienna, Austria.

Brigitte L. Nacos is an adjunct professor at the Department of Political Science, Columbia University, New York, United States.

Cordula Nitsch is a researcher in media and communication studies at the Institute for Social Science, University of Düsseldorf, Germany.

Nel Ruigrok is responsible for the Netherlands News Monitor, Foundation Press Institute, Amsterdam, Netherlands.

Stephan Russ-Mohl is professor of journalism and media management at the Institute for Media and Journalism, University of Lugano, Switzerland.

Clemens Schwender is a lecturer in media psychology and media management at the University of Applied Sciences, Berlin, Germany.

Josef Seethaler is a senior scientist at the Austrian Academy of Sciences, Comparative Media and Communication Studies, Vienna, Austria.

Philip Seib is director of the Center on Public Diplomacy and professor of journalism, public diplomacy, and international relations at the University of Southern California, Los Angeles, United States.

Reinhard Stauber is a professor at and head of the Department for Contemporary and Austrian History, University of Klagenfurt, Austria.

Janet Takens is a PhD candidate at the Department of Communication Science, University Amsterdam, Netherlands.

Wouter van Atteveldt is an assistant professor at the Department of Communication Science, University Amsterdam, Netherlands.

Jürgen Wilke is professor for communication studies at the Department of Journalism and Mass Communications, University of Mainz, Germany.

Romy Wöhlert is a post-doc researcher at the Austrian Academy of Sciences, Comparative Media and Communication Studies, Vienna, Austria.

Index